Organizational Transitions for Individuals, Families, and Work Groups

Organizational Transitions for Individuals, Families, and Work Groups

Louis B. Barnes
Harvard Business School

Colleen Kaftan
Harvard Business School

Prentice Hall, Englewood Cliffs, New Jersey 07632

Library of Congress Cataloging-in-Publication Data

Barnes, Louis B.
  Organizational transitions for individuals, families, and work
groups / Louis B. Barnes, Colleen Kaftan.
    p. cm.
   ISBN 0-13-640590-8
   1. Organizational change—Case studies. 2. Work and family—Case
studies. 3. Work groups—Case studies. I. Kaftan, Colleen.
II. Title.
HD58.8.B37 1990
302.3′5—dc20   90-47934
                                                 CIP

Editorial/production supervision
  and interior design: *The Total Book*
Cover design: *Mike Fender*
Manufacturing buyers: *Trudy Pisciotti/Bob Anderson*

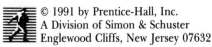 © 1991 by Prentice-Hall, Inc.
A Division of Simon & Schuster
Englewood Cliffs, New Jersey 07632

Printed in the United States of America

10 9 8 7 6 5 4 3 2 1

ISBN 0-13-640590-8

Prentice-Hall International (UK) Limited, *London*
Prentice-Hall of Australia Pty. Limited, *Sydney*
Prentice-Hall Canada Inc., *Toronto*
Prentice-Hall Hispanoamericana, S.A., *Mexico*
Prentice-Hall of India Private Limited, *New Delhi*
Prentice-Hall of Japan, Inc., *Tokyo*
Simon & Schuster Asia Pte. Ltd., *Singapore*
Editora Prentice-Hall do Brasil, Ltda., *Rio de Janeiro*

Contents

Preface

This is a book of cases, comments, and readings about a phenomenon that colors virtually every aspect of our lives: change. In one sense, as the title indicates, the book is about change in organizations. But there are already books about organizational change, many of which describe how someone—often a consultant or a new CEO—came in and saved or ruined the company. This book is a little different. It focuses on the powerful transitions experienced by individuals, families, teams, and organizations as they develop, mature, and face environmental and internal threats and challenges. Sometimes, people in transition pose threats themselves to each other as relationships change.

We developed much of the material in this book for use in the Human Aspects of Business course in the Owner/President Management Program, an executive education program at the Harvard Business School. All the cases are based on actual business and personal situations. They describe the dilemmas, predicaments, and decisions faced by managers who are struggling to balance and develop both their own lives and their often shaken up organizations. Sometimes the cases focus on an entrepreneur or executive member of the company. Sometimes they concentrate on the powerful contexts of family or group history and emotions. Sometimes we simply use the family and its transitions as a good metaphor for operating task-force teams or the organization itself.

The book is organized in three major parts. Section 1 concentrates on changes in the individual as seen against a background of family and/or organizational circumstances. Section 2 shifts the focus to the small family or team group. In many of the situations we have studied, this group represents the nuclear or extended family as it is involved in corporate life. In other cases, the immediate work group or task force is seen as a "family" within the larger organization. Section 3 takes up another step to look at the company as a set of integrated parts encompassing all the earlier units.

This progression from individual to group to organization made intuitive sense to us as we put together the course and the book. In some ways, though, the progression is an arbitrary classification. Each of the cases we include takes place in a tapestry of transitions which occur at every other level of the organization and often in the external environment. Thus, although the "ostensible issue" may bring a single person to the foreground, the reader should bear in mind that the transition is taking place within (or causing) a context of group and organizational change as well. Likewise, families or task forces are affected by their individual members and evolve against a background of the broader agglomeration. And every corporate transition influences myriad changes in individuals and operating units.

Each section starts with a brief introduction to the materials that follow. The introductions describe our reasons for situating each piece in the section, but you should always keep in mind that the foreground for one section is only the background for another, and each represents either context or detail for another arena.

WHY THE CASE METHOD?

A good case study reflects the kind of complexity and interrelatedness among transitioning units we have just described. A good case study presents the reader with a jumble of facts, impressions, and occurrences to sort out in order to understand the situation. Students must grapple with real world ambiguities in deciding what actions should be taken next and how they should be taken. Above all, a good case study requires a personal involvement with the materials as the class discussion proceeds, in the best of circumstances fostering a marriage of analysis and application.

Good cases are wasted if they merely serve as illustrations for a lecturer's favorite theoretical points. A good case is best used as a springboard for debate and dialogue in which class members are the key advocates of one position or another. The instructor optimally serves as a combined symphony conductor and devil's advocate. Using cases in this fashion makes them richer, more dynamic, and more personally compelling than any theoretical presentation can be. As such, a case should be used as a vehicle for questioning, exploring, debating, and practicing the various theories being developed. Again, the depth and learning from a case discussion can be only as great as the participants' willingness to become actively involved beyond the situation as it is described.

The cases we've included do not generally revolve around organizational "heroes" who singlehandedly save the day. Nor will you find "right answers" to the problems our protagonists must face. As you make your way through the book, you will read about—and discuss—real people in real organizations. These people encountered real struggles and made real mistakes, as will *you* upon occasion, if only in debating what they "should" have done. Your discussion of these cases can provide a testing ground for both their mistakes and your own.

In addition, you will be asked to put yourself in the position of one or more individuals with imperfect knowledge but with very human commitments and responsibilities. Your greatest opportunity to learn will come from examining your own reactions to these situations and then working with classmates and instructor to achieve a deeper and sometimes common understanding of what the case is "all about." Like any really creative discussion, that can take time, energy, and courage.

Don't expect that you will always reach agreement in your discussions! The most effective case-based classes are fraught with conflicting opinions about what has happened and what should happen next. And even if you arrive at a consensus in the classroom, you may find yourselves entirely at odds with the people you're talking about. In addition, as you will sometimes discover in the sequential accounts of many of these cases, the "real outcome" is not necessarily the "right answer."

Most of the cases were written from a particular perspective in time. The time setting is meant to help you focus on the situation and its requirements during a specific period in their evolution. As chronicles of transition, though, all of these cases present a longitudinal stream of events. You will read background information on the history of the current situation. Most likely, too, you will be interested in knowing what actually transpired *after* the events you discuss, but as we said above, don't confuse outcomes with answers.

In many instances, your professor or discussion leader will be able to fill you in on the actual outcomes once you have completed your class analysis. Many of these "debriefings" will pose new debatable questions for student managers—just as in the real world. Again, we want to emphasize that the follow-up sequences are meant to describe real results, *not* the correct answers. The only answers in these discussions are the personal lessons you derive. And those will only be as valid as your own struggle to make sense of and learn beyond them.

THE READINGS

We have selected additional readings to illuminate or enhance the case studies in each of the three sections. The readings, too, could give rise to discussion and debate in the classroom. They can also support your analysis of specific cases and help you make generalizations from the lessons you identify. Or the readings can stand on their own, as thought-provoking pieces on the various aspects of change at different levels of the organization.

Some faculty members will choose to use this book as a supplementary text to assign along with more traditional materials for courses in organizational behavior, management development, family and entrepreneurial management, and organizational change or transition. Some teachers will use it for a stand-alone course. We hope the cases and readings we've included will help breathe life into the concepts you are studying, and we invite you to get acquainted with the people on these pages as we have. Greet them as real actors contending with the complexities of real change in themselves and their surroundings. That's what they were, and that's what they'd like you to be.

An Introduction to Cases

Management instruction involves the development of a set of philosophies, approaches, skills, knowledge, and techniques. Lectures and readings are a highly efficient way to acquire knowledge and to become informed about techniques. Exercises or problem sets are excellent beginning tools for learning about the application and limitations of techniques. But the development of philosophies, approaches, and skills is best served by the case method—a teaching approach that also helps to provide knowledge and experience with techniques. The case method becomes a part of a broad-gauge approach to management education and development. It is therefore generally used in well-orchestrated concert with other approaches.

Most students and executive program participants are quite familiar with lectures, readings, exercises, and problem sets, but the case method is often new to them. The purpose of this note is to help them understand the basis for the case method and to give them some idea of how to approach cases.

The case method is built around the concepts of *metaphors* and *simulation*. Each case is a description of a real business situation and serves as a *metaphor* for a particular set of problems. The situations that a manager faces may differ from the metaphors portrayed in our cases, but taken together, the cases provide a useful and relevant set of metaphors that can be applied to most management situations. The cases were selected to include a wide variety of products and company types, thus assuring that at least some of them would be relevant along those dimensions. The situations analyzed and skills developed in the cases are applicable to almost all management situations, from marketing to manufacturing to finance, and so on.

The use of the case method for management instruction is based upon the belief that management is a skill rather than a collection of techniques or concepts. The best way to learn a skill is to practice in a *simulation*-type process. Just as the swimmer learns to swim by swimming, and the pianist learns piano by playing, so too the skills of management are learned by actively participating in managing—not by readings or lectures. The swimming novice might drown if thrown into deep water after reading a set of books on how to swim. And few of us would want to hear a concert pianist who had never before touched a piano but who had attended many lectures on piano playing. Because it is impractical to have the student manager manage a company, the case provides a vehicle for simulation.

The total case process consists of four steps ordered as follows:

1. individual analysis and preparation,
2. optional informal small-group discussion,
3. classroom discussion, and
4. end-of-class generalization about the learning.

Each of these steps asks the participant to perform related, but different, activities.

While there is no "one ideal way to approach a case," some generalities can be drawn. The student gains the most by im-

This note was prepared by Professor Benson P. Shapiro.

mersing him- or herself in the case and actively playing the role of the protagonist. The protagonist is usually one manager but is sometimes a group. By actively studying the case, the student begins to learn how to analyze a management situation and develop a plan of action, and then to defend and back up that plan of action. By participating in an involved manner in the case discussion, the student learns to commit him- or herself to a position easily and to express that position articulately. The core of management decision making consists of these processes: analysis, choice, and persuasion.

The fourth step, generalization, is also part of good management practice. The smart manager steps back from each situation he or she has experienced and asks, "What did I learn?" and "How does the situation and the lesson relate to my whole experience?" The astute student will want to do the same thing on his or her own, building on the help provided by the instructor. An important part of that process is to relate the cases to the assigned reading material. The reading material generally provides the structure and techniques; the case provides the simulated experience in the application of the structure and techniques. The cases also help to develop a generalized approach to business situations, as well as a set of philosophies.

The case method is demanding of both teachers and students. Participants who get actively involved in each case analysis and discussion, and who attempt to generalize their learning across cases, gain the most from the process.

Each participant should strive to develop the ability to ask "the right questions" about each case. The instructor may provide specific questions for each case. The following questions are among those that are generally relevant to all cases:

- Who is the protagonist?
- What are his or her objectives (implicit or explicit)?
- What decisions (implicit or explicit) must I make?
- What problems, opportunities, and risks do I, as the protagonist, face?
- What evidence do I have to help make the decision? Is the evidence reliable and unbiased? Can I improve it?
- What alternative courses of action are available?
- What criteria should I use to judge the alternatives?
- What action should I take?
- How should I convince others in the case and in the classroom that my approach is best?
- What did I learn from this case?
- How does it relate to past cases and my own "live" experiences?

Action Taking and Action Planning

EDUCATION AND ACTION

Without question, experience either as a manager or as a disciplined student can provide a wealth of analytic techniques and diagnostic tools for any person who wants to use them. Many of these tools and techniques are very sophisticated, and some are bewildering. Academic courses also present a dictionary of buzz words and jargon so that by graduation, most students usually possess dazzling lexicons of business language skills and the confidence to go with them. Graduates are ready to impress the world and themselves with their analytical abilities and verbal wizardry.

But so what? How does any school education prepare you for real action in the real world? Does a little knowledge simply develop more bulls—or worse—for more china shops? And when does analysis become paralysis or abstraction become inaction? What about *real* action taking? At some point, your actions and *how* you take them become major determinants of your influence and success—or failure. Although action habits are not easily learned in the classroom, that's no reason to avoid them. Action taking and action planning cannot simply be left for lives hereafter. Such abdication works only if we assume that action taking and analysis have no important connection. But they do.

An alternative assumption would be that action and analysis are inseparable. Indeed, one form of action *is* one's approach to diagnosis and analysis. That's where our focus on action planning and action taking comes in. Our premise is that *some* action skills are learnable and that *all* action skills benefit from practice and experience.

TWO MYTHS

Most of us consider managerial action taking as made up of individual courage and initiative. The executive action taker is like the military officer who leads the cavalry up the hill—any high hill—in the thick of battle. Most books and articles deriding the MBA experience extol this macho image of the swashbuckling executive—the hands-on manager. "What they don't teach you at any business school," the cynics assert, is street smarts and action savvy. Rugged, and sometimes insolent, individualism is the key.

At some level, most of us buy into this image. It is both exciting and simple, and it puts us in control of ourselves and the world around us. We associate this kind of leadership with dramatic moments when the executive actor or actress is the hard-nosed star of the show. Sometimes, we get aggressive and overplay the role, that is, we adopt the tough-guy image more strongly if we suspect that others don't believe that we are up to it. We see their disbelief as a challenge to our self-esteem and choose to assert hard-nosed behavior. After all, nice guys are supposed to finish last. Thus the hard-charging know-it-all and the marshmallow-inside-posing-as-the-autocrat-outside become caricature embodiments of the myth.

Like all heroic myths, some people come close to the individualist-action model and many more make money talking or writing about how to do it. Examine the literature on self-help leadership and assertiveness training for example. In addition, many companies cherish these myths in their folk histories and executive suites. Others have books, articles, luncheon martinis, and locker room conversations to help "prove" that they live up to their hard-nosed ideals.

The second myth uses a form of logic rather than sentiment for its appeal. This is the myth of the rational decision maker. Once again, emphasis is upon individual action. In this case, though, action takes the form of the clear-headed executive making critical decisions which are implemented by other people. Executive action is more apt to mean executive detachment than executive involvement. Executive action here means keeping a cool head, taking different alternatives into account, getting objective data (the facts) from below, and selecting the option best suited to the situation. Detached analytical judgment is the key to success. The world thus gets divided into critical executive actions (decisions) and more pedestrian managerial actions (data gathering and implementations). This scenario helps us to make another convenient dichotomy—that leaders and managers are different—which, of course, they are according to this assumption.

Not surprisingly, the two myths contradict each other. I may be chasing one myth and you the other. My needs are for heroic actors and emotional charisma. You want cool objectivity and rational thinking. Sometimes the two ideals compete more than the real world data do as different actors take opposing positions on any given issue. Not to possess one or both of these qualities poses real identity problems for many an aspiring manager. Each quality provides values to hang onto, yet neither disconnected ideal is very realistic, even in opposition to the other, if we are honest with ourselves. There are too many other outside variables.

Major problems occur when both models fail a manager as they usually do. Idealistic managers find that a complex world and the people in it are receptive to neither simple heroics nor rational logics. Something goes wrong. Supposedly heroic leaders can't lead, followers don't follow, and admiring colleagues don't cooperate. Instead, they argue or ignore. On the other side, objective managerial logic also fails. Other people seem to be using other forms of logic. Some get immobilized, and "good" managers have been known to give up at this point. Anger, frustration, and withdrawal are the symptoms. The "fact" is that such complex symptoms only reflect the complexities of the "real" world.

AN ACTION NETWORK

Neither of our two mythical perspectives—almost the opposite ends of direct involvement—captures the subtleties of action which this book wants to emphasize. Our premise is that managerial (executive) action is neither heroic involvement nor detached analysis. It is both and more—and sometimes less. Action resides partly in the individual actor's intent and partly in other people's perceptions and responses. In a very real sense, action needs to be thought of as *interactive*. Action involves a complex interacting pattern of people and events mixed in with diagnoses and observations. All these, in a sense, form an intricate action network. In that sense, my actions are probably provoked by my perceptions of your behavior as much as they are by my own initial action plans. However, my action plan roughs out my intentions and objectives and gives me a basis for change or consistency. My action plan *must also recognize your likely action responses and the probable responses of other critical people and forces in my environment.*

Consequently, whenever the topic turns to action, we shall ask you for a *multidimensional, multiperson, multispace, and multitime focus*—almost a contradiction in terms—but that's how complex interaction sometime unfolds. For example, how do *you* see a complex situation (analysis and diagnosis) as it has evolved? How do others see it? What do you want to accomplish? With whom? Where and when do you unwind your actions, and depending upon what? What time constraints are you working within? Is the situation urgent, important, both, or neither? Does it matter whether you meet in his/her office, your own, or in some other setting? During work? After work? How are you trying to set the stage for short-term actions? For actions taken over a longer term? And what if those actions don't work? What do you do then? How might any of these actions be perceived by persons A, B, C, and D? And what about their bosses and their own colleagues, not to mention yours? How do you think they will respond? What if they respond in ways unanticipated by you? Then what do you do (new set of action dimensions)? What are your contingency plans?

Put another way, multiple action thinking is just as important as one's analysis of each basic, elementary part or one's overall diagnosis, which involves broader interpretations of the combined analyses. In this sense, analytical thinking comes from our early Newtonian models of scientific problem solving where we isolate and analyze the separate parts and symptoms. Diagnostic interpretation is more related to the field of medicine. What patterns and syndromes do the parts combine into? Action taking, like medicine, may begin with an analyses of separate symptoms and data but must derive from more complicated combinations of diagnostic thinking.

In addition, actions and diagnoses constantly crisscross over time. They are intertwined and inseparable. You take an action, assess its effects (rediagnose), and follow up with other action steps. Sometimes you take multiple actions so as to get reactions from other parties to improve your own diagnosis. All the time the rest of the world and its players are moving along their own paths, some of which may impact upon you. It gets complicated.

For this reason, treating actions, detailed analysis, and complex diagnoses as though they were temporarily separate like the individual parts of a symphonic passage, is sometimes helpful. This treatment is another myth, though, because none of these parts represents the symphony by itself. The name of the game is relationships—analysis, diagnoses, and actions.

Therefore, this note is written with two thoughts in mind. They seem almost contradictory and, in that sense, become paradoxical. One is to deliberately blur the notions of analytical focus, overall diagnosis, and detailed action planning into an ongoing, interactive process. Analysis, diagnosis, and action all feed together. They are *all* action. However, the most visible indicators of action are those seen, heard, or sensed by other people. These moves involve you and others and occur interactively.

The second intent here is to *separate* these elements—but only temporarily for purposes of focus—because we can't always follow complex, rolling action scenarios in class (although to some extent we can with our comments, discussion practices, sequential cases, and role playing). Therefore, we shall sometimes artificially separate and enlarge the worlds of diagnosis and action to highlight the details and importance of each. Please, though, make no mistake. In the real world, separating and treating diagnoses and action as though they were discrete unrelated parts is often hard and not always useful.

THE ROLE OF VALUES IN ACTION

As each person tries to make meaning and sense out of either a class or personal case situation involving real people only so much of the data come through as facts. *Most* data are made up of opinions, judgments, assumptions, and perceptions, sometimes wishfully treated as though they were facts. To a large extent, those opinions, judgments, assumptions, and perceptions rest on beliefs and values that come out of our individual backgrounds and philosophies. These basic values involve such issues as justice, competence, life, love, and authority, which provide important bases for our behavior and for our similarities and differences with others. Interestingly enough, although values provide the basic framework, action and behavior reveal those frameworks and values to others.

Consequently, we have a curious complex cycle that goes from my values and assumptions to my actions. However, those actions are based partly on my inferences of your values and assumptions coming from your actions. Meanwhile, you are inferring values and assumptions from my actions and behavior which provide a partial basis for your own actions. Needless to say, only parts of this picture are available to each actor during the whole process.

It might help to illustrate the kinds of action taking and action planning we are discussing by drawing on a case that was used for a number of years for teaching and exam purposes. Although presented in summarized form here, the case's issues are very complex, as are most cases of human action and interaction.

THE QUAKER STEEL AND ALLOY CORPORATION CASE[1]

Quaker Steel and Alloy was founded in 1890 in Holderness, Pennsylvania, on the banks of the Ohio River. Usually referred to as Quaker Alloy, or simply Quaker, it became one of the world's major manufacturers ($1.4 billion) of specialized metal alloys. By 1978, it had built an impressive reputation based upon its strategy of high-margin, high-quality alloys, heavy investments in research, development and new plant facilities, customer assistance, and technical service. Its return on investment had been significantly higher than its nearest competitor for over 20 years. Its labor-management relationships were considered to be the best in the industry. It had, overall, a reputation for excellence. In some ways, though, Quaker was different from other companies.

Partly because of its two founders and their Quaker philosophy and partly because

[1]   The Quaker Steel and Alloy Corporation, (copyright 1980 by the President and Fellows of Harvard College) was written by Professor John J. Gabarro from material originally prepared by Professor Paul Lawrence and Research Assistant Andre Ruedi. Harvard Business School case 480-063.

of its small town origins, Quaker had grown in a unique way. With headquarters, R&D facilities, and a third of its plants in Holderness, the founders' original values still lingered, even though most of the town's inhabitants were no longer practicing Quakers. Company norms involved an atmosphere of friendliness, openness in discussing differences of opinion, and influencing through persuasion and competence rather than through formal authority. Considerable emphasis was put on participation in decision making, and on leading by example rather than by fiat. Managers coming to Quaker from other metal producers often found the company a frustrating place in which to work.

Quaker's informal relationships tended to cut across the formal functional boundaries of Mining, Refining, Manufacturing, Research and Engineering, and Sales and Marketing. Top management gave three reasons for this. These were:

1. The small town atmosphere and the informal communications it encouraged.
2. A policy that required all managers above third line supervisor to spend a year working in Holderness. Management considered this policy to be especially important since most transactions across organizational lines were conducted through personal contacts and relationships.
3. The concept of "responsibility lines" which meant that many managers and even whole divisions were "responsible" to other functions, "even though there were no formal lines of authority that linked them." These "formalized-informal procedures" were shown on organization charts as dotted lines, and on Quaker charts there were many dotted lines.

However, outside environments were changing. During the early 1970s, competition, especially from the Japanese, began to challenge Quaker's hold on its larger volume accounts. These large accounts also provided the greatest profit margins. Product managers for the various alloy product lines (steel, cobalt, titanium, tungsten, etc.) became justifiably concerned about these competitive forces, even though customers had typically remained loyal because of Quaker's technical service and support functions.

Maureen Frye joined Quaker Alloys in 1975 with an MBA from the Harvard Business School, a B.S. in metallurgy, and an M.S. in physical chemistry from MIT. Frye was 26 years old when she joined the company and had no previous work experience. After nine months as a market analyst and training in the Sales Representative Training Program, Frye became assistant product manager for the Titanium Alloys product line, the job for which she had originally been recruited. Frye was responsible for all of Quaker's extruded titanium alloy products which accounted for over $100 million in sales in 1978.

During 1977, Maureen Frye examined the competitive market and concluded that Titanium Alloy sales were being lost because sales representatives were spending too much time with their small accounts. She ran a series of computer simulations which suggested that a systematic reallocation of the sales force's time from small customers to larger ones would result in sales increases of as much as $12–25 million in extruded titanium products. Her boss, Hugh Salk, was impressed with Frye's analysis when he first saw it in 1977. With this encouragement, Frye sent a memo to the titanium extrusion sales representatives in late 1977 instructing them to reduce their time in Class 6 (the smallest) accounts by 30% and to reallocate it to larger accounts. The memo included a brief description of the rationale for making the change.

Frye heard from one of the nineteen District Sales Managers for her product line that her memo had aroused a number of complaints from his sales people. Consequently, she arranged to present a summary of her findings to the District Sales Managers

(DSMs) at their annual meeting in January 1978. She also discussed the concept and the simulations with the vice president of marketing, James Bethancourt, who was Hugh Salk's boss—her boss's boss, that is. Even though the DSMs "all agreed to make these changes," according to Frye, the situation was no different 10 months later.

Frye and Salk then arranged to have a meeting with Bethancourt and Lawrence Israel, the vice president of sales (to whom the DSMs ultimately reported with two intermediary bosses) in early December 1978 to get their approval and recommendations. As a result of that meeting, Frye was asked to get a plan prepared by March 30, 1979, for implementation the following calendar year.

The Action Network in the Quaker Steel and Alloy Case

Frye, Salk, Bethancourt, Israel, the DSMs, the titanium sales people, other sales and support people, and others not included in the summary above provide the *multi-person* actors in this case. Many of these people had interaction meaning for each other, partly because of the company's networking traditions and multiple responsibility lines. Unfortunately, Frye tended to ignore these. In addition, each actor came to the situation with personal background attributes which we know little about. There was also a company management context which valued person-to-person persuasion. The case further notes that Frye had spent little time in the field with salespeople or at home with the technical support people who helped to build and maintain customer relationships over the long run. Instead, her time had been largely devoted to perfecting her model and simulation data in 1977 and to assisting Salk with product allocations to districts in early 1978 necessitated by titanium shortages. Di-

agnostically, Frye was in trouble almost from the beginning of her campaign to change sales call patterns.

The *multi-space* dimensions of this case, and the potential psychological walls dividing them, are also apparent. They range from the Holderness community with its traditions to Frye's limited work space involving computer models and simulations to nineteen sales districts scattered around the world. Even beyond these were the individual sales territories and customer locations where Frye's plan would meet its ultimate test. At a still more subtle level were the technical support service offices located in Holderness whose occupants helped a salesperson with customer questions and problems. Some salespeople had better entrees to these technical support offices than others, often because of long standing acquaintanceships. Quaker management tried to minimize these spatial distinctions by keeping people in constant contact with each other.

Any of these locations, or others, provide action settings for the case's actors at various *times* during the case description. The *multi-time* periods for action range from 1975 to 1978 in this case. Each time period contained countless action opportunities, though typically we tend to focus upon a few key action points in a case discussion. For example, in retrospect, what might Hugh Salk have done in each of the following situations or even just before or after them? Equally important, *how* might he have gone about addressing each situation:

- When Frye was first hired?
- Assessing Frye's initial understanding and appreciation of Quaker's values and norms?
- Getting a wider picture of what Frye's model and simulations would mean to those in *other* product line areas?
- Learning of the sales force's discomfort with Frye's proposals and approach when those reactions first appeared?

- Addressing that discomfort?
- Addressing Frye's increasing frustration with her lack of success as time and events went on?
- At the time of Frye's "arbitrary" memo to the sales force in late 1977?
- In discussions with DSMs any time during 1977–78?
- Before Frye's meeting with the DSMs in January of 1978 or when Salk and Frye met with James Bethancourt early that same year?
- Before, during, or after the meeting with Bethancourt and Lawrence Israel in December 1978?
- Making sure that problems like this were minimized in the future?

Likewise, what about Maureen Frye? Beginning as the prototypical rational thinker, she compounded the problem with an autocratic mandate for sales reallocation with little input from the salespeople who were to implement the plan. Were her assumptions reasonable from their point of view? She also missed the warning signals that told her that newer and younger sales people preferred to deal with smaller accounts, because they got a greater sense of accomplishment and competence in those contacts. The newer sales people also tended to get poorer service from technical support people than senior people did. They didn't know how to work the informal networks as well, nor had they been at it as long. In short, Frye missed a whole series of opportunities to make contact with people who could have helped her either implement or modify her sales improvement plan. Instead, she tended to lean upon narrow hierarchical mechanisms in contrast to Quaker's practice of multiple responsibility lines.

In our concern for *future* action taking, Frye is still a key person. She needs to reassess the people she has been in contact with, her own sense of timing, and the ways in which she needs to reach into other space locations. She might very well broaden her contacts— e.g., seek out titanium sales people, spend more time in the field, ask for ideas from technical support services personnel, create contacts between them and the newer sales people, or check with other assistant product managers and the Division General Sales Managers (the DSMs' bosses) to see how her plan would affect other product lines. She might also sponsor new training efforts on large account relationships, ask older sales people for advice on how to build large account contracts, use them as coaches, or ask DSMs for implementation guidance— bearing in mind that according to the case, they expect their sales people to make the majority of their own decisions. Frye has tended to ignore that in the past. She doesn't need to in the future, but it means a whole different series and levels of interactions for her.

In addition, Frye could go back to Hugh Salk, her boss, or even to James Bethancourt and Lawrence Israel, for a better reading on what has happened so far. So far, they haven't functioned too well as guides, and it is useful to speculate as to why. What can Frye do about it? She might learn how to act more effectively in the future by exploring the past through their eyes. For example, why do they want her action plan by March 30th 1979 for implementation *the following calendar year*? Why *that* sense of delayed timing on their part?

All of this inquiry might cause Frye to reappraise her sales reallocation plan or even abandon it. It might also give her a better sense of how to phase it in, where, when, and with which support systems. Because technical support people are so important to the large accounts, she might want to spend a fair amount of short term time building relationships there, both for herself and for her titanium salespeople in the field. With or without her reallocation plan, that would probably help.

There is more that Frye can do. However, the above comments give a rough idea of how each of her actions could trigger responses and new overtures from others in the company. These responses and overtures will probably differ markedly from past reactions if Maureen Frye tries to act according to the norms and values that seem so important in this company. Her own action plan can profit from that kind of understanding and diagnosis. But first, she needs to take action to gain such understanding.

Your Own Patterns for Action Networks

Each of us, like Maureen Frye, is an individual, and in that sense there may be as many action patterns as there are individuals. Why would we evaluate one action as "better" than another? The choice often comes down to the fact that the classroom places certain constraints upon you as an action taker. These constraints usually take the form of balance (*not* compromise—you need to keep them separate) rather than extremism on one side or another. By balance, we mean valuing both task demands and people needs, both superiors and subordinates, both short term and long term realities, both insiders and outsiders in a social situation, and both yourself and others. Further constraints involve an appropriate use of case data, "realistic" assumptions about what one can do in a situation (Don't play God), recognition of

the power held by others, and a relevant sense of timing. Curiosity about what isn't known—as in Maureen Frye's case—can often be a more effective action approach than resolute determinations to clamp down, give in, go back to basics, or damn the torpedoes and go full speed ahead.

In that sense, most case situations provide ample room for creative actions and problem solving. In a sense, Maureen Frye discovered that already. But Frye dealt mostly with creative computer abstractions. She tended to overlook the combined world of ideas and people where conflict and diversity run rampant and where creativity can often resolve conflict and manage diversity only by taking other people's needs into account as well as our own. It's a different kind of creativity than the kind associated with computer abstractions.

Consequently, your own action networks should be based upon your own basic values but also demonstrate an awareness and understanding of what goes on around as well as within you. It should be pluralistic in the sense that you recognize the time, space, and people dimensions that we discussed above. It should be based upon analytical clarity and diagnostic combinations which are credible to a discerning reader or listener. Most of all, it should strike a balance between appropriate detail and a multifaceted perspective which convinces the observer that you have neither your mind in a tunnel nor your head in the stars—even though those stars may look from a distance like heroic, god like, forceful, or rational executives who are—in some wishful and wondrous world—just like you.

1
Individual Transitions

Introduction

Individuals change in many ways and for many reasons over their lives. Some transitions come as a result of natural human development, others by personal choice. Often a change in circumstances—whether pleasant or traumatic—will force a person to change. Conversely, people can act upon and influence the world around them, literally constructing or altering their own reality.

People are both active and passive players in these changing scenarios, evolving out of the world that created them and in turn recreating that world by their active participation. In the process, people often experience confusion, ambivalence, and resistance (their own and others') to the complex phenomena of change.

The cases and readings in this section cover an array of individual transitions. We suspect you will find in them many issues relative to your own lives and to the lives of people around you. Each case is, in one sense, a stand-alone story about a transition in one person's life and surroundings. In another sense, though, the themes from one case are simply recast so that they appear in a different light in another case. Thus, for example, we encounter both Rob Taylor, in a difficult personal situation, and E. J. Wiever, in the midst of a heady career, reflecting on the ways their family context has influenced their own development and the options that are open to them. Although the circumstances of the two cases are very different, some themes are the same for both Taylor and Wiever.

We can trace the development of a person's beliefs, values, and attitudes by examining the significant influences on his or her formative years. That is why many of the people you will meet in this section spend time exploring their own past and the ways in which parents, siblings, and other important people and events have affected their current view of the world.

This exploration not only helps these individuals understand how they developed the attitudes and behavior patterns that characterize them as adults, but it also contributes to people's ability to modify the patterns they choose to change. And when two or more people try to understand each other in the same way, they can create a relationship that is more harmonious, responsive, and satisfying for all concerned.

Several of the case protagonists in this section must use their self-knowledge to resolve personal, interpersonal, or organizational problems. Martha McCaskey grapples with discomfort about the methods she is expected to use to obtain competitive information that some would consider proprietary. John Bak feels forced to reconsider his career and life-style options when working with his boss begins to seem unbearable. Wolf Keller wonders what to do about a poorly performing subordinate whose problems Keller may have helped to cause. Frank Mason struggles with a situation in which his best professional efforts are not allowed to take effect. Milt Kuolt recognizes where his own skills, values, and preferences can be most valuable to the companies he builds and adjusts his activities accordingly.

All these people act and react in an environment filled with other people, with organizational and other constraints, and with varying degrees of opportunity. All must sift through the filters of their own values and perceptions to identify options and choose among them.

In thinking about these characters and their situations, we find it useful to look at their individual transitions in terms of the predictable stages and phases in the adult life cycle. The readings that conclude this section have been chosen to illuminate the effects of life cycle transitions in the cases you will study. By extension, we hope they will serve as a guide for thinking about your own lives and those of the people around you.

Rob Taylor (A)

Anxiety alternated with optimism in Rob Taylor's mind as he sat waiting for his brother. Alex was driving in from Toledo for a meeting with Rob and the counseling staff at the Cleveland Alcohol Treatment Center. Rob was scheduled to be released in two days after five weeks of intensive treatment for alcoholism. The Treatment Center staff had set up the meeting so that Rob, Alex, and two other executives could discuss Rob's treatment and his immediate future with Taylor Trucking, the family enterprise of which Alex was CEO and majority stockholder.

The two brothers had not seen each other since Rob's departure from Toledo some six weeks earlier. At that time, Rob had quit his job at Taylor Trucking in the wake of a stormy encounter with Alex—the last straw, for Rob, in a series of rebuffs that had colored the relationships in the Taylor family for as long as he could remember.

Many possibilities for a future away from Taylor Trucking had gone through Rob's mind in the weeks since his resignation, from the purely escapist to the more feasible and constructive. One option—eliminated relatively quickly—was to take some time off, using the financial cushion from his earlier sale of Taylor Trucking stock to support his family until he found a situation that suited him better. Another was to work with a friend in the same industry in Chicago who wanted to grow a new division of his company. A third was to buy a small fleet of trucks to start up his own new operation.

About half-way through his treatment program, though, he decided it might be better to go back and face the world that had grown so difficult for him in the weeks leading up to his voluntary hospitalization. He recognized that many of the problems he had been experiencing were exacerbated by his use of alcohol, and that things might be easier to negotiate now that he had decided to stop drinking. He also came to believe that leaving Taylor Trucking was a decision too major to be made impulsively.

Still, he was very apprehensive about the reaction he was likely to get from Alex. On the one hand, Rob felt he had never been able to live up to his older brother's expectations. Now he assumed that Alex would be angry and upset about his walking out in the midst of the budget planning cycle. On the other hand, he hoped Alex would share his sense of accomplishment at having undertaken the arduous challenges of the treatment program.

Rob's boss, who had refused to accept his resignation six weeks earlier, would be coming with Alex as would the vice president of Human Resources. Despite his nervousness, Rob felt hopeful that the four of them would be able to come to an understanding about his return to Taylor Trucking—especially if Alex, too, really wanted the situation to improve.

Research Associate Colleen Kaftan prepared this case under the supervision of Professor Louis B. Barnes as the basis for class discussion rather than to illustrate either effective or ineffective handling of an administrative situation.

BACKGROUND ON THE COMPANY AND THE TAYLOR FAMILY

Founded by Rob's father Fred in 1935, Taylor Trucking Company had grown haltingly through the first thirty years of its existence. Fred Taylor had sold the family car in order to buy his first truck so that he could support his young family by making deliveries in the Toledo area. At 31 years old, Fred had a wife Marie, a baby son Alex, and another child on the way. By the time the family was complete, there were six children in all: Alex (born in 1935), Frank (1937), Rob (1940), Bill (1947), Thomas (1949), and Sharon (1951). All but the two youngest eventually joined the company.

Fred and Marie Taylor

Marie Taylor had converted from her Protestant background to Catholicism before her marriage to Fred. The two agreed to raise their children in a strict Catholic atmosphere similar to the one Fred had known. As the oldest of three children, Fred had always exercised considerable authority over his brothers. The brothers claimed that Fred was never interested in any activity—sports, business, or other—unless he could be in control.

Rob Taylor thought the Great Depression had deeply affected his father's way of thinking. In an era of extreme competition for scarce job opportunities, Fred developed the opinion that showing love and warmth was a weakness. Any expression of weakness would eliminate one's chances of being among the few people hired from the huge surplus of applicants for any job opening. A tough, aggressive attitude and a willingness to work hard were the only chances for success, particularly for a man like Fred Taylor whose formal schooling had stopped after the fourth grade.

Fred's severe demeanor had marked the company as well as the Taylor family. Throughout the early years, Taylor Trucking remained in a continuous state of austerity. Taylor trucks were notorious for breaking down en route, because Fred always bought inexpensive, used equipment—he was loath to approach bankers for the loans he would need to purchase a more reliable fleet. The company's survival and later prosperity seemed a vindication of Fred's early dictum: you'll make it in this world only if you persist in working hard, being honest, and refusing all signs of weakness.

At home, Fred created a demanding and highly disciplined atmosphere for the children. Somewhat frustrated not to have participated actively in World War II, he joined the National Guard and applied many of the military's training methods in his own family. Praise was virtually never forthcoming for any of the Taylor children's accomplishments. Fred clearly felt more comfortable criticizing flaws and failings. Years later, Rob recalled:

Even the fun things—like going fishing—were difficult with Dad. He had no way of letting us know when we'd done something well. He could only criticize any slight mistake or clumsiness. I can't begin to count the number of times he told me I'd never amount to anything.

Only Alex, the firstborn, had escaped his father's tendency to make such dire predictions. On the contrary, Fred seemed to believe that his oldest son would naturally assume the leader's position in any situation requiring responsible behavior. Rob later compared this with Fred's role in his own family, describing it as "the old German way—the oldest boy always had to be in charge." But Alex, too, received his share of

Fred's critical comments. Even with his oldest son, Fred felt more comfortable issuing negative reactions than praise.

Years later, while struggling with his own drinking problem, Rob Taylor surmised that his father had probably been a binge drinker himself when the children were growing up. Fred seemed to drink when he found situations too stressful, and Rob recalled that his father was usually quite pleasant under the effects of alcohol—at least until he reached a certain limit. After that point the negative patterns would resurface even more strongly than when Fred was sober. As a result, Rob believed, Fred felt a need to keep close control over his drinking. That very need for control might even have contributed to the anger Fred harbored in himself, according to Rob.

Marie Taylor tried to serve as a buffer between her husband and her children. She lived every day by her favorite maxim: "Treat others the way you want to be treated." With the children she was caring, supportive, loving and philosophic. Rob remembered her as being very sympathetic whenever he had a run-in with his father:

She'd say, "Don't worry, things will get better." If things didn't seem to be getting better, she'd tell us, "That's the way things are. You can't change it." With Dad she had pretty much the same attitude—she wouldn't try to fight it. She always said that marriage was a union of two people— that it wouldn't work unless one of them gives in. Of course, she was always the one to give in. She was always subservient to him.

Sometimes, when he was really unreasonable, she'd try to negotiate with him. I remember a time when we got an invitation to go swimming with the neighbor family. As usual, his immediate reaction was *no*—the implication being that we were going to do something wrong. She talked with him about it, and eventually he came around to say it was o.k. for us to go. But by that time, of course, it was too late—they'd already left hours ago.

High school was a particularly difficult time to live with his father, according to Rob Taylor. For one thing, his mother suffered chronic bouts of diverticulosis—possibly triggered by stress—and was often unable to mediate between Fred and the children. Neither parent gave him any help in overcoming his lack of intimacy. Dating and romance were never discussed in the Taylor household. There was only one phone in the house, located just behind the chair where Fred Taylor always sat. Naturally, Rob found it almost impossible to make calls in front of his father. His social contacts were effectively limited to the time he spent away from home.

Paradoxically, Rob also remembered benefiting from a tremendous amount of freedom during his high school years because his father was always preoccupied with work. All the Taylor children went to parochial schools, and the three oldest boys attended a Catholic boys high school in downtown Toledo. Since the school was out of busing range, the boys had their own car. By the time Rob was sixteen, his two brothers had already graduated from high school and the car belonged to him alone.

Rob could not recall having a curfew during high school. He never abused that freedom, though, partly because athletics and other school activities kept him busy most of the time. Where Alex had been quiet, studious, and uncomfortable in social situations, Frank and Rob both had many friends and were quite involved in student activities. Alex had achieved above-average—but not outstanding—grades, but Frank and Rob were both average students.

Rob excelled in two areas: music and sports. By the time of his senior year, he was starting quarterback on the school's championship football team and was a starter on the basketball team. He also had established an impressive reputation as a trumpet player in the high school band and in a local dance ensemble. At the same time, like his brothers, he spent every summer, holiday, and other bit of free time outside the sports seasons working at Taylor Trucking.

Looking back, Rob realized that alcohol had already been part of his life as a teenager. In the off-season, when he was free of training regulations, he often participated in the beer parties that were practically a tradition among local youth. For Rob, though, the beer drinking did not diminish after high school. It only intensified as he sought ways of getting away from his father and salvaging his self-esteem.

Post-High School Years

Alex Taylor's academic performance soared after high school. He was featured in *Who's Who* as a student at a local Catholic college, where he graduated with honors and a commission from ROTC. Shortly after graduation, he married a young woman from Toledo. By autumn of 1957, he left to serve in the military and then went into an MBA program on his release in 1959. In June of 1961, again having graduated at the top of his class (with a concentration in accounting this time), Alex moved back to Toledo to join the company.

Frank and Rob were not as successful academically. Frank started out at the same college Alex had attended, but dropped out after one semester. He joined the National Guard and worked at Taylor Trucking, managing a small warehouse operation, while waiting to be called up.

Rob was refused admission to Alex's college. The rejection came partly (he thought) because he hadn't taken the admissions process seriously. Fred Taylor was livid: according to him, both Frank and Rob were failures who would be incapable of following in their brother's footsteps.

In September of 1958, Rob left for Columbus to study at Ohio State University.

The memory of his departure was still painful almost twenty years later:

It was just going there cold—I'd been accepted but hadn't talked to any advisors; didn't have a dorm room lined up or anything. Dad was sitting at the kitchen table. I came through with my suitcase and said, "I'm going." He didn't even get up. He just looked at me and said, "You better do well, and not spend all your time drinking. I don't even know what you're going out there for. You're never going to make it anyway." I just said goodbye and left. I was relieved to get away.

The year at Columbus was better socially than academically. By January, he was on probation and in June he was told not to come back unless he filed an official appeal. Without a student deferment, he faced being drafted into the Army. He decided to join the National Guard like his father and his brother Frank. Basic training lasted six months. Just before Christmas, Rob returned home and decided to go to his father's office while still in uniform. Again he felt the pain of rebuff: Fred offered not much more than a brief greeting, and then had to leave to do other work. "It was like I was a thorn in his side," Rob remembered.

Rob worked at the company shop through the spring and summer of 1960, and in the fall he returned to Columbus on appeal. By January of 1961 he was refused the right to return: his grades for the semester had been one point below the cutoff.

When he went back to Toledo that time, his father snarled, "It's just like I told you. You can't make it in college, so you'd better get used to working." Fred gave Rob the dirtiest job in the shop. As a mechanic, Rob remembered getting grease so ground into his hands that it was impossible to wash off.

That October, Rob and Frank were called to active duty for a period of one year. Rob was named administration specialist assistant to the first sergeant in his group. His responsibilities grew steadily over time until the sergeant came to rely on him alone for all administrative information regarding the 278-man infantry command. Rob was also placed in charge of the whole company when the commander was absent or out on maneuvers.

The two brothers returned from active service in the summer of 1962. Frank was dismayed to find that his warehouse management job had been filled by someone else during his absence, and that Alex felt there was no other position available for him at Taylor Trucking. ("Alex didn't think Frank was the caliber of person he wanted in the company," Rob later recalled.)

Fred Taylor accepted Alex's decision but felt a need to provide some security for Frank. He purchased a small trucking operation that Frank could run as a separate business. Rob believed that Frank never got over the bitterness of being forced out of the family company. Years later, Frank was still running his company at about the same size and pace, in contrast to the phenomenal growth at Taylor. Neither Frank nor Alex seemed to have much understanding or respect for the other's personal choices and working habits.

Rob's experience on returning from the National Guard was somewhat more gratifying than Frank's. Rob drove a Taylor truck for one month and then was brought into the office as dispatcher. He lived at home for one year, until age 23. After two years in his job as dispatcher, he was named head of the dispatching department.

During the same period, he played semi-pro football with a team in a neighboring town. As in high school, he held the quarterback's position and led a winning team. He worked hard, played hard, and enjoyed an active social life—which usually entailed fairly large doses of alcohol, unless there was a game the next day.

The National Guard and the football team stood out in later years as exciting, happy experiences in Rob's life. Both activities allowed him to feel as though he could exercise control over his own destiny, as though he really could accomplish something. Neither of them, though, was enough to earn the kind of family recognition his brother Alex got. No family member (except for one uncle, who came despite Fred Taylor's disapproval) ever attended Rob's football games. No one ever commented on the complimentary statements about Rob's performance in the sports press. Fred Taylor only grumbled that the football team was a rowdy group of drinkers and ne'er-do-wells.

The New Generation at Taylor Trucking

Alex had returned from his MBA program eager to apply his new knowledge to the sleepy family company. Treading slowly at first, he was able to win his father's confidence, and by the mid-1960s he had gained considerable influence at Taylor Trucking. Rob was pleased to have his brother back in town, if only for the hope that Alex's presence would make life with their father somewhat more bearable.

The atmosphere at Taylor Trucking remained stern and demanding under Alex. Rob accepted the challenge and worked hard to gain Alex's approval. With a new sense of mission and an expanded set of responsibilities, Rob considered the growth years of 1965-1979 the most enjoyable and exhilarating period of his life.

Under Alex's guidance, Taylor Trucking expanded from a regional carrier within Ohio to a statewide system and later to include several other neighboring states. New controls were established to make the business more profitable; profits were then poured back to finance further growth. By the early 1970s, soon after Alex formally took over as CEO, Taylor operated a nationwide transport network and was authorized to carry virtually any kind of load.

The expanded operations made management a more exacting task than it had been in earlier days. Alex had made it clear already in 1966 that a college education was a prerequisite to a successful management career at Taylor. Rising to the challenge, Rob took an accounting course at Alex's local alma mater. He felt enormous pride to be able to show his brother the B+ he earned on the final exam. Alex seemed impressed with Rob's initiative and the results; Rob began to feel encouraged that the two of them would work well together in running Taylor Trucking.

Both Fred and Alex looked increasingly to Rob for information about the operations end of the business. Alex dealt with the banks and the ICC authorities based on Rob's forecasts of operational needs. Even Fred showed occasional (if indirect) signs of approval about Rob's contribution to the company. He went out of his way to attend Rob's periodic "driver dinners" and always praised Rob's performance in his after-dinner talks. Rob also heard frequent reports of Fred's having complimented him in casual conversations with "old-timers" at Taylor.

Fred still "blistered" Rob if ever there was a problem with service or operations, but Rob felt honored to be placed in that position of responsibility—even if it meant submitting to his father's occasional rage and his brother's stern admonishments. Working 80-hour weeks, the Taylors never lost sight of Fred's original philosophy: Do whatever the customer wants, regardless of the inconvenience to yourself. Do whatever it takes. That's how we built the business; that's how we will maintain the business.

Other happy events also took place during that period. Rob married and started a family. He and his wife determined never to pass on the negative feelings to their own three children that Rob had known at home. The kids were happy and successful in school; the whole family was healthy.

With time Fred Taylor seemed more and more to want to break through his stern exterior. As Taylor Trucking grew in size and visibility, Fred started being tapped for positions of respect in the community. He was particularly proud to be named to the Police and Fire Commission. Rob thought Fred was slowly allowing himself to drop some of his worries about the company and to "think more about living." As Alex and Rob took over the details of running Taylor Trucking, Fred tried to create more positive personal relationships with all his children. Marie Taylor, as always, was a gentle ally in the process. Rob appreciated the chance to be somewhat closer to his dad, but the strains of their past were never very far below the surface.

Rob's younger brother Bill flunked out of college, spent three years in the service, and came back to work part time at Taylor while attending a local university in 1973. After graduating, Bill was put in charge of the service area over mild protests from Alex. The two youngest Taylors, Thomas and Sharon, obtained advanced degrees and settled on opposite coasts. They were the only siblings never to have considered careers in the family company.

Growth and Change

With Taylor's growth came increased competition and other challenges of a nationwide network. By the late 1970s, when annual revenues were nearly $100 million, Alex Taylor became convinced he needed a new layer of professional managers to help him run the company. He brought in a new president with years of experience in a large, well-managed consumer goods company. The new president, Jack Jacobsen, hired several other executives including a human resources manager and a director of organizational development. Together they set about trying to get employees at all levels to take more initiative for decision-making in their areas of responsibility.

In trying to encourage proactive attitudes at Taylor, they were up against forty years of company tradition. Both Fred Taylor and his son Alex had been seen as rather forbidding bosses. As a result, most employees waited to get instructions from above rather than making decisions on their own. Even the more recent hires, the college graduates Alex had chosen, seemed to be more comfortable implementing Alex's edicts than designing their own courses of action.

Rob Taylor had been put in charge of a separate division at the time Jacobsen was hired. He, too, had a tendency to run his ideas past his father or his brother before taking significant action. Fred was now chairman and Alex CEO, but both could still be expected to have an opinion about Rob's business decisions. In Alex's case, the opinions were seemingly more and more critical of Rob as time wore on.

By 1979, under the triple threat of skyrocketing fuel prices, a national recession, and deregulation in the trucking industry, Rob began to feel increasing pressure to perform. Alex's severe attitude did nothing to lighten the load. He found himself drinking more on weekends than he had for several years, probably as a vent for the stress he was feeling. Nevertheless, he maintained strict control over the alcohol: he never drank on Sundays nor during the week. He couldn't afford to be even the least bit impaired on the job.

Later that year his reporting relationship changed. No longer a direct report of his own brother, he was placed under Jack Jacobsen instead. Alex was still very friendly and cordial at family gatherings, but at work he told Rob to address all communication to Jacobsen. (Behind the scenes, however, Rob felt quite certain that Alex was keeping close tabs on his activities through Jacobsen.)

Rob never felt entirely comfortable with Jacobsen, particularly in light of the latter's frequent insistence on a "professional style of management." On occasion, the phrase seemed designed to eliminate anyone who had not benefited from an education like Alex's.

Labor relations were proving to be among the company's biggest challenges in the new competitive environment. Rob's division went through a grueling series of negotiations in order to achieve a 15% pay cut that both Alex and Jacobsen considered essential to the company's ability to compete. In one big industrial state, the contract was not settled until after a painful, thirty-day drivers' strike. Acrimony was also high in other states, but Rob finally managed to achieve his goals with all four unions represented in the division.

A conversation with Jacobsen shortly afterward left Rob somewhat nonplussed about his boss's intentions for him. Jacobsen remarked that Rob looked tired after the ordeal of the negotiations. Rob replied that the three-month process had been exhausting. Jacobsen then asked whether Rob had ever felt he was out of place in the company as it appeared to be going forward. In a statement he later regretted, Rob said, "I'm almost starting to wonder whether I *am* out of place here." Jacobsen shot back, "Well, you know it's never comfortable to be a square peg in a round hole." The exchange ended there, but it rang in Rob's ears for a long time afterward.

A NEW ERA

Fred Taylor died at age 76 in 1983. The founder had never retired and, in fact, had become somewhat disruptive in his last years as he tried to stay involved in most aspects of the business—whether or not he had a full understanding of the issues. On the other hand, he had achieved a considerable improvement in his relationships with most of his adult children during the last years of his life. The only exception, ironically, was Alex. Alex's powerful desire to obtain full control of the company created a serious strain in his relationship with the father who resisted letting go. Fred's will left 50% of his shares to Marie Taylor, and divided the other half equally among his six children.

In 1984, the stock ownership arrangement was changed at Taylor Trucking. Marie Taylor and all the children but Alex sold their shares to a family trust, in which they maintained family ownership. The sale resulted in a welcome cash settlement for the growing next-generation Taylor families without forcing the company to go public. For his part, Alex kept his voting shares in the company, thereby becoming majority voting shareholder.

After that point, life at work became increasingly difficult for Rob. He felt almost constantly on edge, straining to disprove Jack Jacobsen's comment about the square peg in a round hole. His division's performance figures showed slow and steady improvement, but operating costs continued to rise and squeeze profits, requiring further cost reductions in labor and other areas of the company. The unremitting stress was beginning to take its toll.

Alex was still very friendly in social and family settings, and claimed to be capable of separating business from social relationships. Even so, he felt free to criticize Frank for establishing a regular golf game during

the work week and for choosing not to improve his own little company the way Alex was improving operations at Taylor. Alex was equally critical of Rob. An admitted "workaholic" himself, he expected his employees to show a comparable amount of zeal. Yet even the eager middle managers Alex had hired were beginning to feel their enthusiasm crushed by Alex's tendency to behave as if *his* way were the only correct way.

Rob, too, resented what he perceived as intrusions by "Alex's hatchet men" into his own operations. In the relentlessly tight environment the new "professional" team seemed to want to eliminate the more "entrepreneurial" types that had grown up with the company like Rob. On more than one occasion Rob was treated to interference or criticism he found unacceptable for his management position; on more than one occasion he lost his temper with the intruder. Time and/or mutual (if grudging) apologies usually smoothed ruffled feathers after such an incident. Nevertheless, the tone at Taylor Trucking was increasingly strained.

The 1985 contract negotiations in Rob's division proved more acrimonious and stressful than the previous round. For competitive reasons, Rob's division of Taylor Trucking was forced to ask for another 15% cut in driver compensation. Rob spent much of the year trying to explain to the union representatives why the cut was necessary. He prepared comprehensive comparative studies showing the difference between competitors' wage structures and Taylor's. He also assembled several alternate plans for achieving the required savings.

In the end, the rank and file in each of the four state negotiations decided to accept Taylor's final offer. Arriving at that agreement, however, was a long and arduous process. The local that had struck during the previous negotiations rejected Taylor's offer in three separate votes. Only a technicality made it possible to push through a final offer that was structured slightly differently than the first three.

In another state, Rob had to begin laying off junior drivers and to face down the union's international rep before the local finally ratified the sister state agreement. A third contract ran out while the local union leadership stalled a mailing that had to be sent to all Taylor drivers there. And the last of the four contracts was ratified by a margin of just two votes. When the six-month marathon finally came to an end just before Christmas of 1985, Rob was satisfied that he had been able to maintain relatively good relationships with both union reps and the rank and file in every state.

Another challenge during 1985 arose from the discovery of a long-standing accounting error in the books of Rob's division. Neither the accounting department at headquarters nor the auditors had caught the error for several years. In correcting it, Rob was forced to take a substantial reduction in profits for the division for the year. As a result, he would have to report a loss rather than the modest surplus that had been expected.

As in previous years, Alex Taylor scheduled a companywide round of annual reviews and planning sessions for late January of 1986. About two weeks before those meetings were to begin, Alex came to Rob's office for a rare, impromptu conversation. The older brother's comments at that encounter proved to be the final blow for Rob.

Alex started by asking whether Rob thought he would be able to make a credible presentation in front of his fellow executives at Taylor. When Rob probed for the motives behind his brother's question, Alex unleashed a stream of criticism as strong as any Rob had ever heard.

He complained that the four union contracts were technically invalid because they had not yet been officially signed. (The fact that the drivers had voted to accept them and were already working under them was not enough for Alex, although in Rob's opinion it was the only true measure of a completed contract.)

Furthermore, he blamed Rob for not achieving the profit level planned for his division, despite the accounting error that had been missed by the accounting department and—implicitly—by Alex himself. He asked detailed questions about a number of minor line items on Rob's $30 million budget and seemed enraged if Rob did not have every piece of information immediately at hand. Finally, he accused Rob of shirking his responsibilities and of turning in a mediocre performance. Rob's contribution was inadequate, Alex concluded, and there was no room for such mediocrity at Taylor Trucking. Then he left Rob alone to contemplate his remarks over the coming weekend.

ROB'S DEPARTURE

Rob was all but devastated by his brother's attack. He spent the weekend mulling over the conversation, worrying about his presentation, and planning ways of defending himself in front of the other executives who would be present. He also found himself drinking more than usual in order to unwind from the stress of the week.

The following week, he spent two days out of town hammering out a long-term contract with a major customer. He took advantage of the stopover in Chicago on the return trip to have dinner with an old friend from a related industry. The friend knew of Rob's situation and was also acquainted with Alex. The friend's opinion was clear, according to Rob:

He told me I simply had to get out of that mess. He'd been saying it for years, and he even offered me a job developing a new division for his operations. He just kept repeating I'd be nuts not to get out of Taylor Trucking.

But Rob spent a few more days hanging onto his commitments at Taylor Trucking. He worked all day Friday on the presentation and returned to the office on Saturday afternoon. By then, though, his heart was no longer in it. He kept reviewing Alex's comments, and wondering how he would ever be able to highlight his division's achievements for an audience as critical as Alex was sure to be. Finally, late in the afternoon, he gave up. He would take his friend's advice, and get the hell out.

He left the office, returned home, and attended Saturday Mass with his family. That night he drank himself to sleep. He told his wife he was planning to resign, and begged off a party with friends on Sunday afternoon. She agreed to give him the time and space he needed. Rob decided to visit his mother—by now an invalid under round-the-clock care at home—and spent the afternoon drinking while watching the Superbowl on her TV.

During the game, he made several phone calls to people he had admired over the years, to tell them how much they meant to him. He had decided to leave everything: his job, his family, his home town, but he did not mention his intentions to anyone.

On Monday he stayed away from the office while planning his departure. He phoned his boss to announce his resignation, but Jacobsen was out of the office, too. He drank all afternoon and finally reached Jacobsen at home. Jacobsen refused to accept Rob's decision, but Rob told him he was quitting anyway. He was at the airport and ready to go.

Heading for Acapulco, he was forced to change his plans after missing his connecting flight while sitting in the bar at O'Hare. Hawaii was his new destination. He made it and spent another two days drinking in his hotel.

Coming Home

The breakthrough came on Wednesday evening, when Rob decided to call his son to wish him a happy birthday. He rang his brother Bill first, to find out what people were saying about his absence. Bill's only words were, "Rob, call home. Just call home." Alarmed at the thought that something dreadful might have happened in the family he had just left, Rob then dialed his own number.

In fact, the only problem at home was that Rob wasn't there. Renewing contact made him realize he couldn't simply leave everything as he had planned. He decided that night to go home and enter a treatment center to help him stop drinking. His wife agreed to find a program and to meet the first available return flight.

Five difficult, soul-searching weeks later, Rob was preparing to go back to Toledo as a man who had chosen to change. His immediate family had been entirely supportive throughout the treatment. Of his siblings, only Thomas, now a psychologist practicing in California, had been able to get through the telephone screen to stay in touch with Rob.

It was standard practice at the clinic to invite key members of a person's entourage for a group meeting just prior to release. Members of the counseling staff were pleased to learn that Alex had accepted Rob's invitation and was planning to bring Jacobsen and the VP-Human Resources with him to Cleveland.

Despite some lingering ambivalence, Rob felt ready to make a new, healthier commitment to Taylor Trucking. He wondered whether his brother and colleagues would see things in the same light.

Martha McCaskey

Martha McCaskey felt both elated and uneasy after her late Friday meeting with Tom Malone and Bud Hackert, two of the top managers in Praxis Associates' Industry Analysis division. Malone, the division's de facto COO, had said that upon successful completion of the Silicon 6 study, for which McCaskey was project leader, she would be promoted to group manager. The promotion would mean both a substantial increase in pay and a reprieve from the tedious field work typical of Praxis' consulting projects. Completing the Silicon 6 project, however, meant a second session with Phil Devon, the one person who could provide her with the information required by Praxis' client. Now, McCaskey reflected, finishing the project would likely mean following the course of action proposed by Hackert and seconded by Malone to pay Devon off.

Praxis' client, a semiconductor manufacturer based in California, was trying to identify the cost structure and manufacturing technologies of a new chip produced by one of its competitors. McCaskey and the others felt certain that Phil Devon, a semiconductor industry consultant who had worked in the competitor's West Coast operation some 12 years earlier, could provide the detailed information on manufacturing costs and processes required by their client (see *Exhibit 1* for a summary of the required information). Her first interview with Devon had caused McCaskey to have serious doubts

both about the propriety of asking for such information, and about Devon's motivation in so eagerly offering to help her.

Malone suggested that she prepare an action plan over the weekend. Ty Richardson, head of the Industry Analysis division, would be in town on Monday to meet with Malone and the two group managers, Bud Hackert and Bill Davies. McCaskey could present her plan for completing the Silicon 6 project at that meeting. Malone said all of them would be extremely interested in hearing her ideas. Silicon 6 was turning out to be a very important project. The client currently accounted for 15-20% of the division's revenues. In a meeting earlier that day, the marketing manager representing the client had offered to double the fee for the Silicon 6 project. He had also promised that there would be 10 more projects for the division to do that would be just as lucrative, if they could come through on Silicon 6.

By Saturday afternoon, McCaskey had worked up several approaches to completing the Silicon 6 project. With the additional funds now available from the client, she could simply have Devon provide analyses of several alternatives for manufacturing state-of-the-art chips, including the one used at the competitor's Silicon 6 plant. The extra analyses would be expensive and time-consuming, but Devon most likely would not suspect what she was after. Another option was to hand the project over to Chuck

This case was prepared by Assistant Professor Bart J. van Dissel as a basis for classroom discussion rather than to illustrate either effective or ineffective handling of an administrative situation. The circumstances described in this case are reported entirely from Martha McCaskey's point of view and do not necessarily reflect the perceptions of others involved. All names, places, and companies have been disguised.

Kaufmann, another senior associate. Chuck handled many of the division's projects which required getting information that a competitor, if asked, would consider proprietary.

McCaskey felt, however, that no matter which option she chose, completing the Silicon 6 project would compromise her values. Where do you draw the line on proprietary information, she wondered? Was she about to engage in what one of her friends at another consulting firm referred to as "gentleman's industrial espionage?" McCaskey reflected on how well things had gone since she joined the Industry Analysis division. Until the Silicon 6 project, she felt that she had always been able to maintain a high degree of integrity in her work. Now, McCaskey wondered, would the next step to success mean playing the game the way everyone else did?

PRAXIS ASSOCIATES

Praxis was a medium-sized consulting firm based in Chicago with offices in New York, Los Angeles, and San Francisco. Founded in 1962 by three professors who taught accounting in Chicago area universities, the firm had grown to nearly 350 employees by 1986. Over this period, Praxis had expanded its practice into four divisions: Management Control and Systems (which had been the original practice of the firm), Financial Services, General Management, and Industry Analysis. These expansions had taken place within a policy of conservative, controlled growth to ensure that the firm maintained a high level of quality of services and an informal, "thinktank" atmosphere. Throughout its history, Praxis had enjoyed a reputation for high technical and professional standards.

Industry Analysis was the newest and smallest of Praxis' four divisions. It had been created in 1982 in response to increasing demand for industry and competitive analysis by clients of Praxis' Financial Services and General Management divisions. Industry and competitive analysis involved an examination of the competitive forces in industries, and identifying and developing ways in which firms could create and sustain competitive advantage through a distinctive competitive strategy.

Unlike the other three divisions, the Industry Analysis division was a separate, autonomous unit operating exclusively out of San Francisco. The other divisions were headquartered in Chicago, with branch operations in New York and Los Angeles. The Industry Analysis division had been located in San Francisco for two reasons. The first was that much of Praxis' demand for competitive analysis came from clients based in California, and particularly in Silicon Valley. The second reason was that Ty Richardson, the person hired to start the division, was well-connected in Northern California and had made staying in San Francisco part of his terms for accepting the job. Richardson reported directly to Praxis' executive committee. Richardson had also insisted on hiring all his own people. Unlike the rest of Praxis' divisions, which were staffed primarily by people who were developed internally, the Industry Analysis division was staffed entirely with outsiders.

THE INDUSTRY ANALYSIS GROUP

By 1986, the Industry Analysis Group consisted of 15 professionals, 12 analysts (called associates) and six clerical staff. In addition to Richardson, who was a senior vice president, the division had one vice president, who served as Richardson's chief of operations, and two group managers. The remaining 11 professionals formed two groups of senior associates which reported to the two group managers (see *Exhibit 2*).

The two groups of senior associates were distinctly different. The senior associates who reported to Bud Hackert were referred to as the "old guard." Several years earlier, they had all worked for Richardson when he had run his own consulting firm in Los Angeles. In contrast to the old guard, the senior associates reporting to Bill Davies all had MBAs from well-known schools. Consequently, the "new guard" had significantly higher starting salaries. Another difference between the two groups was that the new guard tended to spend their time equally between individual and team projects. The old guard worked strictly on individual projects.

Senior associates and group managers received their project assignments from Tom Malone, Richardson's chief of operations. For the most part, however, roles and reporting relationships among the professional staff were loosely defined. Senior associates often discussed the status of their projects directly with Malone or Richardson rather than with the group managers. Both group managers and senior associates served as project leaders. On team projects, it was not unusual for the group manager to be part of a team on which a senior associate was project leader. The assignment of associates to projects, determined by a process of informal

bargaining among associates and project leaders, served to further blur the distinction between senior associates and group managers.

Malone and the two group managers also had previously worked with Richardson. Hackert and Richardson met when Richardson, who had a PhD in business administration, left academia to join the Los Angeles branch of a well-known consulting firm. Richardson left shortly thereafter to start his own firm in Los Angeles, consulting to high-tech industries. Malone had managed Richardson's Los Angeles operation.

Clients and employees alike described Richardson as an exceptional salesman. Very sharp in all his dealings, he had a folksy way with people that was both disarming and charismatic. Richardson was also a highly driven person who rarely slept more than four hours a night. He had taken major risks with personal finances, making and losing several fortunes by the time he was 35. Some of these ventures had involved Hackert, who had not made it in his previous employer's up or out system, and had gone to work for a major Los Angeles real estate developer. By age 40, the demands both of being an entrepreneur and running his own consulting business had played havoc with Richardson's personal life. At his wife's insistence, Richardson switched careers and moved to San Francisco, where his wife started her own business and he accepted a high-level job with a major international consulting firm. Within the year, though, Richardson had grown restless. When Praxis agreed to let Richardson run his own show in San Francisco, he left the consulting firm, taking Bill Davies and several of the new guard with him.

MARTHA McCASKEY

Martha McCaskey, 29 years old and single, had been with Praxis for 18 months. She joined the firm in 1985, shortly after completing her MBA at Harvard. Prior to the MBA, McCaskey had worked at a major consumer electronics firm for three years, after graduating from CalTech with a degree in electrical engineering. In the summer between her two MBA years, McCaskey worked as a consultant to a young biomedical firm in Massachusetts that specialized in self-administered diagnostic tests. While there, she developed product strategy and implementation plans for a supplement to one of the product lines, and assisted in preparation of the firm's second equity offering. McCaskey thoroughly enjoyed the project orientation of the summer work experience and her role as consultant. The firm indicated a strong interest in hiring her upon completion of the MBA. McCaskey, however, had decided to pursue a career in consulting. In addition, she had grown up in the Bay area, and wanted to return there if possible.

Praxis was one of several consulting firms with whom McCaskey interviewed. Her first interview at the San Francisco branch was with Tom Malone, the division's vice president. Malone told her that the Industry Analysis division was a wonderful place to work, especially emphasizing the collegial, thinktank environment. He said that, as Praxis' newest division, they were experiencing tremendous growth. He also said they were just beginning to get involved in some very exciting projects. The interview ended before McCaskey could push him on specifics, but she wasn't sure that such questions would have been appropriate. Malone had impressed her as very dynamic and engag-

ing. Instead of interrogating her, as she expected, she later commented that he had made her feel "pretty darn good."

The rest of her interviews were similar. Although she grilled the other people she met, they all told her what a terrific place it was. McCaskey was surprised that many of the senior associates, and even the two group managers, did not seem as sharp as she had expected. In one of the interviews, McCaskey was also surprised to see Jeff McCollum, a former classmate she had known slightly at CalTech.

Upon returning to Boston, McCaskey had a message from Ty Richardson, who had called to say he would be in town the following night and was wondering if she could meet him. Over dinner at one of Boston's most expensive restaurants, Richardson told her he was quite impressed with what he had heard about her. They were looking for people like her to help the business grow, and to handle the exciting new projects they were getting. He also said that, for the right people, the Industry Analysis division offered rapid advancement, more so than she would likely find at the other firms she was talking with.

The next day Richardson called McCaskey with a generous offer. Later that afternoon she received a call from Jeff McCollum, who once again told her what a great place it was to work, that Richardson often would take everybody out for drinks Friday afternoon when he was around. In fact, he laughed, there had been a golf outing the day before McCaskey's interview, and everyone had still been a little hung over when she arrived. McCaskey called Richardson early the next week to accept the offer.

WORKING IN THE INDUSTRY
ANALYSIS DIVISION

McCaskey's first day at work started with a visit from Malone. He explained that the division was experiencing a bit of a crunch just then, and they needed her help on a competitive analysis study. In fact, she would have to do the project by herself. It was unusual to give a new person their own project, Malone continued, but he had arranged for Davies to provide back-up support if she needed it. McCaskey reflected on her first project:

It was relatively easy and I was lucky, it was a nice industry to interview in. Some industries are tough to interview because they tend to be very close-mouthed. Some industries are easier. The consumer electronics industry, for example, is pretty easy. Other industries, like the electronic chemicals area, can be really tough. People making chips are very secretive.

Although it was her first assignment, McCaskey gave the client presentation and wrote a formal report detailing her analysis and recommendations. A few days later, Richardson dropped in on a working lunch among Davies's group to compliment McCaskey on her handling of the project. He went so far as to say that both he and Malone felt that her analysis was the best they had yet seen by anyone in the division.

Two weeks later, McCaskey was assigned to a major project involving a competitive analysis for a company that made printed circuit boards. As with her first assignment, she was to work alone on the study, consulting Davies if and when she needed help. It was during this period that Malone began suggesting that she talk with two members of the old guard, Dan Rendall and Chuck Kaufmann, about sources of information. The project involved gathering some fairly detailed information about a number of competitors, including one Japanese and two European firms. The old guard handled many of the projects that involved gathering sensitive information on target firms; i.e., the client's competitors. This was always information that was not publicly available, information that a target firm would consider proprietary. It appeared to McCaskey that Dan Rendall and Chuck Kaufmann were the real producers in this group, often taking on projects when other members of the old guard had difficulty obtaining sensitive information.

Rendall was the recognized leader of the old guard. He could often be seen coming and going from Richardson's office on the infrequent occasions that Richardson was in town. Recently, Richardson had been spending about 80% of his time on the road. When McCaskey approached Rendall, however, she felt him to be difficult and uncooperative. McCaskey found subsequent attempts to talk with Rendall equally unproductive. Chuck Kaufmann was out of town on assignment for two weeks and thus unable to meet with McCaskey.

Given her difficulty in following through on Malone's recommendation to work with old guard, McCaskey developed her own approach to the printed circuit board project. The project turned out to be extremely difficult. Over a period of six months, McCaskey conducted nearly 300 telephone interviews, attended trade shows in the U.S., Japan, and Europe, and personally interviewed consultants, distributors, and industry representatives in all three countries. Towards the end, McCaskey remembered working seven days a week, ten to fifteen hours a day. Her European contacts finally came through with all the necessary information just three days before the client presentation. Despite the results that her efforts produced, McCaskey felt that Richardson and Malone disapproved of how she handled the project, that it could have been completed with less time and effort:

The presentation went really well. Towards the end, I began to relax and feel really good. I was presenting to a bunch of guys who had been in the business for thirty years. There were a few minor follow-up questions but mostly a lot of compliments. I was really looking forward to taking a break. I had been with the company at this point for nine months, and never taken a day of vacation, and I was exhausted. And then, Richardson got up and promised the client a written report in two weeks.

Davies was very good about it. We got in the car to go back to the airport, and he asked me wasn't I planning to take a vacation in the near future? But it went right by Richardson. Davies didn't press it, of course. Even though he had an MBA from Stanford, he was a really laid-back California type. That sometimes made for problems when you needed direction on projects or firm policy.

The next day, I was a basket case. I should have called in sick, I really should have. I managed to dictate about one page. Richardson came by at the end of the day and said, well, what's the hold-up? I was so mad I got the report done in ten days.

The rate at which McCaskey wrote the report was held up by Malone as a new standard for Industry Analysis projects.

McCaskey's handling of the written report on her next project led to an even tighter standard for the division's projects. Hoping to avoid a similar bind on the project, McCaskey planned to write the report before the client presentation. Malone had told her she would not have any other responsibilities while on the project because the deadline was so tight. Two weeks later, however, Richardson asked her to join a major project involving the rest of Davies's group.

He kind of shuffled into my office and said something like: Damn, you know, ah, gee Martha, we really admire you. I'd really like to have you on this team. We're a little behind schedule and we could really use your expertise. I've also asked Chuck Kaufmann to join the team and I'd like the two of you to work on a particularly challenging piece of the project.

Despite the dual assignment, McCaskey managed to complete the report on her original project before the client presentation. That also became a standard within the division.

In mid-1986, several senior associates left the firm. Bill Whiting and Cory Williamson took jobs with competing firms. Doug Forrest was planning to take a job with one of Praxis' clients. Jeff McCollum left complaining that he was burned out and planned to take several months off to travel before looking for work. Over the previous six months there also had been high turnover among the associates. It had become a running joke that Tuesday's edition of the *Wall Street Journal*, which carried the job advertisements, should be included in the set of industry journals that were circulated around the office.

While some of the turnover could be attributed to the increasing workload and performance expectations, a number of people had also been upset over the previous year's bonuses. Richardson and Malone had met with each senior associate prior to Christmas and explained that the division was going through a growth phase, and wasn't the cash generator everybody seemed to think it was. Each person was then given the same bonus and told how valuable they were to the firm, regardless of the time they had been with the firm or what they had accomplished. But, as McCaskey recalled, what really got to people was when Richardson and Malone showed up at the New Year's office party in a pair of brand-new Mercedes.

Chuck Kaufmann had gone to see Malone about the personnel situation. He warned Malone that unless something was done to improve things, several more people would leave. Malone responded that he could put an ad in the paper and get ten new people any time he wanted. Chuck had been shocked. For McCaskey, however, Malone's response was not surprising. In the lighter moments of working on team projects, conversation among members of the new guard had naturally drifted to views on Richardson and Malone, and what made them so successful:

Malone was good looking, married with two kids. He usually drove a Ferrari instead of the Mercedes. He was very aggressive. You could hear this man all over the building when he was on the phone. We decided he was just really driven by money. That's all there was . . . he'd go whip someone and tell them to get work out by the end of the month so we could bill for it. And have no qualms about doing it, all right, 'cause he's counting his bucks. He was also a very smart man. If you spent a couple of hours with him in the car or on a plane explaining a business to him, he'd have it. The man had amazing retention.

Both he and Richardson were great salesmen. Malone could be an incredible bullshitter. At times, though, you wondered how much credibility you could put in these people. They kept saying they wanted you to be part of the management team. But then they'd turn around and wouldn't even tell us where or when they would go on a client call, so you really couldn't make a contribution.

Chuck's shock at Malone's response to the personnel question was also typical. McCaskey had worked with Chuck on a number of team projects and found him to be different from most of the old guard. He was working on his MBA in the evening program at Berkeley and really seemed to enjoy being with the new guard. McCaskey knew that Chuck also had a reputation for working on what were referred to as the "sleaze" projects in the office; projects that involved questionable practices in contacting and interviewing people who could provide very detailed in-

formation about target companies. Even so, McCaskey felt that he did this work mainly out of a sense of loyalty to Richardson and Malone.

Chuck was always torn between doing the job and feeling: These guys need me to help them run their business, because I'm going to be a group manager someday and they really need me. He was torn between that and trying to be, not diplomatic, but objective about his situation, saying: They're paying me less than anybody else but look what these guys are asking me to do.

He wanted to do good in the eyes of people he looked up to, whether it's Richardson and Malone, or peers like Dan or myself, because he has that personal attachment and can't step back and say: They're screwing me to the wall. He just could not make that distinction.

Chuck had been fun to work with, though. McCaskey had observed that many of their team projects had required increasingly detailed information about a client's competitors. These projects had given rise to discussions among McCaskey and her colleagues about what constituted proprietary information and what, if anything, they should do if they found they had to obtain such information. While there was some discussion about the appropriateness of such projects, McCaskey recalled a particular conversation that characterized how the issue was typically handled:

We were on a quick coffee break and Linda Shepherd said she really needed to get psyched up for her next call. Linda was a member of the new guard whom I liked and respected. She had an MBA from Berkeley and had been there about a year longer than I had. We became good friends soon after I arrived and ended up working together a lot on team projects.

I said, "Yeah, I know what you mean. I tried to get some discounting information from a marketing manager this morning and all he would give me was list price. As usual, I started out with general questions but as soon as I tried to get specific he was all over me. Like pulling teeth. Invariably, they slap it back at you. What information do you have? You know, and you don't want to give away the pot because then he'd know what you're doing."

Chuck's advice was pretty funny. He said that he was working on a project that was so slimy he had to take a shower every time he got off the phone, and maybe that's what we ought to do, too.

As was the norm on most of the division's projects, McCaskey usually identified herself as a representative of a newly formed trade journal for the particular industry she was interviewing in. To McCaskey, that was not nearly as dishonest as visiting a target company on the pretense of interviewing for a job, as a friend of hers who worked for another consulting firm had done.

All in all, McCaskey felt that she had been given the freedom to do her work with integrity and quality. It was also clear that her performance was recognized by Richardson. Of the senior associates, Richardson spent the most time with Dan Rendall, McCaskey, or Chuck. While Dan often could be seen in Richardson's office, Richardson seemed to make a point of dropping in on Chuck and McCaskey. For McCaskey, these visits always seemed to be more social than work related. Richardson's comments at a recent consumer electronics marketing research association convention were a typical example of how these meetings went:

We had gone to the dinner but decided not to hang around for the speeches. Instead, he asked me if I'd like to have a nightcap. I said sure. So we went to a bar, and he spent the evening giving me all these warm fuzzies; about how he really enjoyed having me with the company, how I was an important member of the management team of the company, how everything was wonderful with me there, and that he hoped that I would be with them for a long time. And on and on.

At the end of 1986, McCaskey received a substantial increase in pay. She also received a $10,000 bonus. Most of the other senior associates had received much smaller bonuses, in many cases equivalent to what they had received the previous year.

THE SILICON 6 PROJECT

In January 1987, both Richardson and Malone met with McCaskey to talk about a new assignment. The project was for one of Praxis' oldest clients in the high-tech electronics field. Since its inception, the Industry Analysis division had done a lot of work for this client. The project involved a new type of computer chip being produced by one of the client's prime competitors, a company that had also once been one of Praxis' major clients. The project had originally been assigned to Lee Rogoff, a senior associate who reported to Hackert. The client was interested in detailed information about manufacturing processes and costs for the new computer chip. Although he had made numerous calls to the target company's clients and distributors, Lee had been unable to obtain any of the required information.

Normally, Dan Rendall would have been asked to take over the project if it had previously been handled by a member of the old guard. Instead, Malone explained, they had decided to approach McCaskey because of her background in electrical engineering. McCaskey had in fact done some coursework on chip design at CalTech. Malone also told her they had been impressed with her creativity and success in obtaining difficult, detailed information on previous projects.

Malone added that there was one constraint on the project. The client had insisted that Praxis not contact the target company to avoid potential allegations of price fixing.

The project was code-named Silicon 6 after the plant at which the chip was produced, the sixth building of an industrial cluster in Silicon Valley. McCaskey began by contacting the Silicon 6 plant's equipment manufacturers. They were unusually close-mouthed. She was unable to get them even to say what equipment the plant had ordered, never mind its operating characteristics. Mc-Caskey also contacted raw materials suppliers to semiconductor manufacturers. Again, she was unsuccessful in obtaining any information. She held meetings nearly every day with Malone, standard operating procedure for problem projects. For McCaskey, the meetings soon began to have a monotonous quality to them:

How's it going? Well, OK. Let's retrench. Did you try this tack? Did you try that tack? Did you try this customer base? Did you try this group of calls?

Malone was especially interested in whether she was having any luck identifying ex-employees. On several of the projects Mc-Caskey had worked on, particularly those requiring detailed data, the best source of information had been ex-employees of target companies. McCaskey had generally found these people quite willing to talk, sometimes out of vengeance, but also at times because there was a sympathetic, willing listener available. People love to talk about their "expertise," she often thought. Industry consultants had been another good source of detailed information. It was not unusual for the Industry Analysis division to hire consultants for $1000 or $2000 a day on specific projects.

McCaskey felt that some of the senior associates had been rather creative in their use of this practice. Several months earlier, Chuck had confided to her that he had hired an ex-employee as a "consultant" to provide him with a list of software contracts for a target company. He said that this was something that Dan Rendall had done regularly on his projects. In one case, Dan had paid an ex-employee of a target company a "consulting" fee of $2000 for a business plan and spreadsheets of a target company's upcoming new product introduction. Bud Hackert was there when Chuck had asked Dan if such information wasn't proprietary. Hackert had a reputation as a tough, no-nonsense manager who prided himself on running a tight shop and on his ability to get the job done, no matter what it took. Hackert said that if someone was willing to talk about it then it wasn't proprietary.

McCaskey had mentioned the incident to Linda Shepherd. They both agreed that Dan's behavior, and Hackert's response, only confirmed what they had suspected all along about the old guard; they routinely paid ex-employees of target companies to obtain highly sensitive information for Praxis' clients. Linda ended the conversation with a comment that, given such behavior, the old guard wouldn't last long when the division really took off and headquarters became more interested in the San Francisco operation.

Many consulting firms had formal, written policies regarding the solicitation and performance of contracts. For example, some firms required that employees identify themselves as working for the firm before beginning an interview. The Industry Analysis division did not have any written, formal policies as such. Richardson occasionally had given lunchtime talks concerning the division's policies, but, as McCaskey recalled, these tended to be quite vague and general. For example, for McCaskey, the bottom line in Richardson's "ethics" talk was quite simply, we don't do anything unethical. Besides, McCaskey knew from her friends at highly reputable firms that people occasionally broke the rules even when formal, written policies existed. After her discussion with Linda, McCaskey considered raising the old guard's use of ex-employees with Richardson but he was out of the office for a couple of weeks. By the time he returned, she was in the middle of several large projects and had all but forgotten about it.

McCaskey's only lead on the Silicon 6 project occurred through a seemingly random set of events. Working through a list of academics involved in semiconductor research, she found a professor at a small East Coast engineering school who actively consulted with several European manufacturers of semiconductors. When she called him, McCaskey found that he could not provide her with any of the information on the list. Malone had suggested, however, that she fly out and interview him because he might have some gossip on the new chip. The interview served to clarify McCaskey's understanding of the manufacturing processes involved but, as she had suspected, did not provide her with any new information. He did suggest, however, that she get in touch with Phil Devon, a consultant in southern California. He did not know Devon personally but knew that Devon recently had been involved in the design and start-up of a plant for one of the European firms.

Upon returning to San Francisco, McCaskey called Devon to set up an interview. During the call she learned that he had been a vice president at the target company some 12 years earlier. When she told Malone about Devon, he was ecstatic. He congratulated her on once again coming through for the division, letting her know that both he and Richardson felt she was the one person they could always count on when the chips were down.

McCaskey met with Devon the following Friday. He was in his mid-forties, very distinguished looking, and relaxed in his manner. McCaskey's first impression of De-

von was that he was both professional and fatherly. Even before getting into the interview, she began to have qualms about asking for detailed information on the Silicon 6 plant. Feeling uneasy, McCaskey opened the interview by saying that she represented an international concern that was interested in building a semiconductor manufacturing plant in the U.S. Devon responded by saying that he couldn't understand why anybody would want to build another plant given the current global overcapacity for semiconductor production. He added, however, that he was willing to help her in whatever way he could.

McCaskey then suggested that they talk about the cost structure for a plant that would be employing state of the art technology. Devon responded that he would need more information to work with if he was going to be of help to her. He explained that there were several new technologies available or under development, and it would make a difference which one they choose. It briefly crossed McCaskey's mind that this was an opportunity to talk about the Silicon 6 plant. Instead, she suggested that they might try to cover each of the options. Devon responded that it would involve an awful lot of work, and that it would be helpful if she could narrow things down. He then asked what kind of chips they intended to produce and whether there would be several products or just a single line. He added that, if he knew whom she was representing, it would help him to determine what type of facility they might be interested in.

McCaskey felt increasingly uncomfortable as the interview progressed. She felt that Devon was earnestly trying to help her. He seemed to have an excellent technical background and to know what he was doing. It was clear that Devon took pride in doing what he did, and in doing it well. By mid-morning, McCaskey began to feel nauseated with herself and the prospect of asking Devon to give her proprietary information on the Silicon 6 plant. As she talked with him, she couldn't help thinking:

This is a guy who's trying to do good in the world. How can I be doing this? I have an EE degree from Caltech, an MBA from Harvard, and here I am trying to sleaze this guy.

At this point, McCaskey settled on a scheme to end the interview but keep open the option of a second interview with Devon. From the morning's discussion, she was convinced that he had access to the information she needed to complete the Silicon 6 project. Instead of probing for the information, she told Devon that her client had not supplied her with adequately detailed information to focus on a specific technology and plant cost structure. She added that his questions had helped her learn a lot about what she needed to find out from her client before she came back to him. She suggested, however, that if they could put together a representative plant cost structure, it would be useful in going back to her client. Once again, Devon said that he was willing to help her in whatever way he could. He said he had recently helped set up a state-of-the-art facility in Europe that might be similar to the type of plant her client was considering. At this point, McCaskey began to feel that perhaps Devon was being too helpful. She wondered if he might be leading her on to find out who she was working for.

Devon provided her with background on the European plant, including general information about its cost structure and other items on McCaskey's list. McCaskey was so uncomfortable about deceiving him about the purpose of her visit that she barely made it through lunch, even though she had contracted with him for the full day. After lunch, she paid Devon the full day's fee and thanked him. McCaskey said that she would get·in touch with him after meeting with her

client to see if they could focus on a particular plant design. Devon thanked her, said that he wished he could have been more helpful, and that he looked forward to seeing her again.

A meeting on the Silicon 6 project was scheduled with the client for the following Friday. McCaskey worked over the weekend and through the early part of the next week putting together her slides and presentation. Malone had been out of the office on Monday and Tuesday on another client presentation. On Wednesday, they met and McCaskey provided Malone with an update on her meeting with Devon and with her presentation. She told Malone that she had been unable to get the information. After Malone left, McCaskey once again reflected on the meeting. Devon had seemed so professional. She really wasn't sure how he would have responded to specific questions about the Silicon 6 plant. She felt sure he could have provided her with all the information they needed. On the other hand, although it sounded farfetched, it seemed just possible that Devon was so straight he might have called the police had she asked him for the information. Or, given his prior employment at the target company, Devon might have called someone there about McCaskey's interest in the Silicon 6 plant.

To her surprise, Malone did not press her to try to get more information from Devon. Instead, he asked McCaskey to go through her presentation. When she came to a slide titled "Representative Plant Cost Structure," Malone stopped her, saying that the title should read "Plant Cost Structure." When McCaskey asked him what he meant, Malone told her to cross out the word "Representative." They would conduct the presentation as if this was data they had gathered on the actual Silicon 6 plant. When McCaskey objected, Malone pointed out that the analysis was general enough that no one would know the difference.

Going into the presentation Friday

morning, McCaskey had only 30 slides. On other projects she typically had used in excess of 100 slides. To McCaskey's surprise, all of the client's senior plant managers were present for the presentation. She had been under the impression that the meeting was to be a dry run for a more formal presentation later on. The plant managers were courteous, but stopped her 15 minutes into the presentation to say that she was not telling them anything new. If this was all she had, they said, it would be pointless to meet with senior management on the Silicon 6 project, although such a meeting was scheduled for the following month. They then asked her to identify all the sources she had contacted. McCaskey did not mention Devon but the plant managers seemed satisfied with her efforts. Malone then explained that the lack of detailed information was due to the constraint of not being able to contact the target company.

The marketing manager in charge of the Silicon 6 project then asked his secretary to take McCaskey and Malone to his office, while he held a brief meeting with the plant managers. Upon joining McCaskey and Malone, the marketing manager expressed his disappointment with Praxis' handling of the Silicon 6 project. Specifically, he said that his firm had never had any trouble getting such information before. Further, he pointed out how much business they provided for the Industry Analysis division, and that he hoped the relationship could continue. Given their progress on the Silicon 6 project, however, he had doubts. Malone then brought up the possibility of still being able to successfully complete the project. Without mentioning Devon's name, he said that they had just made contact with an ex-employee who could provide them with the necessary information if provided with the proper incentives.

McCaskey was struck by how the marketing manager immediately brightened and told them that he didn't care how they got the information, as long as they got it. He then doubled the original fee that the Industry Analysis division would be paid upon completion of the project, adding that the additional funds should provide their source with an adequate incentive. He also told them that if they could come through on Silicon 6, he had 10 more projects just like it for them that would also be just as lucrative.

As they climbed into Malone's Ferrari for the ride back to the office, McCaskey felt stunned by the turn of events. First, there had been the unexpected importance of the presentation; then, the marketing manager's proposition; and, now, Malone's enthusiasm for it. Malone could barely contain himself, delighting in how Richardson would react upon hearing how things had worked out. McCaskey just looked at him, shook her head, and said "You're amazing!" Malone agreed with her, complimented McCaskey in return, and promised her she would be promoted to group manager as soon as she completed Silicon 6.

When they got back, Malone called Hackert into his office with McCaskey and briefed him on the meeting. Hackert's response was that it would be a "piece of cake." All they'd have to do is figure out how to handle Devon. Hackert then suggested that, given the importance of the project, Devon be offered a per diem consulting fee of $4000 instead of the standard $2000. Malone responded that he was unsure if that was how they should approach it, but did agree they should make it worthwhile to Devon to provide the necessary information. He then turned to McCaskey and suggested she think about how to proceed with Devon. He also told her not to overlook the option of having someone else, such as Chuck, meet with Devon. She could still manage the overall project. He grinned, and said it would be good training for her upcoming promotion.

EXHIBIT 1. Martha McCaskey

PROJECT

Develop a competitive profile, in detail, of the Silicon 6 semiconductor manufacturing facility, obtaining:

Detailed cost information per 1000 chips

- Utilities
- Scrap
- Depreciation
- Other materials

Salaries for professionals

Number of people in each category of hourly workers

How overhead is split out between the different chips

Equipment

- Description, including capacities
- Operating temperatures
- Actual production rates and expenses
- Do they use the same lines for different chips?

Raw materials

- Source
- Price
- Long-term contracts?
- How account for captive raw materials—transferred at cost or cost plus?

Marketing and service expenses

EXHIBIT 2. Martha McCaskey. Praxis Associates—Staffing in the San Francisco Office.

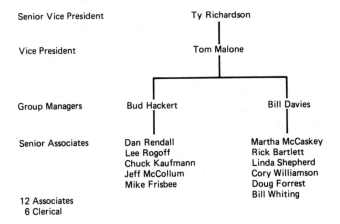

Senior Vice President	Ty Richardson
Vice President	Tom Malone
Group Managers	Bud Hackert · Bill Davies
Senior Associates	Dan Rendall, Lee Rogoff, Chuck Kaufmann, Jeff McCollum, Mike Frisbee · Martha McCaskey, Rick Bartlett, Linda Shepherd, Cory Williamson, Doug Forrest, Bill Whiting
12 Associates	
6 Clerical	

Frank Mason (A)

It was like stepping out of a steam bath into a cold shower," Frank Mason reflected as he recalled the day he left Great Pacific Paper Company. He now wondered if he would have left had he known what awaited him at the Abbot Business Supply Company. Frank sat in his office on Monday morning, September 14, and glanced out his door, noting that Ed Nolan, president of Abbot, had not yet arrived. In recent months, working for Nolan had been the most difficult experience of his otherwise successful career. When Frank had joined the company in March as vice president for marketing and sales, Nolan seemed to be delightful, charming, almost charismatic. Nolan had given Frank a free hand in reorganizing the marketing area and had practically guaranteed that Frank would be president of Abbot within two years. But then, things began to go wrong. He and Nolan no longer got along, his autonomy had been severely limited, company sales were again declining, and things in general were rapidly deteriorating. To make things worse, Daryl Eismann, president of Houston Electronics, Abbot's parent company, would be flying in the following week to review the company's current situation.

The previous week, Frank had decided to take some action before Eismann arrived. It seemed that it was time to have a candid talk with Nolan to try to resolve their differences. Frank had thought that Nolan would surely want to talk these things out before Eismann's impending visit, but even after working for Nolan for six months, Frank still found him unpredictable. On Tuesday, Frank had asked Nolan to have drinks with him that afternoon, but Nolan declined. He also declined Frank's invitations for lunch on Wednesday and Thursday with no explanation. However, Frank noted that Nolan continued to have lunch with some of the other managers in the firm. Frank still felt that a candid discussion about their relationship and the problems of Abbot could no longer be delayed, and he was determined to see Nolan as soon as he arrived. Nolan usually arrived at 9:00 A.M. which gave Frank almost half an hour to review the situation and gather his thoughts.

FRANK MASON

Frank was 35 years old, single, and a native of Peoria, Illinois. He received his B.A. in economics from Antioch College, served four years in the Navy, and earned his MBA from the Harvard Business School. He then joined the Great Pacific Paper Company in Spokane, one of the country's largest and most profitable manufacturers and marketers of consumer paper products. The company sold nationally advertised facial tissue, bath-

This case was prepared by Research Assistant N.J. Norman under the direction of John J. Gabarro as a basis for class discussion rather than to illustrate either effective or ineffective handling of an administrative situation. All names, dates, places, and companies have been disguised.

room tissue, paper towels, paper napkins, and other paper products. It was primarily Great Pacific's good reputation in the consumer products field that had appealed to Frank. His success in the marketing division had been spectacular—product manager in two and a half years (a company record), and senior product manager in only six more months. His salary had more than doubled by the end of his fifth year at Great Pacific.

But Frank also recalled the sense of personal stagnation that was growing during his last months there. Establishing new products had lost its charm; it involved the same procedures again and again, and he felt that there was simply nothing new to learn there. Moreover, because of Great Pacific's strong hierarchical control, ever-present committee work, and endless rounds of required approval, he felt that he had not really tested himself. In fact, with such strong control and competent staff support, it would be difficult to fail. He also recalled Great Pacific's disastrous acquisition of a regional chemical company, which forced them into austerity measures and restriction of expansion and advancement.

For these reasons, Frank left Great Pacific and went to Gleason Pro Shops, a retail sporting goods chain based in Seattle, as VP for planning and marketing, receiving a 15% salary increase over his Great Pacific pay plus a bonus. The autonomy he had there was indeed like an exhilarating cold shower. But corporate financial problems seemed to follow him from Great Pacific, for Gleason fell into a severe cash flow bind a few months after his arrival. Being unable to afford Frank's salary, the company sent him on his second search for employment in less than 18 months.

As he thought back on the experience, there were two things about his 15 months at Gleason Pro Shops that still concerned Frank. First, although he did not consider himself a "job hopper," he found himself

beginning to fit this unattractive mold. Second, none of his co-workers were college graduates, and they all used strong profanity, which seemed crude and unsophisticated to Frank. In retrospect, however, he suspected that he may have been too severe in his assessment of them, which may in turn have caused some of the personal animosities that had developed there.

After he left Gleason, Frank was contacted by an executive search agent, who told him of the job at Abbot Business Supply. The executive search firm had been engaged by Houston Electronics to find a vice president of marketing and sales for its Abbot subsidiary. Abbot had been a family-owned company with a very paternalistic style of management prior to its acquisition a year earlier by Houston Electronics, a producer of military avionics and space tracking radar systems. Abbot was a regional manufacturer of stationery and other paper products, as well as a distributor of related business supply items. The company sold over 2,000 products with annual sales of about $10 million. In addition to stationery and business forms, the product line included envelopes, typewriter paper, machine rolls, folders, loose leaf sheets, pens, pencils, duplicating supplies, staplers, blotters, and stenography supplies. Stationery and business forms were Abbot's largest items, accounting for 45% of sales, and were produced and printed on Abbot presses. About 50% of their orders were received from stationery and business supply stores, 30% from businesses, and 20% from school systems and colleges. Abbot was located in San Francisco, with 70% of company sales in the Bay area, 20% in Los Angeles, and the remainder in Sacramento. School systems, colleges, and businesses were contacted by company salespeople on a regular basis, while stationery and business supply stores sent their orders directly to the sales department. The company had been urgently in need of a vice president of marketing and sales, and the agent offered Frank a salary 20% higher than his salary at Gleason Pro Shops plus a 25% bonus at the end of the year. Although not initially interested, Frank eventually agreed to a luncheon interview later that month with Ed Nolan, the president of Abbot.

INTERVIEWS WITH ED NOLAN

After a discouraging interview for an unattractive job in Burbank, Frank arrived in San Francisco on a beautiful, clear day in late February. It was at the Top of the Mark Restaurant in the Mark Hopkins Hotel that Frank first met Ed Nolan.

Nolan appeared to be in his mid-fifties, about medium height, slightly overweight with large, heavy jowls, and a full head of gray hair. Nolan was originally an engineer and had spent much of his career in high technology companies. He had impressed Frank with his excellent mind, which could accumulate, sort, and evaluate a large amount of information and reach a conclusion in a very short time. Frank was also impressed with Nolan's personal charm, good sense of humor, and attentive interest, which made him seem, at least to Frank, almost benevolent. The one thing that Frank remembered most strongly about the meeting was that it seemed strangely unnecessary to "score points" with Nolan. It was as if Nolan was selling him on the job, rather than the other way around.

Frank also remembered his surprise when Nolan told him he was also president of another division within Houston Electronics, with $300 million in sales. But Nolan had explained that he was only acting as steward of Abbot until he could find an aggressive, intelligent, young manager to take his place there. It soon became apparent to Frank that the next VP for marketing and sales was very likely to become the next president of Abbot within two years. Frank expressed interest in the job and, without making any firm com-mitments, they left the restaurant and Frank took a cab back to the airport.

Ten days later, Nolan called Frank at his parents' home in San Diego and asked him if he was still interested. Since he was, they agreed on a date for Frank to fly up to San Francisco for a visit to the company plant and offices. Nolan told Frank he would pick him up at San Francisco International Airport on Monday morning, March 6. In thinking back to that March morning, Frank was a little amused at the comedy of errors that had occurred. Nolan had not shown up as expected, so Frank called his apartment. Nolan's wife explained that Ed had already left for the office, and a second call to Nolan's secretary revealed that he was not yet in but was expected shortly. Frank felt it would be a waste of time to wait at the airport, so he took a cab to the Abbot offices. Nolan greeted Frank warmly upon his arrival and seemed genuinely sorry for the mixup. Nolan then discussed company operations with him for the rest of the morning. Frank had researched the company thoroughly and was able to conduct an intelligent, knowledgeable discussion. In fact, it had seemed to Frank that he was more prepared to discuss specifics than Nolan.

However, Nolan had some strong general opinions on how to run a business. He was a believer in management by objectives and stressed the importance of good communication among top management. But he was equally convinced that each manager should run his or her own area simply and without help from other functions. Nolan emphasized the importance of the controller as guardian of the company's assets, and he stressed the need for efficiency and tight inventory control in production. He then added, "But in this business, control and marketing are the most important functions." Frank got the impression that Nolan saw people as either competent or incompetent, with great contempt and distrust for the latter. Nolan also talked for quite some time about his experience at Houston Electronics and the importance of accurate cost estimates in caculating required margins for their government contracts. According to Nolan, there were no serious pressures from the parent company, even though Abbot's sales had been declining. Until things were turned around, Houston Electronics could make up any Abbot losses. Frank talked with Nolan until mid-afternoon and then flew back to San Diego.

Two things bothered Frank about his prospects at Abbot. First, Nolan had failed to introduce him to any of the other people in the company (see *Exhibit 1*), explaining that they were busy with the quarterly report. Second, the job was in industrial marketing, which lacked the excitement of surveys, mass advertising, packaging, and so on. However, Nolan had promised the autonomy that Frank wanted, and there seemed to be a very good chance that he might be president within two years. To Frank, the autonomy and challenge of making major marketing decisions seemed to greatly outweigh the less exciting marketing problems of a small, non-consumer company such as Abbot. Additionally, he could live in the San Francisco area, which he had always liked. When Nolan offered him the job the following week, Frank accepted without hesitation.

A TALK WITH ST. CLAIR

On March 22, Frank began his job as vice president for marketing and sales of Abbot Business Supply Company. He soon met Bob St. Clair, a consultant to Abbot, who was also a graduate of Harvard Business School, and had been a consultant to Great Pacific Paper Company. They quickly became good friends, and Frank asked St. Clair to talk with him about the company's background. One afternoon they met for lunch, and St. Clair explained that Nolan was apparently the protégé of Art Lincoln, executive vice president of Houston Electronics (see *Exhibit 2*). St. Clair was on good terms with Lincoln, since they had been college roommates. Nolan had been the only high-level manager in Houston Electronics who was in favor of acquiring Abbot. His influence with Lincoln and his record as a high performer had apparently outweighed objections to acquiring a company in such a different industry.

Nolan was made president of Abbot and was put under heavy pressure from Eismann to improve its performance. St. Clair confided to Frank that Nolan had just told Lincoln that Abbot was in serious trouble. Lincoln had recommended that Nolan spend all his time in San Francisco and leave his division in Houston in the hands of his capable deputies. However, Nolan was still spending half his time in Houston.

St. Clair also told Frank that, while most people seemed to have difficulty getting along with Nolan, Rick Cunningham, the controller, and Lester Metcalf, the administrative assistant, were on good terms with him. They usually had lunch with Nolan three or four days a week. Both men had worked for Nolan at Houston Electronics. A rumor had it that several years earlier Metcalf had been near personal bankruptcy, and Nolan had saved his career. St. Clair added that Metcalf was very loyal to Nolan. Cunningham was an accountant who strongly emphasized cost control but reportedly had no sympathy for salespeople's problems. He, too, was very loyal to Nolan, and they occasionally attended basketball games together. As far as St. Clair knew, these basketball games with Cunningham were Nolan's only social life.

St. Clair knew that Nolan considered Frank a possible candidate for the president's job. However, he warned Frank that Jeff Steele, VP for operations, also wanted to be president of the firm and that Frank could be

in for a difficult time with him. As a final word of advice, St. Clair urged Frank to move into the vacant office next to Nolan's office, "before someone else tries to gain the favored position." Frank thanked St. Clair for the information and advice, and he returned to his office. The next day, he moved into the room next to Nolan's office, as St. Clair had suggested. At first Frank had been apprehensive about St. Clair's warning concerning Jeff Steele. Later on, however, Steele became one of Frank's best friends, while his relationship with Nolan became worse over the summer.

THE FIRST THREE MONTHS AT ABBOT

Initially, Nolan seemed to have absolute confidence in Frank's ability. Franks' recommendations on marketing strategy met no resistance, and he seemed to be the commanding influence on Nolan for his first few months at Abbot. Nolan had given Frank full autonomy over pricing, even though St. Clair had recommended that Nolan retain pricing control over very large orders. Although St. Clair also recommended that Frank be allowed at least two months to gain a foothold in marketing before taking over sales as well, Nolan wanted Frank to take responsibility for sales in early April. Frank was reluctant to take on too much too soon, but he hesitated for other reasons also.

When Frank first joined the company, Percy Little was in charge of sales. Frank saw Little as a highly regimented person who paid careful attention to detail but often could not see the whole picture. He thought that if Little had a personal motto it would be "everything to please the customer." Although Little had excellent relationships with the salespeople, he seemed to have little administrative ability. Nolan would often ask detailed, probing questions of Little, which he could rarely answer without checking his

books or asking one of his salespeople. Little's failure to have the answers at his fingertips invariably angered Nolan, who made it clear to Frank that he thought Little was incompetent and should be fired immediately. Frank also recalled the attitude of the sales force at that time. They were mostly "old-timers," many of them having over 25 years of service with the company. In his initial contacts, Frank found them to be shy, responsive to his questions or requests, and seemingly frightened of him. This was not a situation Frank wished to become involved in at that time.

But Nolan was persistent, and Frank finally yielded and took charge of sales. He felt that he would have to manage the salespeople as best he could, dealing with them primarily through Little. Little proved to be loyal to Frank, even though he, too, was one of the company "old-timers." Little seemed to be relieved when Frank took charge of sales. After this change, the organizational chart for Abbot Business Supply was redrawn as shown in *Exhibit 3*.

In early May, the company had a visit from Art Lincoln, executive vice president of Houston Electronics. The main purpose of his visit was to hear Frank present Abbot's business plan. When Nolan introduced Frank to him, Lincoln remarked, "So this is the guy who walks on water." Frank was somewhat surprised, but replied, "It depends on how deep it is." The presentation for Lincoln was a one-man show, and Frank was the star performer. Much of his presentation concerned a reorganization of the marketing function and its communication needs. He recalled that after his presentation everyone had been happy except him, because he knew that he now had to deliver.

In his first three months at Abbot, Frank had been faced with several difficult decisions. In late May, he found it necessary to release the entire Los Angeles sales force, since the volume for that region was not large enough to justify the operating costs involved. He contacted four large stationery stores and three distributors in the Los Angeles area, which agreed to order exclusively from Abbot. Frank felt that this action would retain most of the volume in Los Angeles without the high operating costs of the salespeople. He appointed James Au, the Los Angeles warehouse manager, to watch over these accounts and to call on them at regular intervals. Although the salespeople were released because of financial considerations and not age, Frank still had mixed feelings about firing them. One salesman was 69 years old, even though the company had a policy of retirement at 65. He reportedly had a private agreement with Nolan to remain in his job past the normal retirement age. Frank felt a great sense of relief when he later learned that all of them had obtained jobs within two weeks of their severance from Abbot Business Supply. Another thing he found necessary to do was to fire Sam Bradshaw, one of the sales managers. Sam was 57 years old with 32 years of company service and was afflicted with Parkinson's disease. Frank had discussed firing Bradshaw with Percy Little, and after a long and labored discussion, Little begrudgingly admitted that it probably wasn't necessary to keep Bradshaw. Although he did not find it easy, Frank eventually gave Bradshaw his notice.

As he began to get the feel of his new job, Frank also made friends with Roger Fields and John Cominski, his two sales managers, who seemed quite happy that Frank was taking the lead role in the company. Both of them also seemed to have considerable difficulty in dealing with Nolan. But Frank had dismissed any concerns they might have had about Nolan, believing that they were simply too unsophisticated to effectively deal with him.

In mid-May, Frank added Steve Lewis to his staff as a product manager. When Frank first met him, Lewis was working for Cunningham in the controller's office. Frank and Lewis were both bachelors in their mid-thirties, and they soon discovered that they were very similar in their life styles and sense of humor. One evening over drinks, Lewis expressed an interest in working for Frank. Frank had been impressed with Lewis's ability, and he remembered Cunningham commenting favorably on Lewis's competence. When Cunningham later returned from a meeting in Los Angeles, Frank indicated his interest in having Lewis transferred to the marketing division. While he could understand Cunningham's reluctance to let Lewis go, Frank was nevertheless persistent, and Cunningham eventually agreed to the transfer.

Frank had also hired Tony Buccini as a product manager in May. Although Buccini often appeared abrupt and stubborn, his enormous energy and his ability with numbers made him a good product manager. Frank recalled the day in mid-May when both Lewis and Buccini were officially assigned to marketing. He remembered how Nolan had emphasized that each manager should be able to run his own area without help from other functions. Therefore, he told Lewis and Buccini that, although their official functions were in marketing, they should keep themselves informed of other aspects of the company as well. The following week, Buccini approached Frank with what he saw as an impending problem in the company's cash position. They discussed it with Cunningham who assured them that there was no problem with the projected cash flow. Neither Frank nor Buccini were convinced, and later that afternoon they met with Nolan to explain the problem. Nolan could see no problem either and, over their objections, dismissed the issue as unimportant. Frank remembered the staff meeting two days later in which Nolan had emphasized the soundness of the company's cash position and how it was not a subject of concern. In retrospect, Frank felt that this incident may have strained Buccini's relationship with Cunningham. Now that Lewis and Buccini were working for Frank, the company organizational chart was again redrawn, as shown in *Exhibit 4*.

After a short time, Frank began to have mixed feelings about his job at Abbot. After searching for greater and greater autonomy, he had suddenly found himself thinking that he almost had too much autonomy. While the Great Pacific Paper Company approach had been tight control, supplemented with strong staff support, the approach within Houston Electronics could be summed up as "self-sufficiency," or as Frank often put it, "parochial functionalism." For Frank, this meant doing his own control, budgeting, planning, and so on. Also, it seemed to Frank that he, not Nolan, was supplying the leadership for the company. The scope of his autonomy seemed a little frightening.

PROBLEMS WITH NOLAN

During May and June, Frank began to see unexpected and unpleasant aspects of Nolan's personality. He recalled how volatile and unpredictable Nolan began to appear, particularly in the way he treated other people, such as Percy Little. Frank's tour in the Navy had taught him that when dealing with subordinates the rule was, "Praise in public, censure in private." Nolan seemed to take exactly the opposite view. It seemed to Frank that Nolan was a Theory X manager—"If something goes wrong, raise hell!" Also, during his frequent outbursts, Nolan would often use strong profanity, even during staff meetings, which Frank found distasteful and at times upsetting. He was shocked that a man of Nolan's stature would use such language at any time, but especially when conducting company business. At first, Frank had attributed such behavior to the other managers' ineptness in dealing with Nolan, but even so, he felt that Nolan's methods and language were unnecessary.

One particular incident stood out in Frank's memory. At a staff meeting in May, Nolan had wanted Jeff Steele to set up the warehouse like a supermarket in order to get away from the computer printouts they were using at that time in inventory control. "When I want to know what we have in inventory," he shouted, "I want to walk through the warehouse and see it with my own eyes!" Steele had argued that the computerized location system was efficient and reliable, and that there was no need to group and display their products in the warehouse like supermarket merchandise. Frank remembered how angry Nolan became during the conversation. Nolan apparently disliked computer printouts and believed that a good manager should have the relevant information in his head. What seemed quite strange to Frank was that Nolan seemed to look to him for assurance as he argued with Steele. Nolan even interrupted the meeting to ask Frank for advice on the matter. Frank responded that from his own perspective there would probably be no problems, but the real issue was whether or not the company would incur incremental costs by changing to the supermarket-type arrangement. The company changed over to Nolan's system within a month.

In June, Frank began to notice that his relationship with Nolan was growing more tense. Nolan had become very concerned about Abbot's recent financial performance, especially the firm's low margin. The low margin was primarily the result of Frank's price-cutting strategy aimed at reversing Abbot's declining sales. Also, the price of paper had sharply increased shortly after Frank took over pricing, which further hurt performance. Although the company's performance was not good when compared to the business plan, Frank pointed out to Nolan that it was still an improvement over the February figures. But his reasoning had little impact on Nolan, who continued to complain about the poor margin.

Frank's relationship with Nolan grew more strained in July, and early in the month they had their first major argument. Frank had approved the sale of an order at below the break-even point. Since he believed that the customer would not pay a higher price, and since the firm was experiencing high inventory levels, he approved a price that at least covered variable costs and provided some contribution, rather than lose the order. Cunningham informed Nolan of Frank's decision, and Nolan became very upset with Frank, since his decision would further reduce the margin. After expressing his anger at Frank for several minutes, Nolan suddenly demanded to know the margin on a small order for desk pens. Since Frank re-

garded his role in the company as strategist, he left details such as this to his subordinates. When he told Nolan that he would have to check, Nolan became furious. During the next few minutes, Nolan also expressed his displeasure that the former owner of Abbot had somehow obtained some sensitive information about their operations in Los Angeles. He was sure that one of the marketing people had leaked this information and he demanded to know what Frank was going to do about it. The entire discussion left Frank feeling very disturbed, confused, and angry, but he managed to tell Nolan that he would bring it up at his next staff meeting.

A few days later, Frank opened his staff meeting with a few words on the sensitivity of company information. He later informed Nolan of this action, but Nolan demanded to be present at the next meeting to see for himself. A week later, Frank presented the same information to his staff, as Nolan had instructed, while Nolan sat by the wall near the head of the table. When Frank finished his opening remarks, Nolan abruptly left the room, slammed the door, and did not return.

At Nolan's next staff meeting, he told Frank that he should send Percy Little to Los Angeles on Mondays to visit the major stationery stores there. Frank protested that there was no need to send Little to Los Angeles, and that he could be of more help in the home office. Nolan became visibly angry at Frank's response and instructed Frank that he wanted Little in Los Angeles on Mondays "even if all he does is sit there!" Then, without looking directly at Frank, he said, "When I tell someone to do something, I expect them to do it!"

Shortly after the incident over the break-even sale, Frank felt the need to talk with Nolan about how things were going. He spoke to Nolan one morning and expressed his frustration and confusion over what was expected of him. Nolan, however, responded that things were going fine and there was nothing to be overly concerned about. This discussion left Frank feeling very unsatisfied. It seemed to him that such a discussion should have had a more powerful impact on Nolan, but instead Nolan had been very calm and approving. Frank decided that it would be better to discuss the matter with Nolan during their trip to Los Angeles the following week.

Frank and Nolan arrived in Los Angeles on a hot, smoggy afternoon in late July. During the ride from the airport, Frank began to tell Nolan about the problems he saw at Abbot Business Supply. He said that since Nolan spent much of his time in Houston, there were communication problems, a lack of central focus, and a power vacuum in the company. Additionally, since Lester Metcalf, the administrative assistant, also went to Houston fairly often, no one was in charge of the company for long periods of time. Frank felt that Nolan needed to be at Abbot either all the time or not at all. Frank also felt that if Nolan could not be there at all, then he should make some sort of power arrangement. After expressing these thoughts to Nolan, Frank suggested that a conference phone hookup from Houston might be feasible. Nolan listened to Frank and seemed to be very understanding of the problems and frustrations Frank was experiencing. He agreed with Frank's analysis and seemed appreciative of his candor; Frank began to feel optimistic, since Nolan seemed ready to make some needed changes.

THE CONSTRUCTION PAPER INCIDENT

After their conversation, Nolan casually mentioned to Frank that the company ought to sell more school construction paper because of its current margins. Frank agreed and, upon his return to San Francisco, began to gear up for increased construction paper sales. One week later, Frank was surprised to discover that there was no construction paper in inventory. For an explanation, Frank went to Jeff Steele, who told him that Nolan had ordered him to stop purchasing construction paper a few days earlier. Frank then went to Nolan and expressed his distress that he had not been informed of this decision. Nolan remarked, "This is a small company. When I tell one guy something, he should tell the others." He had little else to say, so Frank returned to Steele's office and they discussed the matter for over an hour.

The following Tuesday, a salesperson from a major paper producer offered to sell 40,000 reams of construction paper to the company at a very good price. Frank talked to Steele and then to Nolan, explaining that the supplier would guarantee the order to the company's specifications and would allow Abbot to inspect the shipment before delivery. Nolan, however, didn't think it was a good idea. Although 40,000 reams was a small amount of construction paper, Nolan still said no, stating that "I don't want to go into it. I've talked to paper experts and they say we're too small to be hedging in the paper market." The next day, Steele asked Frank about the order and Frank told him of Nolan's decision. Steele responded, "I want to talk to Nolan," and went straight to the president's office. Twenty minutes later, Steele returned to say that Nolan had changed his mind and had decided to buy the 40,000 reams of construction paper. When Frank confronted Nolan about this reversal, Nolan explained, "For that amount, we can sell it. Besides, Frank," he continued, "you didn't give me all the facts about this deal. You never told me that we could reject the order at no cost to us, if it wasn't prepared to our specifications." When Frank pressed him, Nolan simply dismissed the issue, saying that Frank needn't be concerned about it. Frank left Nolan's office feeling angry and frustrated.

THE NEW PRICING SCHEME

In early August, Nolan took control of all pricing. The margin for July was as poor as that of May and June, and Nolan decided to remedy this problem with his own pricing scheme for Abbot's products. His pricing scheme was based on a required, overall company margin of 24%.[1] Since the cost of each item was known, Nolan could calculate a price for each of the company's products that would produce a margin within two or three percentage points of the required figure.

However, Frank felt that this scheme was far too simple. It treated every product the same, regardless of differences in demand, competitive situation, or unique qualities of each item. Also, it had the effect of lowering the price on high margin, low volume goods and raising the price on low margin, high volume goods. Since stationery stores often carried thousands of items, they could not absorb large orders and, therefore, would be unable to take immediate advantage of a lower price on the high margin, low volume items. Furthermore, if prices were raised on high volume, low margin items, which were typically price competitive, the company might lose those sales to lower-priced competitors. Although Frank voiced these objections, Nolan insisted on going ahead with his plan. When Frank saw the new price list, he protested that he couldn't possibly generate the volume at these prices. Nolan replied, "When did I expect you to worry about volume?"

As Frank had expected, Nolan's pricing scheme proved to be a complete failure, and the company's performance for August was even worse than it had been for May, June, and July. Nolan received the August performance results on September 4 and since that time had spoken to no one but Cunningham and Metcalf. Since Frank's autonomy was now very limited, and since Nolan was no longer speaking to most of his managers, it seemed to Frank there was no longer any leadership in the company.

RICK CUNNINGHAM

It occurred to Frank that his deteriorating relationship with Nolan was paralleled by his deteriorating relationship with Cunningham. During April and May, he and Cunningham got to know each other fairly well, and they would occasionally have drinks and dinner. Although they got along well after working hours, it seemed to Frank that Cunningham was a completely different person at the office. Frank felt that "apple-polisher" would be too kind a word for Cunningham, who blamed everyone else for any problems and always answered Nolan with "Yes, sir," "No, sir," and "Right away, sir." Cunningham also saw Percy Little as a major problem in the company because he was "giving the

---

[1] Margin, in percent, was calculated by dividing gross margin by sales revenue. Gross margin = Sales revenue–cost of goods sold.

products away" with low prices and easy credit terms.

It seemed to Frank that Cunningham and Nolan were always on the same side of every issue. After Nolan's reprimand over the break-even sale, Frank discovered that Cunningham had informed Nolan of Frank's decision to approve the order. That afternoon, Frank had found Cunningham in the hall and had asked him why he had gone directly to Nolan without coming to him first. Frank made it clear that if Cunningham didn't have the decency to deal with him directly instead of running to Nolan, then he too could play that game. In response, Cunningham demanded that Buccini mind his own business and accused Frank of letting Percy Little operate in his usual way, which was causing the company to lose money. After a short time both men calmed down and returned to their offices.

After this incident, Frank's relationship with Cunningham became more openly hostile. A few days later, Buccini drove to Sacramento and returned via San Rafael on company business but neglected to get receipts for the bridge tolls. The controller's office had recently established a new policy that specifically prohibited reimbursement of expenses for company business without a receipt, and Buccini's request for $2.35 was refused. Buccini explained the situation to Frank, who was amazed at the pettiness of the refusal. Frank was so angered by it that he went directly to the company clerk and complained. However, the clerk argued that he could not make the payment under the company's policy, and Buccini never received payment for this expense. A few days after this incident, Frank received a memo from Cunningham which said, essentially, "If you have a complaint, don't talk to my people, talk to me." To Frank, the note seemed to be the last straw. By the time he reached Cunningham's office, Frank was so angry that he simply crumpled up the note, dropped it in Cunningham's wastebasket, and told him, "I got your note."

THE CURRENT SITUATION

The most recent problem facing Frank involved Nolan's insistence that he dismiss James Au, the Los Angeles area representative. Frank had put Au in charge of the Los Angeles accounts after he had released the Los Angeles sales force. He had felt that the volume of business there was large enough to warrant a company representative to service these accounts. It seemed to him that, without a local representative in Los Angeles, the company would probably lose these accounts to competitors. Nolan, however, felt that these accounts could be serviced equally well from San Francisco, and that Frank should dismiss Au to cut costs. Although Frank had recommended that no raises be given to himself, his product managers, or his sales managers in an effort to reduce costs, Nolan still insisted that Au be fired. Frank felt that this problem, as well as the pricing problem, had to be settled before Daryl Eismann arrived. The impending visit of the parent company's president gave an added sense of urgency to resolve these and other problems that had developed over the previous few months.

Over the weekend, Frank had even considered resigning from Abbot. At first the idea seemed appealing, under the circumstances, but the more he thought of it, the more distasteful it became. A resignation, to Frank, would be an admission of failure, and if he took another job it would be his third in less than two years. Additionally, he had recently purchased a house overlooking the Bay, and the prospect of being without income again for an undetermined period of time would strain his resources. Frank had invested most of his savings in the property, and he did not have enough cash to sustain a prolonged job search. Also, he liked the Bay area and did not look forward to leaving it, if he could not find a job nearby.

Frank leaned back in his chair and tried to put the last six months into perspective. He had taken a job with substantial autonomy, a good chance for advancement, and a very good relationship with the company president. But the relationship had deterio-rated, his autonomy had been severely curtailed, and his chances for advancement looked dim. Nevertheless, he felt that he could no longer continue with things as they were. Some immediate actions were needed to improve the situation with Nolan and Cunningham. Frank became lost in his thoughts for a few minutes until he heard the familiar sound of Nolan's heavy, purposeful footsteps down the hall. Frank looked up and stared at the president's door, waiting expectantly.

EXHIBIT 1   Partial Organization Chart—Abbot Business Supply Company, March 1.

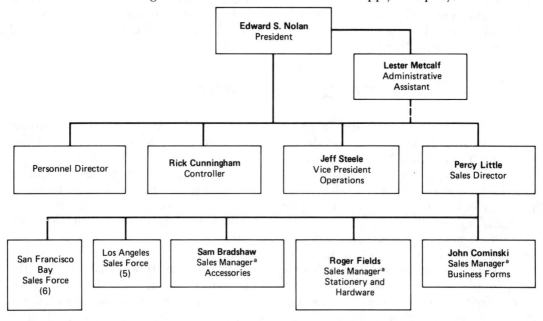

a. The company was divided into three product groups, each with its own product manager:
- The Accessories Group included bulletin boards, rubber bands, paper clips, maps, and art supplies (18% of sales).
- The Stationery and Hardware Group included stationery and envelopes, appointment books, scratch pads, calendars, card indexes, stenography supplies, fasteners, and paper punchers (39% of sales).
- The Business Forms Group included business forms, business envelopes, machine rolls, typewriter paper, indexes, folders, and expanding envelopes (43% of sales).

EXHIBIT 2 Partial Organization Chart—Houston Electronics Corporation, March 1.

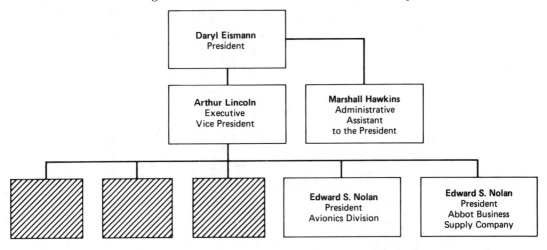

EXHIBIT 3 Partial Organization Chart—Abbot Business Supply Company, May 1.

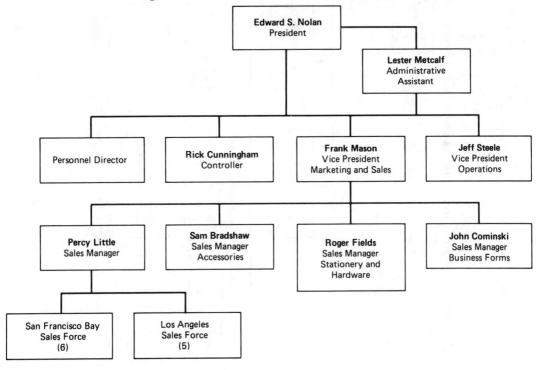

EXHIBIT 4 Partial Organization Chart—Abbot Business Supply Company, May 25.

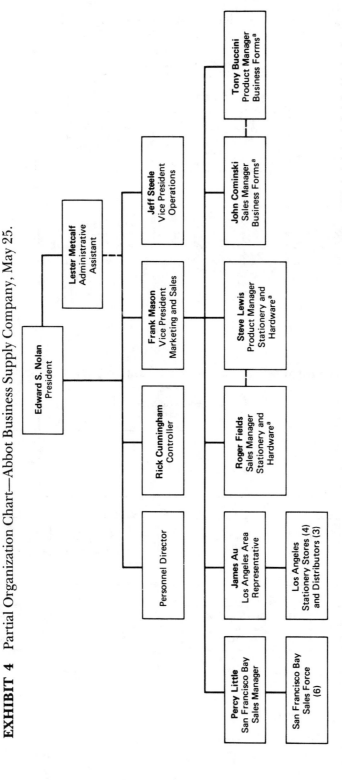

a. The products in the Accessories Group were absorbed by the other two product groups. The Stationery and Hardware Groups (49% of sales) then included rubber bands, paper clips, and bulletin boards, and the Business Forms Group (51% of sales) included maps and art supplies.

John Bak

In February 1988, management consultant Martin Drost received a phone call from his friend John Bak, executive vice president of Château Rouge Corporation, a Montréal-based firm which made heavy production machinery. Bak wanted to know if Drost could meet him after work. Drost already had plans that evening, but was happy to change them in order to see Bak, as he'd been planning to contact him for a while.

Drost thought he knew what Bak had on his mind. About eight years earlier, soon after they had met, Drost helped Bak find a new job when Bak abruptly resigned from Château Rouge. Bak had been persuaded to go back to Château about two years later. The new job at his old company was a big improvement for Bak in terms of compensation, explicit definition of responsibilities and authority, and a title that clearly indicated his position as number two in the company hierarchy. Drost knew that things had been much better, from Bak's point of view, during the years since his return, although there were recent rumors that some of the difficulties had resurfaced between Bak and Maurice Tremblay, the president of Château Rouge.

Shortly after six o'clock they met at a restaurant on Place Jacques-Cartier, and talked through dinner and into the evening. Bak opened the conversation with the remark, "I expect you know what's up, Martin. Maurice can't seem to stop meddling any longer, and this time if I quit it'll be for good!

I want to plan ahead for it better than I did last time."

Drost said, "How long can you hold off? You sound really upset."

"I am," Bak replied, "but I managed to leave today without calling a showdown. Tonight's Friday, so I can calm down over the weekend. Also, I've had two good offers recently; they're only waiting for my answer."

"That should help you, John," Drost said. "I also have a third offer that was made with you specifically in mind. I was going to call you next week about it." After giving their orders to the waiter, Drost asked, "Why don't you bring me up to date with what's happening at Château? You didn't have any complaints when we spoke last August, so I thought your troubles were over."

Bak said, "They *were* over, Martin, until about a year ago! Then Maurice started postponing approvals, ones I needed quickly or they wouldn't be worth acting on. He questioned a lot of my decisions, things I'd been doing for years without his objection. They aren't important by themselves, except to show how he's purposely interfering. He makes more and more comments about how I should handle my staff . . . comments he knows damn well I won't listen to! I've never treated people the way Maurice does, and I never will."

After taking a deep breath, Bak continued talking. "Well, that's how it's been for just over a year. This morning, when I met

This case was originally written by Professor Joseph C. Bailey, and has been revised by Nicole Michellé Jordan under the supervision of Professor Louis B. Barnes. It is intended for use in class discussion rather than to illustrate either effective or ineffective handling of an administrative situation.

with Maurice to go over the next budget for my divisions, he said he'd been studying it and thought I should cut the marketing figure by three million dollars. I said, 'Not unless I cut the figure for projected sales by three times as much.' Maurice didn't like that but wouldn't argue; we've already gone over it too many times. So he went back to the three million he said I could save. I wouldn't take it without the sales cut back. Finally Maurice said, 'You aren't Château's president yet!' I just said, 'That's right.' Then he said, 'I think you ought to cut three million off that figure. Think it over.' I told him I would and walked out, and here I am."

Drost only asked, "What do you think he wants?"

After a long pause Bak answered, "I hate to say this because it shouldn't be true, but I think Maurice is afraid of me. He really shouldn't be! He's the top person in the industry; one of the old-timers, too, out of the rough-and-tumble era. Maurice owns a lot of the stock and controls most of the company directors. He's very wealthy and has been for years. It's taken me a long time to admit to myself that he might be afraid, but it's the only explanation that fits his behavior."

He continued, "My divisions' figures are turning out the way I predicted them to Maurice almost two years ago. I've pulled two of our chronic money losers out of the red. They're in the black now, and next year both will be making money. I think he's scared that everyone involved with the company will see the positive results from the work I've done over the last four years." Bak leaned closer to Drost across the table, and lowered his voice as he said, "Maurice is afraid they might decide he wasn't needed. Every day he's touchier about that, ever since he passed his 70th birthday."

Drost replied, "He can't last forever, John, and you're the only possible successor in the whole organization. Everyone in the company knows it, and a lot of them are looking forward to the day. You've put in 25 years all over the company, overseas and here, getting ready to take over when Maurice retires. You've spent much of the last ten years as his heir apparent; he chose you and trained you personally. Don't you think you can take the punishment a little longer?"

"It's not that simple, Martin," Bak answered. "I've never taken any 'punishment' from Maurice, except lots of hard work and tough assignments, and I asked for those. It's most of the other VPs who've taken the punishment; I mean, the ones who stayed on for the high salaries. The ones who wouldn't have all left. I guess I'm the only one who's still with Maurice who won't put up with his slave tactics."

Drost said, "Maybe that's why he picked you as his successor."

"Maurice chose me because I thought about problems until I was sure what the trouble was," Bak said. "Once I'd done that, a couple of likely solutions were always easy to find. When I went to Maurice, I always had ideas ready and then fought for them. I usually won because I checked everything several times. Those battles never bothered me, and I don't think they bothered him, either. The other VPs would generally tell Maurice the problem, and then ask him for an answer. That's why they got into trouble."

He picked up his glass, put it down without drinking from it, and continued, "He'd give them the answer, all right, and say they were stupid or dumb or incompetent. Right in front of their own people, too! Sometimes I'd feel sick over it. But when they'd come to see me afterwards I'd say, 'You asked for it, going in like that.' I'd try to show them that the only way to avoid being shot down was to have their own plan ready, and then fight for it."

"You know Maurice lives for nothing but Château," Bak said. "He and his wife, Anne, live in a hotel downtown on Sherbrooke Ouest, so he can be close to the office. They don't own a home, and there aren't any children. Anne's been a confirmed neurasthenic for ages, going from doctor to doctor looking for a cure. A few years ago she started with fads, cults and faith healers."

"In the middle of the night," he continued, "or on weekends or vacations, Maurice'll phone any Château officer he wants to, and either order them in to work while the office is closed, or keep them on the phone to solve a problem. He tried it on me not long after I got back from that Sydney assignment. I was expecting it because I'd heard some rumors. I just told him I had some guests over, and would see him first thing in the morning. Maurice never said anything to me, and didn't try it again."

"So you see, Martin," Bak concluded, "I'm not the one who's been taking that kind of punishment. It's the other VPs. Actually, it's the whole executive structure."

Drost replied, "We've gone over some of this before, but I'm still confused. With salary and bonuses you're earning well over $300,000. You don't put up with Maurice's bullying; in fact, you're indispensable to him. You've been working hard for a long time to get what's almost in your hands; it can't be long now. Why don't you go along until the company is yours?"

Bak answered after another long pause. "Age is one reason, both his and mine. I'm 50, and if I'm going to do anything important in an organization as big as Château Rouge, I've got to have a free rein as soon as possible. Ten years is hardly enough. Fifteen might be. At least I'm still ready to try hard, but I may not feel the same when there's less time."

"Maurice is over 70 years old," he went on, "although his close relatives had long lives. Many of them lived into their nineties. I think he's going to hold on as long as he can, but I may be wrong. Maurice often talked with me about his retirement and I think he meant it. But he hasn't mentioned it in a long

time. I'm not sure why he clammed up, whether it was his 70th birthday or the way I saved those losers that he couldn't rescue."

Bak stopped talking as the meal was served. When the waiter left, he continued, "Maurice still works like a horse, though he's slowing down and won't admit it. He may keel over one of these days, but I just don't know. His retirement is a big question mark, Martin. I've wondered about it for years. Now that I've reached 50, I realize I'm the one who's got to make the decision."

Drost said, "John, suppose Maurice died tonight. What would you like to do with Château? Why would you stay there rather than go to one of the three openings you've been offered? What's Château got for you that Peerless can't top?"

Bak quickly leaned back in his chair. "You've got an offer from Peerless?" he said, almost before Drost could finish the question.

"I've got the executive vice presidency for you," Drost replied. "Not at once but explicitly within one year, so that Charlotte Johnson has a decent amount of time to move back to the Chair. It has a salary, bonuses and deferred payments, plus a tentative pension to meet your requirements. I also have authorization to meet any offer you get from any other firm in the industry on each of those points."

Bak didn't say anything. He wasn't prepared for such an offer from the chief rival in his field. Bak's thoughts had been so preoccupied with his difficulties at Château Rouge, he found it hard to grasp his friend's statements. Finally he asked, "Is that true?"

Drost gestured towards his briefcase. "I have the papers with me when you're ready to look at them. Now how about my question? What does Château offer that Peerless doesn't?"

"Well, for one thing," Bak said, "I know Château like the inside of my own house. I know every move I want to make, who I want to make the moves, and when and how. I know what our weaknesses are, and things that can be done to correct them. I also know where we have untapped strengths which I'm sure can be developed until we're the industry leaders." He continued, glancing at Drost, "That means we could overtake Peerless's 10% sales' lead and end up 20% to 25% ahead of them. That's one thing Château's got for me."

Bak went on, "Another thing, and I should have said this first, I could bring out the potential in a lot of good people that Maurice has used as gofers. I could also attract and hold on to good employees who'd never come through our doors as long as Maurice's policies are followed. This is something I've wanted to do at Château longer than anything else. I feel I owe it to the ones who never got a fair chance to show what they could do. I owe it to some friends whose lives were made miserable because they worked at Château."

Bak paused briefly and then said, "That's a serious thing to say, but I mean it. The funny thing is that I owe more to Maurice than I do to anyone else. He gave me a chance in sales when I asked to be transferred out of accounting over 20 years ago. Maurice sent me to Sydney to take over sales when that subsidiary looked weak, and then put me in full charge in less than a year, when they had to replace the general manager. He gave me total freedom to run it for nearly a decade. Sure, he asked for results, but I'd do exactly the same thing. During Maurice's yearly visit we took our operations apart, down to the last cent, and I learned as much during his inspection as I did over the rest of the year."

"Maurice is a tough and often ruthless man," he continued, "but you've got to remember the times he went through. He grew up during the Depression. I've often told Maurice that he's a holdover from the old-time Hudson Bay Company skinflints."

Drost said, "That's quite a compliment to pay your boss! How did he take it?"

"Sometimes he'd look irritated, sometimes he'd laugh," Bak answered. "Don't forget that Maurice is probably the greatest promoter and salesman our industry has produced; nobody could compete with him ten years ago. He merged the first truly international organization in our business, at least from a Canadian base, and he carried competition into every profitable market. There's no personality like Maurice left in our field."

Drost smiled and said, "Sounds like hero worship to me."

Bak replied, "I guess it does. I've felt that way about Maurice for years. But I don't any longer. At least not much, not since I've been at headquarters and seen him in action with the staff. I was in Australia for nearly ten years, you know, and when I got back he sent me out again to put the São Paulo subsidiary on its feet. I didn't really get to know him, or the situation at home office, until about six years ago."

"I think maybe Maurice has changed, too. I'm sure he has in the last two or three years. He lies to me now, and goes behind my back and then denies it. He never used to do that. I've lost my respect for him."

Drost said, "Well, are you ready to look over the material I've got on Peerless?"

"Not yet, Martin," Bak said, "I can't swing around that fast. Or that far."

He continued, "What I mean is, I never expected that kind of offer from Peerless. Except for two years, I've worked all my life for Château Rouge. I can't just go over to the enemy that I've spent most of my time fighting all over the world. It sort of makes me feel like a deserter."

"Although," Bak added, "it might be a good kick in the pants for Maurice; make him put things back into perspective. On the other hand, he was really decent to me the first time I left. Remember how I just walked out? Well, Maurice said I had to keep my title and office until I found a new job. He was still going to pay me, too, but I didn't feel right taking it. He also met all my terms when I was rehired, and he kept them until a few months ago."

"What about the two positions you mentioned earlier? What do they offer?" Drost asked.

"You'll laugh when I tell you about the first one," Bak answered. "At this point their annual sales are barely $30 million a year. Château and Peerless are both well over $1 billion."

"Still," he continued, "they made it very attractive for me personally and for my family, too. It's MacRae & Sons. They've got this great country club type of place, out past the suburbs. I could live in the country and have a relaxing 20-minute drive to work. I'd get to spend more time with my family. I've hardly seen them in the last four or five years, ever since I started putting so much time into saving those divisions. My kids are in college now, and if Katie and I don't see them as much as possible while we can, it's going to be too late."

"I think I owe something to Katie in all this," he explained. "We were very close in Australia, and saw each other nearly as much after the São Paulo transfer. But since this last deal got underway, she must think I'm turning into the kind of husband Maurice is! Although Katie doesn't say much, I know what she thinks about how the Tremblays have lived their lives. We found a lot of new interests in Australia but recently I've had to neglect them. There's no point driving yourself the way Maurice does, especially since it's taxed away almost as fast as you earn it. I don't know if Katie would make the choice, but the MacRae setup is the closest thing to what we both feel is ideal. Can I tell you a bit more about it, Martin?"

Drost nodded his head, so Bak said, "The presidency is opening up soon, and that's what MacRae is offering me. The salary is $120,000 with a profit-sharing deal that should add about $90,000 after the couple of years we'd need to increase sales. There's a capital gains opportunity through an option of 5% of their total stock, which is very attractive. The stock is currently low, but has a growth potential that I think would triple the price before I needed to sell. All in all, I see almost a million dollar gain between the buying and selling price. The pension scheme is limited, though; I'd have to build my own retirement fund some other way."

"It's a big salary drop, especially over the next five years. So, financially, I'd have to balance the short-term versus the long-term considerations at MacRae against the immediate gains with the other openings."

"I'd probably have more freedom at MacRae because of its size, for one thing," Bak continued. "In a year I'd know its people as well as or maybe better than I do my own at Château. The executives are all decent people, and the company has an excellent reputation for its business standards. It's one of the oldest in our line, and I'm sure there's a good base for doubling its share of the market. Most of all, I'd be on my own again, and the directors who I've talked with will accept any reasonable conditions I have for running things the way I want."

"It's very tempting, all right, Martin," Bak said. "The country, getting back to my wife and family, a chance to make a good record and a dependable nest egg . . . all without killing myself like I have been.

Drost asked, "What about the other offer?"

"It's another presidency, after a year, with Grande Étoile," Bak answered. "I'll start as executive vice president at $180,000 which would go up to around $340,000 when I take over the presidency. There's a bonus that's about 10% of the salary each year. I'd retire with $90,000 annually from the pension alone. The stock option proposal is complicated, but it works out so I can buy it on a basis which almost guarantees that I double my money. And if the stock goes up in value, I'd secure that increase."

Once more the waiter arrived. They stopped talking as he cleared the table, and took their orders for coffee. The conversation started again after they'd been served. "From a financial angle it'd be hard for me to beat," Bak stated. "The salary and bonus are less than what I'm getting now. But about three years ago, I found my bonus that year was only about $8,000 after the government took its bit. As a matter of fact, I bought tax anticipation warrants with what was left, just to remind myself that a big bonus often doesn't mean a thing."

Étoile is an old, reputable company known for honesty and integrity, something that appeals to me more and more as time passes. All the officers are polite and respectful. I've known many of them for years, and admire the atmosphere of goodwill and cooperation they work in. They know what teamwork means, and it's an asset I'm counting on when I consider what can be done for the company."

Bak continued, "They have a line of staple products. Some of them are nearly monopolies, not only because of worldwide preference and brand prestige, but also because of entrenched marketing setups. As an old marketer, I have a feeling that there's a lot of potential both in the company's position and the products, and they're ready for expansion." Bak finished his coffee and pushed the cup aside. "The stock is closely held," he said, "and hasn't missed a dividend in over two generations. The financial standing is edged in gold. Actually, all that's necessary is some concentration on promotion and sales, exactly what I did successfully in those three assignments at Château. Sales are close to $90 million annually, and I can see at least a dozen ways to raise that figure nearly 10% a year."

"I can't tell which excites you the most," Drost said, "MacRae & Sons or Grande Étoile. Aren't there any drawbacks in the last one?"

"That's the question, Martin," Bak replied. "I asked it myself after a private talk with Sylvain Laurier, the president of Étoile. I'm sure there must be a drawback, but I haven't found one yet, and I've gone over it again and again."

"In fact," he said, "all I've found are more pluses. Their offices take up part of a company-owned building, which leaves room for easy expansion. It's located in Centre-ville, the part of Montréal I like best, and it's easy to reach from where we live now. We're finally becoming part of a community, so a move would be upsetting. The president's office even has my favorite view of the city, looking out over Vieux-Montréal. And the executive office layout somehow creates a mood which feels good, and will probably make me work better. Maybe I'm oversensitive to these things right now; I guess it's silly even to mention them. But I'll bet there are lots of considerations hidden in these kinds of decisions. I'm just trying to look at mine, and to me the location and the offices I'll get are a plus."

Drost asked, "John, is it any use showing you the draft proposals from Peerless?"

"I don't see why," Bak answered. "At least not this evening. It's getting late, and I've got a lot of thinking and deciding to do this weekend. I know the essence of the offer, that they'll give me a better financial package than anyone else."

"They'll go further than that," Drost started to say. "They're ready to . . ."

Bak interrupted him. "I know a big organization, Martin. I know what they can and can't deliver. Money they can. The rest is only a chance to try to turn a whale around. Maybe I'll want to; it's the kind of animal I'm most familiar with! Maybe these smaller companies are just 'greener pastures' to me right now. I'm grateful to Peerless, though I guess I should thank you since you've been the prime mover. But it's good for my morale, coming from my friends, the enemy."

Bak stood up and took the check. "Thanks for the evening, Martin," he said. "I did all the talking, but it helps organize my thoughts. I wanted to talk with you before going to Katie, because she's more involved now than in any other decision of my whole business career. I want Katie to say honestly what kind of life she'd like for the next 15 years. Then I have to make the choice that satisfies both of us. Doesn't that make sense to you?"

Drost smiled and said, "It makes sense to me, all right. But I'm not the one you have to make sense to from now on! Good luck. And call me if there's anything I can help you with."

EXHIBIT A   Chronology

1917	January: Maurice Tremblay born in Trois-Rivières, Québec.	
1929	Beginning of the Depression era.	
1937	November: John Bak born in Winnipeg, Manitoba.	
1939	Canada enters World War II, effectively ending the Depression. World War II ends in 1945.	
1955	Bak enters McGill University, majoring in business administration and specializing in accounting.	
1957	Bak meets Katie deMurias, a transfer student from University Laval, Québec.	
1960	Bak graduates from McGill University at the top 10% of his class. He starts work as a cost accountant for a Toronto based firm which makes heavy production machinery.	
1962	John Bak and Katie deMurias get married. Several businesses, including the Toronto firm where Bak is employed, are merged to form Château Rouge Corporation. Bak requests a transfer to foreign	

sales, because he feels it is the department where the quickest career advances are made. Bak gets moved to domestic sales in preparation for his eventual promotion.

1963	Château's yearly sales are about $15 million.
1966	Bak is promoted to sales manager of the Sydney, Australia, subsidiary, and then almost immediately promoted to general manager. During this period, Château's sales are approximately $30 million/year.
1970	The Baks accept the fact that they cannot have children of their own and adopt two Vietnamese babies, a girl and a boy, born eight days apart.
1975	An unexpected and sudden changeover of the Australian Government causes a political and economic upheaval in that country. Maurice Tremblay, president of Château, decides to retrench. He temporarily closes the Sydney subsidiary, and calls Bak to the company's Montréal head-

quarters, which has grown much larger. They work together briefly, and then Tremblay entrusts Bak with the liquidation of an unprofitable, old-line subsidiary in São Paulo, Brazil. Soon after his arrival in Brazil, Bak discovers ways in which the subsidiary can save money; he incorporates some new systems and ultimately increases sales. Tremblay encourages Bak to continue his efforts. Château's sales are just over $250 million/year after several major acquisitions.

1979   Tremblay again calls Bak to headquarters, and makes him assistant to the president with the title of vice president. Bak is given troubleshooting assignments throughout the corporation, a job he soon dislikes. On several occasions Bak requests from Tremblay some definite responsibilities, with which Bak feels he could make his own record. Bak states that when he finds problems it makes other vice presidents look bad and, alternatively, if he doesn't find problems it would be assumed he's incompetent. Once or twice Tremblay dissuades him from pushing for this explicit definition of duties. Eventually, however, Tremblay

agrees but then never gives them to Bak. At the end of the year Bak abruptly resigns from Château. Yearly sales are $750 million, although net profits have risen much more steeply since 1975.

1980   Bak meets and becomes friends with Martin Drost, a management consultant. Shortly afterwards, Drost helps Bak find another job in the heavy production machinery industry, with a smaller firm that indirectly competes with Château.

1982   Early in the year, Tremblay offers Bak the vice presidency over all of Château Rouge, which Bak accepts. Soon thereafter Bak is promoted to executive vice president, and by late that year is given direct responsibility for the two most problematic divisions in the company.

1987   January: Maurice Tremblay's 70th birthday. The work relationship between Bak and Tremblay begins to deteriorate, and progressively worsens during the year. John Bak turns 50 years old in November.

1988   Château's yearly sales are well over $1 billion. In February, the conversation between Bak and Drost occurs as detailed in this case.

Königsbräu-Hellas A.E. (abridged)

After a two-month temporary assignment in Brazil, Wolfgang (Wolf) Keller was returning to Europe, where he would meet his family in Switzerland for a 10-day ski vacation. His boss, Dr. Hans Haussler, had insisted that he take the time off before returning to Greece, where Keller was managing director[1] of Königsbräu's Greek subsidiary, Königsbräu-Hellas A.E. The parent corporation, Königsbräu A.G., was a Munich-based brewer of premium beers with worldwide sales of $2.6 billion in 1981. Königsbräu was known as one of the best-managed and most profitable brewers of premium beer in the world, and its brand enjoyed high recognition and prestige on almost every continent.

During the flight from Rio to Zurich, Keller decided to review several problems that would need his attention when he returned to Athens in two weeks. The most pressing problem concerned Dimitri Petrou, Königsbräu-Hellas's commercial director (a title roughly equivalent to vice president of marketing and sales in North America). Petrou had joined the firm two years earlier, and his performance had increasingly concerned and annoyed Keller. After several difficult discussions with Haussler, Keller felt that he could no longer delay taking action on the matter.

As Keller saw it, he had three options. One option was to fire Petrou or, at the minimum, not give him an annual salary increase, which might have the same effect. Keller suspected that firing him would not be well received by Königsbräu's corporate headquarters, and Petrou's voluntary departure might also raise questions. A second alternative was to try, once again, to help Petrou improve his performance. The third alternative was to try to organize around Petrou to compensate for his inadequacies, perhaps by splitting marketing and sales.

WOLFGANG KELLER

Wolf Keller was 34 years old and a graduate of Harvard Business School. His undergraduate work had been in business economics and chemistry at the University of Cologne. Upon finishing business school, Keller joined a large German manufacturer of food products as a strategic planner. This assignment was short lived, however, and within six months he was made general manager of a small subsidiary in Greece that was in serious economic difficulty. Keller turned the subsidiary around in less than two years and was subsequently promoted to general manager of a $20 million subsidiary in Germany that was also in trouble. By the time he had turned around the second subsidiary, he had

---

[1] Outside of North America, the titles managing director and director were generally equivalent to president and vice president, respectively.

This case is an abridged and redisguised version of Königsbräu-Hellas A.E. (A), which Colleen Kaftan prepared under the supervision of Professor John J. Gabarro as the basis for class discussion rather than to illustrate either effective or ineffective handling of an administrative situation.

Copyright © 1984 by the President and Fellows of Harvard College. Harvard Business School case 9-484-080.

a reputation as a successful hands-on manager.

After less than two years in this assignment, Keller left the food manufacturer to join Königsbräu as managing director of its Greek subsidiary, which at the time was losing $2 million per year on sales of $80 million. In the three years since taking charge, Keller had increased the Greek subsidiary's earnings to $5 million per year on revenues of $100 million. This effort involved changing the marketing strategy, hiring a new top-management group, restructuring the sales force, and acquiring a fourth brewery in Salonika. Keller was pleased with the results and found the turnaround to be one of the most exciting experiences of his life. He accepted the job with Königsbräu because of the responsibility and challenge it offered, and also because he had very much enjoyed his earlier stay in Greece and spoke the language fluently. His friends often joked that he was more Greek than German in both temperament and business style.

Keller loved his three years at Königsbräu-Hellas. He also knew that his success in Greece had been noticed in Munich, and he had heard rumors that some people saw him as having the potential of someday being promoted to the firm's *Vorstand*. (This consisted of a small group of corporate officers which, under German law, served as a corporation's collective chief executive office. For many German executives, being a member of the *Vorstand* was equivalent to being named CEO in the United States or Canada.)

Keller had spent the preceding two months in Brazil as head of a start-up task force for a joint venture that Königsbräu A.G. had begun with a Brazilian brewer. The start-up went smoothly, and its success pleased Keller. Nonetheless, he was eager to get back to Athens. He had been gone for nearly three months because Haussler had insisted that he take a three-week vacation before leaving for Brazil, arguing that the start-up would be so demanding that he had to arrive well rested and ready. During most of this time, Keller had no contact with his subsidiary except for a briefing he had received six weeks earlier. This was routine. When an executive was assigned to a task force, he or she was expected to devote full time to the assignment.

KÖNIGSBRÄU-HELLAS

Königsbräu's Greek subsidiary was founded in 1953 as part of the parent company's postwar reconstruction and expansion effort. For most of the ensuing 20 years, Andreas Carellas, the company's Greek partner, had managed Königsbräu-Hellas. Carellas took the title of chairman when the parent company bought out his share in 1971, but he continued to be active in the subsidiary's management.

Keller's predecessor as managing director was transferred back to Germany because of his inability to work with Carellas. Both Keller and Carellas reported directly to Haussler, who was a member of the *Vorstand*.

Keller was in charge of all operations, and Carellas was in charge of external relationships with banks, trade associations, and government agencies. Keller believed that this worked quite well, although he suspected that Carellas sometimes missed being involved in daily operations (see *Exhibit 1* for partial organization chart).

Commercial Strategy

The keystone of the marketing strategy that Keller introduced was to consolidate and strengthen Königsbräu's distributors and to offer them heavy support and service, even at the retail level. The approach was essentially a high-margin, quality-service, and heavy advertising and promotional strategy. Distributors were provided with various services, including information systems and logistics support as well as conventional sales support. Keller felt that because consumer preferences were relatively undifferentiated among premium beers, distributors could play a pivotal role in affecting sales. Moreover, important market trends reinforced his belief in the service-oriented commercial strategy. The number of beer distributors in Greece had been steadily diminishing over the years as the industry consolidated. In Keller's view, this tendency made it critical to identify and cultivate ties with the distributors most likely to survive. This included helping viable distributors through difficult stages and making business suggestions that would enhance their ability to survive.

Distributors, and the brewery's relationship with them, were important to a beer's success, regardless of strategy, because the distributors sold directly to the taverns, hotels, restaurants, and other retail outlets that ultimately served the consumer. As an executive of a competing brewer stated:

If there's any business that needs hands-on contact with distributors, it's the liquor game. They're tough people, entrepreneurs who will play hard. Personal relationships and trust really matter. In a country like Greece, you've got the additional problem of converting people from wine and hard spirits to beer. That's a hard selling task, and you need aggressive distributors for it. It's also a game in which entertaining, eating, and drinking are an important part of doing business.

Keller intended to continue strengthening relationships between the company's sales force and distributors. He believed that salespeople would have to cultivate personal contacts with distributors, concentrating less on trade discounts and emphasizing the help and advice customers could expect from Königsbräu-Hellas.

The strategy, though not yet totally implemented, had significantly increased market share and greatly improved profitability. In some respects, Keller felt that the strategy was succeeding despite Petrou's efforts as commercial director.

DIMITRI PETROU

The highly cultivated and intellectual Petrou was 10 years older than Keller. He had held influential positions in two large consumer-oriented multinationals. Before joining Königsbräu-Hellas, he was the commercial director of the Greek subsidiary of a large U.S.-based toiletries firm. Before that he had worked in the United States, Greece, and France. Petrou was hired because his experience and maturity would balance the largely young group of managers that Keller had attracted during his first year. Petrou maintained a distant but cordial relationship with Carellas. Unfortunately, his dealings with Keller were strained and occasionally stormy almost from the outset.

Problems with Petrou

By the end of Petrou's first year, Keller had serious reservations about Petrou's skills and management style. Keller believed that Petrou had excellent analytical skills and that he had done a superb job of redesigning the sales force organization and of developing a comprehensive set of information and control systems. However, it took him over six months to do so, and Keller suspected that it might have taken even longer, had Keller not put a freeze on sales hires until Petrou completed it. Petrou's thoroughness was offset by what Keller saw as an almost total incapacity to react to problems expeditiously. Keller had to step in several times to handle a situation himself, simply because Petrou refused to take action when a deadline seemed impossible. This happened in mid-September 1980, when rumors of a government price freeze forced the company to change the formula and brand label of its newly acquired brewery within two weeks. The phaseout of the local brand was originally scheduled to occur over a year. Because it was a lower-priced beer, however, Keller felt that they either had to act immediately or be stuck with a lower-margin product.

Keller also believed that Petrou's formal and distant management style hurt his effectiveness as the commercial director. Petrou's formality and distance pervaded his dealings with his peers and subordinates as well as with customers, competitors, and other outsiders.

In fact, Keller suspected that Petrou's emphasis on the use of administrative systems served, above all, to minimize his need for face-to-face contact with subordinates. Keller preferred to create a much closer relationship with his employees and to cultivate their loyalty and enthusiasm through personal contact. He felt that camaraderie was fundamental to the creation of a vigorous and aggressive company. It was partly this concept of management that troubled him about Petrou's distant management style.

Petrou's desire to keep his personal life separate from his professional life also bothered Keller. This circumspection was not characteristic of most of the other managers at Königsbräu-Hellas. Petrou rarely talked about his family with his colleagues, even though many of them had met his wife at official company functions, nor did he participate in social outings, such as evening get-togethers or weekend sailing or fishing trips with other managers. Even during the workday, Petrou did not join in when the others lunched together or shared a beer after hours in the company bar while rehashing the day's events. He was the only Management Committee member who declined to use the familiar *esi* form of "you" when addressing his peers. He preferred the formal *esis*, which the others found slightly stilted in the close working environment at Königsbräu-Hellas.

Petrou's formal interactions also extended to his relationships with the field sales staff and with Königsbräu-Hellas's customers. Keller considered this to be more problematic for the company than the reserve Petrou maintained with his colleagues in Athens. Keller was convinced that the new commercial strategy required a closer, hands-on management style.

First, the sales force needed considerable guidance during the transition, and Keller thought that Petrou should spend much of his time in the field. Petrou, however, did not feel that this was so important. He claimed that the head office should not interfere with the sales function so as to encourage greater autonomy and responsibility in the field. In fact, Keller thought Petrou purposely refrained from visiting sales representatives to avoid getting involved in the daily sales and marketing problems.

Second, Petrou's refusal to get his feet wet in dealing with customers annoyed Keller. The distributors were critical to Königsbräu's future in Greece. Yet Petrou was characteristically reluctant to develop personal ties with them: consequently, Keller feared that business would suffer. Thus, Keller intervened with customers in several instances where he thought Petrou's relationship was inadequate.

Conflicts in Style

These different management styles fed the conflict. Petrou tended to be analytical and deliberate in his actions and preferred to delegate as much as possible. In contrast, Keller tended to be impatient and action oriented, using a hands-on approach when dealing with problems. These differences led to several conflicts because Petrou felt that Keller was intruding on the commercial department's activities.

Keller acknowledged this tendency and knew that it was not confined to Petrou's department. During one particularly heated meeting, the Management Committee drew up a new "organization chart" while Keller had stepped out of the room. When he saw the chart, he could not help laughing, as it presented a particularly amusing and accurate caricature of his management style. Keller liked it so much that he hung it in his office (see *Exhibit 2*).

PETROU'S PERFORMANCE APPRAISAL, 1980

Keller's first annual appraisal of Petrou's performance occurred in November 1980. The explosive meeting lasted over three hours, while Keller walked through the evaluation form with Petrou (see *Exhibit 3*). Some items took more time than others because Petrou sought further explanation or defended himself against Keller's criticisms. He particularly objected to Keller's comments concerning his inability to motivate the sales force because "of a low level of leadership and no personality." Petrou countered by saying that he could be a leader if only Keller would stop interfering in the sales and marketing function.

After a lengthy discussion, Petrou convinced Keller to change the wording of the remark on sales force motivation. The revision read as follows: ". . . due to an average level of leadership and personality not completely adequate to our specific situation." Another negotiated change raised Keller's initial overall rating of Petrou from "sufficient" to "good."

Petrou did not take advantage of Keller's usual practice of having a follow-up meeting. Instead, he wrote a memorandum for the record and sent it to Keller two weeks later, requesting that it be attached to the official appraisal form that would be filed in Athens and sent to Haussler in Munich.

The memorandum gave a detailed list of his accomplishments during his first year as commercial director and took issue with Keller's criticisms of his management style. Petrou also defended his delegatory management style, arguing that it was essential for the development of his subordinates.

Further Problems

Unfortunately, Keller's assessment of Petrou's performance did not change during the following year, despite the firm's increased growth and profitability. Keller felt that the commercial department's success was less a result of Petrou's efforts than of his own interventions in problems that Petrou either had failed to act on or had refused to address. These interventions included Königsbräu's annual distributors' meeting, the collection of bad debts, the resolution of a pending lawsuit by a distributor (which would have cost the subsidiary over $900,000 per year from 1981 onward), and Königsbräu-Hellas's relationships with several of its key distributors.

For example, on the Friday before the annual distributors' meeting, Keller discovered that over half of their distributors were not planning to attend. By the time Keller reviewed the list, Petrou had left for the weekend and was unreachable at home. Keller immediately telephoned all of the area managers to devise an action plan, because the meeting was scheduled for Monday. He and they spent much of the weekend personally inviting distributors by phone and making arrangements to have them met at the airport or railroad station. Keller felt it was critical that the large and powerful distributors from the rural areas attend. The weekend's effort more than doubled the attendance.

Keller was equally disturbed by Petrou's handling of the distributor's lawsuit. Petrou first sent a sales representative to talk to the customer, who was one of the firm's largest distributors. Only after the sales representative had failed did Petrou himself contact the distributor. As a result of the meeting, Petrou concluded that the distributor's position was unchangeable. Keller felt that the issue was too important to drop and made a point of sitting next to the customer en route to the firm's annual convention of top distributors in Munich. By the end of the flight, the customer agreed to drop the suit in its entirety. Keller was certain that Petrou could have settled the matter had he devoted more time and personal attention to the distributor.

Several other, though admittedly minor, incidents also reflected on Petrou's lack of judgment and ability. For example, for the flight to Munich that was just described, Petrou had assigned all the seats in the front of the airplane to Königsbräu's sales and marketing personnel and all the seats in the back to its key distributors, making it impossible for the two groups to communicate with each other.

A second incident related to the Munich trip disturbed Keller even more. During one of the social events, Petrou joined in when several important distributors and three of Königsbräu's managers decided to switch from calling one another by *esis* to the more personal *esi*. This was marked by everyone toasting each other with wine. A few weeks later, however, Petrou declined to join the same group on a weekend sailing excursion. As a gesture of friendship, some of the distributors decided to visit Petrou at his home after the excursion. One of the distributors told Keller that Petrou's formality surprised him, especially when Petrou used the more formal *esis* after their agreement to use *esi* in Munich.

Another small, but telling, incident concerned a distributor whom Petrou wrote off as a bad debt of $60,000. Keller urged him to meet with the customer and demand payment. Keller suspected that the distributor was sheltering the money in other businesses while allowing the distributorship to slide into insolvency. He feared that if they did not act quickly they would risk getting nothing when the firm went bankrupt. Petrou resisted the idea but finally called the customer. He again concluded that nothing could be done until the distributor became solvent or filed for bankruptcy.

Annoyed by Petrou's response, Keller drove three hours one Friday evening to confront the distributor. After a long and heated discussion, he returned to Athens with a check for the full amount. Petrou reacted first with surprise and then with anger at Keller's interference in what he considered a departmental affair.

As the year progressed, another complication arose around Keller's relationship with Petrou's marketing manager, Nico Chorafas. Chorafas, a 31-year-old MBA, had previously worked for Keller in the Greek food subsidiary. Over the years, Keller and

Chorafas had developed a social relationship that persisted after Chorafas joined the firm. Although Petrou had hired Chorafas a year earlier, he quickly resented Keller's relationship with him and accused Keller of playing favorites. A confrontation, over this and other issues, resulted in still another exchange of letters for the record in which Petrou complained specifically about Keller's interference in his operations. These letters went into Petrou's personnel file.

Because of their personal relationship, Keller felt that he demanded even more from Chorafas than he did from the others. He also noted that Chorafas was heavily involved in both sales and marketing and that several middle managers seemed far more comfortable dealing with Chorafas than with Petrou. Petrou explained that this resulted from his delegating tasks appropriately to Chorafas.

Keller had thought of splitting marketing and sales and making Chorafas sales director and Petrou marketing director, assignments that he felt were better suited to their strengths and styles. He was not yet convinced, however, that Chorafas had the seasoning to do the job, and he was certain that Petrou would resist the change and make an issue of it with Munich.

Keller's problems with Petrou had, in fact, become one of several issues that Haussler focused on during Keller's performance appraisal review in Munich in May 1981. Keller was disappointed with Haussler's overall assessment of "sufficient," which meant that his performance was adequate for his current responsibilities but not promising enough to indicate advancement. Haussler sent a letter to Keller, summarizing the key points of their conversation shortly after the interview (see *Exhibit 4*). Keller, in turn, sent a letter back, thanking him for the feedback and attempting to clarify some of the issues that were raised (see *Exhibit 5*).

PETROU'S PERFORMANCE APPRAISAL, 1981

Before departing for Brazil, Keller held performance appraisal interviews with all of his subordinates in November 1981. With Petrou, however, he decided not to finalize the appraisal and to withhold the actual form (see *Exhibit 6*). Instead, he prepared a letter (see *Exhibit 7*) to use as a basis for the interview and told Petrou that he would not discuss or submit the final form until he returned from Brazil. Keller did this for two reasons. First, it enabled him to go over Petrou's performance problems without having to commit a final judgment on his performance to the personnel file (and, therefore, to Munich). Second, Petrou's efforts and cooperation with other departments during the preparation of the 1982 budget had impressed him. The budget had required considerable work by everyone. Profits for 1982 were projected to be $1 million less than in 1981 because of the economy, inflation, and problems with the newly acquired Salonika brewery.

Petrou's reactions to the letter and to his overall evaluation of "sufficient" were more explosive than they had been a year earlier. He argued that his performance had improved during 1981 and that the company's results showed it. They also clashed over Keller's evaluation of Petrou's leadership ability and Keller's intrusions into the commercial department's activities. Keller finally agreed to change the wording of "you are not a leader for the sales force" to "you are not a charismatic leader for the sales force." Nonetheless, the session ended with little agreement on any of these major issues. After the meeting, Petrou responded, as he had a year earlier, by writing a memo for the record, contesting the drop on his overall evaluation from "good" to "sufficient" and accusing Keller's interventions of constraining his actions.

WEIGHING THE DECISION

As March 1982 approached, Keller felt that he could no longer delay finalizing Petrou's performance appraisal once he returned to Athens. Carellas had urged Keller to fire Petrou, but Keller knew that it would be difficult to find a qualified replacement. The only internal candidate, Chorafas, was not yet ready to take over the sales function, let alone the entire commercial department. Not firing Petrou, however, would require a plan of action for improving his perfor-

mance, either through coaching or reorganizing or both. Moreover, if Petrou stayed, Keller still had to decide how much of an increase to give him for 1982. In Greece's inflationary economy, not giving Petrou an increase was equivalent to a pay cut. If that happened, Keller thought Petrou would probably leave once he secured another job. If Keller gave him an increase, however, he would have to be careful not to send Petrou mixed signals about his performance.

EXHIBIT 1 Partial Organization Chart, December 1981.

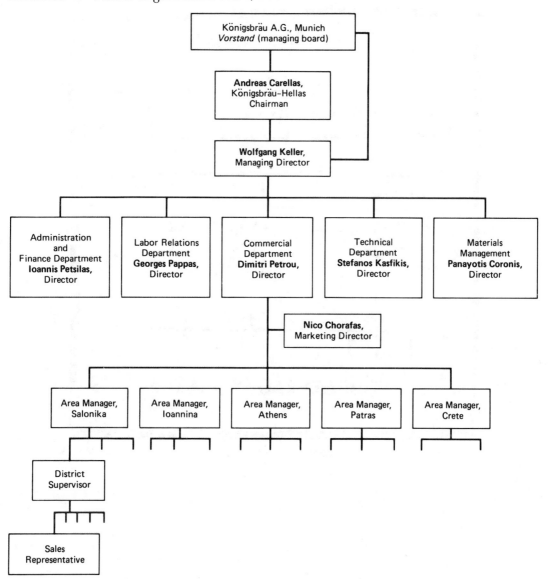

EXHIBIT 2 Organization Chart Hung in Keller's Office.

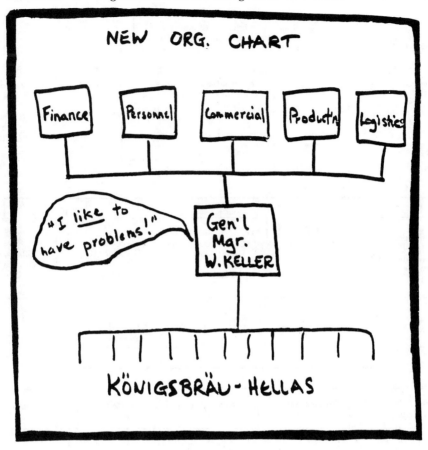

EXHIBIT 3 1980 Performance Appraisal Review for Petrou (original comments).

KÖNIGSBRÄU-HELLAS A.E.

EXECUTIVE PERFORMANCE REVIEW FORM

NAME Dimitri PETROU
DEPARTMENT Commercial Department
POSITION Commercial Director

EVALUATED BY Wolfgang KELLER
POSITION Managing Director
SECOND LEVEL SUPERVISOR Hanspeter HAUSSLER
DATE OF REVIEW November 1980

I. MAJOR RESPONSIBILITIES AND RESULTS

A. RESPONSIBILITY ITEM B. DEGREE OF AUTHORITY (MARK WITH X) C. EFFECTIVENESS IN OBTAINING RESULTS (MARK WITH X) D. COMMENTS

Responsibility Item	Acts On Instructions	Acts After Consulting Supervisor	Acts Independently Reports Results	Acts Entirely Independently	Unsatisfactory	Sufficient	Good	Excellent	Comments
(1) Market and Sales Planning		X					X		(1)
(2) Development and Implementation: – Marketing organization – Marketing strategy		X					X		(2) The responsibility could not be carried out due to our difficulties finding a Marketing Mgr. (beyond Mr. Petrou's control).
(3) Plan and Implement Sales Force Reorganization: – job descriptions – objectives, responsibilities.		X						X	(3) Excellent, very thorough analysis.
(4) Develop and Implement Credit Control Objectives			X				X		(4)
(5) Sales Plan Implementation: – Quality (prices/margins etc.) – Quantity (volume)			X			X			(5) Has not succeeded up till now to realize a motivated Sales Force on all levels in firm due to a low level of leadership and no personality.

69

EXHIBIT 3 (continued).

KÖNIGSBRÄU-HELLAS A.E.

EXECUTIVE PERFORMANCE REVIEW FORM p. 2.

II. OVERALL EVALUATION OF JOB PERFORMANCE

A. OBSERVED STRENGTHS

Calm and methodical, skilled in standardizing and programming his work. Makes decisions based on data.

B. OBSERVED WEAKNESSES

Average personality and leadership in his specific situation.

III. DEVELOPMENTAL REVIEW

A. HAS THE EXECUTIVE'S PERFORMANCE IMPROVED, DECLINED, OR REMAINED CONSTANT SINCE THE LAST REVIEW?

Remained constant.

C. WHAT DEVELOPMENTAL ACTIVITIES WOULD YOU SUGGEST?

More regular contacts in the field, with Sales Force and customers. Mr. Petrou should also try to hire people with stronger personalities to work in his department, as a way of offsetting his weakness.

TRAINING RECOMMENDATIONS ____A public speaking or leadership course____ might be helpful.

RECOMMENDED JOB EXPERIENCES ____

C. OVERALL RATING OF RESULTS AND EFFECTIVENESS

UNSATISFACTORY	SUFFICIENT	GOOD	EXCELLENT
	x		

B. WHAT IS YOUR OPINION OF THE EXECUTIVE'S POTENTIAL FOR ADVANCEMENT WITHIN THE KÖNIGSBRÄU GROUP?

He has the potential for a career within Königsbräu-Hellas or abroad.

D. PLEASE EVALUATE THE EXECUTIVE'S ABILITY TO DEVELOP MANAGERIAL TALENT AMONG HIS SUBORDINATES.

Good.

APPRAISAL INTERVIEW DATE ____14 November 1980____

SUPERIOR'S INITIAL _____   EXECUTIVE'S INITIAL ____

EXECUTIVE'S COMMENTS ____

EXHIBIT 4   Summary Letter Following Keller's 1981 Performance Review.

DR. HANSPETER HAUSSLER
MITGLIED DES VOSTANDES DER
KÖNIGSBRÄU A.G.

> Herrn Dipl.-Kfm
> Wolfgang Keller
> Königsbräu-Hellas A.E.
>
> GR - *Athens*
>
> München, den 20. May 1981

Dear Mr. Keller,

Further to our meeting last week, I would like to summarize the highlights of our discussion about your personal development as a Königsbräu manager.

Let me repeat my overall evaluation that your performance for the last year has been sufficient. You have a tremendous capacity and enthusiasm for work, and you always try to make sure that Königsbräu comes out on top. Aside from these dynamic qualities we have also appreciated your willingness to admit you have made errors and to accept criticism, at least in your relationship with corporate headquarters. I believe that this openness will allow you to avoid misinterpreting corporate policies and to provide us with more frequent and ample reports in the future than in the past.

We understand that you may occasionally feel caught between two cultures; that is, between the orderly directness of our German style and the more flexible attitude you must have to be successful in Greece. Even so, you must bear in mind that Königsbräu-Hellas is an integral part of the total corporation and must be articulated into its operations like all other non-German operations. Working together with corporate staff and service functions is a case in point. I am confident that you are skillful enough to bridge the gap when necessary.

Because you have been so busy trying to restore financial health at Königsbräu-Hellas, I have not always felt fully informed about your working relationships there. However, I hope you will keep in mind that this company is bigger than the ones you have managed for your previous employers and that you may have to force yourself to delegate more authority than you learned to do in the past. I have observed that you seem to prefer to have direct personal contacts with most of your employees and important customers, and that you enjoy doing many jobs yourself. Although this can be a good quality it also sometimes gives us the impression that you don't believe in "teamwork".

You may also have to pay more attention to your way of working with Mr. Carellas. I mentioned to you that I think co-managing an enterprise with him could be a difficult job in itself. But you must remember you are not Greek and there may be some situations in which he, as an older man, knows better what to do in Greece than you do. My advice is to try to involve him more fully in the general management work, and especially to keep him informed of your activities.

You can see that whatever flaws I have mentioned are actually the "other side" of your many strong points. Indeed, it might be difficult for you to change the weaknesses without affecting your overall positive performance, but I am confident that you will try to do so.

I would like to repeat that we feel you have contributed very adequately to the company over the past year. I am eager to follow your progress as you develop your managerial skills further within the Königsbräu organization.

Let me also transmit the *Vorstand*'s best wishes for success in your forthcoming temporary assignment with the Königsbräu start-up team on the Brazilian joint venture.

With best greetings,

Häussler

Note: This letter's text has been translated from the original German.

EXHIBIT 5   Keller's Letter, A Response to His 1981 Performance Review.

KÖNIGSBRÄU-HELLAS A.E.
  WOLFGANG KELLER,
  Managing Director

Herrn Dr. Hanspeter HÄUSSLER
Mitglied des Vorstandes der
Königsbräu A.G.
D -   *München*

Athens, May 25, 1981

Dear Dr. Häussler,

First of all let me thank you for your frank and thoughtful review of my
activities during the past year. I would like to take some time to respond
to some of the details of our discussion and to tell you informally about my
own position. I'll organize my comments according to a few themes from our
interview.

Delegation of authority at Königsbräu-Hellas

Your remarks did not surprise me because I've been thinking about the
question for a long time. Of course each incident is a special case, so
it would be a waste of time to try to explain further each one of the
episodes you mentioned. As far as Petrou is concerned, I believe our
problems are normal in any boss-subordinate relationship, although my
actions may sometimes be controversial. I have behaved exactly the same
way towards my other subordinates and have never had problems with them.
Even though I may occasionally make errors in my analysis or judgement, I
believe I have always acted in an honest and professional way.

I agree completely with your conclusion that I have interfered too often in
line responsibilities. Part of the reason is my background in smaller
companies, as you suggested. Here at Königsbräu-Hellas it is not the same,
and I need to learn to step back from functional responsibilities. But there
are also other reasons for my direct management style:
  1. I *love* being involved in operations. I enjoy it; I think it's fun.
  2. I can't sit still if I see a problem that could have real financial
     consequences. I need to hammer away at it until things get done the
     way I think they should be.
  3. We had so many things to change in the beginning that I worried more
     about getting the job done than about lines of responsibility. This
     tendency got even stronger since most of my managers were new.
  4. Things move too slowly for me sometimes (or maybe I'm too fast and
     don't give the others the time to be convinced and to follow me).

My plans for improvement

1. I intend to try to take things more slowly and to step back if possible from immediate problems.
2. I'll also make an effort to allow others to do things their own way, even if I disagree, provided the results are there.

There is, of course, a danger that we will become a bit sluggish as an organization and that we will make mistakes or miss opportunities. But I do agree with you that Königsbräu-Hellas is no longer in urgent difficulty and that I should turn my attention to general management rather than to keep worrying about day-to-day details.

Contacts with Munich

When you explained to me some of the mistakes I have made in my dealings with corporate staff, I understood that I should be more careful in this area. As a result, I shall try to pay more attention to the staff people's recommendations in the future. To tell you the truth, I am quite sensitive to criticism and I am eager to have good working relationships within the company.

Admitting my shortcomings

You said this was one of my strong points. I have always found it very easy to confess my faults, perhaps because I am young and not handicapped by my experience. I sometimes tell my managers that a wise man has a different opinion every day. I hope to stay this way. Incidentally, you are the first person to tell me you consider this a positive trait.

Working with Andreas Carellas

I've thought it over again since we talked, and I'm convinced our current division of responsibilities is the best one. I *do* keep him involved in my plans. If he agrees (as he always told me he does), I'd like to continue working under our present arrangement.

I'd like to thank you again and to tell you I'm very pleased to have been chosen to lead Königsbräu's task force for the new Brazilian joint venture. I'm looking forward to the project with great pleasure.

Yours sincerely,

Wolfgang Keller

Note: The letter's text has been translated from the original German.

EXHIBIT 6 1981 Performance Appraisal Review for Petrou (unfiled as of early 1982).

KÖNIGSBRÄU-HELLAS A.E.

EXECUTIVE PERFORMANCE REVIEW FORM

NAME Dimitri PETROU
DEPARTMENT Commercial Department
POSITION Commercial Director

EVALUATED BY Wolfgang KELLER
POSITION Managing Director
SECOND LEVEL SUPERVISOR Hanspeter HAUSSLER
DATE OF REVIEW November 1981

I. MAJOR RESPONSIBILITIES AND RESULTS

A. RESPONSIBILITY ITEM   B. DEGREE OF AUTHORITY (MARK WITH X)   C. EFFECTIVENESS IN OBTAINING RESULTS (MARK WITH X)   D. COMMENTS

A. RESPONSIBILITY ITEM	ACTS ON INSTRUCTIONS	ACTS AFTER CONSULTING SUPERVISOR	ACTS INDEPENDENTLY REPORTS RESULTS	ACTS ENTIRELY INDEPENDENTLY	UNSATISFACTORY	SUFFICIENT	GOOD	EXCELLENT	D. COMMENTS
(1) Market and Sales Planning			x				x		(1)
(2) Development and Implementation of Marketing Strategy			x			x			(2) *See explanatory letter
(3) Implement Sales Force reorganization; guide and develop sales personnel		x			x				(3) *See explanatory letter; Mr. Petrou designed an excellent plan but we need to see the results now.
(4) Develop and Implement credit control objectives			x				x		(4)
(5) Implement Sales Plan - quality (price/margins) - quantity (volume) - sales and distribution		x					x		(5) Excellent and thorough plan now needs to be carried out with Sales Force.

EXHIBIT 6 (continued).

KÖNIGSBRÄU–HELLAS A.E.

EXECUTIVE PERFORMANCE REVIEW FORM p. 2.

II. OVERALL EVALUATION OF JOB PERFORMANCE

A. OBSERVED STRENGTHS

Good, methodical analysis,

able to standardize and program

his work.

B. OBSERVED WEAKNESSES

Low personality and leadership.

Low creativity and fears change.

Insecure and consequently slow

in making decisions.

C. OVERALL RATING OF RESULTS AND EFFECTIVENESS

UNSATISFACTORY	SUFFICIENT	GOOD	EXCELLENT
	x		

III. DEVELOPMENTAL REVIEW

A. HAS THE EXECUTIVE'S PERFORMANCE IMPROVED, DECLINED, OR REMAINED CONSTANT SINCE THE LAST REVIEW?

Remained constant.

B. WHAT IS YOUR OPINION OF THE EXECUTIVE'S POTENTIAL FOR ADVANCEMENT WITHIN THE KÖNIGSBRÄU GROUP?

Mr. Petrou is more suited to a staff position than to line respon-

sibilities. He could work in the central staff at higher levels.

C. WHAT DEVELOPMENTAL ACTIVITIES WOULD YOU SUGGEST?

--

D. PLEASE EVALUATE THE EXECUTIVE'S ABILITY TO DEVELOP MANAGERIAL TALENT AMONG HIS SUBORDINATES.

--

TRAINING RECOMMENDATIONS --

RECOMMENDED JOB EXPERIENCES --

APPRAISAL INTERVIEW DATE _____

SUPERIOR'S INITIAL _____ EXECUTIVE'S INITIAL _____

EXECUTIVE'S COMMENTS _____

EXHIBIT 7 Explanatory Letter for Petrou's 1981 Performance Review (original wording).

KÖNIGSBRÄU-HELLAS A.E.
  WOLFGANG KELLER,
  Managing Director

> Mr. Dimitri Petrou
> Commercial Director
> Königsbräu-Hellas A.E.
>
> Athens, November 1981

Dear Mr. Petrou,

As we approach the end of your second year with us here at Königsbräu-Hellas, I should like to express to you my impressions of your performance in the role of Commercial Director.

First of all I would like to congratulate you on the excellence of the systems and plans you created within your department. However, it will come as no surprise to you that I have not been as happy with your ability to handle the implementation aspects of your duties. My overall evaluation of your results for the year is that they are sufficient.

In the remarks that follow I shall try to give you a more detailed review of your performance.

Strengths

You are a good analyst and you prepare your plans and reports in a sound, complete way. Theoretically most of them are perfect. You are also a very loyal employee, and you give adequate follow up even when you have to implement a decision with which you were not initially in agreement.

I feel that it is not necessary to discuss more in detail strong points, but rather to spend some time illustrating your weaker sides.

Weaknesses

You are not a "leader" for the sales force, and you seldom act directly with them. The same goes for your internal department. Your personality is not fit to maintain personal contacts with our most important customers and to serve as a guide for the sales force. Consequently, you never solve problems personally and avoid dealing with complicated questions on the spot. You do not like personal contacts with customers and the sales force, and you rarely have them. Perhaps because of this propensity and your resulting lack of experience in the field, you are slow in decision making.

You are not well integrated into the management team. You give the impression that you do not accept suggestions, ideas, or collaborative efforts from your colleagues within your functional areas, perhaps out of fear that you will be unable to control their influence as a result.

Consequences

1. Due to these weaknesses, you tend to manage your department not as a line manager/leader, but rather in a more staff-oriented way. You over-organize your department with rules, procedures and hierarchy.

2. Since I am aware of these weaknesses, I do not give you complete autonomy for the operations of your department. I try to compensate for your deficiencies whenever possible and to check closely on your activities where there are risks involved for the company.

Personality Differences Keller - Petrou

I am aware of the fact that my personality and style of leadership can condition your performance. In the last eight months I have tried to interfere only when I believed it was absolutely necessary for the benefit of the company.

Steps to be taken

In my opinion, three things would help you:

1. Integrate and collaborate closely with Chorafas, who has an easier contact with the sales force and the customers.

2. Integrate and involve your colleagues from the Management Committee. Every problem always has another functional aspect, and together you will be able to find sound solutions quickly.

3. Plan and make "field trips" on a regular basis, so as to have the needed contact with the sales force and customers.

Being certain that it will be possible to achieve a better performance and collaboration, especially after the results of the last weeks and our recent discussions, I remain,

Your sincerely,

Wolfgang Keller

E. J. Weiver (A)

Columbia Products Corporation, where E. J. Weiver worked as a product manager, was situated 40 miles from New York City in a pleasant suburban community. The casewriter visited E. J., a transplanted New York advertising executive, to discuss the job demands of being a product manager for two nationally known products in the company's Toiletries Division (see Exhibit 1 for the division's organization chart).

SUPERVISOR'S VIEW OF WEIVER

Before meeting with E. J., the casewriter talked to E. J.'s boss, Tom Bird, a product group supervisor who supervised E. J. and several other product managers.

CASEWRITER: If I understand you correctly, you don't really have a specific problem with E. J., but you do wonder what's going to happen to E. J.'s career and how to help in planning it?

BIRD: That's right. E. J.'s a hard charger and that's been just great. We had two new products to get out on the market in a short time and how they got there wasn't important—E. J. got them out. But now, as the pressure is easing off, I'm trying to see how to give E. J. new challenges as a product manager and beyond that how to help E. J. develop into a good general manager. It's a question of style, in part.

CASEWRITER: Do you think a mid-career executive training program would help?

BIRD: I can't spare E. J.'s time. Those products are out on the market, but they have to be monitored for at least another year. I have to figure out something to do right here. You see, E. J. has a very responsible position in charge of two new toiletries products. Now E. J.'s just beginning work to pep up another set of older products. The toiletries products are grouped together with each product being managed by a product manager. Some, like E. J., manage several products. People in my job work with the product managers by seeing not only that the products are produced and marketed but also that the product managers themselves get a chance to develop.

CASEWRITER: Tell me about E. J.; how long have you two worked together?

BIRD: For four years—not all of them here. E. J. was at our ad agency as our account executive and then came here. We've had

Nancy N. Wardell, Research Assistant, prepared this case under the supervision of Associate Professor Larry E. Greiner as a basis for class discussion rather than to illustrate either effective or ineffective handling of an administrative situation.
Copyright © 1972 by the President and Fellows of Harvard College. Harvard Business School case 472-067.

no problem in going from the agency relationship to the company one.

E. J. is proving to be one of the most effective people in moving this business ahead —in cutting through lethargy and shaking people up a little bit—and with lots of management support for it. E. J.'s assignment was to get some products out fast. If it took some waves to do it, we took them. But E. J.'s maturing now—still making waves, but you might say the surf is not as violent as it used to be. E. J. has a very definite style and I have to figure out how to utilize it effectively. Talk to E. J.; you'll see what I mean.

INTERVIEW WITH WEIVER

E. J. was talking on the phone when the casewriter appeared at the door; a hand was waved toward one of the three leather chairs in the office. While waiting for E. J. to finish the phone call, which was accentuated by desk pounding and arm waving, the casewriter had time to read the motto on the wall, written in gothic script: "I will walk through the valley of the shadow of death and fear no evil, for I am the meanest son-of-a-bitch in the valley." On the desk was a wooden nutcracker, a gift from some sales promotion employees. It was inscribed: "Nutcracker Award. E. J., for outstanding performance, from the sales promotion group." E. J. plunked down the phone, leaned across the desk to shake hands, and said, "So you want to see how a product manager operates! Stick around. I'll try to fill you in on what I do."

CASEWRITER: How did you get started in all this?

WEIVER: After graduating from the Harvard Business School eight years ago, I accepted a job with an ad agency in New York. [See Exhibit 2 for E. J.'s resume.] I was in a two-year training program, which sounds unappealing to most new graduates, but we were in each department long enough as a functioning member so that we really got to know it well. At the end of the training period, I asked one of my friends what would be a good account to get onto. My friend suggested an airlines account, saying, "If you live through that, you'll live through anything." And he was right. I guess I lived through it.

I worked on consumer products after that and did public service accounts, too. Then, I had an offer from Columbia Products and I took it. One difficulty I'd had with advertising was that, as an account executive, I never felt as if I created the end product. The account executive represents the agency to the client and presents someone else's copy, art, and so forth. You never represent your own thing and I wanted involvement with the actual end product. Here I have that. We do as much R&D as we can afford, but we have seat-of-the-pants type thinking, too. I can actually point to my brands and say that I invented them.

Initially, my job here was unusual since I was given new products. You develop a rationale for marketing the products in the first place—talking to R&D, then working with market research to see if there is a viable concept that will motivate people to buy it. Then you work with advertising. You work with everybody to get all the elements together into a cohesive piece or program. You have to see that the product is good, that it fits a need, that its ability to fill the need can be communicated to people. Then you have to make the product right and get it to the people. There are a lot of details that have to be covered. For example, ordering the change parts on the assembly line for bottles takes six months' lead time.

Now, with the new products essentially launched, my role is shifting to that of planning a total ongoing program for the brands. We plan from a profit point of view and a brand is judged on its profit program. I have ongoing profit and market responsibility for the brands that are out now.

I enjoy strategy most of all in this job. For example, last October we found out another major toiletries company was bringing out a competitive product at exactly the same time as ours. We had to react to this—it's fascinating. You'd try to guess what they were doing. You do a lot of figuring out of the most profitable positioning for your brand—do you try to be first with a new product on the market, or what are the implications of being second?

Because of Tom's style, I've made more decisions than usual. I attribute a lot of this to Tom—he knew he could trust me and he let me have more responsibility. Some other product managers don't feel they have as much, but they're not working for Tom, either.

You have to spark the things that are done. There is a difference between just doing the things that have to be done and making the spark. You have to motivate people. Now I'd like to get into the broader planning areas, thinking of broader implications for the division, I'm trying to make my job into more; I'm finding out more —about knowing how our products are formulated, and building on that knowledge to get a broader sense of our divi-

sion's place in the total toiletries market. What are our limitations on sales since we don't have many salespeople? Are there other ways of selling? It's a broader investigation. I try to think of a future strategy for our division. Understand that none of this is my responsibility, but I want to help Tom who in turn can help his boss. It's not my job directly, but I enjoy thinking about it. We have not traditionally had innovative products, but we may decide for once to be the first ones out with a product. These are the types of questions that interest me.

CASEWRITER: How would you describe your style?

WEIVER: Halfway between a bulldozer and a Mack truck. It depends on what I perceive other people's attitudes are toward their jobs. There are some people I trust with their jobs, and others I constantly tend to push. If I feel that the person in question agrees with something I've given him, then I'll just go down later and say, "How's it coming—can we help?" If he doesn't agree, or I sense that he's hesitant, then I'll push him to find out what he's thinking.

I came here not knowing anything about packaging, manufacturing, or sales promotion. I had to jump in and make a lot of decisions in these areas, and I found that my judgment is pretty good. Looking back, I can see one poor strategy decision, but on the whole it's been pretty good. So now if I believe I'm right, the chances are I probably am. And if being extremely forceful and directive is the only way to get it done—to get two new products out in one year—then I feel the ends justify the means. There's so much to be done, I often sacrifice personal relationships in order to get the job done. Like with sales promotion—there I give directions down to crossing the t's. I may sacrifice some people's feelings to get the job done as completely and thoroughly as possible. I was brought here to do a job, though.

But now I have to train people who report to me. It's a different task. Now that we've got the basic job done, my assistant, Bill Walton, can get training. Now more time will have to be spent helping him become a complete product manager. My role will begin to be that of backup or consultant to him, helping him when he needs help, but he'll have to tell me. He used to come in and say, "I have a problem." I'd say, "I'll solve it." That has to stop. It will be interesting to see if I can be as good a leader as I was an activist, because as far as supervising is concerned, I still get uneasy in delegating authority.

CASEWRITER: How do you find supervising Bill?

WEIVER: I'm judging him on how much he can pick up with these new products. I can't do everything. I want someone who will say no to me. It's not been a good training period for him, though, because of the rush we're in. However, I am now forcing him to write our reports and to take a more active part in policy decisions. It bothers me when I realize there are things that haven't been done, but I will have to get used to delegating. It's tough when you're used to doing everything yourself.

CASEWRITER: Has Bill worked for someone like you before?

WEIVER: Oh, no. He said to me that he'd worked for someone with whom he could work for a month and the guy would make one decision and you'd know how he made it. Bill said to me, "You made 30 decisions and I don't know how you got there." He's a really nice guy, and I haven't leaned on him too much and I've tried not to be too directive. It's tough, since you have to be up on every detail of every other department. Like market research—know how it's done so you can evaluate it—and adver-

tising, production, and so forth. I can recognize what is reasonable and what isn't. You have to know so much about so many things I'm convinced that you just have to wade in and do it.

CASEWRITER: You feel he's been wading.

WEIVER: Yes. But he has a different motor. It runs at a slower speed than mine.

Bill Walton came in and E. J. mentioned that a meeting was going to be canceled. Bill said, "Pending further notification?" E. J. said, "Yes, let's try on Monday. Then why don't you talk to Mr. X? There are too many dates floating around—I don't know. Double check with Linda and apologize for this. Cancel the room so Time-Life doesn't expect us. Double check his schedule. See if Mr. Y can come."

CASEWRITER: What priorities do you put between your job and the rest of your life?

WEIVER: My free time is limited to one or two nights a week, but I often have last minute delays. I have a tough time making the transition from a work personality to a social personality. I have a bad temper. Poor performance irritates me, and in my performance reviews I've had it said that I am intolerant of people less smart than I. I'm really very intolerant of dummies, I guess. I can explain something one or two times, that's OK. The third time I get curt, and the fourth time is a bad time. I have no patience. I tend to lose my temper. If you know someone isn't bright—then you're tolerant. But if someone's been 15 years on the job and he comes in from 9 to 5 and has the dullard mentality with no pride in his work—that's what really irritates me. I get to be a table pounder—I curse and shout. My losing my temper, when I really do it, unfortunately is really effective. There are types here who after I do it will really produce for at least two weeks. I use it as a little management tool. It's theory X. Normally we like to be theory Y. But sometimes it's X time.

CASEWRITER: What lies ahead do you think?

WEIVER: Having achieved some success, it gives you confidence. The divisions go through cycles of where executives come from. Our division is currently experiencing accelerated growth and profitability. So, we can see unlimited possibilities for us, and our bosses moving up. Also, Columbia just bought a related company. So the opportunities will be there, too.

I know how to get things done across—that is, horizontally. I need to learn how to develop people, how to convince people, how to work vertically. My career path coming up appears to have two forks. Either I'll stay in a corporation like this, having people work for me, and having management responsibilities to develop them to function well within the organization. Or, I could go to a small company where I'd have ownership interest. And there I'd be an activist, particularly if it was my money. I've gotten self-confidence this year in my marketing ability. I'd get to know it all—whatever business I was in. I'd devote 15 hours a day and be totally absorbed. [See Exhibit 3 for the casewriter's observations on a typical morning for Weiver.]

WALTON'S VIEWS ON WORKING FOR WEIVER

WALTON: Before coming here, I spent two and a half years in training at a major cosmetic marketer. I wanted to go into international marketing, but there weren't any jobs, so I accepted one with the marketing group here. I moved here because I liked the idea of coming into a smaller, less structured situation where you could do it yourself. Here there are only 8 to 10 product managers. Basically, I'm in a training period. I've always felt like an interloper on the two new brands because they were already in process when I came, but I have a chance now for creativity with the third new product we're developing.

E. J. has a fairly important job, with about 30% of all the division's advertising dollars. This means there is horrendous detail and a lot of opportunities for panic. Before, I worked on a couple of old brands, but here, working on new brands we're constantly putting out fires. This job makes you capable of holding 360 balls in the air at the same time. At my other company, I spent 90% of my time on advertising and promotion duties. This job is filling in my experience in a lot of areas—financial, production, and working through the manufacturing department.

Implicit in the system here is a strong brand product manager system. The other departments don't resent us because they know we're supposed to be involved. The thread of continuity comes from brand management people. The brand managers set the key dates for each element of the program, for example.

E. J. goes at such a pace the list never quits. At first, I was bothered by it, trying to juggle all the things, trying to select which thing to do. It was very frustrating. Now I'm not frustrated by it. I try to select the important things and do them.

E. J. is very thorough—never satisfied until knowing that things are being done E. J.'s way. This may be going overboard. E. J. tends to get into such detail that people who'd normally do a job on their own end up waiting to be told exactly what to do, or exactly what E. J. wants, because they know it will have to be done that way in the end. For example, suppose we were to do a merchandising piece for a magazine. Ordinarily, the product manager would call in someone from the sales promotion area and outline the whole thing briefly and say, "You coordinate it, draft up a merchandising piece and let me see it." Generally, what they draft up would be OK. But with E. J. it's not that way. If it's not precisely what E. J. would have written, it's changed. So pretty soon these guys stop trying. They're tired of doing something and having it rejected, and so they come to think, "Why put myself out?"

CASEWRITER: What would you do differently in that instance?

WALTON: If I were doing it, the merchandising piece, I'd be a little more charitable. I'd accept their work from them more readily. I wouldn't agonize over one or two words if the piece basically said what I wanted it to. Because you'll never find anyone who is exactly like you.

CASEWRITER: What would you borrow from E. J.'s style?

WALTON: E. J. has made me much, much more aware of details. I'll be aware of details when I'm on my own, but I'll stop short of caring that much. To die over one or two words is not my style. After all, how much time is there to devote to the job?

Generally you try to minimize the small things so you have more time to devote to the important. However, if you're willing to work from 7 to 7 every day like E. J. does, you can give time to the minutiae. Not many people can work that way.

The job of being a product manager best utilizes the talents of an entrepreneurial-type person. E. J. is this type. But if you're truly an entrepreneur, you can't be happy in a corporation. The product manager job seems to attract the entrepreneurs, but it can't keep them satisfied forever. Product managers are always looking for a better situation. Because it's not truly entrepreneurial, they tend to get frustrated. If you're an entrepreneur, you want to do it yourself. You can't do it in a larger corporation, because you have to work through groups and things are beyond your control. A person like E. J. is much more used to the corporation than the corporation is to E. J.

I think ultimately E. J. would be happier as an entrepreneur—with a finger in every pie. The mistakes would be of E. J.'s own making. On the other hand, in a corporation, other people do make mistakes for you. There are things that you have no control over. For example, you have no real control over the assembly line in a plant, but if things go wrong, it affects you.

OTHER VIEWS OF WEIVER

To gain impressions from other people who worked with E. J., the casewriter talked with Sam Bodkins, assistant director of market research, and Pat Miles, who like Tom Bird was a product group supervisor.

BODKINS: E. J., in particular, is much more inquisitive than most product managers— very demanding and very bright. E. J.

understands research, always asking, "What about this or that?" More often than not, E. J. is right, which is sort of annoying. All product managers suffer from wanting answers to come out the way they want them to. Product managers, including E. J., are interested in research only for short-run solutions and justifications—on the grounds that (a) they may not be here next year, (b) they may forget about it by next year, and (c) there are so many things mucking up a situation that you can't blame anybody. If something goes wrong, is it advertising, distribution, and so forth—whose fault is it? A product manager is judged by how well a product does. You can be a hero this year and a bum the next.

CASEWRITER: What makes a good product manager?

BODKINS: It's hard to say. Essentially a product manager has to be a tremendously diversified person with a diversified background. A lot of it is gut feel. Knowing when to do things. You have to rely on the ad agency and on a sales force—and you have to nudge them. You're a traffic cop. You're a monitor with a lot of curiosity and sensitivity. They usually tend to be strong-willed and egocentric, but I'm not sure that's a necessity. E. J. is. I wonder sometimes if it doesn't work against them. Working with E. J. can develop into a pain in the ass. It's nice to work for someone who isn't always after you. What's more amazing is E. J.'s being right most of the time. Usually you get a tough time from the product managers and they don't know what they're talking about. But E. J. is usually right, along with being tough, bright, strong-willed—everybody admits E. J. is bright, but every once in a while you have to get slapped down.

MILES: E. J.'s style is successful and effective. The majority of the people around here are financial marketing types, rather than merchants. They don't have a feel for products; they feel the balance sheets and the charts. So they need someone who is constantly whipping and nudging, who has a sense of the product. E. J. wears everybody down—it doesn't make for great friendships, but it gets the job done.

E. J.'s one of the few who has the capacity to learn all aspects of one job. But as promotions come, E. J.'s going to have to temper that pushy style.

E. J. would be fantastic as an entrepreneur. But I don't see E. J. putting up with a corporate structure or a political structure—E. J. is a person with too much to do.

EXHIBIT 1 Division Organizational Chart.

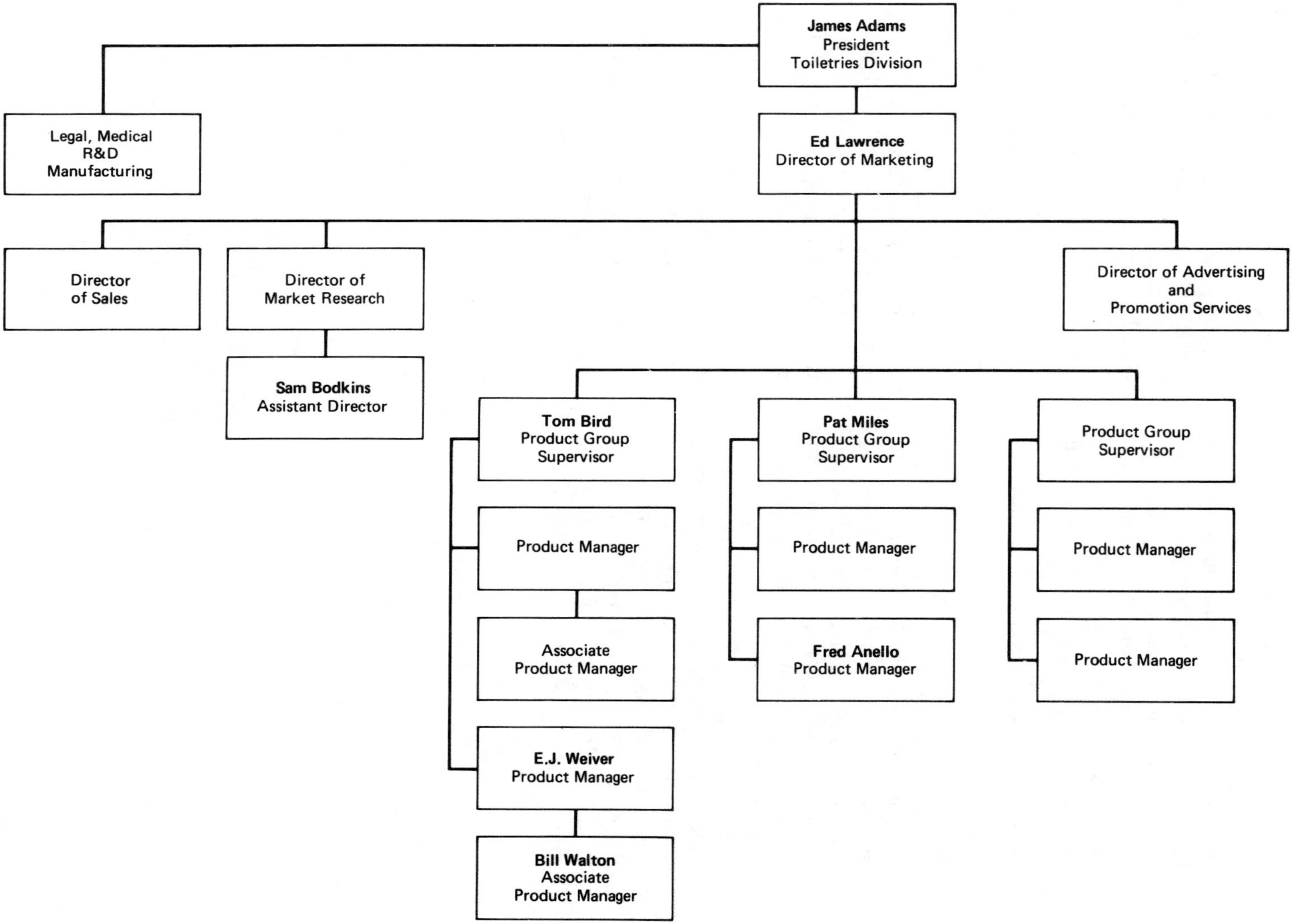

James Adams
President
Toiletries Division

Legal, Medical
R&D
Manufacturing

Ed Lawrence
Director of Marketing

Director of Sales

Director of
Market Research

Sam Bodkins
Assistant Director

Director of Advertising
and
Promotion Services

Product Group
Supervisor

Product Manager

Product Manager

Pat Miles
Product Group
Supervisor

Product Manager

Fred Anello
Product Manager

Tom Bird
Product Group
Supervisor

Product Manager

Associate
Product Manager

E.J. Weiver
Product Manager

Bill Walton
Associate
Product Manager

EXHIBIT 2 E. J. Weiver's Resume.

EXPERIENCE

Columbia Products Corp., Toiletries Division—one and one-half years

Product Manager: Responsible for the conceptual development and market introduction of two new toiletries products in 1971 and for assorted other brands.

Advertising Agency—six years

Senior Account Executive: Two years in toiletries, clothing, and public service accounts, including Columbia Products. Responsible for planning and executing plans in marketing, advertising, promotion, and collateral areas.

Account Executive: Two years on airline account. Responsible for planning and executing all sales promotion materials, also for development of their segmented approach to the special travel markets (ethnic, sports, honeymoon, youth).

Executive Trainee: Two years' training in research, traffic, media, and marketing departments. Program included six months of sales experience with client. Accounts included magazines, toiletries, automotive, food, clothing, furnishings, and public service.

Summers, part-time positions

Trainee positions at department store in Washington, D.C., and bank in Boston, Massachusetts.

EXHIBIT 3 E. J. Weiver's Morning Routine.

8:30 A.M.

- Sales department employee visits E. J. for social purposes.
- Market researcher, Sam, comes in to discuss note he left that morning.
- E. J. calls New York City ad agency.
- Bill comes in to discuss what E. J. told Sam earlier.
- Manufacturing person comes in to discuss labels for box and says memo is coming down about the cost and the making of applying labels.
- Sales planning person comes in to get information.
- Call from agency to E. J. re marketing. E. J. discusses conversation held with agency member the day before, raising the fact of feeling strongly on an issue that should be discussed seriously.
- Bill comes back. E. J. tells him how to cut the paper to fit the xerox machine.
- E. J. calls back agency to continue conversation. Tone of conversation is reasonable and friendly. E. J. acknowledges personal feelings, "But I can be overruled, this is my own feeling, but I want to know your feelings and also how to use the test scores." Reviews a production schedule for TV shooting.

9:30 A.M.

- In the next half hour, E. J. reads three memos and then writes a one-page reply very quickly, with a quick phone call to check some data. E. J. calls Bill in and gives him some directions to pick up samples from manufacturing, and to check on the status of some concepts from the medical division; then E. J. makes two more phone calls.

10:00 A.M.

- Call from a salesman for Good Housekeeping; E. J. searches files for information.
- Agency employees calls and long, detailed discussion follows on market test results, the amount of time needed to make a film, and methods needed to get the film done on time.

11:45 A.M.

- Four more telephone calls and a meeting, initiated by E. J., for sales promotion.
- E. J. goes to comptroller's office for some financial data and is back just before noon to drive to New York City for meeting with the ad agency.
- E. J. paces a lot, reads everything that comes to the desk, and scribbles a note, discards the item, or puts it off with a notation into the out basket. Nothing sits on the desk very long.

Note: This exhibit contains the casewriter's observations of E. J. Weiver's morning routine.

Kuolt's Complex

LUCIEN RHODES

Milt Kuolt had been through all this before—that agitation of the spirit, that spasm of discontent. It had driven him out of Thousand Trails, Inc., the first company he had founded, and now it was haunting him again, this time at Horizon Air Industries Inc., his second. It was a strange malady, a kind of occupational disease peculiar to entrepreneurs. Paradoxically, it always seemed to strike at a moment of triumph, when the dream that had given birth to the company was emerging as full-blown reality. In the glory of that moment, a troubling question presented itself: Had the company outgrown the person who had founded it?

Kuolt had been wrestling with this question for two years when I first met him back in 1981. At the time, he was chairman and chief executive officer of Thousand Trails and—to all outward appearances—the picture of entrepreneurial success. That success dated back to 1969, when Milton G. Kuolt II (his last name is pronounced "Colt") had finally lost patience with the state parks and other verdant glades that he and his family frequented in their 16-foot Terry Travel Trailer. The campgrounds were too crowded; maintenance was deplorable; and they weren't safe, what with the boozing and pot smoking and all manner of raucous hooliganism.

Kuolt had pondered this sad predicament for a while and had struck on what was then a startling innovation. He would build his own campground, called a "preserve," replete with cozy travel-trailer pads in the woods, a pool, a clubhouse, and other amenities. He would then sell nature lovers a lifetime membership in the preserve, giving them the right to use it and any others he might build in the future. If his own preferences were any guide, he figured, there would be thousands of takers for his "modest man's country club."

As it turned out, he was absolutely right. Starting with a few sites that he cleared with his kids, he had built Thousand Trails into the largest membership campground system in the country. By 1981, the company had 27,600 members who had paid average membership prices of up to $5,795 for the right to enjoy a patch of sylvan splendor in any one of 19 preserves located in five states and British Columbia. From Milt and the kids whacking away at the underbrush, the company had grown to more than 900 employees, with annual sales of $40 million and profits of $3.3 million. Thousand Trails was as big a success as the great outdoors it sold.

"But," says William Peare, then president and chief operating officer, "Milt wasn't comfortable. He wasn't happy. How'd I know? Well, he said so. You know him, he always speaks his mind. At least once a week for two years he'd say, 'I don't like this. I can't get my hand around this anymore.'"

The company had become too big, an institution. "You had to take on a bureaucracy, whether you liked it or not," Kuolt says, "and I've never cozied up to bureaucracies. I get upset with them." There was, he finally decided, no way to relieve his discomfort short of leaving the company. "I felt that I was much better in the formative stages of a company, in the creative stages, in coming up with new concepts, as opposed to taking a proven product and making it 5 or 10 times its size. I felt that takes a whole new type of discipline, a new type of management thinking."

After a year of discussion, he brought in another chairman and CEO, sold most of his stock, and walked. Now a multimillionaire, Kuolt announced he would start Horizon Air Industries, a new regional airline based in Seattle, serving the Pacific Northwest. It seemed, in some ways, an odd selection, given the restless, impulsive nature of the man and the grinding technicalities of the airline business. But, the choice of industries aside, Kuolt had no doubt about his decision to leave Thousand Trails. "The worst mistake an entrepreneur can make," he told me back then, "is to think that the abilities he had to run a company of 20 employees are good enough to run a company of 850 employees."

To be sure, the dilemma that Kuolt faced in 1981 is hardly unique. It is part of a pattern that every successful entrepreneur can recognize. You take an idea and a little money, find a handful of believers, and together set out to build a new enterprise against all odds. The quarters are cramped, the hours are long, the pay is thin, but it doesn't matter. There is a magic in the work, a special shine. You are a family, bonded together in common purpose and commitment. Exuberant, enthusiastic, and dedicated, you accomplish prodigies of endurance and self-sacrifice. The idea takes hold, and the company grows—the first million dollars, 5 million, 10, and still rising.

Then it strikes—let's call it "Kuolt's Complex." In the fullness of your accomplishment, you find it strangely hollow. The company is too big, too complex. What is that

person's name? Where did that family feeling go, and where the magic? You find yourself stranded in the breach where impulse and improvisation must give way to systems and planning, and the fires of creation are cooling on the routines of disciplined technique. You sense—vaguely at first, but more certainly as your awareness deepens—that your own talents by themselves, so productive at the start, are no longer of the kind and quality to carry the enterprise further. Others around you see that as well. But it's your enterprise, isn't it? You birthed it. You are its loving parent. How can you let go? What can you do?

To listen to business school professors, management consultants, and other such experts, there is an easy solution to this dilemma. "Recognize your limitations," they say. "Face up to the fact that the company has outgrown you, and bring in professional management before it's too late."

That is, indeed, what Kuolt had done at Thousand Trails, although it had been anything but easy. Now he was at the helm of another young company, Horizon Air—one that appeared every bit as successful as Thousand Trails. In four years, the airline had grown from three planes shuttling commuters between Seattle, Yakima, and Pasco, Wash., to become the fourth largest of the nations' 200 regional airlines, with more than 30 planes and more than 20 destinations throughout the Northwest. Its prospectus of June 1985—for its second public offering—reported that in fiscal 1984, the company had 847 employees serving some 660,000 passengers, with $48.7 million in revenues and $3.4 million in profits. Horizon was, in short, roughly the same size in revenues and employees as Thousand Trails had been when Kuolt left.

So how, I wondered, was he dealing with "Kuolt's Complex" the second time around? Did he find it easier to face up to his own limitations, having been through the experience once before? Was he already making plans to bring in professional management, without the agonizing soul-searching that had accompanied his decision to leave Thousand Trails? Or had he discovered new strengths in himself—strengths that allowed him to remain at a company that had soared beyond the start-up phase?

With such questions in mind, I called Kuolt and asked him if I might come out for a visit. "OK," he said. "Can you meet me in Sun Valley?"

"Sure," I replied, "but isn't the airline in Seattle?"

"Yes, but I bought a ski resort here, Elk Horn. We're having a party, black tie. You'll love it."

"Sounds great," I said. "But what happened to the airline?"

"I've still got it," he said. "This is just something extra I got into. Listen, we'll talk about it when you get here."

Elk Horn Resort is located in the heart of Sun Valley, Idaho, within schussing distance of Dollar Mountain and Mount Baldy, two of the most famous ski slopes in the United States. In this case, "resort" is not a euphemism for a roadside motel with an aboveground swimming pool and a miniature golf course. Elk Horn offers 350 rooms and condominiums, 18 tennis courts, two Olympic-size pools, and a 7,100-yard championship golf course. Its roofs and chimney tops are sharply angled to conform to the surrounding mountains and, faced in white stucco, its buildings gleam. Kuolt estimates that he has sunk about $10 million into Elk Horn, which has yet to break even. Currently, it is a separate corporation owned by Kuolt himself, apart from Horizon Air, although the two advertise each other's existence.

The black-tie affair Kuolt had mentioned was billed as the Elk Horn Lodge Second Annual Birthday party, an intimate affair for about 250 people, where he could thank various politicians and businesspeople for their kind words and support. After dinner, Ruth M. Lieder, the mayor of Sun Valley, stepped to a speaker's rostrum and read a passage from Charles Dickens's *A Christmas Carol*. The passage ended, "And God bless Christmas." Then Lieder, looking to Kuolt seated at the head table before her, said, "And God bless Milt Kuolt for all he's done for Sun Valley." The audience stood up and cheered. Kuolt, sitting there next to his wife, Kathy, was utterly abashed, working his face rapidly to accommodate various expressions of pride, properly toned with humility and heartfelt gratitude.

I think it was at this moment, amid the hurrahs and applause, that I first recognized the connection between Elk Horn, Horizon Air, and Thousand Trails, although I admit I had had some inkling of it before. During the two hours we had spent together before the party, it had become increasingly apparent that Kuolt was feeling the strain of his commitments. To be sure, he was still very much the man I had met five years ago, but the tone and focus of his considerable personality had shifted.

Over the years, Kuolt's trademark has been his contagious energy. "Milt has the ability to get people excited because of the pace he runs at," says his friend, Joseph Clark. "His leadership is by his tenacity and his strength in working so hard. He doesn't say, 'Show me.' He says, 'Watch me, watch me run.'" Standing still, Kuolt looks like what a quarterback sees when he peers over the line at a crouching linebacker. He has no neck to speak of, a bristling mustache, and broad, square shoulders, so that, at any given moment, particularly when he's excited, he seems poised to jump in your face. When his colleagues at Horizon describe his management style, they say it is personal and inspirational; tenacious in its goals, yet impulsive in its execution; open and bluntly honest. They also point out that, on occasion, it can be intrusive, overbearing, unpredictable, intim-idating, and insulting.

And yet Kuolt was not as fearsome, or as feral, as I had remembered him. He is 58 years old now and knows that he looks tired. This bothers him. "You know," he says, "when I was at Thousand Trails, I used to go out and cut down trees and clear trails by myself. I loved that. I was in shape. Now what do I do? I go to my office and sit on my ass. I put on 25 pounds since I quit smoking, my hair's gone gray, and I look 10 years older."

I was even more struck by the change in his attitude. When he was leaving Trails, Koult had been all self-confidence and un-daunted optimism: build a new company, take over the market, unlimited prospects, a "slam dunk." Now he is more humble, cau-tious, and questioning. He said he was pleased to be in the airline business, but then he talked about how the industry had sur-prised him, how he should have known more about it from the start, how difficult it was to serve customers. He mentioned heavy finan-cial losses, dissension on his management team, and the need for a different kind of management. Above all, he sounded frus-trated.

"What I really wanted to do," he said, "is to show people that I can build an airline different from all those other dipshit airlines out there. That's a tough son of a bitch. . . . We still lose bags, we still piss off passengers, we still don't answer the phones at reservations fast enough, we still have late flights, we still have mechanical breakdowns, we still have all those things like other air-lines, and ours ain't no better than. I can't stand that. You know, sometimes I wish I could be happy being number five, but I can't. I can't stand mediocrity. I can't stand incompetence."

His frustration was enormous, and I did not have to look far to find its source. It could be traced directly to the ferocious and turbulent growth of Horizon Air itself.

By all accounts, the first two years of Horizon Air were one of those magical peri-ods wherein dwells the stuff of legend. Every-one involved remembers it as a time of heroic deeds, selfless commitment, total immersion in a common goal, and complete personal fulfillment. "It was," says Thomas E. Cufley, 42, currently assistant director of flight oper-ations and a member of the start-up team, "absolutely electrifying." To Kuolt, fresh from the trials of Thousand Trails, it was like being born again. "God, I love it," he says. "That's what I live for. Take something that everyone else is absolutely convinced will never succeed, and then make the son of a bitch work, make it come alive. I love it."

In the beginning, at least, nobody was thinking about building an empire. Indeed, neither Kuolt nor his two co-founders, Scott Kidwell and Joe Clark, had any experience running an airline. "It was only going to be two airplanes in three cities," says Kuolt. "Just a little thing. That's all I wanted to do. There was no plan to take over the whole goddamn Northwest."

But what had started out as casual con-versation among friends quickly developed a momentum of its own. In the late spring of 1981, Clark began assembling a start-up team out of a small office on Boeing Field, and, by the end of the summer, most of the preparations were complete. To this day, no one is quite sure how it was all done. Says Donald P. Welsh, 29, vice-president of sales, "We didn't have a manual on how to start an airline so we just kinda stumbled across things."

Yet it was productive stumbling, lead-ing to the arrival, one afternoon, of the most conspicuous sign of the team's progress: the first of three used Fairchild F-27's, pur-chased from Quebecair Inc., in Canada. From a long bay window in the Blue Max Restaurant & Lounge, the start-up team, Kuolt, and 20 of his personal friends watched Cufley land the plane on Boeing Field, and then ran out to the runway cheering. Early the next morning, Kuolt, Cufley, and several pilots began scraping the aircraft's body, getting it ready for a new paint job and the Horizon Air logo—a blazing sunrise in hot orange, burning red, and smoldering maroon. "Milt was involved in everything," Cufley says. "We'd be cleaning the plane on the outside, and there'd be Milt washing a window on the inside."

On September 1, 1981, about 25 people walked along a red carpet stretching from Gate C-2 at the Seattle-Tacoma International Airport to Horizon's first flight, to Yakima in eastern Washington, 120 miles away. On board the plane, they received champagne and an inaugural flight certificate. Watching from the runway were Welsh and Dianna Maul, vice-president of stations, who had stayed up all night fretting over some last-minute details. "It was like our baby," Welsh recalls. "There was a real feeling of pride. That sounds real corny, but it was like the baby walked for the first time." Maul cried. "It was a relief," she says. " 'My God,' I thought, 'we did it.' "

Kuolt was aboard the flight as well, having left Trails that same day to become chairman, president, and CEO of Horizon. He had even greeted passengers at the gate. But he was already learning some hard lessons about the airline business. "I thought if we started an airline," he says,"we'd have to turn people away from the flights. Well, I think we had about half a dozen customers on that first flight. With the assistance of about 20 friends, we managed to put 26 passengers on a 40-passenger airplane, so when the press showed up, it looked pretty decent."

Out of the start-up experience came Horizon's extemporaneous, entrepreneurial style of management, which guided it for the next few years. It is perhaps best summarized by Kuolt himself, to wit, "When I see things working smooth, kinda good, I say: 'Shit, let's do some more.' " This approach offered the singular advantage of not cluttering intuitive flashes with market analysis. When a new market opportunity looked "kinda good," the folks from Horizon went after it—family-style, everybody grab hold wherever you can.

When, for example, they wanted to begin service to a new city, they would list on a large easel pad what had to be done, and then divide up the tasks according to areas of expertise. "If one person finished first," says Cufley, "he'd help somebody else. We never asked if we were going to get any extra money for it. We just did it." At the same time, they would stage what Welsh calls a "city blitz," sending in a team of managers and sales representatives who would split into two groups and walk down the main street, introducing themselves to as many businesses as they could cover in a day's march. "We always brought along a pilot and a flight attendant in full uniform," Welsh says. "That's what really does it, the pilot and the flight attendant. You should see that work on a cold call."

It all happened very quickly. City by city, Kuolt's modest plans broadened in scope. He was like a wolf turned loose in a sheep fold, who—once there—finds his appetite suddenly growing.

There were, he discovered, other small airlines operating a few planes on limited routes throughout the Northwest. For the most part, they had been created by wealthy investors who bought the planes and then leased them back to the airline for the cash flow and investment tax credits. Horizon soon acquired two of these airlines, Air Oregon Inc. and Transwestern Airlines of Utah Inc., adding more planes and cities to its system.

In part, the determination to grow reflected the heightened competition throughout the industry, brought on by deregulation. "We were hell-bent on generating revenues and developing market share," says

William S. Ayer, 31, Horizon's vice-president of scheduling and planning. "That was the name of the game for the first three-plus years. I'm not saying that was wrong. You've got a certain window with deregulation, and you've got to jump, or somebody else is going to beat you to it. So you jump when you can and figure out what you're doing later on."

After nearly two years of heavy start-up expenses, Horizon fianlly became profitable in the quarter ending September 1983 and, for the next four consecutive quarters, reported rising net income. Then, suddenly, the profits not only stopped but turned into steep losses. Horizon, barely three years old, was fighting for its life.

The major obstacle to Horizon's continued progress was a company called Cascade Airways Inc., based in Spokane, which had been in the business since 1969. Cascade had been flying head-to-head with Horizon on certain routes almost from the beginning, and had shown no signs of tiring. "I began to realize," Kuolt says, "that the two of us cannot survive. One of us is going to have to go. I say to myself that we've got to make the moves that will eliminate one of us—either suicide or murder. You've got to run yourself into bankruptcy or run the other guy into bankruptcy, one of the two."

Cascade itself had signaled the onset of mortal combat in the fall of 1984, when it announced the introduction of five recently purchased BAC1-11 Jets, small planes capable of carrying 79 passengers. Kuolt and his managers, who had been considering a similar move, were both stunned and relieved. Granted, the jets represented a potentially significant competitive advantage, but they were also unusually expensive to maintain and operate. From what Kuolt knew of Cascade's financial condition, the company would be unable to support the combined weight of operating expense and debt service on the planes unless the jets were immediately successful.

Horizon rose to the challenge, mobilizing itself to keep Cascade from realizing its advantage. "It was exactly like a war between two opposing generals," Welsh says. "Kuolt was one and the president of Cascade was the other." Once again, Horizon's officers entered the fray with the family-style initiative that had characterized the company's entire brief history. Ayer, for one, became so obsessed with the jets that he drove out to Walla Walla, Wash., where they were being refurbished and skulked about, surreptitiously writing down each plane's identification numbers. Then, for six months, he spent most of his lunch hours at Cascade's gates in the Seattle-Tacoma airport, noting the competition's flight frequency and passenger count, and comparing them with Horizon's.

Meanwhile, Horizon was countering with an assortment of defensive strategies. It offered discounted fares. It held special promotions with travel agents. Above all, it increased its number of flights. When, for example, Cascade introduced 3 jet flights a day on the route from Seattle to Portland, Eugene, and Medford, Ore., Horizon responded by offering 12 flights a day along the same route.

The battle raged intensely for about six months, and then it was over. Cascade withdrew its jets. Soon afterward, Kuolt reached an agreement with Cascade's principals to acquire his major competitor. "I suppose we could've let it go under," he says, "but this way it's done once and for all. You know, dead airlines have a strange way of coming back to life." As it was, Cascade filed for Chapter 11 protection soon after agreeing to the acquisition.

The triumph over Cascade marked the end of a period of Herculean accomplishment for Horizon. In less than five years, it had grown exponentially by nearly every measure in the book—number of passengers carried, number of stations opened, flights per day, cities served, number of employees, fleet size, revenues. In addition, the company had negotiated three acquisitions and made two public offerings. Along the way, it had clearly established itself as the dominant airline in the Northwest.

And yet most of Horizon's managers remember their victory as an unexpectedly anticlimactic event—one, moreover, for which they had paid a steep price. "Chasing [Cascade] got very tiring," says Ayer. "You felt like it wasn't a productive way to spend time, but—if you didn't do it—they'd get an advantage. It was like we were playing a little game that was important, yet it wasn't."

The dimensions of Horizon's Pyrrhic victory soon became evident. For the first six months of fiscal 1985, the company had reported a loss of $3.2 million, the bulk of which was directly related to the struggle with Cascade. At the time, there were hopes that the second half of the year would show a return to profitability. But when the year ended on September 30, 1985, Horizon was forced to record a loss for the year of $4.9 million on a 35% increase in revenues to $65.9 million—this despite an operating profit of $345,000 in the fourth quarter. As it turned out, the operational profit was more than offset by two extraordinary charges against earnings, one of them an unexpected inventory write-down.

Horizon clearly had its work cut out. That point was driven home in November 1985, when Edward Keaney, a securities analyst at Burns, Pauli & Co., in St. Louis, released a report that, among other items, presented selected operating statistics for the "top 10" commuter airlines in the country during comparable reporting periods. Even in fiscal 1984, its best year, Horizon placed only ninth in one vital measure of operating efficiency (the breakeven load factor) and eighth in another (yield per revenue passenger mile).

In Horizon's defense, vice-president of finance Michael K. Lowry argues that such comparisons are inherently misleading. He notes, for example, that all regional airlines do not use the same aircraft, and thus their operating expense ratios will naturally differ. But even Lowry admits that Horizon "has substantial room for improvement." Commenting on the swing from a net profit of $3.4 million in fiscal 1984 to a net loss of $4.9 million in fiscal 1985, he says, with only half a smile, "We are a major regional carrier that's forgotten how to make money."

That was an exaggeration, but there is no doubt that the mad rush to squeeze through the precarious "window" of deregulation took a toll. The management team simply did not have much time to concentrate on issues beyond sheer revenue growth. "There were brush fires every hour," says Lowry, "and people's energies were sapped by fighting the fires." Now that Horizon has established its market dominance and operating base, Lowry and his colleagues say that the current year, a year of consolidation, will be devoted to making the company profitable again.

Exactly what this involves remains to be seen. Not that Horizon's managers are oblivious to the problems. They know that they must pay close attention to cost-control procedures, which have lagged far behind Horizon's expansion. They know that the company needs more sophisticated information systems. It also needs better coordination among departments, and a more realistic balance between what customers want and what the company can profitably provide.

Identifying the problems is one thing, however. Solving them is quite another. "Basically," says Ayer, "[the problems are] related to some emotional feelings about the way you know a bigger company should operate, and the fact that we haven't changed our style. We've been acting like we're a brand-new start-up company just sort of making decisions on emotion and not very much information."

And, to solve that problem, they need help from Milt Kuolt.

Kuolt admits that he was shocked to learn of the inventory write-down. "I went simple," he says, referring to an angry, frustrated stupefaction so great that it renders him momentarily speechless, an otherwise unthinkable condition. "Wouldn't you? I mean it makes us look like we don't know what we are doing."

The write-down put a strain on his relationship with Lowry, who bore the news, but there were other things on Kuolt's mind as well. He instantly recognized the significance of the event. Something had to be done. The company clearly needed stronger management. But if the name of the game was now systems and carefully orchestrated departmental maneuvers, maybe it was a game that he could no longer play.

If the truth be told, that unsettling thought had crossed his mind before. He had already tried, and failed, to bring into the company the type of experience that he thought would correct some of these problems. Had he not, in 1984, hired a man with long executive experience in a major airline to become Horizon's chief operating officer? That hadn't stuck. "For a while he was useful and helpful," Kuolt says, "but within a year, the pace was too fast, and he was used to large staffs."

And what about that other experienced fellow, brought in to run the maintenance program? He didn't last either. "He tried to manage through intimidation," Kuolt says, "the old boiler shop, management is 'we,' and you guys are 'they.' All that kinda shit was totally foreign to my style, but I didn't sense it when this person was brought in." Neither man had worked out, Kuolt concluded, because they were big-airline people with the wrong mind-set for a start-up. They weren't

the "shirt-sleeve, hands-on, management-by-shoe-leather-type guys."

So what was he to do now? Here he was, back where he had started, back where he had found himself five years earlier at Thousand Trails. And, Lord, wasn't he just as frustrated as he had been then? All these thoughts frayed the edges of his mind until he began to dwell excessively on the minor irritations he would see in his travels. The free coffee at the gate hadn't been brewed yet. Or, the station attendant was five minutes late, and now there were 10 people in line. "You see the same errors over and over and over," he says. "Your patience runs out. They're minuscule, but I'm absolutely baffled that they keep happening. I can't stand it. I lose my perspective."

Such, indeed, was his state of mind as he sat at the head table at the Sun Valley party, soaking up the applause. For all his composure and his aw-shucks-it-was-nuthin' grin, Kuolt was a man who had just been shot out of a cannon to land in the troubled margin between exultation and consternation. He was not happy.

"Horizon has reached a great transition, a critical turning point in its life," he said as we headed back to Seattle. "It's not a baby anymore. It's a teenager, and it's struggling, like all teenagers do." We were sitting in the tail end of a private plane. Kuolt was dressed in jeans, cowboy boots, and his long, cattle driver's raincoat, which reaches down to his ankles when he stands. Yosemite Sam.

"I think I first noticed it around late 1984 and early 1985," he continued. "What happens is that your growth rate is so high that—when you finally pause to take a look at what's going on around you—you realize, 'Christ, I have not got the foundation I need underneath this thing.' You have to stabilize, get the systems and operations down better, the planning and cost control down better. You know, for a while you think you've got it made, and then you find out that things are kinda unraveling. You find that your management team is not pulling together as it should. And a lot of times we, as managers, have to take a look at ourselves to see if we're not part of the problem."

The symptoms were clear. Here, high above the newly formed dome of Mount St. Helen, Kuolt was describing the onset of the Complex. And as we talked, I could see him struggling with it.

He would say, for example, that, in the beginning, he intentionally avoided people with a lot of major airline experience because the "old traditional airline thinking is so screwed up." Then he immediately went back, adding, "but I probably should have brought in a little more than I had." He'd say he was happy at the airline, and then counter with, "but that's when things are good. When they're bad, there's nothing that can be much worse."

Or, "Overall, the first year or two I think we did everything kinda right." And then, "No, I would say we could have done a lot better job, had a lot more planning."

Or, "I drive my people. You've got to understand that. I work them hard, unmercifully." And then, "I'd probably change that today, because you strain the limitations of the people that are putting everything together, and I guess, if anything, I would have gone a little slower."

He said his management team held a planning meeting without him, "but I know what was going through their minds. They want to run an end play . . . . They're out there fishing for an opening. A palace revolt is all it is, a palace coup." Then, "When my senior people get together and want to have their own planning meeting without me being there, then I kinda know that maybe I'm not leading as well as I need to."

He'd say, "I'm quick to let go when I know the competence is there." And then,

"But the competence has got to be so high that maybe I gotta lower my standards just a little to allow that person to take hold. I've got to work hard at letting go."

It was an altogether curious experience, listening to Kuolt think out loud. At no time, however, did I get the sense that he really expected anything to change. Rather, he seemed to be dealing in resolutions and possibilities that might happen at some point in the distant, unspecified future. It made me sad to watch him—a kind of faltering hero figure, his usual blustering bravado now broken in places by moments of quiet self-doubt.

Nor did it seem to help much that he had been through the experience once before. Indeed, his plight was probably worse this time around, if only because the airline business is less forgiving than campgrounds of an entrepreneurial management style. Horizon, for example, depended heavily on market share; Trails did not. Cost control was crucial at Horizon; at Trails, it was much less important. Horizon's business is technically complicated, involving route structures, flight schedules, and maintenance requirements; Trails's business was straightforward by comparison.

During Horizon's start-up, Kuolt and his team had been able to overwhelm these differences with sheer energy, largely because the business was, at that point, still drawn to human scale. But as the company grew, it began to demand more premeditation and greater control. Inevitably, the old ways—the family-style initiatives—were put to the test and found wanting. So, for that matter, was the impulsive, peripatetic style of the company's founder.

As usual, no one knew this better than the management team.

When a founder is in the throes of Kuolt's Complex, everyone within reach is affected. In the case of Horizon Air, many of the company's managers found that they shared their boss's symptoms. They remember, for example, the early days of the start-up with a keen sense of loss at their passing. "Have you ever talked to someone who grew up with a big family in a 2-room house?" says Dianna Maul. "You know how they say, 'As crowded as it was, it was great.' That's what it was like here. Now we've got a 10-room house, and everybody's spread out, and things are a little more distant, colder."

"There was magic here," says Donald Welsh. "It was a Camelot. I mean pilots would come in on their days off and wash airplanes. Everybody was there for the cause. There was no distinction between management and employees." Not only has growth "robbed" Horizon of its magic, Welsh says, but he has also come to question his relevance as a manager.

Welsh and Maul were not alone in such thoughts. According to most accounts, management's frustration reached a peak in early October 1985, when senior managers rented a suite at an airport motel for a three-hour meeting, to which Kuolt was not invited. "It was a lot of emotion and frustration coming to a head," William Ayer recalls. "People just felt they needed to get away from Milt and talk about what was going on. My contribution was [to point out] that Milt is the way he is, and he's always going to be that way, and we either ought to figure out how we're going to cope with it or go do something else for a living."

Ayer says that, as a result of the meeting, managers have begun to communicate with one another more effectively. Its primary accomplishment, however, lay in the affirmation of solidarity, an understanding that "we're all in the same boat." Meanwhile, the managers are hoping that Kuolt will change enough to bring in a strong chief operating officer, who would relieve him of the day-to-day details with which he is obviously uncomfortable. Failing that, they are prepared for the possibility that Horizon might get a new COO another way—through acquisition by a larger airline.

Not that they question Kuolt's value to the company. "The whole irony of the thing is that we wouldn't be where we are now if it weren't for Milt and his style," says Ayer. "I mean the growth and the good things that have happened to this company. His style was completely appropriate for the first two or three years, but now [we need a] a different style, a more traditional organizational style of managing a going concern. We're no longer this entrepreneurial deal, flailing around and growing and trying to find itself. We're a major company that needs to be managed."

"It's such a goddamn challenge," Kuolt is saying as we drive to a late dinner in Seattle. "We're a teenager trying to be an adult, that's what we are." But help is on the way, he says. Yes, even as we speak, he says, he has plans to add experienced people to his management team. Granted, it didn't work out the last time, but now the company's "personality is stronger," Kuolt says. "They won't be so tempted to come in and say, 'Well, this is the way we did it at TWA.' I never gave a shit how they did it at TWA anyway." Then, too, he says, he is "more willing to accept help."

(That's true, says William Peare, the former Thousand Trails COO who recently joined Horizon with a broadly defined marketing assignment. "I'd guess that Horizon today is basically where Trails was in 1981. But here, Milt is confronting issues, which he wouldn't do at Trails. At Trails he'd say, 'I just want out.' He couldn't see light at the end of the tunnel. Here he's willing to try ways to make himself more comfortable.")

Yes, says Kuolt, he's been thinking a lot recently about the similarities between his situation at Horizon and the situation at Thousand Trails before he left. But there is one major difference, he explains. "When I left Trails, I felt that we had built an excellent company, the best in the country, primed beautifully to move to its next level of accomplishment. It's very different with this airline. Here we are about the same size as Trails was, but I do not feel the same way about it as I did about Trails. This company is not anywhere near the best airline of its size. I think we've got all the ingredients, but I have not been able to bring the whole thing together yet. I'm going to bring in outside talent to address these things. When I let go at Trails, I brought in somebody who I thought was better than myself to run the company. I don't feel I've got that person yet, here at Horizon."

"What will happen when you find that person?" I ask.

"When I find that person," Kuolt says, "I guarantee you, he'll run the company."

"And what will you do then?" I ask.

The answer to that question has to wait for a plateful of enchiladas. We are having dinner at the Azteca restaurant. José "Pepe" Ramos, the owner and a friend of Kuolt's, is sitting with us. Kuolt has been complaining that he doesn't take enough time away from business. He says that the further away he gets geographically, the more relaxed he feels. Ramos laughs. He says that, this summer, he took Kuolt to Cuautla, the village where he was born in Mexico, which is pretty far away from just about everything. But it hadn't helped Kuolt relax. Kuolt, he says, had tied up the only two phones in the village, trying to reach Horizon.

"Well," says Kuolt, "don't you worry, Pepe. Maybe in a year or so, there will be a chance for me to relax."

"Oh, really," Ramos says, "and where are you going to do that?"

"At Elk Horn," Kuolt says. "Maybe I'll be spending a lot more time at Elk Horn."

And it occurred to me then that maybe Koult had discovered a cure for the Complex after all. In his own roundabout way, he seemed to be saying that there are some people in this world meant to start things and then move on to start something else, and that the most they can do in between is to find their own replacement.

At least, I think that's what he was saying. The ways of Milt Kuolt and his Complex are sometimes hard to figure.

Maps for Adult Development (Part 1)

LAURENT A. PARKS DALOZ

Asked to imagine a map of America, most of us conjure up a vision of a multicolored United States—pink Massachusetts, yellow Texas, green Florida. But as every cartographer knows, a political map is only one of dozens of possible maps. A geographic map might ignore state lines entirely, emphasizing mountain ranges, rivers, and lakes; a historical map might draw boundaries in sharply different places than our more familiar contemporary one; and a demographic or weather map would look different in still other ways. What goes on a map clearly depends on what interests the cartographer; and the map we choose depends on what we wish to know.

The same goes for theories of human development. Although developmentalists, like cartographers, may assert at times that their maps are value free or strictly descriptive, they have made choices in constructing their schemes to highlight some elements and to ignore others. Those choices inevitably affect the traveler who is using the map. In preferring one road over another, travelers do not simply trace differing paths to reach their destinations; they may often be led to a new destination. Thus, when Carol Gilligan (1982) offered women an alternative map to the prevailing ones, suggesting that optimal development need not mean ever-increasing separateness, she caused many women—and men as well—to reconsider the importance of striving toward a stance of detachment and abstract principle and to value instead those parts of themselves calling for connectedness and relationship. The very existence of a map stirs the traveler in our bones, and the places on that map color our dreams.

Yet good maps also offer choice; they are not mere formulas. And while developmental theories do imply direction, none insists that the journey can be taken in only one way or, indeed, that it be completed at all. Just as a map frames the setting for a journey, so does a developmental theory offer a context for growth. It indicates landmarks, points out dangers, suggests possible routes and destinations, but leaves the walking to us.

One of the best-known maps is the one offered by Daniel Levinson and his associates in *The Seasons of a Man's Life.* . . . As a member of that family of developmental studies that have come to be known as psychosocial or phase theories, the work is mainly concerned with the question "What happens to people psychologically as they grow older?" It is closely related to the earlier thinking of Carl Jung and Charlotte Buhler as well as contemporary research of people like Bernice Neugarten, Robert Havighurst, and Roger Gould. What unites this family is that each of these writers sought to understand common tasks that people confront as they face the problems associated with aging. The theories are thus chronologically and culturally determined to a significant extent. By the same token, few of Levinson's colleagues have

These excerpts were taken from Chapter 3 of Effective Teaching and Mentoring, *by Laurent A. Parks Daloz. (San Francisco: Jossey-Bass, 1986.) Reprinted with permission.*

locked life changes as tightly into specific ages as he has. Most have found considerably more room for variation according to gender, age cohort, life task, or ethnic and economic status (Knox, 1977).

A second map, offered in Robert Kegan's *The Evolving Self,* represents another major branch of developmental theory, often called stage theory. Jean Piaget is generally accorded fatherhood of this family through his contribution of the idea that we pass through distinct and qualitatively different stages in the ways we construct our childhood experience. This notion gained greater sophistication as applied to adults in the work of Jane Loevinger, Lawrence Kohlberg, and Carol Gilligan, each of whom suggested that as we develop, we move first from a "preconventional" stance, in which our own personal survival is paramount, into a "conventional" orientation, in which our main concern is to fit into and be accepted by society, and later (if our development continues) into a "postconventional" position, in which we derive our decisions from broader considerations than personal survival or a wish to conform.

What is exciting about this family of theory is that it asserts that growth involves more than becoming a well-adjusted member of society (moving from the first to the second level). It also means coming to see one's own culture from a critical stance and establishing loyalties that go beyond one's immediate community (moving from the second to the third level). In many ways, Kegan's book provides the most carefully honed elaboration of stage theory to date.

Most stage theorists focus their attention on a kind of growth that does not inevitably come with age. They are less concerned with the process of becoming older than they are with the question of growing wiser. That is, Piaget noticed that some children seem to be able to comprehend the world in more adequate ways than others, and he saw that the difference has less to do with static "intelligence" than with dynamic "development." The stage theorists extend this observation throughout the life span. Some adults seem to "understand" a complex world in a more complex way than others. Rather than see intelligence as a fixed condition, developmentalists suggest that we all have the potential to evolve toward increasingly integrated and differentiated ways of making sense of the world. Thus, while two forty-two-year-old men may share common tasks in relation to their culture, they may interpret that experience in sharply different ways, depending on the framework of the particular stage they are moving through. Because later stages are by definition more conceptually inclusive and discriminating, are "better" in some sense than earlier ones, this family brings with it both exciting prospects and considerable dangers. . . .

We begin with Dave, at forty-three struggling to understand why his priorities have begun to shift under his feet. . . . Notice how he describes the direction of change in how he sees himself and thinks about what is "true." And take note of how these changes affect those around him.

THROUGH THE HOURGLASS

He looks tired. I nudge the tape recorder closer to his bowed head, hoping to be unobtrusive. It's unlike Dave to mumble, and I find myself straining to catch his words. He still speaks in that same somewhat inflated yet disarming style, and the passion is still there, but it is subdued in a way that astonishes me. He speaks to the floor, to himself.

. . . a very, very dramatic change that I witness inside myself. No longer am I boisterous—you know, take an initial, active part. Not interested in that at all. Very quiet mannerisms as compared to very loud, robust type. I have an extremely hard time making decisions that I never had before, even though there used to be a lot of wrong ones. Now I don't make any if I don't have to. I wait as long as possible and think about it. That's what stands out for me.

We are sitting in the community college office where I had asked him to come for an informal, follow-up interview. Dave and I have known each other since we met eight years ago. He stood out then, a tall, handsome man in his mid thirties, radiating confidence, a gunslinger of the construction industry. Owner of a highly successful small business, he had fathered three sons, was Little League coach, and a respected member of the church community. He had gone about as far as he could, learning on his own, and wanted to "get more formal-type learning." With the kids mostly out of the way now, he could. On the basis of an unusually high award of experiential credit, Dave entered the external degree program and became my student. At almost exactly the same time, to the consternation of his wife and friends, he sold his business and began work for a large industrial firm. He felt a need, he said, to "try something with more of a challenge."

Not long afterward, he was selected to participate in a study of adult development and gave us two intensive interviews a year apart. In the first interview, he spoke of returning to education as a way of "filling voids" in himself. When he had attained the knowledge he sought, he told us, he would achieve his goal: "peace of mind."

A year later, though still undaunted in his quest, Dave had begun to entertain doubts. For the first time, he spoke of an "internal" self that seemed to be asking unsolicited questions: Why change careers? Why go back to school? Why am I feeling these feelings?

Internally I've been in combustion. I've been, I've got an internal upheaval, OK? Crazy thoughts, a lot of questions to be answered. Outwardly, I've been very, very energetic, trying something different. . . . I've always been in control of my external self. I thought about what I was going to say; my appearance was always right for the situation; I made sure the proper tools were always at hand . . . and suddenly, uncontrollably, the internal Dave Hyssop began to take ahold of his life. And all of a sudden the tools of the external weren't important; they didn't do the job, they didn't bring me any of that peace of mind I've mentioned so many times. It was the internal that had control of me. . . . It kept reaching out and taking ahold of my life and shaking the hell out of me, OK? and saying, "No, you don't need this business, you don't need these tools, you don't need this appearance anymore. That's not what life is about."

I ask him about that now. How does he see his movement over the years since that conversation? How might he describe it? He looks at me sideways, wry grin baring a straight row of teeth, his eyes show our brotherhood. We both know the territory.

"I'd still sketch it with my old hourglass theory," he says, squinting out now through the dusty window of the old office building to the brick facade of a tenement hotel across the street. "You know, there's a coming into life so easily in the big bottom bubble. . . . I remember in my thirties being very self-satisfied with where I was going, and tremendous energy, confidence in myself and feeling of success. . . ."

His voice trails off; there's a long silence for both of us. Finally, I ask, "When did it start? I mean when did you enter the neck of the hourglass?" More silence. Slowly, he turns to me, then back to the window.

"The hourglass? Oh, I guess, I'd say . . . I've been in there maybe five years."

"So you were about thirty-eight?"

"Thirty-eight. Yeah. And getting into

the neck, I suddenly realized for the first time what an individual I was. I didn't need a lot of things that I depended on before. I began to question a lot of things that I was always taught to believe in or that always seemed to be right. I remember for a long time in there, just questioning everything."

We talk then for some time about what it's like "in there," for me as well as for him. He speaks of the struggle within himself between an "old self" that always seemed to be in control, and a "new Dave" who seems to be more passive. Yet while his former self was more decisive, it was also less genuine, obsessed with "tangible things" at the cost of the "general concern for humanity" growing in importance now. "I was a bastard!" he says of himself. "A real bastard." And I begin to realize that when Dave calls himself passive he simply means that he no longer feels such a need to control his outside circumstances. He is drawing back, making way for the emergence of a more "internal" self, a self he calls more real.

"Did your education have anything to do with all this?" I ask, not sure I want to hear the answer. He looks at me, a twinkle in his eye, jaw set.

"Well, I'm very disillusioned about it right now. I was extremely disappointed in what I thought my education would do for me in terms of where I was in life when I began, some of my objectives, I mean. It's not going to do much for me in terms of employment or money, and [long pause] I'm not even sure I like myself anymore."

Somehow I had expected this, perhaps because I've heard it enough before, and yet I hear a "but" coming. I nod and keep my mouth shut. After another long pause, it comes.

"The one thing it did for me is make me realize how little I know, how little learning I did have, and how much there is to learn and understand. You know, I read a lot more than I ever did before—all kinds of things

interest me. I'm an entirely new person now, and I'm having trouble living with myself. Other people too—my wife and my kids." He smiles to himself. "The other day she said she wished I'd never gone to college."

"What did she mean by that?" I ask.

"Well, I'm not the strong man in the family anymore. She wanted me to tell Ted, our youngest, to mow the lawn, and when I asked him, he said he wanted to work on the basketball court first. So I said, 'Fine, but the lawn's got to be mowed.' I got home that night and the lawn was mowed—no big deal. Now my other kids, I'd beat their ass if it wasn't mowed right then and there. I was a bastard, I tell you. My wife got used to living with that."

We talk on about how much strain there is on our relationships when we are going through changes ourselves, how hard it is on marriages, on friendships. And he speaks of his own changes as a journey. I ask him what he feels he is moving toward.

"I'm beginning to see the whole world as being relative," he replies. "It's like, like . . ." searching for the words, "time means nothing to me anymore. Like Einstein, you know; it's only a measurement of space. It's got nothing to do with beginnings or endings." He falls silent a moment, then grins and shakes his head. "Man, you can go any way you want. You know, all of us, we get thinking about our thinking and we immediately start to judge our thinking—why we're thinking that way or if it's all right to think that way. And, you know, you suddenly realize that in your mind you can think about anything you want to think about. You're a self-entity, irregardless of what you were before or what you're going to be tomorrow."

"Sounds like you've been traveling."

"Oh yeah," he says, grinning broadly at me now, the old Dave back. "I've traveled a long, long ways. You know, my education was like a catalyst when I think about it. I always enjoyed that word: *catalyst*. I always thought it was fantastic ever since I took a science course in junior high—a catalyst, you know? Something that starts something, helps something burn brighter, or you know, gives something more energy. Yeah, that's what I think my education was, a catalyst."

"Can you describe that a little more?" I ask. "A catalyst?"

"I think it brought to the surface things that were probably always inside me," he replies, sending a chill down educational spines at least as far back as Plato. "Maybe I lived a kind of phony life before; you know, it wasn't the real me. My education, how I studied, working with other adult learners, that was a catalyst. You know, look in the mirror and be truthful with myself. At least I'm being truthful with myself because that's the real me. My education brought out those things; it provided me with the confidence and the freedom to see things as they are, truthful about everything, not hide and act other than the way it actually is. . . ."

Dave's hourglass is a fitting metaphor for the midlife transition described in *The Seasons of a Man's Life* (1978). Levinson and his associates divide men's lives into four major eras. Like a stairway, they ascend through time, the risers representing periods of consolidation with relatively little change, the steps indicating disruption and what he calls structure changing. As he sketches it, our lives move rhythmically back and forth through periods of building, breaking, building, breaking, and building again as we grow older and accommodate to the changing circumstances of our lives. (See *Figure 1*.)

Levinson pays particular attention to the middle two eras of the life span, the years from about seventeen to sixty. The defining task of the late teens and early twenties is to move into the adult world and become accepted on its terms. For men in our culture, this means getting a job, establishing a household, and developing a sense of competence. During the twenties, says Levinson, men de-

vote their energy to exploration and tentative commitment. Many of those he studied began to form a "dream" of how and who they wanted to become—a kind of projected script for their lives. Often they would find a mentor who embodied that dream and who could help them move toward it. Mentors, in Levinson's ground-breaking research, are closely linked with the dream. They are living proof that it can be attained, and they usually help their protégés toward it. Appearing most frequently during one's twenties and thirties, mentors tend to be a half-generation older and remain in the role from three to ten years. Because much developmental research has looked at men and women in the workplace, it is perhaps not surprising that mentors are more commonly associated with the working world, with the building of competence and career rather than with development of the awareness and emotional maturity more appropriate to caring for oneself and others. Levinson's study of the lives of women will be published shortly, but whether it will deal with the meaning of mentorship for the whole lives of women remains to be seen.

The BUILDING period of the twenties ends with the midcourse correction that Gail Sheehy called "Catch 30." It is a time when we ask, "Is this really what I want?" and may be surprised to discover that when we thought we were asking the same question years before, we had actually asked, "What *should* I be doing?" In effect, we grow more serious about our lives, hearing an inner voice that urges us to make our commitments, "for soon it will be too late to turn back." Depending on the answer, this BREAKING period may be relatively mild or tumultuous, but typically it involves the act of self-assessment: "Is this what I want?"

This transitional time bridges our thirtieth birthday and comes to an end with the beginning of the settling-down time, around age thirty-three. Now we begin to act on the commitments we have come to, spending the next five or six years BUILDING again— establishing a business, settling into a job, raising a family.

Then, beginning in the late thirties and extending into the early forties, comes the notorious midlife transition. It represents the elbow joint of our lives, squarely in the middle, separating spring and summer from fall and winter. For many men the most dramatic transition, it prompts us to reappraise our life, not simply against our dream as we did years before but against our whole life span, cast with growing sharpness against the backdrop of our death. The neglected parts of ourselves call out more loudly to be heard, and for many, a longing for wholeness begins to replace the ideal of perfection. It is during this time, says Levinson, that we address more fully the polarities that lie within us like scales seeking their balance.

What tends to throw us off balance is our impulse to hold onto one end of those scales. By midlife, their imbalance can be such that only a major jolt can right them again. Such a jolt has the twin possibilities of either deadening our systems entirely, sending us down the remainder of our lives in slow despair, or refreshing us and pointing the way toward something like wisdom. Writing about this possibility, Carl Jung termed it *individuation,* the process by which we differentiate (yet again) our selves from our surrounding culture in a way that leads not to isolation but paradoxically to a greater sense of membership in the whole. Levinson "operationalizes" the term by suggesting that individuation happens as we redress imbalances along four polarities. Although he discusses these in detail in the context of the midlife transition, he makes it plain that the stuff of each polarity is always with us, and each transition requires tinkering with our little imbalances. To the extent that we maintain a reasonable equilibrium through early transitions, our midlife crisis will remain relatively placid. The more fully we can throw ourselves into the tumult of one crisis, the more fully we will grow in our ability to cope effectively with the next. It is essentially like collecting parking tickets—regular glove compartment cleaning keeps the Big Fine down.

The tension between being at once both *young* and *old* is the first and most apparent polarity. To address it, we must first acknowledge that we have changed since we last looked. Since the change is inevitable and since at all ages we contain within ourselves some aspects of both youth and age, the important question is "In what ways am I older and in what ways young?" To retune the balance each time, we need to draw out those parts we call young and old and label them afresh. "The task in every transition," Levinson reminds us, "is to create a new Young/Old integration appropriate to that time of life" (1978, p. 212). A similar process of introspection and redefinition is at work with the other polarities: Creation/Destruction, in which we come to acknowledge our capacity for evil, Masculine/Feminine, in which we question a sexuality formed by earlier needs, and Attachment/Separation, in which we reassess the boundary between ourselves and others.

Different cultures tend to value one end of each polarity more than another. In American society, for instance, youth, masculinity, creativity, and separateness are almost universally more weighted than their counterparts. To right the balance, to "develop" in Levinson's terms, then, implies that we must swim upstream against our culture. . . .

By the mid forties, Levinson writes, we have begun to move out of our midlife wilderness and we begin BUILDING a new "life structure" for the second half of our lives. It is time for the realignments that took place during the last transition to settle in and give more lasting meaning to our relationships, work, and spiritual commitments. There was great variability among the men studied at this period. Some, consolidating the gains of a lifetime, entered more deeply and richly into their lives than ever before; others seemed simply to be marking time until retirement; and still others seemed to find it a time of great pain, of "constriction and decline."

Although Levinson delineates several further phases, the work loses much of its power after this period, in part because the research grows thinner but primarily because the authors have outreached their own experience and simply lost their passion. In any event, those portions of the life span that they illuminate most thoroughly stand out with great vividness and provide guides and pilgrims alike with a valuable map.

There is, however, one important caveat. Levinson studied men. I find his work strikingly useful for understanding major aspects of my own and my male students' development, but its value for women is less clear. For one thing, women's life paths are different (Baruch and others, 1983). Our culture's expectation that they will take time out as mothers wreaks havoc with the neat, linear male trajectory. How a woman decides to juggle her "family responsibilities" has major ramifications for when she returns to school (Bernard, 1981; Evans, 1985). For another thing, recent (and long overdue) research is increasingly demonstrating that women define themselves in relation to others differently than men do, placing more emphasis on connectedness, less on separateness (Choderow, 1978; Dinnerstein, 1976; Gilligan, 1982; Baker-Miller, 1976; Rubin, 1983; Klein, 1985). This fundamental difference holds major implications for education, implications that are only now being spelled out in a call for a "connected education" to counteract what some consider an undue emphasis on detachment as a prerequisite to

"rational thought" (Belenky, Clinchy, Goldberger, and Tarule, 1986).

But Dave too seems to be feeling the effects of too much separation. Let's return to him and consider what we see through Levinson's overlay. It should be apparent that Dave was squarely in the midst of a rousing midlife transition. The hourglass metaphor was a unique and effective way to make sense of what he was feeling as he moved from the confidence, self-satisfaction, and tremendous energy of his early thirties into the neck of the hourglass, a time he traces to his late thirties when he sold his business and returned to school. Though he physically remained at home, in a metaphorical sense, he had left. His friendships fell away; he spent more time with studies and work, less with his family and community. In a real sense, he found himself wandering alone in a wilderness of questions, dancing, as he put it, in a twilight zone.

It was during this time that the sea change he describes as a shift from active to passive occurred. Although there are hints in his description of Levinson's male-female shift, the change seems more profound than this, more encompassing. Dave links the changes in a number of aspects of his life: from interest in tangible to intangible things, from material to humanitarian considerations, from external to internal concerns, and from being in control to being out of it. He describes an "old self" who was a "bastard" and a "new Dave" whom he's not sure he likes but who is at least much more "real," no longer obsessed with appearances. And although he acknowledges that he is not as satisfied as he once was, he is more content now than he has ever been. A superficial happiness is no longer the goal of his life. Dave is clearly hearing new voices in himself and is listening with rapt, if sometimes uneasy, attention.

Transformations rarely, if ever, come

about abruptly. Rather, they slip into place piece by piece until they become suddenly visible, often to others first, only later to ourselves. Yet it is possible sometimes to see key moments that seem central to the change. In Dave's case, the discovery that "in your mind you can think about anything you want to think about" is such a moment. Able now to think about thinking (a capacity Piaget considered of critical importance for the higher stages of intellectual development), Dave realizes perhaps for the first time, that *what he thinks can be separate from who he is—*that he can *have* his ideas rather than simply *being* them. This new capacity is both liberating and frightening, for while he is free to have his own thoughts, he can no longer hide behind the old beliefs. All at once, the givens of his life—patriotism, the work ethic, his boyhood religion—come up for scrutiny. With confirmation that "the whole world is relative" comes a new kind of responsibility. Dave's reluctance to act impulsively, or even decisively, is grounded in this discovery.

FIGURE 1 Levinson's Developmental Periods.

(Late Adulthood)

65

LATE ADULT TRANSITION

60

Culmination of
Middle Adulthood

55

Age 50 Transition   Middle
                           Adulthood

50

Entering
Middle Adulthood

45

MID-LIFE TRANSITION

40

Settling Down

33

Age 30 Transition

28   Early Adulthood

Entering the Adult World

22

EARLY ADULT TRANSITION

17

(Childhood and Adolescence)

Source: Daniel J. Levinson et al., *The Seasons of a Man's Life,* New York: Alfred A. Knopf, 1978, p. 20.

Maps for Adult Development (Part 2)

LAURENT A. PARKS DALOZ

A quite different set of questions confronts Sandy, at thirty-three working hard to replace her old roles as daughter, mother, and wife with a new relationship to her family—one that includes herself as an independent person. As she talks, listen to her description of where she is coming from and where she is headed. Note the function of her studies in that movement. And try to see how she is redefining the boundary between herself and others.

JOINING THE WORLD

Although it is only three in the afternoon, what little light the day has to offer is fading fast as I shut off the engine, hoping it will start again in the subzero cold. I step over a frozen snowbank and stiffen against the sound of branches crackling overhead. To my relief, Sandy opens the door quickly and gestures to the kitchen table where I sit, a bit too far for comfort from the compact wood-stove against the far wall.

"That's where I do most of my work," she says, smiling toward the table with gentle irony. "Coffee?"

We make small talk for several minutes, and then feeling the press of the growing darkness outside, I remind her that I have stopped by to listen to her talk about what it is like for her, at the age of thirty-three, to be back in school studying again after twelve years. She explains that she had spent much of that time after acting school trying to find work, to prove to herself that she could be a successful actress. She had also married and borne a child. At her husband's urging, she began to think about resuming her educa-tion. Staying at home seemed stifling to her; she felt an intense desire to "participate in the world." The program in which she had recently enrolled seemed right. She liked its flexible structure, liked being treated as a unique human being, felt that "it was time," she says, laughing somewhat self-consciously, "to prove to myself that I wasn't dumb."

"Has it worked?" I ask, drawn to her laughter.

"Well" she pauses, catching a breath, hearing it as a serious question, "yes, I think so. I mean I'm finding out that I have my own thinking process and I have my own way of learning and that I have my own way of understanding myself and learning how to deal with things in life. I'm finding what that is now. I think that I had previously . . . I hadn't developed that side of myself at all. I feel like that the way I guided myself through life was to go back to my family and say, 'Tell me what to do. Am I OK?' you know, rather than seeing, looking, understanding how *I* operate and finding out how *I want* to think

These excerpts were taken from Chapter 3 of Effective Teaching and Mentoring, *by Laurent A. Parks Daloz. (San Francisco: Jossey-Bass, 1986.) Reprinted with permission.*

and *I want* to deal with myself and how *I want* to treat other people from my own perspective and my own point of view."

I'm struck, as I listen, by the contrast in her voice, dark and somehow burdened as she speaks of that earlier self who turned so often to her family and to others for guidance, hardening to a kind of driven urgency as she tells of her new self, underlining *want*, nailing it home, setting each word of "my own point of view" up on end for display.

"And I feel like that it's just happening. I'm starting to see who I want to be, and it's really, it's getting away from my family and getting away from all that security. I was really cowering late in my twenties and realizing I had to find a way out or I was going to get smothered by it." Her voice drops, and she looks down at her hands, laughing softly, wryly. "And I don't know if I'd like that."

"Away from all that security?" I ask, curious about the tension in her words.

"Well," she replies, "my last study was about family systems, and I know my family has a definite system of how it operates to keep its members secure. There's a loyalty in families that gets so ingrown and so protective that its members all stop growing. And I've had to find out what my philosophy is and how I want to live as a separate person. It's all in letting myself think and feeling secure enough to think."

She goes on to describe her experience with feminism, her struggle to understand it not simply as a woman's issue but as a source of power for both women and men. It has changed her relationship not only with her husband but also with her family, separating her from them in still another way.

The language of movement suffuses her speech. At one point, I ask her whether some of the changes she describes have been easy for her.

"No, but it's been forward moving; it's been exciting; it's been . . . more and more I feel that I'm being pulled with a current. I'm connected now with where I'm going, and I wasn't before."

"Where's the current going?" I ask.

"Well, I guess that what I *want* is to feel that I am . . . to know that I am independent. And that I am responsible for myself emotionally and intellectually, and that I stand alone." She is choosing her words carefully now and rounds off that word "alone" like a sculptor her clay. "That I can support myself, support myself and my kids if I have to, that I'm not at the mercy of greater forces, that I've got some control, and that I've got a vehicle to express myself—you know, to participate in the world rather than isolating myself and putting it down. That's what I want: I want to be *a legitimate member of the world.*"

She laughs at this, disarming the considerable power of her speech, but I can feel the chill on the back of my neck. Perhaps she senses it too, and we both fall silent for a moment. On cue, the phone rings, and I take a deep breath.

The conversation goes on for some time after that, illuminating corners like a flashlight in the attic. Sandy's sense of motion is striking, the more so as she chooses to describe her adviser as a guide, moving ahead under some mysterious force, leading the way on a voyage she cannot take alone. Her use of the journey metaphor is quite explicit. She sees herself moving toward a clearer sense of independence, a self defined more by her own actions than others' expectations, away from a security that no longer protects so much as constrains. Far off, too dim to make out, there might be an edge to the horizon of independence and self-rule— kind of reblurring of distinctions, a new sort of legitimate dependence. But it is dark off there, and she can't be sure. For now the struggle is to feel responsible for the shape her life has taken, for what she does in her life, for her*self*. Never again will she allow someone else to do that for her.

How best to understand this drive toward independence so powerfully described by Sandy? . . . One of the clearest thinkers in this field is Robert Kegan, like many developmentalists, a former literature scholar turned psychologist. In *The Evolving Self* (1982), he describes with charm and eloquence his vision of the meaning of growth. Although clearly derived from the work of Kohlberg and Piaget, Kegan's model avoids the sometimes boxy quality of the earlier theories, substituting for the ladder metaphor an upward-spiraling helix. . . .

Several things are worth noting about Kegan's map (see Figure 1). First, what is important for our purposes here is not the particular balances so much as the overall direction of movement. That is, as we cycle through these levels, we go through times when we are preoccupied primarily with our relations with "the other" and times when we are mainly concerned with our "self," apart from the other. In an important sense, our lives can be understood as a series of transformations of how we see ourselves in relation to others, how we negotiate the twin claims of what David Bakan has called agency and communion (Bakan, 1966). Thus, the early stage "impulsive" child is unable to distinguish his own impulses and wants from those of anyone else. We *are* our impulses, says Kegan; we don't *have* them. It is very difficult, as any parent knows, for a four-year-old to see through any eyes but his own. The "imperial" ten-year-old, however, knows what motivates her younger brother because she is more able than he to get outside of herself. She understands the importance of reciprocity (and the power of bribes) in a way he cannot. More self-possessed than her brother, she *has* her impulses; what she can see less clearly are her needs. With movement into the interpersonal balance, however, we open up in a whole new way as we seek to redefine ourselves through others, often as teenagers but frequently later in life

as well. This is the time of falling in love ("I am *nothing* without you"), of conforming to the ways of the tribe, and of transforming the earlier mutual back-scratching morality into a more communal group ethic of trust. A more fitting paeon to interpersonal virtues than the Boy Scout law would be hard to find: trustworthy, loyal, helpful, friendly, courteous, kind, obedient, cheerful, thrifty, brave, clean, and reverent. Now we *have* our needs, but we *are* our relationships. With the swing back and upward toward what Kegan calls the institutional balance, we "zip up" in a sense, drawing our boundaries more clearly, struggling (often against the inner and outer voices of our culture) to define ourselves in terms less borrowed from others than earned of our own effort. Loving becomes more an act of will than of self-denial; responsibility is redefined to include oneself; loyalty to the tribe is based less on friendships than respect for abstract principles; and guilt replaces shame as a form of social control. Finally, we swing back in a new yielding to something greater than ourselves, dissolving our boundaries once again as we work to let go of a self that may have grown too narrow. We reach out again to others in an effort to heal the wounds of too much separateness with a new compassion and often a new spirituality. Each transformation, each move involves a swinging outward, away from the familiar world into the strange, a leaning into uncertainty, a risk. Often we experience that move as a kind of impulsion toward our own opposite, our dark side, and we go at times unwillingly.

More than any other stage theorist, Kegan respects the motion in our lives, and he has focused the chapters of his book not on the stages but on the quality of the transitions between them, emphasizing how our movement involves both a reaching out and a letting go. Development is not a self-contained process that takes place inexorably. How readily we grow—indeed, whether we grow at all—he says, has a great deal to do with the nature of the world in which we transact our lives' business. To understand human development, we must understand the environment's part, how it confirms us, contradicts us, and provides continuity. . . .

Consider Sandy again. Clearly, her story tells of transition out from the "security" of her family—an interpersonal world that defined her for years—toward the "security" of a more self-conscious and deliberately constructed identity. Her tale reverberates with the voices in numerous current feminist writings about the struggle to define a new self apart from the reflections of a male-dominated society in which her place was to keep her place. Alice Koller's *An Unknown Woman* is a particularly effective portrayal of the anguish this can entail. As such, the appeal *and importance* of feminism to Sandy should come as no surprise, for the movement is a powerful cry for an ideology of self-affirmation to enlarge the personalized world of face-to-face contact with family and friends. It calls us to identify also with people we do not know, thus defining a new and broader sense of our place in the world.

But beyond this, Sandy's frequent return to the theme of separation, of emergence from embeddedness in her family's expectations, of a sense of breathing again after being almost "smothered," is striking in its evocation of liberation. There can be no doubt that she is moving into Kegan's period of self-authorship, feeling her oats, reveling in the new promise of independence, of control, of participation in the world. This is the time when people think of career rather than simply job; goals and a sense of achievement take on a new power; a feeling of purposefulness and the capacity to achieve what one sets out to do makes itself felt more strongly than ever. Those who return to school at this time tend to see the value of education not as a means simply of gaining new status (a concern more strongly felt at earlier stages) but as a way to achieve career goals or sometimes as a way to expand and develop that precious new inner self that they are beginning to discover and value so highly. All of these are movement "out" as the inner self comes more clearly into view. At the same time, recall that "separation" for women at this point may have a different quality than for men. Carol Gilligan's work suggests that Sandy may not so much be splitting herself off from her family as attempting to redefine her relationship so as to include *herself* as one of those deserving of care. . . .

Ahead for Sandy lie a new career, new friends, and perhaps a new basis for friendship. Her marriage may experience strain as she redefines the terms of relationship, taking her own needs into account in a new way. Her mentor might do well to stand back and watch carefully before moving too precipitously, for Sandy needs her head. Her question is about who she wants to become, and she must answer that by herself.

FIGURE 1 Kegan's "Helix of Evolutionary Truces."

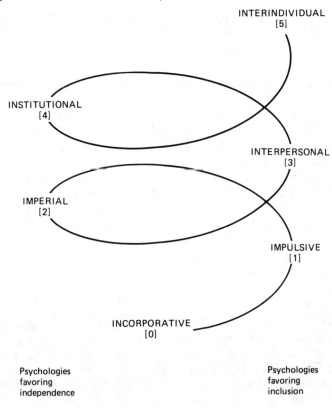

Reprinted by permission of the publishers from *The Evolving Self: Problem and Process in Human Development,* by Robert Kegan, Cambridge, MA: Harvard University Press, Copyright © 1982 by The President and Fellows of Harvard College.

Taking the Mystery Out of Change

NANCY K. SCHLOSSBERG

A local television reporter recently asked me about the midlife crisis. "It's an artifact of the media," I said. "Crisis, transition and change occur all through life." The interviewer was shocked and crestfallen. I had wrecked a story. But I hope I paved the way for a better understanding of the adult years.

Based on my research and that of many others, I have come to believe that there is no single predictable, universal adult experience—there are many, and they frequently involve transitions. From childhood through adulthood, people are continually at the beginning, in the midst of and resolving transitions—some expected, others not. We initiate some but are forced to weather others. At times, we feel comfortable in our roles, at other times uncertain about what is ahead. Although we all experience transitions, our lives are so different that one person may go from crisis to crisis while another may experience relatively few strains. These differences depend on many factors, but one of the least telling is chronological age.

I believe it is less important to know that a person is, say, 50 years old than to know that the person is a newlywed, the parent of adolescent children, recently divorced or about to retire. People facing retirement encounter many of the same problems whether they leave their jobs at age 50, 60 or 70. Newlyweds of any age are engaged in similar tasks of bonding, discovery and negotiation.

In short, transitions are more important than chronological age in understanding and evaluating a person's behavior. And because the adult years are so variable, we cannot assume that particular transitions will necessarily occur at specific ages.

The transitions in our lives are those events—or nonevents—that alter our roles, relationships, routines and assumptions. They include:

- *Anticipated transitions:* the major life events we usually expect to be a part of adult life, such as marrying, becoming a parent, starting a first job or retiring.
- *Unanticipated transitions:* the often-disruptive events that occur unexpectedly, such as major surgery, a serious car accident, a surprise promotion or a factory closing.
- *Nonevent transitions:* the expected events that fail to occur, such as not getting married, not having a baby or living longer than expected.

Transitions such as the birth of a first child or taking early retirement appear to have little in common, but both change a person's life. It's not the transition per se that is critical, but how much it alters one's roles, relationships, routines and assumptions, and how able one feels to cope with the situation. Psychologist Richard Lazarus finds that we cannot understand the impact of a transition unless we look at the way the individual appraised the transition and his or her resources for dealing with it.

Nancy K. Schlossberg, Ed.D., is a professor in the Counseling and Personnel Services Department, College of Education, at the University of Maryland-College Park.

Transitions take time, and people's reactions to them change—for better or worse—while they are under way. At first, people think of nothing but being a new graduate, a new widow, a new parent or newly jilted. Then they begin to separate from the past and move toward the new role, for a while teetering between the two. A year, sometimes two years or even more pass before moving from one transition to another. While some transitions may be over and forgotten, others never seem to end. In a study looking at men whose jobs were eliminated, I found that once men obtained new jobs they felt the transition was completed, while the men unable to replace what they had lost felt stuck in the midst of the transition.

Clearly, people differ in how they cope with what seems to be the same transition, and often cope well in one transition but feel ineffective in the next. How, then, do we handle this journey, live through it and learn from it?

To help answer these questions I have developed a systematic way to predict, measure and modify people's reactions to change. By examining the features common to all transitions, however dissimilar they appear, some of the mystery can be taken out of change.

Studies of change—whether job loss, geographical moves, returning to school, caring for aging parents or retiring—have shown that people in transition have both strengths and weaknesses. I have clustered these potential resources or deficits into four major categories, the four S's: situation, self, supports and strategies. By looking at the balance of people's resources and deficits in each of these categories, it is possible to predict how they will cope.

- *Situation:* Does the person see the transition as positive, negative, expected, unexpected, desired or dreaded? Did the transition come at the worst or best possible time? Is it "on time" or "off time"? Is it surrounded by other stresses? Is it voluntary or imposed? Is this the transition's beginning, middle or nearly the end? Is this a personal transition or a reaction to someone else's?

- *Self:* There are many ways to gauge a person's inner self or strengths for coping with the situation. What is the person's previous experience in making a similar transition? Does the person believe there are options? Is the person basically optimistic and able to deal with ambiguity? If so, he or she will bring to the transition the greatest resource of all: a strong sense of self.

- *Supports:* External supports and options include both financial assets and potential emotional support from family, close friends and coworkers. Dealing with transitions successfully requires that those close to us offer more support than sabotage. Unfortunately, this is not always the case.

- *Strategies:* Understanding the nature of transitions can help us find ways to cope with them. Sociologist Leonard Pearlin points out that there is no "magic bullet" coping strategy. Rather, the creative coper uses a number of strategies, including those that change the situation or the meaning of the situation, as well as those that help the person to manage stress.

By taking readings on the state of the four S's we can target the problem area, then ease the pain of change by modifying that area. Consider, for example, the case of Mary, a middle-aged graduate student whose recent life is a study in transitions. Before she had a chance to grieve the deaths of both her parents, her aged in-laws decided it was time to move to a nursing home. Because her husband, the breadwinner, couldn't afford to take leave, she commuted regularly out of town to help his parents plan their move. At the same time, her daughter, unable to afford her own apartment, moved back home, and Mary's son and daughter-in-law had a baby just as he lost his job. To an outsider, Mary's situation was obviously overloaded with transitions. Yet she was so unaware of the additive impact of these changes on her life that she could not understand why it was so hard to complete her graduate degree!

Merely evaluating the four S's made Mary realize that she had three strengths: supports, self and strategies. Her personal strengths included her maturity and resourcefulness, and she had the support of a collaborative, loving relationship with her husband, as well as a sympathetic church group. She added prayer to her many coping strategies to help herself get through these difficult times, and developed new supports by seeking professional counseling. Just realizing the many resources she had helped Mary deal with a very stressful time in her life.

We know transitions are inevitable and recurrent, but their specific form, timing and intensity cannot always be anticipated or controlled. We can, however, control how these changes will affect us. By systematically sizing up transitions and our own resources for dealing with them we can learn how to build on our strengths, cut our losses—and even grow in the process. With a lifetime of practice, some people even get good at it.

2

Family, Work Group, and Team Transitions

Introduction

Families and work groups often share the label "family" as a descriptive metaphor. The concept of family implies a closeness of ties and feelings. However, the concept and the reality often differ as we shall see in some of the cases included in this section. Family tensions all too often invade the work setting, and work tensions invade the family. Neither setting remains easily isolated from the other.

Yet the family metaphor continues. Each of us needs to belong to a home setting which provides us with primary membership and affiliation. It shouldn't be too surprising that sometimes those memberships are stronger at work than they are in our homes of origin. Or if they aren't stronger, we wish they were.

Groups, like families, find it easy to establish boundaries around themselves. There's "us," and there's everybody else, who become "them." There are the insiders and the outsiders, those who are like me and those who are not and those who share with me common tasks, bonds, norms, animosities, and pressures. Some group ties are stronger than family ties, and many managers hope to keep them strong.

Both the family and the work group face inevitable transitions—from one generation to the next, from one struggle to another, and from threats either inside or outside. The so-called permanent or primary work group has almost become a rarity these days in that membership turnover and environmental change conspire to upset stability and foster new company and task relationships. In addition, as cross-functional cooperation becomes more and more necessary in organizations, the concept of teams has augmented the concept of groups. The team concept implies ever greater degrees of cooperation, commitment, urgency, and a desire to win. From this athletic metaphor to the military metaphor is only a small step too: companies turn groups into teams and teams into task forces.

From family to teams and task forces seems like a far journey. It isn't. In modern organizations, the similarities outweigh the differences. In each case, the sentiments for cooperation and commitment are basic. Norms of cohesion building across differences are expected to outweigh those differences of opinion, special interests, and background. And yet, just as in families, those differences do exist and go along with a variety of role preferences and assignments: parent and child roles, sibling rivalries, specialists and generalists, and family feuds as one branch disagrees with another. There are established leaders and emergent leaders, hierarchies and networks, task concerns and people concerns. There are efforts to keep the family, group, team or task force "working together" and there are inevitable needs for separatism and individuality. In some respects, the cries for family unity have become even stronger in the workplace as our so-called nuclear families go through their own variations and upsets. In that sense, transitions have replaced traditionalism in both work groups and families.

In this section, we shall begin with the world of family dynamics as they affect the workplace, much more often than we typically acknowledge. Garcia y Mora describes the wrenching experiences of a tradition-bound Spanish family as dissension and bitterness take their toll on both the family and its business in an international context. Henry Manufacturing and Precista Tools AG are both accounts of the youngest child struggling against family hierarchies. In the Henry case, Gene Harms is the CEO and youngest son in a company where two older brothers represent tradition and two seats on the board of directors. In Precista, Greta Hubler is youngest daughter in a precision tool company located in Switzerland and dominated by a father who can't let go and whose chosen son doesn't want to enter the company—at least until recently. In both cases, not only tradition but mixed role demands are important issues.

Newby Motors is a case where the tyrannical father browbeats the rebellious son and his wife almost into acquiescence. As in the Precista case, one can only wonder how families hold together under such pressure. Blood ties and money may provide part of the answer, and yet the costs seem enormous in these families where anger, dissent, and rivalry seem pervasive and out in the open.

Sometimes, these conflicts are more muted but still-powerful influences on both family and nonfamily members as in the Frank Reardon case. In each of these family-in-business cases, the essence of so-called family spirit seems to be lost. One could argue that these kinds of family experiences in business are atypical aberrations. We suggest otherwise. Although not necessarily typical, these experiences are neither unique nor uncommon. Families in business are often no better at building "family" spirit in the enterprise than anyone else.

Those same tension-ridden patterns are seen in the Wood Structures and Datavision cases. In each case, the CEO is struggling to build team spirit and cooperation norms. In each case, he cannot figure out where the problems come from or why they persist. Those chores are left up to ingenious instructors and their insightful students. In Section 3, you will get another taste of these team and task force issues in the John Hancock Mutual Life Insurance Company case, where the Inflation Strategy Task Force is charged with developing the bases for a whole new company strategy.

As in each of the cases in this book, we ask you to think multidimensionally. In this section, the cases ostensibly focus on relationships within basic groups and families. However, that, as usual, is only a part of the picture. Person-to-person relationships make up groups, and person-group-to-group relationships make up organizations. All these relationships provide both basis and context for other issues of importance. Acting upon both bases and context requires both vision and explorations beyond vision.

Precista Tools AG (A)

April 30, 1986

Dear Mami and Papi:

Before I leave again for the United States, I think that I have to write to you. Papi asked me to let him know what my decisions are concerning my employment with Precista. He set the deadline.

I have decided to leave the company.

After a long period of thinking, I came to the conclusion that my attitude, my inner beliefs, and how the company should be managed to achieve its set goals are all basically different from the ideas that Papi has. Peace in our family has the highest priority, and I'm convinced that this step I take will keep peace and that you will understand my feeling and wish.

After my return from the United States, I will write to the Board and give formal notice. You can be assured, I promise, that I will stay with Precista until you have found a new solution. I still feel very responsible for the future of the company.

Now that I have made the decision—written down the words—I feel myself free, and I'm looking forward to a new environment in which I will be able to develop myself again. I hope that you will take me just as I am. I would just like to be a happy, content family member—nothing else.

With all my love,
Yours, Greta

BACKGROUND

Precista Tools AG was founded in Glarus, Switzerland, just after World War II by Mr. Franz Huebel who was born in 1913. Mr. Huebel and his wife, Sophie, were running a small international trading company out of Glarus. As Mr. Huebel said of Precista's origins:

At the time we started the business, we had little money, a great deal of credit, a lot of ideas, and the will to make more money and work hard at it. But Precista could only become and stay leaders in the precision tool field if we were able to invest more money in product development than the average company could.

In order to raise money for product development, the Huebels poured the profits from the trading business into developing specialized precision tools for export out of the new business. By 1985, the company had 100 employees and 60 sales representatives throughout the world. Mr. Huebel had developed excellent marketing contacts in other countries where Precista became known for its sophisticated and well engineered special purpose precision tools. Precista became very successful and was still fully owned and tightly controlled by Franz Huebel.

A former OPM (Owner President Management Program) participant and Professor Louis B. Barnes wrote this case as a basis for class discussion rather than to illustrate either effective or ineffective handling of an administrative situation.

On a personal level, Mr. and Mrs. Huebel had four children, three daughters and a son. Mrs. Huebel continued to work in company management, while a grandmother took care of the children. As one of them said: "Mother always played the mother role in the company and did whatever our father told her to do." Mr. Huebel, meanwhile, encouraged their son, Peter, the third child, to come into the business when he grew up. In 1975, however, at age 25, Peter decided to seek a masters degree in engineering and not to enter the business. Among other things, Peter did not want to work for his father. However, the youngest daughter, Greta, did join the firm shortly after that as her father's assistant after graduating from college with an economics major. She not only worked with Mr. Huebel in Glarus but often accompanied him on sales trips to foreign countries. The two oldest daughters, both married, expressed no interest in becoming part of the company. Mr. Huebel seemed to value Greta's help, even giving her a Porsche convertible one year as a birthday present.

In 1980, Mr. Huebel had a serious heart attack and had to have triple by-pass surgery. After a three-month recovery, Mr. Huebel returned to the business, but his board of directors, particularly Dr. Riegel, a lawyer, tried to convince Mr. Huebel that he needed help in running the company. This was not the first time that Mr. Huebel had tried to bring in executive assistance. On three previous occasions, the effort had not worked out. Mr. Huebel also tried to interest Peter again in joining the company, but Peter was still involved in his engineering studies.

This time, the other members of the board, Dr. Hausman, an economist consultant, Mrs. Huebel, and Greta Huebel joined Dr. Riegel in putting pressure on Mr. Huebel. They not only wanted to hire a new general manager but they also wanted to reorganize the company so that Mr. Huebel was less directly involved in detailed operations. Mr. Huebel eventually agreed.

Consequently, a professional general manager, Mr. Paul Schmeed, was hired. Mr. Schmeed came to work in March of 1983 after being employed in a large technical products firm. Mr. Schmeed was an engineer with considerable international management experience. Greta Huebel, then aged 30, was put in charge of Finance and Administration along with Dr. Riegel's advice that:

It is important for a family business to have a family member in charge of the finances, but you know that for all the rest of the business, we need a man who has technical training.

After that, Mr. Huebel stayed out of day-to-day management more. He would often come to work about 10:00 A.M. Later in the day he often walked around talking with engineers in the product development area. However, he also continued to read the minutes of all meetings, and received reports from Greta at least once a week. Board of Directors meetings were held in Mr. Huebel's weekend chalet, but only after his daughter and Paul Schmeed had carefully gone over the agenda with him. Mr. Huebel would also attend one or two informal luncheons each week with his managers or engineers. He would often invite the chief engineer to his office, and the two would work out major product decisions informally.

The arrangement worked fairly well for awhile. But then Mr. Huebel and Mr. Schmeed began to have disagreements. Mr. Huebel felt that Mr. Schmeed was interfering too much in some areas of product development. On one occasion, Mr. Huebel encountered a new engineer who was working on one of Mr. Huebel's favorite products. The engineer was making changes in the design which he said had come from the general manager. There were other similar incidents. By the fall of 1985, Mr. Huebel had decided that Paul Schmeed was not competent.

THE BOARD MEETING OF NOVEMBER 24TH

At the November 24th board meeting Mr. Huebel proposed that Mr. Schmeed be removed from his job. Excerpts from minutes of the board meeting are shown in *Exhibit 1*. At the same meeting, the board had a long discussion about two new organization plans. Neither involved hiring a new general manager. One plan set up a management committee of three functional department heads reporting to Mr. Huebel. The three departments were technical, finance/administration, and sales/marketing. The second plan divided the business into two major areas, commercial and technical. Greta Huebel would be made managing director of the commercial area, and Dr. Klaus Olander, the chief engineer, would be managing director of the technical area. The board adopted the second proposal by a four to one vote with only Dr. Riegel, the lawyer, opposing the new plan. Dr. Riegel explained that his vote was not so much a vote against the plan as it was to call attention to its two major weaknesses that he saw being exacerbated by the second option. One concern was over whether the chief engineer, Dr. Olander, could take on new production technology and administrative duties effectively. Dr. Riegel said that:

At this point, some production technology changes have to be made, and I doubt that Dr. Olander will be able to make them. I also question whether the production manager can help him.

Dr. Riegel's second concern related to the new reporting relationship of marketing and sales. They had previously been a separate department reporting to the general manager. Under the reorganization, they now reported to Greta Huebel. Dr. Riegel worried about this because:

Precista needs a professional in that position who has a degree in engineering and who has done extensive course work in sales and marketing.

Only if these two major points are covered will this new organization proposal be useful. As it currently stands, there is too big a gap between any experienced generalist and middle management.

FAMILY COMPETITION

In December 1985, Peter Huebel, now 35, graduated from the university with a masters degree in mechanical engineering. Although he and Greta had been close as children, they had grown apart in recent years as their lives and interests had taken separate paths. Earlier that year, Peter had done a school project at Precista on software optimization for one of the new electronic tool projects. He had satisfied the course requirements, but promised to come back and do more work on the company project in January and February of 1986. According to Greta:

At the end of February, I was going to go on a one-week skiing vacation. Peter had finished his work and was going to take a one-month holiday. I left on a Thursday night, and on Friday my father signed an employment contract with my brother. When I came back, I knew that my father had a hard time telling me about it, but when he did, I asked him why he didn't talk about it before. He said, "I don't have to ask you about anything. It's my business and I run it the way I want to run it." He had never done anything like that before. During that same week I was gone, he had scheduled a meeting with some tax accountants, even though I was in charge of finances. I made special arrangements to come back from skiing for a day and called him to say so. His reply was, "Well, if you really want to, but we've held these meetings for 40 years without you. Don't think that we can't do it alone."

It was like he really wanted to hurt me which was entirely new. I couldn't understand this after all of those years when we had been so close together when there had been nothing that he didn't tell me. It had been such an open relationship. I think that it was partly because, for my father, Peter's joining the company was like a dream fulfilled. Not only did he now have a son for a successor, but it was a son who had a graduate degree—something my father never had. It was like a second life for him, even though his health was getting worse.

Some of the problems had nothing to do with the fact that I am a woman. It was a combination of things. It was being young, being a daughter, being a nonengineer, and being a woman. So some of these things would have happened anyway. When you're in the position that I was in—number two or number three in the company for 10 years—then when you get into your father's shadow, you're competing with him. Until 1986, I wasn't really competing with my father but from the time he made me managing director, I was competing—not from my side, but from his.

But being a woman did make a difference, and I talked with Peter about this. We both agreed that when it came down to making decisions, tradition said that leaders should be men. Also by tradition, if you have an only son—no matter how many daughters there are—then the man should be the one who takes charge. That was very deeply ingrained, not only with my father but with Dr. Riegel and Dr. Olander. It was even what my older sisters expected. My father started talking with them about the business, something he'd never done before. He was trying to turn them against

me—telling them how I was trying to run the company differently. I think that it will take a long time before that will change.

Also in Switzerland, its expected that you can only be head manager in a company like that if you're over 50. You can't be a young manager. You're too young. How could you be a leader at only 33 or 34. It's not possible.

Greta also felt that her problems were made worse because some employees felt that a high-tech company had to be managed by a technical person. In addition, she tried to get the sales people to become more marketing oriented by developing market information and new product ideas as well as selling products. That was a change at Precista where marketing traditionally tried to sell whatever the technical department designed and produced. Greta went on to say:

My father was a pioneer in the industry, and he didn't want to give up control. I came in and wanted to make decisions too, but he wanted to be in charge and directly involved in the daily business. He became very angry when he read the minutes of those sales meetings, because he wanted to be the one to decide which products were created. When that happened a lot of people in the company became insecure, because they didn't know who was supposed to be doing what or who was the leader.

THE BOARD MEETING OF APRIL 11

At 4:00 P.M. on April 10th, 1986, the day before the combined board meeting and annual meeting, Mr. Huebel called Greta into his office and said that he didn't agree with the agenda items that she had proposed. Greta wanted the board to reconsider its November 24th, 1985 reorganization decision. She wanted to bring in a new finance and administration manager who would also be on the management committee so that she could devote more time to sales and marketing. Mr. Huebel told his daughter that if she didn't like the way he was running the com-

pany, maybe she should go out and look for another job. Greta reported:

That's when I changed. I knew my agenda proposals would stir controversy, but I also knew that I couldn't let him get to me that way. I was trying to get someone new onto the management committee who would be more on my side, because I wasn't getting any support from the technical people. Even when any of the other managers agreed with me, they were under enormous pressure to go along with him. And I wasn't going to let him pressure me. So I said that I'd always considered us a partnership, but that if that's the way he felt that he should say so the next day at the board meeting. Then the others could hear his words and know that he didn't want to put up with me. I also asked—and I know it sounded a little bit arrogant—is that all you want to tell me? He was shocked. I didn't argue. I just said, if that's what you want, you repeat it tomorrow at the meeting, and that made him mad. Then, I left his office.

When I got outside, though, I just couldn't believe what he had said. I was mad and sad and hurt.

At the April 11th meeting, the board rejected Greta's proposal for three management committee members. They did request that she hire a subordinate finance/administration manager and also a new sales/marketing manager. Excerpts from the board minutes are presented in *Exhibit 2*.

A week later, Greta asked Dr. Karl Tappe, a lawyer who was an old family friend, if he could help. Dr. Tappe had once worked as counsel for a company which had business dealings with Precista. He said that he would try to help if Mr. Huebel wanted

him to do so. According to Greta:

I went to my father and said that I thought we shouldn't argue any more and that we should talk with each other, but that we were having a hard time doing that. I proposed that we ask Dr. Tappe, and my father said, "Yes, I like him, but before we do that, I have to talk with Mami."

I think that was really the turning point for me. Until then, I knew that my father had never, never, in his whole life asked my mother for any advice, especially in business things. He always did only what he wanted to do.

Two days later, he called me into the office and said that he'd talked with my mother and with the other two members of the board. The two men said that if we had that talk with Dr. Tappe, they would resign from the board, and he said, "And you know what that means." I said, yes, but I asked him to call Dr. Tappe and say that he didn't want to have this talk. He did call and say that he didn't want anyone else involved in this situation, but that he would appreciate it if Dr. Tappe would talk with me, and that he could send the bill to my father. And that was it. I don't think that my father even talked with the other directors. He just made it up.

MR. AND MRS. HUEBEL'S RESPONSES

During her time at the Owner President Program in May of 1986, Greta Huebel received the following separate letters from her father and mother.

May 9, 1986

Dear Greta:

Mami and I have read your letter of April 30th. There are just the two of us who know about it. We think that you should really think everything over again—really very quietly. When you return from the U.S., you should give us your final decision.

Love,
Mami and Dad

May 13, 1986

My Dear Greta:

To write you my promised letter, I am once again using my beloved little typewriter. Hopefully, you don't mind. I still don't know how to make the new one work—you know changes are not so easy to do at my age. Dad and I were very pleased to get your phone call. It was good to hear your voice. We haven't waited so anxiously for a phone call for a very long time. We hope that the course is a good one and watch, with a lot of respect, your taking on another work load. We really hope that you enjoy this time of studying.

Papi and I were very sad about your letter. We haven't talked a lot about it. We kept it to ourselves. At least once each day I can feel how he is worried—really worried—seriously.

As he did, you have worked very hard, my dear Greta, for Precista. It is not a gamble, we all know. Would selling the company be the answer to the struggle?

The crisis with "the good old man" is not over, and it will not be for awhile. But I really do hope we find a solution. It really makes no sense to think of selling after you have both given everything you have—not for your father and not for you, my dear Greta.

Yes, it is true. Too many things are depending upon you. It is more than time to make changes. All of the struggles with Papi, with the board members, and most probably with the personnel, have ruined your nerves—well how could it be any different?

You need time until you are really in your good old form again—in good health—and I think that you should be given that time.

I would be really sorry if you couldn't find a way—especially being surrounded by so many "smart men." Just give them some time. (I personally don't think that it does them any harm to be left in the dark for some time. They don't know that.)

Try not to over challenge yourself. I know that it is easier to write than to do. I wish you strength for your decisions. Papi and I want only the very best for you.

Right now, I won't give this letter to Dad to read. With all of my dear wishes and love.

Mami

EXHIBIT 1 PRECISTA TOOLS AG (A): Excerpts from Board of Directors Meeting—Minutes of November 24, 1985

POINT 6.2

The analysis by Mr. Huebel shows that Mr. Schmeed has neglected or not fulfilled the following tasks according to the organization rules, Article 5.

- To give clear orders to the department heads so as to provide appropriate controls.
- To guarantee an appropriate personnel structure.
- Introducing cooperative management.
- Regularly informing the board and chairman of the board.

These observations are based upon the following facts:

1. The management committee is not functioning well.

2. The high cost of introducing the latest new product which did not function well at all shows that management is not working well together.

3. Motivation among employees is not high. It begins with a lack of information. Mr. Schmeed, despite mutual agreements is not improving this. Nor can we overlook the fact that Mr. Schmeed gave instructions to the development department without consulting the chief engineer. If this were to continue, Precista could be in great danger. It is important not to lose any of our talented staff nor to have them frustrated.

4. The chairman (Mr. Huebel) is not able to exercise appropriate controls, because Mr. Schmeed does not provide appropriate information.

POINT 6.3

The obvious key to this problem is that Mr. Schmeed is, by his nature, a rather introverted and not very communicative person. This leads to too many miscommunications. The situation will not improve.

POINT 6.4

The Board unanimously votes that the chairman should tell Mr. Schmeed that Precista will fulfill his contract until the end of 1986, but will immediately release him from the position of general manager.

(Five other points covered severance arrangement details.)

EXHIBIT 2 PRECISTA TOOLS AG (A): Excerpts from Board of Directors Meeting—Minutes of April 11, 1986 Meeting

POINT 7: ORGANIZATION

Greta Huebel submitted organization Plan #1 again, even though we had decided to go for Plan #2 at the November 24th meeting. We can't see any need for a change to Plan #1.

There were no other formal resolutions, but from the discussion, it can be stated that:

1. Mr. Huebel, Dr. Riegel, and Dr. Hausman don't think we need a separate Finance and Administration manager who would also be on the management committee. . . . Finance and Administration has to be managed by G. Huebel, and is so represented on the management committee. On the other hand, G. Huebel should be allowed to get a F&A manager whom she thinks is capable for the task.

2. The gentlemen (Huebel, Riegel, and Hausman) are also convinced that the Marketing and Sales position has to be held by an experienced person—an engineer who has an understanding of marketing. This does not mean that G. Huebel will not have anything to do with marketing and sales. Her position as the chairperson of the management committee gives her enough room to get involved in any questions concerned with marketing.

3. Besides being chairperson of the management committee, there are more than enough responsibilities for her in the field of Finance and Administration.

4. G. Huebel is asked to give her opinions on the above proposal. She will do so, and at the same time consider looking for a position and a career in another enterprise.

Newby Motors of Portsmouth (A)

Business was booming for Newby Motors of Portsmouth. With three showrooms and four separate dealerships, the company employed over 135 people and had an annual turnover greater than ever before in its 50 years of existence. But for Chairman and Managing Director Eric Spence, the impressive figures were not as comforting as they appeared. While the company's total sales had risen dramatically over the last ten years, the return on sales had been slowly deteriorating over the same period. Strong competition in the market for mid-sized passenger cars had forced all mid-sized car dealers to accept smaller margins on each sale. At the same time, increasingly heavy overhead costs were beginning to make Newby's large organization seem more like a burden than a source of pride. And there were no signs that the trends would reverse themselves in the near future.

After weeks of painstaking analysis, Eric had arrived at a difficult conclusion: the only way to improve profits would be to reduce the size of the company. In Eric's opinion, Newby Motors needed to terminate two of the four franchises in order to concentrate on the higher-margin sales of luxury autos. The move would entail severing a 44-year-old relationship with the manufacturer that had served as Newby Motors' sole supplier of autos and commercial vehicles throughout the company's early years. It would also reduce the number of new motorcars sold from nearly a thousand per year to under two hundred, at least until the luxury end of the business could be developed to its fullest potential. Worst of all, it would make redundant some sixty staff members—many of whom had been with the company for twenty or thirty years.

Eric's calculations showed that Newby Motors could expect to lose about £100,000 for the first year after implementing the change. The second year would see the company break even, and in the third year Eric expected to earn about £100,000 in profits. After that, according to Eric's plan, Newby Motors would be well-situated to continue as a smaller, more profitable enterprise.

The transition would certainly be a difficult one. But for Eric, the challenge of explaining the plan to his father would be even harder. At 79 years of age, Tristan Spence was still acutely interested in the day-to-day activities at Newby Motors. Although he had "retired" three times and hardly ever visited the company premises any more, the senior Spence still demanded that Eric phone him twice a day to report on developments in the business. Rarely, if ever, had he fully agreed with anything Eric tried to discuss with him.

Nevertheless, since Tristan held two-thirds of the shares in Newby Motors, no important decision could be made without his express approval. Eric and his wife Jessica owned the remaining third of the company. The Board of Directors included Tristan, Eric, and another Portsmouth businessman

This case was prepared by Research Associate Colleen Kaftan, under the supervision of Professor Louis B. Barnes, as the basis for classroom discussion rather than to illustrate either effective or ineffective handling of an administrative situation.

who was an old friend of Tristan's. While the board would have the final decision about the direction the company would take, Eric knew he would have to convince his father before he could even hope to introduce the matter at a board meeting.

FAMILY BACKGROUND

The son of a naval officer who was absent or ill for long stretches of time and who died relatively young, Tristan Spence had never know his own father very well. In particular, according to Eric, Tristan had "never learned what it was like to be an adult and to have to deal with a father." As a result, Eric thought, Tristan had been unable—or unwilling—to develop a close relationship with his own son. As the younger of two children, Eric had always believed his parents both preferred his sister Rose, their "blue-eyed daughter who could do no wrong." In fact, at one point Rose had told Eric that their father had been disappointed to have a boy instead of another girl—which would have left Tristan as the last bearer of the Spence family name.

As a result of the difficulties between his father and himself, Eric had never really planned to join Tristan to work at Newby Motors. Having left home to attend boarding school at the age of fifteen, Eric found that the highly disciplined training of the CCF (Combined Cadet Force) was his favorite part of the curriculum. He also excelled in sports and considered himself "more the sportsman than the scholar." In fact, Eric believed that sports was the only area in which he had been able to attract his father's interest. Tristan always went to the games and matches when Eric was playing, even if he had to travel some distance to attend. Unfortunately, Tristan had never seemed willing to praise Eric for his good performances. With criticism, though, he had always been quick to comment.

As the end of his four years at school approached, Eric found himself contemplating further military training. For one thing, a stint in the army would give him many opportunities to participate in sports events. Eric believed that attending the national military academy at Sandhurst would allow him to be as close to a professional athlete as possible. To the great surprise of both his parents, he began studying for the Sandhurst entrance exams.

Eric's mother, Sarah Spence, came from a troubled family herself. The eldest of five sisters who were estranged from their only brother, she had worked as a shop girl before her marriage to Tristan. Sarah had always been reluctant to talk about her modest origins, and—perhaps as a result of them—she worked hard to create a respectable, and even "elegant" household for her own family. She seemed genuinely concerned about Eric's activities and choices, and Eric had often thought of her as an ally in his relationship with his father. On learning of Eric's plan to enroll at Sandhurst, she had asked him to reconsider, and had planted the idea in Eric's mind that he might think about working at Newby Motors. She surprised Eric by mentioning that Tristan actually hoped to see him join the company, a message that Eric had never received directly from his father. When Eric finally decided, at age nineteen, to enroll in a Motor Trade training program, he realized he would be coming into Newby Motors at a time when the company was beginning to be quite successful.

HISTORY OF NEWBY MOTORS

Established in 1926 in a small warehouse outside of Portsmouth, Newby Motors was originally a distributor of lubricating oils and tires for trucking and bus companies in the area. Founder Martin Newby had hired young Tristan Spence in 1932 to work as a travelling salesman and to deliver oil and tires to his customers. After Martin Newby's death, ownership in Newby Motors was transferred to his two grown children, Stanley and Jeannette. The Newbys decided to open a garage in Portsmouth proper where motorists could come to have tires fitted and for minor servicing to their autos.

For the next thirty years, the business had been managed jointly by Tristan Spence and Jeannette Newby. Mr. Spence, as the employees called him, had been general manager and Miss Newby handled the administrative end of the business. Stanley Newby maintained a financial interest in the company without participating in day-to-day activities.

Shortly after taking charge, Mr. Spence and Miss Newby decided to expand Newby Motors' activities still further. They obtained an exclusive distributorship in the Portsmouth area for one of the nation's leading car and truck manufacturers, and offered 24-hour servicing for large trucking companies. Just before the outbreak of World War II, the company also took on the franchises for a number of imports, including Citroen from France and Fiat from Italy.

With the loss of the import business in 1938, Newby Motors turned to another English manufacturer, the Rootes group, to fill the unused space. Sales grew quickly enough to require an expanded showroom within the first year, and soon afterwards, the Newbys approved a second construction project to house the sales and service business for commercial vehicles. Before the building could be completed, however, it was requisitioned by the British Admiralty, only to be destroyed by enemy action later in the war.

Having survived the war by repairing military supply trucks and refurbishing old commercial vehicles to help their former customers stay in business, Newby Motors was offered the franchise for the entire Rootes group, including Humber, Hillman, Sunbeam, Commer, and Carrier vehicles. By 1945, with over a hundred workers in the company's employ, Jeannette and Stanley Newby decided to form a corporation, and offered to let Tristan Spence buy a one-third share. At last, the senior Spence was able to become a full-fledged partner in the business he managed.

In the early 1950's, Mr. Spence and Miss Newby jointly purchased a filling station near Newby Motors' main showroom, thus establishing a "complete motoring service" for their customers. Shortly thereafter, Stanley Newby decided to sell his part of the company in order to make further investments in another business he had founded. Tristan Spence bought Mr. Newby's share, thereby increasing his own holdings to two-thirds of the company.

Eric Spence's Career

When Eric Spence joined the company at 22 years of age, he still felt that the relationship between himself and his father was "terrible." Although Sarah had assured him that Tristan was pleased with his decision to come into the business, Eric got no direct encouragement from his father. In fact, without specific assignments for his first several years at Newby Motors, Eric recalled feeling "in a complete and utter wilderness." He was extremely frustrated at the lack of responsibility until he was given the commercial vehicle service center to run a few years later. On being named a director of the company, Eric began to feel more satisfied and more involved in his work, although he invariably found it difficult to come to an agreement with his father about any direction Eric thought the company should take.

As Tristan and Miss Newby approached their early sixties, they began to consider selling the business. When asked whether he would agree to go on managing the garage if they sold Newby Motors to a group of competitors, Eric felt obliged to voice his strong disagreement. By that time married to Jessica, with a two-year-old son and another child on the way, Eric took his responsibilities to his own young family very seriously. He pointed out that he had come to Newby Motors with the idea of becoming an owner some day. Luckily, Tristan and Miss Newby had second thoughts about the sale, and the buyer group fell apart before a deal could be made.

The "turning point" in Eric's professional life came only a few years later. Tristan suffered a severe heart attack and was forced to stay away from work for a full twelve months. Toward the end of the same period, Miss Newby fell ill and died of cancer. Eric was left to manage the entire operation on his own, with only minimal input from either owner. To his great relief and pleasure, Eric found that the business continued to prosper under his direction.

A Difficult Partnership

Although he had recovered almost completely from his heart attack by the time Miss Newby died, Tristan Spence never came back to work full time at Newby Motors. Under the company's articles of association, Tristan's two-thirds ownership gave him the right to choose a potential buyer to whom Miss Newby's shares would be offered after her death. He exercised this right by designating Eric. With two children in school and a mortgage on his house, Eric found it difficult to negotiate an additional loan with his bankers, but at last he put together a deal that brought him into partnership with his father. Owning a third of the company, however, did not make it any easier for Eric to get on with Tristan.

Even Tristan's rare words of praise were usually tainted with negative feelings. For example, in a letter congratulating Eric for his success in his first full year as managing director, he wrote, "I hesitated writing because any praise I've given you before has gone to your head and you've reacted the wrong way." Indeed, Tristan seemed to think his son was arrogant—an idea that baffled Eric, who had always felt more a lack of confidence than a surplus of it.

Newby Motors continued to grow—almost in spite of the ongoing clashes between Eric and Tristan. According to Eric, his father seemed to disagree with him as a matter of course:

The majority of our arguments are over things so minor that it's stupid. We never seem to agree on anything where the business is concerned. It's easier for us to talk about sports than about the company. But even then, any slight word you say can be taken out of context. He'll jump on it and use it against you. He has the most remarkable memory for things that happened ages ago—he'll bring up your "prior offences" in a row when you can't even remember the occasion, let alone what you've said.

Tristan *did* seem willing to commiserate about the difficulties Eric had whenever the automotive business went through a downturn. Still, on happier occasions, he seemed to take particular pleasure in pointing out that Eric's successes were not as important as his own:

If you have a difficult year, he will sympathize. But if you produce a better figure he'll say, "It's not as good as in our time."

On the other hand, Eric recognized that his own behavior might sometimes provoke the altercations:

What I do is probably wrong, too. I'm sometimes combative too, when there might not be a need to say anything at all. I go to him for approval; he disapproves, and I get my hackles up. If I say my figures aren't bad, he'll say "They're not as good as when I ran it." But in a way I suppose I shouldn't have said such a thing. I suppose I've got as much a temper as he has. I never feel relaxed at all with my father.

Family Relations

At least part of the father-son dispute seemed to reflect a broader family conflict. Neither of Eric's parents had ever approved of his marriage to Jessica. The daughter of a prominent public servant, Jessica was active in community affairs herself and had always taken an interest in Eric's work at the company. In Jessica's opinion, Eric's mother resented her family's status in the public affairs of Portsmouth. Moreover, having remained at a distance from her own husband's professional life, Sarah disapproved of Jessica's involvement with the business. In fact, Sarah insisted that (aside from Miss Newby) "women should not be allowed in the showroom," and had asked Tristan to promise that Jessica would never be made a director of the company.

According to Jessica, her problems with her mother-in-law had started early in her married life:

Once, when we were first married, I was hauled up in front of the "tribunal" and told how disappointed my in-laws were with Eric. I said, "Disappointed in what way? Is he a womanizer? Does he drink? Gamble?" They had absolutely no reason

to criticize him. In fact I think she wanted Eric to marry a nondescript girl she would be able to dominate.

Her illnesses of the last several years had not made Sarah any easier to please. Severe arthritis and other painful complications had kept her bedridden most of the time. Even extensive medical care—including a full-time private nurse at home—had not seemed to attenuate the discomfort, and Sarah felt increasingly bitter about her state. Since Eric's sister, Rose, had moved to the United States, Jessica had taken over many of the "duties" a daughter would normally perform, but her in-laws remained critical of her even so. For example, they seemed to resent any good thing that happened in Eric and Jessica's life. As a result, Jessica found it necessary to hide the fact that she or one of the children had got a new coat, that her grandmother had given her an heirloom ring, that Eric had installed a telephone in their kitchen, or any other "petty thing" that might evoke Sarah's disapproval.

Worse yet, both Sarah and Tristan seemed jealous of Jessica's father's accomplishments and of the family's close relationships on Jessica's side. While Sarah and Tristan had few, if any, close friends, Jessica's family took great pleasure in the wide net of relationships they enjoyed. For his part, Eric often felt closer to Jessica's father than he did to his own. Eric, Jessica, and the children shared vacation trips and many other activities with Jessica's family, but every time, Eric could expect a "dressing down" from his own father:

Whenever we go on holiday there will *always* be a row to spoil it. I'll go over to see him, not because I want to, but because I've been summoned, and I'll have to answer a hundred questions: "Where are you going? With whom? What makes you think you can take a three-week holiday?" Even though he'd been away for a month at a time in the early days.

On one occasion, Tristan's caustic remarks had led Eric to submit a formal resignation. The "summons" to appear at his father's house had come when Jessica was in London to attend a ceremony celebrating her father's being awarded the title of "Commander of the British Empire." Tristan had wanted to complain about a business decision Eric had made:

I can't even remember the subject of his lecture—there had been so many before it that I was more or less punch-drunk. I should have said nothing and walked out, but I stayed and tried to defend myself. He said,"I'm going to take this business away from you and then see how your friends laugh at you. I'd like to see you with nothing, see what friends you have left." He and my mother had dropped all their friends by then, and were happy with each other's company. So I wrote him a letter, saying I was sorry to have failed him but that I wouldn't go on in that way.

Like most others, that quarrel had finally been resolved, and Eric maintained his position as director, continuing to call Tristan at home at least twice every business day. Still, Eric felt some bitterness in recalling the incident:

If I was more confident in myself I'd have gone off. But then it was too late—there were the children, and we had everything tied up in the shares we owned. And you kept thinking that with some help, with some time, it would be better . . .

Further Developments

In the years that followed, Eric had resigned at least once more, and Tristan had retired (complete with going-away parties and presents) three times. In spite of the motor trade's usual cyclical difficulties, Newby Motors continued to grow and prosper throughout. The Rootes group franchise eventually brought in a Chrysler-Talbot dealership and, in the former commercial vehicle showroom, Eric added Mercedes-Benz and Audi. When Audi franchisors were required to take on Volkswagen with their dealerships, Newby Motors dropped Audi and took on Peugeot as a mid-range companion to the Mercedes line. More recently, they had decided to add a BMW dealership in the showroom adjacent to the original premises. All of the changes had required long negotiations with the manufacturers. Since many of the ideas for expanding had originally come from Tristan, the senior Spence had agreed with the development plan in general, and had even used his contacts to help smooth the discussions with the Rootes-Chrysler group.

Perhaps most exciting, though, had been the growth of the Mercedes business. In a triumphant 50th anniversary celebration for Newby Motors, in 1976, Eric and Tristan had dedicated the company's brand-new ultra-modern Mercedes showroom, custom built on the outskirts of Portsmouth. Even that occasion had been marred by family conflict. Miffed by Jessica's editing of a company history she had encouraged him to write for the press release, Tristan had threatened not to attend the opening if Jessica would be there. Although both Eric and Jessica were uncertain until the last minute whether Tristan would come, they were relieved to see him drive up just before the ceremony was to begin. His backing down had saved considerable embarrassment, because the Mercedes-Benz organization had planned a special surprise ceremony honoring Tristan's fifty years in business, and had brought an engraved plaque to present to him.

THE DECISION

Convinced as he was that his analysis was correct, Eric still felt knots in his stomach as he faced the task of presenting the plan to his father. In order to concentrate on the higher-margin Mercedes and BMW lines, Eric proposed to drop the Chrysler-Talbot and Peugeot lines. While Peugeot had been a fairly recent addition to the company's business, Chrysler-Talbot represented his father's oldest relationships in the trade. Moreover, many of the employees that would be made redundant had been hired by Tristan before Eric could walk or talk. Beyond those problems, Eric expected Tristan to resist scaling down the business at a time when Sarah's medical bills would probably continue to be a considerable drain on his personal finances. Finally, if Tristan reacted in his usual irascible manner, Eric would be hard put to find any argument that could persuade his father.

Nevertheless, with his own and his family's future tied up in Newby Motors, Eric felt determined to make the best economic decisions possible. By his estimates, both falling volume sales and declining margins on the mid-range franchises would begin to take drastic effect on the company's profits within a relatively short time. So far, only Jessica knew of Eric's carefully formed opinions. As he nervously planned how to approach his father, she offered to help in any way she could.

Meeting of the Board of Directors, Henry Manufacturing Company, Inc.

After three days of concentrated effort early in September 1973, Gene Harms, president of the Henry Manufacturing Company, placed the finishing touches on his Five-Year Growth Plan. As he reviewed the contents, Gene was pleased that finally, after 20 years of operations, the company had an explicit and comprehensive plan outlining its strategic objectives. Nevertheless, he realized that the plan was solely a result of his efforts and those of his key managers. It had yet to face a complete review by his management team as well as that of the board of directors.

COMPANY BACKGROUND

In 1953 at the age of 60, Harold Henry ("H.H.") Harms decided to go into business for himself. For the previous 15 years he had been a successful industrial salesman in the field of filtration equipment. He sold large mechanical filters to heavy industrial manufacturers who used them to filter metal filings and other particulate matter out of the coolant fluids circulating through their production plants. Working closely with his customers, H.H. came to understand their problems so well that he began designing new machines and turning these designs over to his employer. Although the employer appreciated his innovative designs and put them into production, H.H.'s requests for equity participation or royalty agreements were refused.

As a result, H.H. started the Henry Manufacturing Company based on a unique product—a nonmedia filtering device that was unlike any sold by the competition. Henry equipment did not employ a costly disposable filtering medium; instead, the principle of gravity was applied to separate the particulate matter from the coolant fluid circulating through metal-working equipment. In this way, the waste and dirt were removed from the coolant, and the clean coolant recirculated. To the customer, the somewhat higher initial price of the Henry separator was far outweighed by the elimination of expenses associated with other machines due to the periodic replacement of the filter and coolant.

Gene Harms, H.H.'s youngest son, considered the company to be part of the machine tool industry. Henry's product line, however, was primarily filtration and separator equipment. The market consisted of industrial customers who had recently become increasingly interested in this type of equipment as environmental concern became more vocal and as government bodies responded with environmental protection acts and regulations. Henry was aware of this

Simon A. Hershon, research assistant, prepared this case under the supervision of Professor Louis B. Barnes as a basis for class discussion rather than to illustrate either effective or ineffective handling of an administrative situation.
Copyright © 1974 by the President and Fellows of Harvard College. Harvard Business School case 475-031.

trend; in fact, the company had already sold one pollution-control system, a scaled-down model of one developed by a large customer of Henry filtration equipment. However, none of the sales force really understood it and no other sales had developed. In 1972 Henry developed a new addition to the prod- uct line, the BOS separator. This unit was designed to kill bacteria and remove tramp oil from central coolant systems. Much en- thusiasm was generated by the development of this product, but it was too early to tell how it would fare in the marketplace.

ORGANIZATION

From the start, the Henry Manufacturing Company was a family affair. Two of H.H.'s six sons, Don and John, joined him in the initial stages of the firm's development. By 1958, however, the relationships among the two sons and their father made working together difficult. Don left the filtration field entirely but stayed in the area, becoming a teacher. John, on the other hand, moved to Florida, where he soon designed and devel- oped a cartridge filter for swimming pools which was manufactured for a time by Henry. Later, he started his own firm to both produce and sell the filters. A third son, Bob Harms, became an attorney and as part of his law practice served as Henry's corporate counsel.

In 1959 H.H. brought another son, Dick, into the business as a salesperson. De- scribed by Gene Harms as "clever, reads people, and is primarily interested in *his* customers and *his* commissions," Dick had no interest in management but quickly became the lead salesperson. Meanwhile, Gene Harms, the youngest of H.H.'s 10 children, had earned his MBA at the Harvard Business School in 1957. He joined General Motors in its foreman training program and planned a career in the automobile industry.

Other families were involved with the growth of Henry, too. Clyde Brown, still with the firm in 1973 as vice president of manu- facturing, began on a part-time basis by su- pervising the welding shop after he finished work at his full-time job. Clyde's brother, Kenny, worked at Henry, too. Over the years, many other employees encouraged their relatives to join Henry. Even H.H.'s wife was involved. Each time one of the employees had a child, she would knit a baby blanket and present it to the child.

In 1959 H.H. visited Gene and con- vinced him to join Henry as general man- ager. Gene quickly instituted a more liberal guarantee and service policy, a marked de- parture from industry practice. Then, by adding several experienced filtration sales- people on a manufacturer's representative basis, he was able to build sales from $100,000 in 1959 to $1,500,000 in 1966 (see *Exhibits 1* and *2*).

Soon after Gene joined Henry, H.H.'s health began to fail. Although H.H. re- mained active until his death in the early 1970s, his efforts were primarily in the inven- tion and design stages of product develop- ment. In fact, many of Henry's products in 1973 were either exact models of H.H.'s designs or ones that had incurred only minor modifications from his original conceptions.

Gene continued to assume greater re- sponsibility as H.H. withdrew from the oper- ational aspects, becoming both president and general manager in 1970. This was accepted enthusiastically by the employees, though to a lesser degree by Gene's older brothers, of whom two were still active—Dick as key sales- person and Bob as corporate attorney. Both were also on the board of directors.

As the management of the business

grew more complex, Gene felt that his executive team would require greater sophistication. In 1968 he convinced the board of directors that Steve McEwen, the executive vice president, should go to the Program for Management Development (PMD) at Harvard; however, Steve turned down the opportunity. Later, in 1971, Steve asked for more responsibilities but Gene reminded him of his earlier decision. This time, Steve took the opportunity and went off to the PMD in Boston. When he returned, Gene noted, his attitude had changed markedly—Steve began to look at Henry from the viewpoint of a general manager.

Soon Steve, Bill Losey, and Blaine Wiley (see *Exhibit 3* for data on the management team and board of directors) began to push Gene for greater company growth. Although Gene was not really clear on how he felt about the question of growth, he embarked on an ambitious program to develop and educate his executives. (His schedule for management development is shown in *Exhibit 4*.) An up-to-date organization chart did not exist at Henry, largely because Gene did not believe in such charts. However, *Exhibit 5* is the casewriter's picture of the reporting relationships at Henry.

SALES DEVELOPMENT

Henry's early growth came primarily from a sales volume of relatively small units. In 1967, however, Henry began designing and producing large central-filtration systems, increasing sales to $2.2 million. Sales continued to grow in 1968—reaching $2.9 million—and remained at that level through 1969 to 1970. The product mix continued to show a trend toward larger units. Expansion was aided by a good relationship with the local bank which had allowed Henry to get funds pretty much on an as-needed basis.

To handle the large volume, Henry built a new factory in 1970 at a cost of $450,000. Shortly after it was completed, the country entered a recession and sales plummeted to $1.4 million. Belt-tightening policies were instituted to limit losses to $39,000. Large dollar savings were realized when the sales force's commission rate, which some managers felt was inordinately high, was cut by 20%, and the executives' bonus plan was eliminated.

Sales rebounded in 1972 to $2.7 million, contributing the largest profits to date—$124,000. Projections in 1973 were for modest growth to $3.2 million, but a more realistic appraisal indicated that sales would run near $4 million with profits of $250,000. A sales growth of such magnitude would also create some production capacity constraints. Thus, a new 7,200-square-foot manufacturing bay was proposed and built at an estimated cost of $110,000.

These changes all brought attention to the fact that, over the years, company policy had developed out of Gene's personal philosophy of offering a quality product, including a generous service policy and completely custom-designed equipment. As a result, Gene and his managers decided that the time had come to do some more explicit planning. Financial summaries can be found in *Exhibits 6, 7,* and *8; Exhibit 9* shows Henry's pro forma growth projections.

BOARD OF DIRECTORS

The board of directors consisted of four managers: Gene Harms (chairman), Steve McEwen, Bill Losey, and Clyde Brown; two salesmen: Dick Harms and Carl Cutright; and Bob Harms, the corporate attorney. Ownership of the firm remained in the hands of the Harms family and, to some extent, a few key employees as shown in this list of stockholders:

	Number of Shares (as of December 31, 1972)
Eugene (Gene) Harms	418
Eleanor Harms (wife)	133
Robert (Bob) Harms	10
Richard (Dick) Harms	99
Helen Harms (wife)	10
Clyde Brown	25
Stephen McEwen	40
Carl Cutright	20
	755
Treasury stock	245
Total	1,000

The board typically met once a quarter in the law offices of Bob Harms. One such meeting was scheduled for Saturday, September 15, 1973, to discuss management's long-range plans for growth. To some degree, this plan had come out of the pressures applied by Gene's younger managers in a series of planning meetings which were held earlier in the summer. The plan had also evolved from the feedback Gene himself had received from classmates in August 1973 when he attended the second three-week phase of the Smaller Company Management Program at the Harvard Business School. To produce the Five-Year Growth Plan, Gene had taken these ideas, escaped from the office for three days, and devoted himself entirely to conceptualizing strategic objectives for Henry. The plan was circulated to the members of the board before the meeting; excerpts are presented below.

PREPARATION FOR THE BOARD'S MEETING

As he did before each board meeting, Gene prepared financial summaries and thought about an agenda. He reviewed his Five-Year Growth Plan and tried to set it in perspective. Gene realized that the other board members had their own ideas about Henry's growth, but he felt that his plan was a set of well-reasoned, rational objectives. Although he expected a fair amount of criticism, Gene was expecting the board to adopt and authorize its general contents. With this in mind, he prepared an agenda (shown here) for the meeting which included a motion to adopt the Five-Year Growth Plan. Under the company's charter, Gene needed a majority vote of the board before the proposal could be adopted.

Board of Directors' Meeting September 15, 1973 (Agenda)

1. Presentation and discussion of Five-Year Growth Plan.
2. Adoption of Five-Year Growth Plan by means of the following resolution:

   Be it Resolved, that the management of Henry Manufacturing Company, Inc., is directed to take the necessary actions to implement the Five-Year Growth Plan, reporting to the Board of Directors quarterly on progress.

3. Resolution to authorize $10,000–15,000 for a 40′ × 80′ steel-clad unheated pole building with concrete floor, to be used for storage of all types and is necessary as we are losing our Daybrook storage facility.

Believing that he had done what was necessary to prepare for the meeting, Gene was stunned when he arrived at his brother Bob's law office on the morning of the meet- ing and received a letter from Dick Harms, his other brother and Henry's leading sales- person, announcing Dick's resignation from the board. Gene called Dick on the phone and Dick indicated that his resignation was definite. Gene wondered how this announce- ment would influence the board meeting, and whether he should manage the meeting any differently because of it.

EXCERPTS FROM THE FIVE-YEAR GROWTH PLAN

The goals for Henry Manufacturing shall be an average growth for the next five years of 10–15% per year or between six and eight million by 1978. This growth should come from a combination of existing products, new products such as the BOS and pollution equipment, as well as penetration into new markets, such as Europe. The organization must be flexible enough so that growth in any one year can be handled at an increased rate of 35–40% or a decreased rate of 35–40%. In order to capitalize on this growth potential the following steps shall be taken:

1. *Sales Organization:* The sales organization shall be reorganized and reconstituted over the next two to three years as follows:
   a. Present commission salesmen shall be brought into the corporation on a salary basis plus expenses, plus override, perhaps 5% on all sales above their breakeven.
   b. The reason for the above approach is that we have indications that sales of basic Henry filtration systems can be increased through greater market penetration.
   We have checked the going rate for indus- trial capital goods salesmen, and we think that we can get a pretty good sales force with a potential earnings of 35 to 45,000 dollars per man. Also, to sell pollution control equipment, we think a highly trained chem- ist or chemical engineer is required. In or- der to have this pollution control sales force be effective, it will be necessary for him to cut across territorial lines.

2. *Sales Growth in Europe:* The next area of sales growth potential is Europe and the Eastern Bloc countries. We have been approached by two different firms concerning the possibility of licensing.
   The time required for the European venture and talent required would depend greatly on how we go about setting it up. Three alterna- tives exist:
   a. Licensing, which takes the least time.
   b. Joint venture, which will take about me- dium time.
   c. A wholly owned subsidiary, which of course would take the most time and talent from Henry.
   The potential, however, for Europe and the Eastern Bloc countries looks to be sub- stantial and if the problems can be resolved, it would seem to be worthwhile.

3. *Manpower and Facilities:* In order to attain the growth indicated we are going to need addi- tional manpower both in the office and in the shop. Additional facilities will also be required which will be constructed as needed.

4. *Sale of Stock:* In order to provide additional incentives and essentially deferred income op- portunity to the inside key management, part of the treasury stock shall be made available to these people as well as the salesmen who join Henry.

5. *Dividend Policy:* In order to finance the growth anticipated, a conservative dividend policy shall be adopted whereby 10% of the after-tax earnings shall be paid as dividends.

6. *Reorganization of Henry:* In order to benefit the shareholders, the people who have made Henry what it is and who are going to contrib-

ute to its further increased growth, we will reorganize Henry Manufacturing in 1974.

This reorganization will consist of setting up two wholly owned subsidiaries called the Henry Real Estate Company and the Henry Filter Company. Both will be wholly owned divisions of Henry Manufacturing, Inc.

I personally feel that by keeping our options open, by developing a strong sales force, by developing a strong management team, by developing efficient facilities and new products, by developing a market in Europe, we have the greatest strength and flexibility to accomplish the goals we have set for ourselves. We will be a profit-generating company that will provide high job satisfaction and opportunity for advancement, and high financial reward for all who help provide this growth.

EXHIBIT 1 Annual Sales Data, 1955–1972

Henry Sales

Average order............................	$3,800	4,600	4,650	5,300	5,000	6,000	8,250	8,900	8,100	12,500	19,600	19,200	22,500	26,380
Percent of successful proposals....	15	25	20	23	24	25	30	30	44	49	38	42	16	27
Number of proposals..................	169	262	374	444	440	525	545	600	568	415	362	324	336	380
Number of successful proposals....	26	65	76	106	95	133	161	182	268	212	135	137	57	104

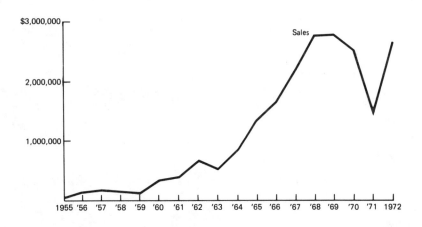

EXHIBIT 2   Annual Sales by Salesperson

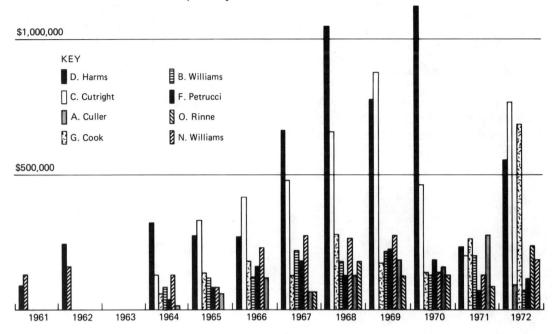

EXHIBIT 3 Background Data on Executive Personnel and Board of Directors

Name	Position	Age[a]	Education	Joined Henry	Previous Experience
Gene Harms[b]	President and General Manager	42	B.A. Bowling Green State Univ., 1955 MBA-Harvard, 1957	1959	Foreman—General Motors, 1957–1959
Steve McEwen[b]	Executive V.P.	41	B.S. General Motors Inst., 1954 PMD-Harvard, 1972	1963	Plant Engineer—General Motors, 1950–1963
Bill Lafayette	V.P.—Engineering	41	B.S. General Motors Inst., 1955	1967	Engineer—General Motors, 1951–1967
Blaine Wiley	V.P.—Proposals, Installation, and Construction	41	B.S. Notre Dame, 1957	1968	Architect—Mosser Construction, 1957–1968
Bill Losey[b]	V.P.—Finance and Treasurer	35	B.S. Albion College, 1960	1966	Accountant—General Motors, 1960–1966
Clyde Brown[b]	V.P.—Manufacturing	50	H.S.	1955	Foreman Supervisor—Young Daybrook, 1940–1955
Bob Brandt	V.P.—Research and Technical Services	32	B.S. Capitol Univ., 1962; M.S. Bowling Green State Univ., 1968	1970	Teacher—Capitol Univ., 1962–1968
Keith Norton	V.P.—Sales and Product Development	48	H.S.	1973	Salesman—Delpark, Commercial, Monbon, 1953–1973
Jack Muir	Director of Purchasing	46	H.S.	1972	Salesman—Katy Steel, 1965–1972
Bob Fox	Director of Service	28	H.S.	1965	Welder, Draftsman, Chief Draftsman, Dir. of SVC—Henry, 1965–1972
Dick Harms[b]	Salesman	59	H.S.	1959	1955–59, Salesman, CUNO Filters; previously owned and operated ice cream business
Carl Cutright[b]	Salesman	54	B.S.M.E. Univ. of Michigan	1963	Pump salesman—Y.C. Smith Co.
Bob Harms[b]	Attorney	61	B.A. Bowling Green State Univ., J.D. Univ. of Denver	1953	Private law practice

[a] Age in 1973.
[b] Member of the board of directors.

EXHIBIT 4   Schedule of Management Development

	1973	1974	1975	1976	1977	1978	1979	1980
Gene Harms, President	II	III						
Clyde Brown, V.P. Manufacturing	I	II	III					
Bill Lafayette, V.P. Engineering		I	II	III				
Blaine Wiley, V.P. Proposal, Installation, and Construction			I	II	III			
Bill Losey, V.P. Finance				I	II	III		
Bob Brandt, V.P. Research and Technical Services					I	II	III	
Jack Muir, Purchasing Agent						I	II	III

Note: All professional training was scheduled at the Harvard Business School in the Smaller Company Management Program (SCMP). The program is expressly designed for men and women who are owner-presidents or hold other top-level positions in smaller companies. The program consists of three units of three weeks each—I, II, and III.

EXHIBIT 5 Organization Chart

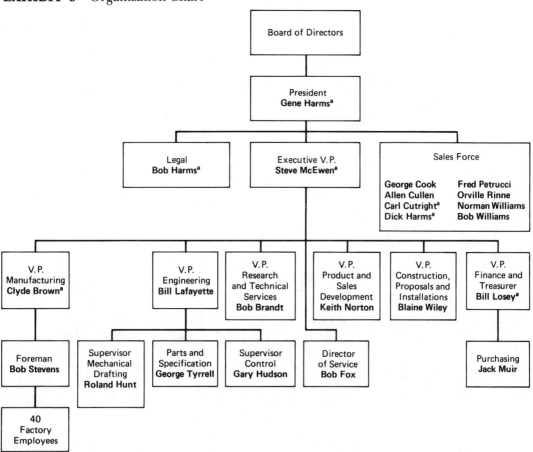

a. Member of the board of directors

EXHIBIT 6   Balance Sheets, 1971–1972

Assets

At December 31	1972	1971
Current assets		
Cash	$2,903	$7,763
Accounts receivable		
Trade	535,288	440,308
Other	1,792	–
	537,080	440,308
Inventories		
Raw materials	191,563	152,869
Work in process	55,798	19,198
Finished goods	18,587	12,805
	265,948	184,872
Prepaid expenses	10,761	16,243
Total current assets	816,692	649,186
Other assets		
Cash surrender value of life insurance	36,227	26,560
Investment	1,000	1,000
	37,227	27,560
Property, plant, and equipment at cost		
Land	84,000	84,000
Land improvements	2,231	–
Buildings	433,418	433,418
Machinery and equipment	250,400	232,055
	770,049	749,473
Less accumulated depreciation and amortization	185,283	137,126
	584,766	612,347
Patents, at cost less amortization	30,179	36,378
Total	$1,468,864	$1,325,471

Liabilities and Stockholders' Equity

At December 31	1972	1971
Current liabilities		
Notes payable to bank	$211,000	$230,400
Stockholder	17,117	41,678
Other unsecured	27,459	27,459
	255,576	299,537
Accounts payable	60,373	85,407
Commissions payable	116,915	106,368
Federal income tax	75,581	–
State and local income, less tax deferred	9,128	–
Accrued liabilities		
Salaries and wages	4,046	2,625
Other	30,889	9,168
	34,935	11,793
Long-term debt due within one year	47,067	47,067
Total current liabilities	599,575	550,172
Long-term debt due after one year		
5% note, unsecured, due $1,400 monthly to 1977	50,876	64,110
Building mortgage bond	394,750	412,250
Other—unsecured	9,527	25,861
	455,153	502,221
Stockholders' equity		
Common shares, without par value; 1,000 shares authorized and issued at stated value	25,000	25,000
Capital in excess of stated value	10,634	10,634
Retained earnings	420,027	278,969
	455,661	314,603
Less 245 treasury shares at cost	41,525	41,525
	414,136	273,078
Total	$1,468,864	$1,325,471

EXHIBIT 7 Comparative Statements of Income, 1969–1972

	1969 $	1969 %	1970 $	1970 %	1971 $	1971 %	1972 $	1972 %
Sales, net	$2,863,241	100%	$2,520,751	100%	$1,390,965	100%	$2,741,725	100%
Cost of sales								
Material	1,237,970	43.2	965,322	38.3	511,203	36.8	989,139	36.1
Labor	204,075	7.1	189,143	7.5	114,588	8.2	257,339	9.4
Commissions	574,931	20.1	532,146	21.1	262,252	18.8	457,406	16.7
Gross profit	846,265	29.6	834,140	33.1	502,922	36.2	1,037,841	37.9
Manufacturing expense	283,847	9.9	269,449	10.7	199,169	14.3	334,829	12.2
Sales expense	20,900	.7	21,734	.9	17,746	1.3	17,549	.6
Engineering expense	144,723	5.1	142,260	5.6	89,270	6.4	137,701	5.0
Laboratory expense			10,185	.4	14,428	1.0	32,530	1.2
General and administrative expense	164,523	5.7	207,135	8.2	168,124	12.1	229,950	8.4
Net profit	232,272	8.1	183,377	7.3	14,185	1.0	285,282	10.4
Miscellaneous income	9,411	.3	30,204	1.2	5,895	.4	9,170	.3
Interest expense	25,423	.9	49,545	2.0	56,216	4.0	68,516	2.5
Operating profit	216,260	7.6	164,036	6.5	(36,136)	(2.6)	225,936	8.2
Bonus	109,665	3.8	82,430	3.3	–	–	–	–
Income tax	50,174	1.8	31,761	1.2	–	–	101,105	3.7
Net profit	$56,421	2.0	$49,845	2.0	$(36,136)	(2.6)	$124,831	4.5

EXHIBIT 8 Financial Ratios Analyses, 1968–1972

Year	Current Assets/ Current Liabilities	Current Assets Less Inventories/ Current Liabilities	Inventory Turnovers (per year)	Average Collection Period (days)	Debt to Total Assets	Return on Assets (%)	Return on Investments (%)
1968	1.1	.7	9	43	.75	6.3	26.8
1969	1.1	.8	11	47	.77	4.2	19.6
1970	1.4	.8	10	49	.72	3.9	15.0
1971	1.2	.9	7	54	.80	(2.7)	(11.7)
1972	1.3	.9	9	44	.71	8.5	36.3

EXHIBIT 9 1972 Pro Forma Projections for 1972–1976 ($ thousands)

Years Ended December 31	1972 $	1972 %	1973 $	1973 %	1974 $	1974 %	1975 $	1975 %	1976 $	1976 %
Sales	$2,800	100%	$3,200	100%	$3,600	100%	$4,200	100%	$4,500	100%
Cost of sales	1,663	59.4	1,888	59.0	2,110	58.6	2,444	58.2	2,610	58.0
Gross profit	1,137	40.6	1,312	41.0	1,490	41.4	1,756	41.8	1,890	42.0
Expenses										
Sales commissions	448	16.0	512	16.0	576	16.0	672	16.0	720	16.0
Selling expense	28	1.0	32	1.0	36	1.0	42	1.0	45	1.0
Engineering	168	6.0	192	6.0	216	6.0	252	6.0	270	6.0
General and administrative	196	7.0	224	7.0	252	7.0	294	7.0	315	7.0
	840	30.0	960	30.0	1,080	30.0	1,260	30.0	1,350	30.0
Operating profit	297	10.6	352	11.0	410	11.4	496	11.8	540	12.0
Other income	12	.4	16	.5	20	.6	25	.6	25	.6
	309	11.0	368	11.5	430	12.0	521	12.4	565	12.6
Interest	68	2.4	62	1.9	57	1.6	50	1.2	45	1.0
Net income before tax	241	8.6	306	9.6	373	10.4	471	11.2	520	11.6
Provision for tax	110	3.9	141	4.4	172	4.8	217	5.2	239	5.3
Net income after tax	$131	4.7	$165	5.2	$201	5.6	$254	6.0	$281	6.3
Number of sales force			11		12		14		15	
Office personnel			24		28		35		38	
Factory personnel			36		40		48		51	

Frank Reardon, Jr.

FRANK REARDON, JR.: "Good morning, Jack, what can I do for you?"

JACK MCDONALD: "Well, Mr. Reardon, I've got a few problems I'm hoping you might be able to help me out with."

FRANK: "Jack, you know I'm always available. Shoot."

JACK: "Well, conversion to the computerized accounting system for the Buick dealership is not progressing as smoothly as I had hoped it would. I'm not getting complete cooperation from your brother, Art, in the way of his assistance and his time, and frankly, I'm really having problems with my own time because Mr. Reardon, Sr. is in here with me almost constantly, questioning me and even harassing me on occasion. You know he's dead set against computers. Says he's operated quite successfully for years without them—doesn't trust them. I want to get this system instituted by our deadline. You know I intend to make that bonus."

FRANK: "Yeah, I sympathize with you on that. The old man was once a great businessman, but now he's old and a little out of touch with modern times. I think I can talk to him, though, and help you out there. But this bit about Art not giving you his full cooperation bugs me. Look— why don't you meet me for lunch at The Encore tomorrow at noon. I'd like to get to the bottom of this, before I discuss it with my brothers."

HISTORY OF REARDON MOTOR ENTERPRISES

In 1933, Frank Reardon, Sr. purchased a Buick franchise from General Motors and established his dealership on a main thoroughfare of downtown Hartford, where the company stands to this day. With the arrival of the New Deal, Mr. Reardon firmly believed that the economy would quickly revive and that business activity would soon return to a prosperous level. Previously a stock broker, Mr. Reardon had always wanted a company of his own and when the opportunity to obtain a GM dealership presented itself, he gathered all his financial resources and invested in the automobile industry. Frank Reardon felt that the restrictive franchising system employed by the largest auto producers would prove to be extremely profitable for all authorized dealers. He also saw the value of being a duly authorized representative of the manufacturer. In most communities, the dealership was the only place where the consumer would purchase a product of the manufacturer and obtain competent service. Further, Mr. Reardon believed that re-

This case was prepared by William L. Coleman and Chris Gwin under the direction of Associate Professor Jeffrey A. Barach, as a basis for class discussion, rather than to illustrate either effective or ineffective handling of an administrative situation.

stricted entry into the distribution sector of any industry would yield a greater rate of return than unrestricted markets, where the number of franchises was not limited.

Although the company did not progress as rapidly as Mr. Reardon had hoped, the post-war boom of the late 40's and early 50's generated record sales and profits. Relying on his entrepreneurial instinct, Mr. Reardon decided to use the excess capital of Reardon Buick to create the Reardon Leasing Company (RLC). With the cost of automobiles rising and an average depreciation rate of 30% over the first two years of ownership, Mr. Reardon felt that the American public deserved an alternative to buying their cars. While the leasing concept was not widely recognized or accepted in 1954, Frank Reardon saw many advantages to leasing, both to the individual and corporation. For example, leasing involved no down payment, only a fixed monthly installment; leases could cover maintenance and licensing; and, above all, leasing was a convenience to the customer—one could take his transportation needs to one person who could handle all automobile problems. Although leasing provided no clear tax advantages, allowable deductions for automobile use could be easily identified from the accounting point of view. Mr. Reardon knew that a lease would produce no more profit than a sale, on the average, but it would provide a customer service that he saw as essential for the future. Despite these numerous beliefs, RLC did not show a profit for several years. In 1959, however, a large Hartford corporation decided to lease their company vehicles through RLC. This proved to be the necessary break in launching the Reardon's most successful enterprise.

During the years of continuing prosperity for Reardon Buick and the expansion of RLC, Mr. Reardon hoped that he would be able to realize his dream of having his three sons join him in a family business. He deeply felt that a strong family like the Reardons would produce natural leaders and executives. The Reardon family tree contained several generations of Hartford's community and political leaders and Frank Reardon expected his sons to carry the family tradition forward. Beside the personal reward of watching his sons learn the automobile business, he believed that the future success of any Reardon enterprise would be insured by the strong sense of responsibility and loyalty that could be created through family ties. Thus, in 1953, Frank Reardon, Jr. came to Reardon Buick as new-car sales manager. This facilitated the necessary shift in focus of Mr. Reardon, Sr.'s attention from the auto dealership to RLC. Three years later, Tom entered RLC as manager of wholesaling all cars returned after lease expiration. In 1958, Art, the youngest son, joined Reardon Buick as a member of the sales force. Mr. Reardon expected his sons to master their own jobs, as well as to become familiar with all aspects of the two companies' operations.

In 1962, Frank Jr. suggested the acquisition of an available Cadillac franchise to his father and brothers. Based on the high probability of success and growth of a Cadillac agency, the decision was made to acquire the franchise and finance it from the profits of the two existing companies and a sizable bank loan. Frank Jr. was installed as president of Reardon Cadillac. Under his able management, the Cadillac dealership grew and prospered.

Following Mr. Reardon, Sr.'s seventieth birthday in April of 1965, the three brothers decided that their father should be retired from the family business. Their decision was based largely on his advanced age. Although they had the deepest respect and admiration for the "old man" and his accomplishments, the Reardon brothers felt his desire to cling to the conventions of the past was restricting the further growth and operation of the three companies. For example, in recent years Mr. Reardon had continuously insulted GM district and zone officials when they visited Reardon Buick. He felt that the growing volume of rules and directives regarding dealership operations was interfering with the efficiency of the company. At the same time, the Reardon brothers were becoming antagonistic toward their father because of his double-checking of their work and the resulting petty corrections. Finally, Mr. Reardon dismissed a representative of Datsun, who was seeking Reardon Buick as a potential distributor, with the comment that, "he should take his 'tinker toys' and go back to Japan." Tom Reardon had made a substantial effort to gain a Datsun distributorship, which he and his brothers believed would be very profitable. When the Reardon family learned of their patriarch's behavior, they agreed it was time to relieve him of his business duties.

By August of 1965, Mr. Reardon reluctantly accepted, as terms of retirement, a life salary of $35,000, two company cars and gas, and a generous travel and entertainment expense account. He did retain the right to visit the businesses regularly and to consult with his sons on substantial financial decisions. In return, Frank Reardon, Sr. agreed to distribute his stock holdings, over time, equally among his sons. This equal distribution of the ownership of the three elements of the family business continued to be the basis upon which the pooled profits of the three companies were shared. Frank, Jr. presided over Reardon Cadillac, Tom over RLC, and Art over Reardon Buick. The profit contributions of the three enterprises were disproportionate, but personal incomes were identical according to the ownership agreement. (See *Exhibit 1*.)

FRANK REARDON, JR.

Frank Reardon, Jr. had always been admired and respected by his brothers, friends, and business associates. His determination and analytic ability had been the tools that he used to achieve his successes in school and in the business world. Frank had received several awards for achievement and outstanding performance from the social and business organizations in which he was a member. He was also a fine athlete and the current men's golf champion at the Maple Hill Golf Club. Frank and his wife, Ellin, lived in an exclusive Hartford suburb with their daughter and two sons.

Upon graduation from college in 1948, Frank decided to start a business career of his own with a large, national food company rather than join his father's automobile dealership. Frank progressed rapidly in the firm's marketing division and after five years, he was offered an important management position. The offer of a divisional management post was a gratifying one because Frank knew his hard work and excellent performance record were being rewarded. Frank had developed a sense of company responsibility and fully recognized that his company's value system was oriented to personal achievement and recognition of ability to accomplish company directives. The innovative nature of the business and Frank's dedication to his job indicated an exciting and rewarding future.

Within a week of the divisional manager offer, Frank received a call from his father, who made his son an attractive offer to return home to Reardon Buick. Mr. Reardon explained to his son that he needed someone capable of taking the reins of the dealership while he devoted full time to the new leasing company. Frank realized that by accepting this generous offer, he would be fulfilling his father's dream of creating a family business. Frank was also aware that, with some financial sacrifices by the family, large capital resources could be available to further expand the business. Many of the marketing techniques Frank had previously learned could be applied at Reardon Buick. In addition, a family business would have the advantages of a unified management and a definite policy of future growth. But, Frank was concerned about a possible conflict developing between the family, its business, and its financial interests. Frank knew that

his wife would undoubtedly voice her opinions about the company and its policies and he wondered about the relationship between family and business priorities.

After considerable deliberation, Frank decided to join his father's company as new-car sales manager, a position of authority and responsibility. As far as Frank was concerned, the benefits of a family business far outweighed the disadvantages. Frank's capable management and hard work were rewarded in 1962 when the family obtained the Cadillac dealership. Frank Reardon, Sr. was extremely proud to install his son as president of Reardon Cadillac. The second Reardon automobile agency became a model of efficiency, cooperation, and managerial control under Frank's leadership. (See *Exhibit 2*.)

TOM REARDON

Tom was Frank Reardon, Sr.'s second son. He was a rugged individual and still showed some of the bumps and bruises from his college wrestling career. Tom was a complex person and, at times, contradictory. He was frank, cautious, shrewd, and enthusiastic while retaining a skeptical nature. His lack of sensitivity had often impaired his relationship with others, particularly his two brothers. However, Tom's business acumen and gift of vision had brought about RLC's greatest successes and he was respected by his father and brothers for his financial abilities.

Tom's decision to join his father and older brother in business was based solely on money and opportunity. He saw in RLC the

chance to get in on the ground floor of a rapidly expanding company and to build it into the Reardon's most profitable enterprise. Although the credit for establishing the company belonged to his father, Tom always felt that he, alone, had been the driving force behind the business. As the leasing field began to grow competitive in the early 60's, Tom often got the jump on his competition by creating the necessary innovations to gain large and lucrative contracts. For example, RLC was the first Hartford leasing firm to utilize an open-end agreement.* It was also upon Tom's insistence that RLC entered the truck leasing field in 1967. By 1975, Tom hoped to expand RLC into the

*The *open-end* agreement allowed the lessee to turn in the leased vehicle at any time during the term of the contract. If the vehicle was returned early, the lessee would terminate the agreement or immediately enter into a new lease with a new vehicle. This arrangement allowed greater flexibility than the closed-end lease, which required that the full duration of the lease be completed. Most leases were of a 24- or 36-month length.

heavy construction equipment market. (See *Exhibit 2.*)

Although Tom was a highly successful businessman, he did not have nearly the same skill at managing his family life. His somewhat sensuous nature often had placed him in awkward situations. As a result, Tom's first marriage ended in a brutal divorce proceeding, after eleven years. Ruth was a beautiful and intelligent woman from a wealthy New England family, and although many believed theirs was the ideal marriage, it took only a few years to reveal its true colors. Following the divorce in 1967, Ruth and the four children were given support by the Reardon family in addition to alimony.

Against the strong objections of the family, Tom remarried almost immediately.

Tom's divorce and remarriage alienated him from his father and brothers and particularly upset the wives of Frank, Jr. and Art. Serious family trouble arose in August of 1973 when Tom refused to continue payments for his children's education. At the same time, he made serious attempts to lure the children away from their mother by offering them expensive gifts. The resulting family uproar had no visible effect on Tom's actions. He had the ability to keep private concerns separated from the family's business concerns.

ART REARDON

Art was the youngest Reardon brother. He had always looked up to Frank and had felt more of a rivalry with Tom, only three years his senior. Art was a flambouyant personality, loved parties, and was somewhat regarded an amateur comedian. It often seemed that nothing could lower his spirits; he was an eternal optimist. Art's close friends also knew him as a compassionate and sensitive individual. He and his wife, Joan, were also very active in several charitable organizations. On more than one occasion, Art had received special commendations for his work in this field.

Throughout college, Art had envisioned himself as a corporate executive. But with some persuasion from his father, Art came into the family business in 1958 as a member of the Reardon Buick sales staff. His gregarious nature and ability to exude confidence and sincerity made him an immediate

favorite with the customers. Within a year, Art became a top salesman. Although Tom and Frank worried about their youngest brother's less-than-business-like nature, they were glad to have the family totally involved in the pursuit of profit.

Even though Art proved to be an excellent salesman, he never was enthusiastic about learning all the intricacies of the two Reardon businesses. Art had a thirst for swift success. He wanted to have a management job, as his brothers had. Despite the fact that Mr. Reardon, Sr. assured his son that the next opening would be his, Art was impatient. He felt he had paid his dues during his three years as a salesman and customer relations man.

Prior to the acquisition of the Cadillac agency, Frank and Tom began a search for a capable person to fill the new-car sales manager's position, should Frank be moving to the new agency. They had found an experienced and capable man and were about to make him an offer to join Reardon Buick when their father learned of their intentions. Mr. Reardon wanted Art, his youngest and favorite son, to fill the vacant management job. In order to avoid a family controversy, the two older brothers consented to their father's wishes. Frank and Tom hoped that the responsibility of a management position would create a willingness in Art to fully learn the automobile business. They discounted his inexperience because of the strength of the family.

Following Mr. Reardon's retirement in 1965, Art assumed the primary management function at Reardon Buick. Within several years, problems began to develop. In order to help Art maintain control of the business, Mr. Reardon returned to take an active role in the daily operations of the company. Inefficiency, stiff competition, high overhead, and location (downtown) were draining profits from the dealership. (See *Exhibit 2*.) Yet, more than five years later, the same problems remained. With growing businesses occupying their full attention, Frank and Tom accepted the many explanations and excuses for the lack of improvement. They had also opposed the re-entry of their father into family business affairs but felt that his presence could be helpful to Art. At the same time, sales were increasing, the tire department was making large profits, and a small foreign car was added to the sales line. (See *Exhibit 3*.) In May of 1974, a respected accountant, Jack McDonald, had been hired to restructure the accounting department and to convert the system to a computerized one, based on GM accounting principles. At this point, Art was sure the company was on the road to recovery. . . .

THE LUNCHEON MEETING

FRANK, JR.: Hey, Jack, how's it going?

JACK: Got some bad news for you, Frank. Yesterday afternoon, before I was about to leave for home, Art came in and showed me this letter from GM. Here, take a look.

FRANK: (reads for a moment). I should have known this was eventually going to happen. A friend of mine in Minneapolis—a Pontiac dealer—was told two years ago by GM that if specific financial standards weren't maintained, he would face a substantial cutback in new-car allotments. Same damned thing here for "all Buick dealers in the Hartford zone area." That's a hell of a way to let you know you've got problems. I've been on Art's back constantly trying to get him to straighten out this floundering situation. If this cutback goes through, it might lead to a total collapse of the dealership.

—Oh, two martinis, please.

JACK: You know, Frank, in the short time I've been with the company, I've developed a few thoughts along those lines, and if you don't mind my being perfectly frank and honest with you, I'd like to discuss some of them with you.

FRANK: Sure, Jack, go right ahead. I certainly respect your twenty-five years of experience with GM dealerships and the specific knowledge you've gained about how the other two companies worked. I'd like to hear what you've been thinking.

JACK: Thanks. You know—you say that you've been constantly on Art's back to straighten things out. But Art is your brother, and he happens to be one of the nicest guys you could ever want to meet. It occurs to me that maybe you haven't taken the same position with him that you might have were he not your brother—say if he were some guy with a hot-shot reputation who just hasn't panned out as you'd hoped. Do you think there's any merit to this thought? I mean, do you think you've always been so objective about this as you should?

FRANK: Well, I suppose you could be right. I never really considered that. I've always told him what I thought—but it's quite possible my reactions and remarks have been restrained a bit because we've been so close since childhood. And our brother Tom has never been too kind towards Art. I guess you could say I've been defensive with him in response to Tom's harsh criticism. Also, I've always believed, as my dad believed, that brothers are more likely to feel a stronger sense of responsibility to the business than most non-relatives would. In guiding Art, I've always felt persistent prodding would eventually bring that quality out in him.

JACK: Those are reasonable assertions, Frank, and I can see how and why you could believe in them. But I feel an equally likely situation can arise where you have a brother who—and Frank, I'm saying things now as honestly and candidly as I know how about your brother and my boss, hopefully for the good of all of us; are we in confidence here? (Frank nods yes.)—as I was about to say, your brother is an intelligent man, not without ability, but his motivation for and his fulfillment of that responsibility to the family business are lacking, and nothing is being done about it. What I'm suggesting is that occasionally a family member tries for a free ride in a family business. He knows the more motivated members will not let him fail and

takes advantage of their unwillingness to be tough with him.

FRANK: I don't buy that. I know my brother Art well enough to know he's not taking a free ride. He may not be applying himself fully. Indeed, he may not even be capable, but one thing we must remember. Art is running the toughest of the three businesses—the one with the most strikes against it. You know the problems—downtown location, stiff competition, and so on—those things are beyond Art's control.

JACK: Maybe I overshot on that. You're probably right. Art's lack of cooperation with me may be getting on my nerves a bit, but there is one very important fact you need to consider. Employees look up to their leader, to the president of the company they work for. It is well known around our shop that Reardon Buick, Reardon Cadillac, and Reardon Lease Company form a "family business." They think the only reason Art is chief here is because he is Frank and Tom's brother. The image they have of him is lousy. They think he is lazy—why, he isn't even here half the time. Even when he is around, he sometimes goes across the street to play pool with some of the salesmen. Now, what do you think all of this does to morale? What do you think goes on in a mechanic's mind when he considers that he's working his butt for a company that is losing business, and its president is out playing golf?

FRANK: Well, I certainly didn't know that feelings against my brother were so intense. When he talks to me he seems very interested in the business and even gets excited describing certain events that have taken place. (Reflecting a bit.) You know we were all educated at the same schools, got the same advice from dad, and, in general, have had very similar backgrounds which we all believed had led to similar thinking and perception of established policies. In turn, we thought the attributes of these similarities would be to our advantage in running three companies under common ownership. Until lately, this setup served to build our morale as a management team. I felt my brothers to be more loyal and dependable than anyone we could hire, and indeed they probably are, but it looks as though, in Art's case, no advantage is being gained.

JACK: Frank, I know how you feel, but let me add just a couple more thoughts before lunch is served. My son, Duane, who is currently going to business school out west, recently sent me an article from the *Harvard Business Review* with some very interesting thoughts on family businesses. I jotted down some notes which I'll give to you as soon as I get back to the office. (See *Exhibit 4*.) But one thought in particular seems particularly relevant to Art's case. Regardless of how capable a relative may be, he may find that the pressure to live up to others' expectations of him inhibits his self-development. That relative may come to doubt his ability to succeed without his brother's help. This is something which

Art probably wouldn't admit, but it might really be affecting his performance. You might want to try to make him aware of this. . . . And another thing which seems apparent to me, though I can't claim to be totally informed, is that the company has no particular long-range goals, outside of annual sales forecasts. I should think that you would want to seriously consider a way in which you can establish definite management policies and guidelines, especially concerning discipline and hiring of family members, to insure the future of the family business. Such measures would certainly serve to reduce or minimize conflicts between brothers where no particular policy prevails.

FRANK: (Pause.) I appreciate those thoughts, Jack. They sound quite valid. Kind of things you just don't think about all the time when you're one of the brothers. My family spends a great deal of time with Art's. It's tough to be genuinely critical in a situation like that. And it's true, we don't have any particular vision into the future—I can assure you I am convinced that I must take some kind of action. Let's eat.

CONCLUSION

As a result of the letter of warning from GM and its financial implications, and the McDonald discussion, Frank knew that specific and substantial action must be taken, and soon. A family stockholders' meeting was scheduled for the following week, and Frank was determined that one of the following actions would have to be taken.

1. *Fire Art outright.* In order to do this, however, Frank would in effect be joining Tom to vote

Art out. By terms of the stockholders' agreement, if any one of the brothers ever departed from the business for any reason, his share of the ownership would be surrendered to the remaining brothers. Tom had wanted this for some time. But the potential disruption in Frank's own home, not to mention Art's, made this alternative a severe one in Frank's mind. What would the family think if Art were removed and replaced by someone who proved to be no better? What would the ultimate effect be on Art? Possibly, the ouster could be softened by supporting Art financially for an adequate period of time and actively helping him to find a new job.

2. *Demote Art*. This would also be a difficult move because Art would certainly lose face among family and friends. Any effort to change his position would have to minimize this loss to Art. Perhaps a new position could be created for Art with an executive function in all three companies. Tom had indicated in the past, however, that he would prefer not to have Art interfere in his lease company. But Frank believed he could persuade Tom to accept Art in a new position if it meant saving Reardon Buick and thus substantial revenue. The possibility of an outright demotion was not considered to be viable because a similar action involving a non-relative would rarely be exercised. The resulting total loss of respect for Art would serve no advantage to anyone.

3. *Reorganization of the family business*. A plan to integrate all three businesses under the single management team of all three brothers, a sort of triumvirate, seemed like a rational solution. This alternative had been actively considered once several years ago when Tom had been hospitalized for several months and couldn't operate his business. Three factors served to dismantle the plan although Frank and Mr. Reardon, Sr. both had thought implementation of such a plan would be the ideal way to run the business. First, Tom had made it quite clear that personality conflicts might impede the smoothness of operation if the triumvirate went into effect. Second, it was understood that GM, as a matter of general policy, was opposed to any such arrangements, insisting that all franchises be singly owned and operated. Third, the costs involved in a major reorganization, including legal fees, changing accounting systems, etc. were considered a substantial barrier to the plan.

4. *Sell Reardon Buick now*. The currently realizable value of selling the dealership now was considered less than the value of continued ownership, considering that future operations would be resolved of the current problems that the dealership wouldn't be faced with a cut in new-car allotments, and that Reardon Buick would improve its competitive standing in relation to other dealerships in town. Both Tom and Frank felt this to be attainable if a more effective manager were brought in to replace Art. But, of course, one major problem loomed. What to do with Art? The problems involved here were discussed with the first two alternatives. Another problem would surface if the decision were made to sell the franchise. Frank Reardon, Sr. would explode. Reardon Buick was his life's work and to see it sold as a result of mismanagement, especially from within the family, just wouldn't set with him. The agreement to transfer his stock equally to all sons had not yet been completed, and he might try to terminate the ultimate transfer of the balance if the sons tried to sell Reardon Buick. It was clear to Frank, however, that the current value of selling the dealership now, in view of the possibility of a cutback from GM, would have a considerably favorable financial impact.

5. *Switch companies*. One way to circumvent most of the problems in the preceding alternatives would be, in effect, to play musical chairs with the management of the three companies. This would provide for a more effective allocation of managerial talent. But, some very practical considerations prevailed. First, neither Tom nor Frank really wanted to attempt to cure the ailing dealership. They were getting along in years themselves and to change lifestyles for any reason would be opposed by them. They knew Reardon Buick was the toughest of the three. What if they failed? And further, since Reardon Cadillac and RLC were operating successfully, both financially and from the management standpoint, it might be a greater risk than Frank would wish to take to have Art take over either of the two.

6. *Keep Reardon Buick and work with Art*. The most desirable solution to the problem *might* be to do exactly this. Frank remembered what Jack had said toward the end of their luncheon conversation about possible reasons behind Art's weaknesses. The thought hit hard that a preponderance of consideration for this problem revolved about financial impacts of various alternatives, all at the *expense* of his *brother*. How could he ever clear his conscience if Art really did have the ability, but he failed to bring it out in him? On the other hand, for years now Frank had tried to help and encourage Art, usually with fair short-term success, but the major problems had never been solved.

EXHIBIT 1   Contribution per Dollar Profit to the Reardon Family Business from Each Company

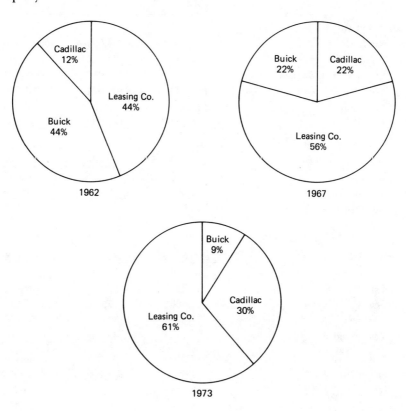

EXHIBIT 2   Frank Reardon, Jr.: Profit & Loss Statements

	1962	1967	1972
Reardon Buick			
Net Sales	$4,120,000	$5,233,000	$6,542,000
Gross Profit	515,000	604,411	680,368
Tot. Var. Sel. Exp.*	101,120	128,058	142,221
Tot. Pers. Exp.†	144,800	165,524	201,300
Tot. Semi-Fix. Exp.‡	103,600	123,069	136,219
Tot. Fixed Exp.¶	111,240	145,990	174,103
Net Op. Income	54,240	40,770	26,525
Other Inc., Net	4,200	4,600	4,496
Net Profit, B-Tax	58,440	45,370	31,021
Income Tax	19,869	15,429	9,926
Net Profit, A-Tax	$38,571	$29,941	$21,095
Reardon Cadillac			
Net Sales	$ 990,000	$1,932,000	$3,291,000
Gross Profit	118,800	255,990	476,176
Tot. Var. Sel. Exp.*	23,740	52,236	102,606
Tot. Pers. Exp.†	39,600	77,280	152,212
Tot. Semi-Fix. Exp.‡	17,820	34,912	71,057
Tot. Fixed Exp.¶	26,730	48,300	90,103
Net Op. Income	10,910	43,262	60,198
Other Inc., Net	4,624	4,200	15,593
Net Profit, B-Tax	15,534	47,462	75,791
Income Tax	5,436	18,895	20,463
Net Profit, A-Tax	$ 10,098	$ 28,477	$ 55,326

EXHIBIT 2 *(continued)*

	1962	1967	1972
Reardon Lease Company			
Revenues:			
Regular Rentals	$3,221,496	$4,732,191	$7,339,651
Interest	413,944	615,184	779,777
Other	390,018	421,293	552,181
Total Revenues	$4,025,458	$5,768,669	$8,671,609
Expenses:			
Depr., Leased Equip.	$3,221,496	$4,732,191	$7,339,651
Int., Leased Equip.	386,579	559,103	760,758
Sel., Gen. & Adm. Exp.	343,948	388,121	409,116
Total Expenses	$3,972,013	$5,679,415	$8,509,525
Net Op. Income	$ 53,445	$ 89,253	$ 162,084
Other Income	19,530	31,013	40,088
Net Income, B-Tax	72,975	120,266	202,172
Income Tax	33,997	45,701	84,912
Net Income, A-Tax	$ 38,978	$ 74,565	$ 117,260

*Total Variable Selling Expenses include: salesmen compensation, delivery expense and policy work.

†Total Personnel Expenses include: owners' salaries, all other salaries, employee benefits, and pension fund.

‡Total Semi-Fixed Expenses include: company vehicle expenses, advertising, travel and entertainment, supplies.

¶Total Fixed Expenses include: rent, heat, light and power, depreciation, insurance, leasehold amortizations.

EXHIBIT 3 Frank Reardon, Jr.:
Sales Trends (Volume in New
Units Sold/Leased)

Year	Buick	Cadillac	Lease (cumulative)
1962	598	180	225,198
1963	623	195	289,143
1964	720	216	305,616
1965	688	243	422,382
1966	752	257	479,509
1967	795	285	602,114*
1968	830	298	701,995
1969	565†	194†	745,223†
1970	873	345	857,096
1971	960	370	926,777
1972	1012‡	392	1,101,327
1973	1207	445	1,101,327
1974 (forecast)	1420	468	1,198,467

*Trucks incorporated.

†UAW strike.

‡Small foreign car added to sales line.

EXHIBIT 4 Frank Reardon, Jr.: Notes from HBR Article

ADVANTAGES IN FAMILY BUSINESSES

1. Family members, bearing the names of present or past owners, have a better chance of impressing prospective customers.

2. In the words of a Texas oilman, "Certainly this closely held family corporation has the *right* to retain management in the family, and assuming family people are qualified, this usually works out best because the nepot feels an added responsibility to the family and will frequently be more conscientious."

3. There are vast advantages in having similar backgrounds which lead to similar thinking and preclude the need for explaining the why's of policy every time.

4. Relatives in management help to assure continuity and effective carry-on of corporate policies.

DISADVANTAGES IN FAMILY BUSINESSES

1. There is a definite tendency that family concern discourage outsiders from seeking work in the company. (This you well know—the man who would have had Art's job had Art not been around.)

2. If a relative is hired as an executive and proves to be inadequate, he cannot be fired or demoted as readily as others can.

3. Family and personal interests sometimes tend to be put ahead of corporate interest since there is no "impartial" boss looking over the nepot's shoulder. (63% of respondents to HBR questionnaire regarding this topic agreed.)

4. Presence of relatives in management can be a drain on company efficiency, growth, and profitability as problems arise with the nepot's ability to earn the respect of other employees. They tend to suspect that his authority was not earned.

5. Often-times pressure is exerted by wives, mothers, sisters, etc. to give the relative "another chance."

Harvard Business Review, The Editors. "Is Nepotism So Bad?" Jan.–Feb., 1965.

Garcia y Mora S.A.

Juan Mora was nearly at the end of his rope. For years he had been trying to establish a viable working relationship with his partner, Ramon Ballester. It seemed as though there was nothing Juan could do to make things better. Ramon appeared to thrive on negating anything Juan said or did. Rarely, if ever, did Ramon offer any positive suggestions or seem willing to cooperate on company business. Most of the time, in fact, Ramon behaved as if Juan were his enemy rather than his partner.

At 38 years old, Ramon now owned 50% of Garcia y Mora S.A., the company of which he was Chairman and Juan Mora—age 43—was president. Juan and his two older brothers, Pablo and Jorge, owned the other half of Garcia y Mora. Ramon and the Mora brothers represented the fourth generation of partnership between the families of the two men who had founded the company some ninety years before. The two families had managed the company successfully together through good times and bad, and in 1985, Garcia y Mora was one of Spain's foremost rice millers. Juan's biggest concern was that unless he and Ramon found a way to get along better, the company would go into a decline from which it would be difficult to recover.

Already in 1983, a management consultant had pointed out that the "conflicts of approach and opinion" at the top of Garcia y Mora were having negative effects throughout the organization. People were confused about the lines of responsibility and the direction the company would be taking. According to the consultant, the lack of cooperation at the top was demoralizing for the operating executives and for lower level employees as well. Now, more than two years later, the conflict between Juan and Ramon had not abated even though many of the consultant's suggestions had been implemented. If anything, matters had gotten worse. In Juan's opinion, the only progress he had made over the two years was to convince his brothers (who both lived in Thailand where the Mora family had another rice company) that there was indeed a problem at Garcia y Mora S.A. Even with his brothers' support, though, Juan found the situation demoralizing too.

Only a few solutions seemed possible, and none of them was especially attractive to Juan. He could carry on with the situation as it was, trying once again—most likely in vain—to find an arrangement by which he and Ramon could continue to work under the same roof. He could threaten to dissolve the company at the next Board meeting, when Ramon would be certain to contradict him regarding virtually every subject on the agenda. Or he could consider buying Ramon's half of the company or pushing Ramon to buy out the Mora brothers' half.

Dissolving the company would mean heavy tax liabilities and considerable financial losses for all parties. Selling out to Ramon would leave the Mora family without a con-

This case was prepared by Research Associate Colleen Kaftan, under the supervision of Professor Louis B. Barnes, as a basis for class discussion rather than to illustrate either effective or ineffective handling of an administrative situation.

crete base in Spain and would deprive Juan of the position he had pursued for more than a dozen years. Moreover, if Ramon bought the company, Juan believed that most of the key employees would want to leave to form a new organization under the Mora family's management. In that event, Garcia y Mora would be nothing more than an "empty box," and the prestigious old firm would be sure to fail under Ramon's erratic leadership. Even worse, by selling out to Ramon, the Moras would lose control of the strong brand image the company had developed over the years. To promote a new brand now would be far too expensive a proposition. As a result, all three brothers considered selling to Ramon an unacceptable option.

On the other hand, buying Ramon out seemed nearly impossible too. For one thing, Ramon would be very suspicious of any offer the Mora brothers made, and would most likely demand an exhorbitant price for his shares. Lately Ramon had begun to claim that his grandfather—Pedro Garcia—had been cheated by Juan's father, Enrique,

when Enrique bought Pedro's share of Garcia y Mora's Thai operation in the mid-1930s. Pedro Garcia had been unable to travel to Thailand because of the political situation in Spain at the time, and had no sons to send in his place. Since he also felt quite skeptical about the future of the business in Thailand, Pedro offered to sell his half of the Thai operation to Enrique, who agreed somewhat reluctantly to buy. Jose Ballester later expressed regret about his father-in-law's decision to sell to the Moras. A generation later, Ramon started claiming that the transaction proved the Mora family wanted only to take advantage of the Garcias and the Ballesters. If Ramon were willing to sell at all, the Moras would probably have to borrow heavily to pay for his shares, and the charges might be too great for the company to bear.

Yet Juan was convinced that something had to change if the company—and its top managers, including himself—were to survive. He worried which path to take, and how to ask his brothers to support the choice he would make.

COMPANY BACKGROUND

The Garcias and the Moras had been rice millers for as many generations back as the family histories could be traced. In the late 1800s, Vicente Garcia and Pere Mora had set up their own rice trading operation in a small town Southwest of Valencia. The founders' sons, Pedro Garcia and Luis Mora, decided to incorporate and called their company "Hijos de Vicente Garcia y de Pere Mora S.A." ("Sons of Vicente Garcia and Pere Mora, Inc."), and in the following generation the name was shortened to Garcia y Mora.

Pedro Garcia's daughter, Dolores, inherited Pedro's half of the business and signed all of her shares over to her husband, Jose Ballester. Their son, Ramon, inherited

the shares on his father's death in 1980, and was given full responsibility for the financial well-being of his mother and his sister, Pilar.

On the Mora side, the inheritance had passed from Pere Mora to his son Luis, and to Luis' son Enrique, the father of Juan, Pablo and Jorge. The three brothers now owned equal shares in both the Thai and the Spanish companies.

All three Mora brothers had worked closely with Jose Ballester at one time or another. Since Jose was nearly fifteen years younger than Enrique, he had served as a mentor and role model for each of the three Mora boys. When Enrique Mora retired in 1967, he set up a system by which each of his sons would spend three years in Spain working with Jose Ballester in order to learn the Spanish company's operations and to look after the family's interests there. As a result, Pablo had lived in Spain between 1967 and 1970, Jorge had taken over Pablo's job between 1970 and 1973, and Juan had moved to Spain in 1973. When Juan's three-year tour approached its end, the brothers agreed that Juan should remain in Spain with his family, while the other two families carried on with the business in Thailand.

Juan had appreciated the chance to learn from the senior Ballester, as had Pablo and Jorge before him. A large, convivial man with little formal education, Jose Ballester had come to Garcia y Mora in 1954 from an import-export office he had managed before his marriage to Dolores Garcia. His acute business sense and the rich web of friendships he soon developed in the rice industry had served the company well. Jose had earned a reputation as one of the region's most knowledgeable buyers and sellers of bulk rice. Many rice millers and almost all of the wholesale distributors counted him among their closest acquaintances.

For the most part, Jose's intuitive sense combined well with the Moras' more formal training. On occasion, however, the Moras had trouble convincing Jose to adopt ideas they had tested successfully in Thailand. Jose's resistance was similar to the attitude his father-in-law, Pedro Garcia, had shown towards a marketing strategy suggested by Enrique Mora in the late 1940s. Enrique believed (and experience in Thailand had shown) that end-users would pay more for rice if they could identify specific brands of a known type and quality. Pedro Garcia had been skeptical of the idea that rice could be anything other than a commodity, to be traded in bulk bags.

In order to convince Pedro to try the brand strategy, Enrique Mora had contributed the packaging machines himself. Boxes of rice were marketed under the brand name "Arroz Lola" with a picture of Pedro's daughter, Dolores, on the box ("Lola" was a nickname for Dolores). The color of Dolores' dress on the box indicated the type and quality of the rice inside.

The strategy had been extremely successful: "Arroz Lola" put Garcia y Mora on a steady growth curve, and branded retail sales were still showing the biggest profit margins almost three decades later. The rice named for his wife was already quite popular by the time Jose Ballester joined the company, and Jose himself chose to support the brand strategy rather than to follow in his father-in-law's footsteps by concentrating on bulk distribution and wholesale operations, which (at the time) represented more volume than brand sales.

Like his father-in-law, though, Jose was hesitant to implement any new ideas the Moras brought from Thailand. Once Jose was convinced, he generally threw his full support behind a project or strategy (as with the "Arroz Lola" brands), but reaching that commitment almost always required both patience and persistence on the Moras' part. For example, when Jorge wanted to introduce a new rice processing technology, the Moras again had to contribute the technology free of charge in order to convince Jose that the resultant rice products could be successful. By the same token, Jorge and Juan had been forced to act alone to develop the export market by pushing sales to major European breakfast cereal manufacturers. Later, as usual, Jose had come to support the new marketing plan, and was even enthusiastic about retaining a sales consultant with considerable experience in international markets.

Juan recalled that—apart from the few instances where he and his brothers decided to forge ahead against Jose's judgment—his working relationship with the senior Ballester had been generally favorable, and even quite rewarding at times. In the rare event that the two disagreed on some routine aspect of the business, Juan usually deferred to the older man's experience and judgment.

Such was not the case, however, in Jose's relationship with his own son Ramon. After a stormy childhood and a heavy involvement in anti-Franco demonstrations during his university years, Ramon had worked for four years as an electronics engineer, designing switching systems for the Spanish telephone company. When he joined Garcia y Mora in 1975, he seemed still to be harboring ill feelings toward his father. In fact, in the early days, Juan Mora had occasionally been placed in the position of mediating between father and son.

Even then, the Mora brothers had also been frequent targets for Ramon's disgruntled feelings. In one altercation, Ramon told Juan that Jose was the only person doing any work in the company, and that Juan and his brothers were simply taking advantage of the Ballesters' contribution. On hearing about his son's accusation, Jose suggested that Juan should be Ramon's boss, so that Ramon could see for himself just how much effort the Moras were putting into the company.

The arrangement lasted only a short while, until Ramon came to Juan to ask for a salary increase for his low-level management job. Juan refused the increase, noting that Ramon was already being paid at competitive market rates for the type of work he was doing. As a result of the ensuing blow-up, Jose decided that Ramon should take a job outside the company in order to get some business experience and to gain a better understanding of commercial relationships.

With the help of another consultant, Ramon was hired as a junior department manager in a nationally-known retail chain. Despite the consultant's forewarning to the hiring officer, Ramon performed extremely well during his two years outside Garcia y Mora. Even his visits home were more pleasant than they had ever been before, according to his parents and his sister. But when Ramon came back to the company after losing his position in a major restructuring, the conflict started up all over again.

RAMON RETURNS

Ramon was given general management responsibilities for a small operation packing rice for use in *paella,* a regional seafood specialty. In his new position, he had very little reason to be in contact with Juan Mora, but Juan often heard the loud, argumentative meetings Ramon had with his father in the adjacent office. The discussions frequently went beyond the subject of business, with Ramon hurling accusations at his father for grievances dating back to Ramon's childhood. Nevertheless, when Ramon suggested changing the processing technology at the *paella* plant, Jose was pleased to support his son's initiative.

As Ramon started to research the new processing technology, Jose's illness began to be apparent to everyone who worked with him. While the project went forward, Jose grew sicker and sicker, and eventually Juan was forced to take over some of the older man's responsibilities. When it became obvious that Jose was dying of cancer, Juan started trying to shield him from any unpleasantness in the business. Whenever Jose asked how his son was doing, Juan gave him a positive report even though he and Ramon were beginning to be in conflict again.

The issue this time was whether there should be a pilot project before the whole *paella* plant was switched to the new technology. Ramon wanted to start with a complete operation, while Juan thought it would be more prudent to test the new processes on a smaller scale first. In the end, Juan conceded and the new equipment was inaugurated shortly before Jose's death in early 1980.

Juan Mora had already taken over most of Jose's work by the time Jose died. When Ramon inherited Jose's shares and became a full-fledged partner, though, a whole new set of challenges arose. For one thing, Ramon was suspicious of every statement Juan made about the company's performance. Ramon began insisting on more detailed accounting and budgeting procedures, intimating that the simple, "entrepreneurial" system that had been used until now had actually served to cover up inequities that favored the Moras. Moreover, when the new *paella* plant was judged to be a complete—and uncorrectable—failure within a year of its opening, Ramon insisted on closing the plant and taking a more central management position in the company. According to Juan, Ramon's coming to work at the head office marked the beginning of a new era of conflict between them.

Continuous Clashes

In Juan's opinion, Ramon slowly transformed his hate for his father into a hate for the company and, in particular, for Juan himself. The situation deteriorated steadily from the moment, a year after his father's death, that Ramon took the office adjacent to Juan's. From his suspicion about the accounting systems, Ramon's distrust spread until it covered everything Juan said, did, or suggested about the business. With time Ramon began to idealize his father's memory, and said that all of the Ballesters' problems had been, in fact, the fault of Juan Mora and his brothers.

For Juan, the greatest difficulty was Ramon's constant tendency to go against anything Juan tried to do. If Juan made a proposal, Ramon would negate it, seemingly for the sheer pleasure of thwarting Juan's efforts (or so Juan thought). Nor was Ramon willing to give reasons for his vetoes: he simply said he didn't agree with Juan's idea. Worse yet, Ramon only rarely made any positive suggestions himself, so Juan felt completely stymied in his task of growing the company. And when he tried to explain to his brothers the problems he was experiencing, he always got the same response: "We understand it's difficult to work with him, both of us had hard times with his father too. You simply have to find a way to work around his stubbornness."

One way Juan "worked around" Ramon's stubbornness was to use "reverse psychology" in any discussion with him. Whatever action Juan thought the company should take, he would suggest the opposite to Ramon. Nine times out of ten, Ramon would insist on the opposite—the outcome Juan had originally wanted.

When reverse psychology didn't work, Ramon's negative attitude could cause real problems for the company. For example, on one occasion, the Mora brothers and several top executives identified a German rice distributor as a perfect acquisition for Garcia y Mora. Not only would the German company help to expand Garcia y Mora's distribution network, it would also provide easy access to the large German market. Ramon had refused to sign the final purchase contract, saying he needed more time to think about whether he could agree with the acquisition or not. For three months Ramon found excuses to avoid any discussions about the proposal, saying he needed more time to analyze the relevant numbers. Ramon had still not completed his "analysis" when the German company decided to accept another offer— allegedly lower than the one Garcia y Mora had made—from an Italian competitor.

Ramon's stalling reflected the attitude

he had taken about diversification in general. While Juan was interested in pursuing any expansion opportunities that would make sense for the company in the long run, Ramon seemed to care only about diversification outside of the rice industry. For example, he resisted the proposals for acquiring rice interests outside of Spain (including the German company) but seemed more willing to consider expanding into non-rice or rice-related businesses (such as the ill-fated *paella* plant) within Spain. An acquaintance suggested to Juan that Ramon might be trying to insure that any new business would be in an area about which both partners were "equally ignorant" at the outset. Any expansion of rice operations would increase the size of the domain in which Juan had more experience than Ramon. If the growth came from outside the rice industry, Ramon could be on equal footing with Juan. Juan was willing to consider any projects Ramon would propose, but he deplored the idea of limiting Garcia y Mora's options simply to protect Ramon's ego.

Another long-term dispute developed around the issue of advertising for the "Arroz Lola" brands. Ramon rejected several ad campaign proposals, saying they didn't fit the image his mother's name should carry in the marketplace. After two months of stalemate with Garcia y Mora's longtime advertising agency, Ramon decided to take over the ad campaigns himself. He assigned the task of writing copy to one of the senior executives, and for a full year all ads were created "in house." The executive himself later said he had accepted the task only to avoid further problems between Ramon and the advertising agency. Writing the ad copy took enormous amounts of his own time, and resulted in "the worst series of ads we've ever had," in the executive's own opinion. For the following season, Ramon lost interest in the problem, and the outside agency was hired again. Juan made no attempt to demonstrate whether Ramon's campaign had directly hurt sales, but he believed that a direct negative effect would have become obvious if Ramon had insisted on managing publicity much longer.

As the situation deteriorated, Juan found himself adopting methods that he never would have imagined himself using with anyone. He tried being very kind with Ramon, attempting to establish a more personal relationship. On those occasions, Juan discovered, Ramon usually reverted to a contrariness worse than before after only two or three days. On the other hand, when Juan tried being "mean" with Ramon—that is, saying things and making personal accusations Juan had never imagined saying to anyone—Ramon would dissolve into tears, agree with Juan and try very hard to be conciliatory for at least a month and a half. Then Ramon would revert to his previous negative and suspicious behavior.

Auditors and Consultants

When the books were closed for 1982, Ramon asked that an auditor be brought in for the first time in the company's history. The request was tantamount to a public accusation, but Juan welcomed the chance to disprove Ramon's theory about the Mora family's intentions. The auditor found only minor irregularities, all of which were corrected immediately. For the following year, Ramon decided to change auditors. In the meantime, he ordered a personal computer and began tracking the company's financial records with his own parallel system. Juan found himself feeling relieved that Ramon had a new distraction.

Juan and Ramon agreed to bring in a new consulting group early in 1983, so that the advisers could evaluate the current organization and make suggestions about a new structure as well as a new, more detailed cost accounting system. After an introductory meeting with Juan, the organizational specialist came in to interview employees at all levels of the organization. His initial findings, presented in a memo for Juan and Ramon only, suggested that unless the conflict at the top were settled in one way or another, no other organizational changes would be helpful. The report continued:

The two of you have profound differences of character, of working styles and of experience. . . . Today there are disputes about the way Mr. Mora has chosen to run the company because Mr. Ballester, after an "apprenticeship" (as he himself has called it) of a couple of years, would like a more collegial style of management and more management by objectives. In other words, Mr. Ballester insists that Mr. Mora has established a principle of "greater authority" by which, in the case of disagreement between the two partners, the opinion of the President [Juan Mora] prevails.

Mr. Ballester rejects this practice and would prefer a more collegial management where the solution to every problem and the operant decisions should result from a consensus to which both partners feel committed.

Furthermore, according to the consultant:

These conflicts and this difficult relationship between the two people who are expected to guide the company are, at this point, so obvious and widespread as to make everyone who works at the company aware of them and willing to talk about them. . . . The executives react normally to the difficulty of getting clear, rapid, and non-contradictory responses to their requests—that is, they are frustrated because they feel constrained to use indirect methods to get results that should be coming directly from the top. . . . Their discontent is evident, openly declared, and already so hard to bear that the risk of losing qualified personnel must be considered very high.

Losing qualified personnel would be particularly troublesome in the small town more than an hour out of Valencia where the company was located. Not many people wanted to move that far from the city to work, and the few highly qualified managers Garcia y Mora had developed would be difficult to replace.

The consultant did make several recommendations of ways to circumvent the problem, most of which were immediately put into effect. First, the most qualified of Garcia y Mora's managers, Carlos Perez, was appointed Chief Executive Officer. He was told that Juan Mora and Ramon Ballester would have distinct areas of responsibility in the future, and that henceforth he would report to each one only for questions in the appropriate area of responsibility. Any strategic or long-range issue about which there was not immediate agreement between the two partners would be brought before the Board of Directors.

Unfortunately, the areas of responsibility were never completely defined nor agreed upon. As a result, many potential disputes had to be solved either by Carlos Perez or at frequent Board meetings.

Carlos Perez was respected throughout the industry for his keen sense of management and his understanding of the local rice business. He, too, had nearly reached his limit in frustration as a result of the disputes between his two bosses. When he was offered the CEO's job, his first reaction was that it would not be worth the adversity that would surely be attached. However, remembering that he personally had hired at least 20% of the company's 130 employees and that he had spent the major part of his career working there, he made a pact with Juan Mora "not to leave until the situation was solved."

Carlos later found himself using a tactic he normally would have deplored. When he needed Ramon's agreement to proceed, he presented the issue as a question about which Juan disagreed. It was the only method by which Carlos could be sure to get Ramon's agreement. Carlos also thought the opposite approach might work if ever he had trouble getting Juan's approval.

Board Meetings

Like the share ownership, the Board of Directors was divided evenly between the Garcia-Ballesters and the Moras. On Ramon's side were his brother-in-law, a prominent attorney in Valencia; another well-known attorney and politician who had been one of Jose Ballester's closest friends (but who was also a friend of the Moras); and a third businessman who was a good friend of Ramon's father-in-law. On Juan's side were another prominent lawyer who had been a friend of Enrique Mora and who had a close relationship with Jorge; a cousin of the Moras who was a friend of Ramon's father-in-law; and Juan's brother-in-law, who was a well-respected corporate lawyer. Finally, by legal requirement, three non-voting auditors were required to attend every Board meeting.

Juan found the Board members extraordinarily patient about the disagreements at Garcia y Mora. All of the Directors were busy, successful people in their own right, and the only material benefit they derived from their positions on the Board was an occasional dinner (remuneration for directorships was insignificant) and the chance to meet regularly with each other. The Board composition had been unchanged for some fifteen years, and Juan thought the Directors stayed on partly out of loyalty to Jose Ballester and Enrique Mora. Juan felt almost as comfortable with the Directors from "Ramon's side" as he did with his own. Still, it seemed that neither side had yet acknowledged the true gravity of the situation. Like Juan's brothers, the Directors could see there were frequent clashes between Juan and Ramon, but they had not yet had any open discussions about the problem. Meetings were frequent after the consultant's 1983 study. In most cases, there would be a dispute between Juan and Ramon about some strategic or operational question; the

Board would be asked to meet to resolve the problem, Juan would present the issue at the meeting, and Ramon would decline to voice his complaints with anyone else around, so the Board would approve Juan's proposed course of action. Partly because of this pattern, Juan's brothers in Thailand had found it difficult to believe Juan's reports about how difficult it had become to manage with Ramon.

However, as things got worse and Ramon started being more vocal about his disagreements, Pablo and Jorge began to be more sympathetic about Juan's laments. When Jorge came to Spain for an extended visit late in 1984, he finally began to grasp what Juan had been saying and what the consultant had confirmed: it had become nearly impossible to work with Ramon.

By that point other employees were willing to tell Jorge what Juan had been trying to convey. The offices had taken on the atmosphere of a nineteenth century organization, as one secretary put it. People whispered to each other behind closed doors, afraid that their conversations would fall on "enemy ears." Nobody knew what to believe about the immediate or long-term future; all that was known was that the two directors did not agree. One could always use that knowledge to one's advantage if one was clever enough. But the situation was putting a strain on everyone. If more jobs were available in the area, even many old-timers might consider leaving.

The Board members too were seeing more and more examples of Ramon's stubbornness. First, meetings were called more often to resolve relatively minor issues. Then Ramon started to break his previous pattern of remaining silent at Board meetings. Although he still generally acquiesced in the end, he spent more of the Board's time presenting what Juan considered to be irrational arguments. Lately he seemed to be almost as recalcitrant at Board meetings as he was in the office, and Juan feared that things would deteriorate even further. In a few weeks time the Board would be asked to consider the business plan for the coming year, and Juan suspected that Ramon was planning to turn the occasion into an all-day battle.

Another Incident

On one occasion when Juan was out of town for the day, another blow-up occurred which seemed to beg for action. Carlos Perez, exhausted by several hours of "paranoid" questioning from Ramon, had finally told Ramon to leave him in peace and to "stop driving me crazy." Ramon had stormed out of Carlos'

office and had sent the memo translated in *Exhibit 1*. Carlos had responded with the memo in *Exhibit 2*. Juan received copies of both memos from the executive secretary (who had typed both of them, all within a half hour of the disagreement) on returning to the office at the end of the day. Clearly the problem had reached crisis proportions, and still Juan had no idea how to resolve it. Unless he took decisive action soon, Juan feared losing the very organization he and his ancestors had strived to build for four generations. Yet any action he might take risked making the situation worse. He wondered if he'd ever see the end of this frustrating set of problems.

EXHIBIT 1   GARCIA Y MORA S.A.: Memo from Ramon Ballester to Carlos Perez

---

TO: Carlos Perez
FROM: Ramon Ballester
CC: Juan Mora

Yet another time there is inadequate information, this time about the [...] project, which you now tell me has entered into the operational phase without the kind of clear analysis you agreed we should do.

I remind you that it is your specific duty to keep me informed about everything that happens in the company. Your failure to do so is particularly serious in cases where there is a commitment to study a question further before proceeding.

You will also please have the courtesy to avoid future use of unpleasant language in your dealings with me as well as with other persons.

[Translated from the Spanish original.]

EXHIBIT 2 GARCIA Y MORA S.A.: Response to Ramon Ballester from Carlos Perez

---

TO: Ramon Ballester
FROM: Carlos Perez
CC: Juan Mora

I have received, through proper channels, your communication of this morning. Through equally proper channels, I respond.

With respect to such a communication, I reject both the contents, which are untrue, absurd, and undeserved, and the tone, which I consider offensive and injurious to my professional and human dignity. I also note that there was no reference to the expressions *you* used this morning.

What you have written, which comes after a whole series of other episodes, is absolutely explicit in its significance for my career at Garcia y Mora. I must and will have to take the obvious action.

[Translated from the Spanish original.]

Datavision (A)

Datavision, a small computer-company, had grown rapidly since its birth in 1969. By 1977 the organization was a leader in the process control monitoring industry. Despite the fact that Datavision's business was flourishing, its President, Dr. Larry Campbell, was concerned with some existing and potential problems inherent in rapid growth situations. He was particularly concerned about Datavision's high turnover rate, the lack of collaboration between functional areas, and "morale" problems within the organization. In general, Campbell was disturbed by a lack of sense of vitality both in the executive wing of Datavision's office building and across the organization. To deal with these issues specifically and to improve their ability to manage organizational issues generally, Campbell and his Vice President of Finance, Matt Leona, enrolled in a two-week executive education program held in August 1977 at the Harvard Business School.

At the seminar, participants met in large classes as well as in small, 8 to 10 member, action planning groups. By the end of the two weeks Campbell and Leona had gained perspective on Datavision's needs and identified an appropriate course of action. The focus of their plan was to set in motion a process designed to get problems out on the table, increase the executive group's ability to communicate, and plan more effectively. They did not have any clear ideas about what particular changes in management, in managerial roles, or in organizational structure might result, from this process. At the suggestion of other managers in their action planning group, they planned to use an organizational development consultant to play a catalytic role in their effort to identify and address issues.

DATAVISION'S BUSINESS

Datavision Incorporated is an organization involved in the design, development, manufacturing, and marketing of process control monitoring systems; such systems provide real-time visual feedback of process type manufacturing operations. Datavision has pioneered the use of color graphic displays in process monitoring. Their mini-computer-based systems replace older dial and strip-chart recorder monitoring methods.

Process control monitoring systems are used in a number of different industries. Datavision has directed its marketing and sales efforts towards large companies in the chemical processing, food processing, and utility plant industries. A Datavision system sells for approximately $250,000.

This case was prepared by Emily Stein, Research Assistant, under the supervision of Michael Beer, Lecturer, as the basis for class discussion rather than to illustrate either effective or ineffective handling of an administrative situation. It was made possible by a company that prefers to remain anonymous. Company data have been disguised.

HISTORY OF DATAVISION

Datavision began in 1969 when Larry Campbell, Walter Jackson, Luther Beale, and Paul Winters, four engineers from Lincoln Labs at MIT, decided to go into business for themselves. Campbell became President, Jackson, Beale and Winters became Vice Presidents, four other people were hired and headquarters were set up in Campbell's living room. Datavision's engineers worked closely that first year and in 1970 introduced the first color graphic process monitoring system ever to appear on the market. The systems were well received, particularly in the food processing industry, and by 1972 Datavision was growing at a rate of 50% per year. In 1977 Datavision was a very different organization than it had been initially. Campbell and Jackson were still involved in company management. Beale, however, returned to MIT in 1972, and in 1976 Winters went to work for another computer company. As Datavision grew, it relocated and finally was housed north of Boston in six separate buildings within 15 minutes of each other. In the spring of 1977, the company employed a total of 470 people.

Despite rapid growth and profitability, the company was not without problems. In an industry where the average turnover rate is from 12 to 15%, Datavision experienced a 30% rate in 1975, a 25% rate in 1976 and, still, in 1977 was troubled by 18% turnover. Although the top management team was stable, except for the resignation of Winters, engineers, programmers, technicians, and marketing people would come and go quickly. Datavision's business is characterized by high and ever-changing technology. Employee loss can be a serious problem in that type of situation because qualified people are in high demand but limited supply. The process of recruiting, interviewing, and hiring costs the company both time and money.

Despite the turnover problem Datavision has a 31% share of the current graphics processing market. Its five major competitors have 37%, 14%, 9%, 3%, and 6% of market share, respectively. As mentioned previously, the graphic system industry is characterized by a rapid rate of technological advancement. As a result, the industry is highly competitive. To continue to grow, gain market share, or simply maintain its position in the marketplace, Datavision must actively market its product to generate sales. Active marketing is also important to build up order backlog. The organization aims for a steady $5 million backlog of orders. In addition, an organization in the process control industry must constantly develop more efficient, more advanced, and less expensive products. According to one manager,

This is a highly pressurized and competitive industry. To survive you have to be one step ahead of everyone else. Every 6 months there is a significant change in our market place. That kind of activity puts a lot of pressure on everyone, engineering, but particularly sales. People simply don't wait in line to buy a $250,000 computer.

BUSINESS STATUS

Since 1973 net sales at Datavision have grown at a compound rate of a little less than 50% per year. (See *Exhibit 1*, Consolidated Statements of Income, 1973–1977.) When Campbell and Leona left their offices to attend the executive seminar, results of the first quarter of fiscal 1977 were in. (See *Exhibit 2*, Consolidated Operations Report.) Actual total revenues were slightly less than predicted. Income before taxes, however, was slightly higher than predicted for that time of year. By the time the seminar had ended and Leona and Campbell had returned to Datavision there was decided concern about the financial situation. According to Matt Leona (V.P. Finance),

In April 1977 we had just finished a very big year. By August though we were behind our predictions. We hadn't thought the summer doldrums would affect business that year but apparently they did. We had to readjust our thinking and cut down our forecasts for fiscal '78. We had originally predicted a year with $25 million in sales at that point in time (August 1977). We had to cut that forecast down to $22 million.

Datavision's managers were also concerned with company financials. According to a manager in the manufacturing department,

We all know in an industry like this we need a backlog. By the end of the summer of 1977 we had really eaten away and were continuing to eat away at the backlog we had. At that point our backlog was only $2 to $3 million and, from what I understood, we just weren't getting orders.

THE ORGANIZATION

Twenty-nine of the 470 employees at Datavision were executives and managerial staff. The organization was housed in six separate buildings in an area north of Boston, Mass. The President, Vice Presidents of Finance, Engineering, Marketing, and their respective staffs had their offices in building #1. The Vice President and staff of the Manufacturing Department were located in building #2. The Customer Service Department and its functional head, a manager, were housed in building #4. Buildings #4 and #5 were primarily manufacturing. Building #6 housed mostly the N.E. regional sales office. Five of the six buildings were within walking distance of each other. The sixth (a manufacturing building) was only 15 minutes away by car.

Datavision was headed by President Larry Campbell, who was responsible to a 12-member Board of Directors of which he and the other Vice Presidents were members. Reporting to Campbell were five functional managers. (See organization chart and personnel profile, *Exhibits 3* and *4*.)

To maintain contact and disseminate information about departmental and company activities, Campbell's staff met weekly for several hours. Typically, Campbell ran the meeting. He'd ask for informal reports of department activities and problems. Then he would present an idea for some kind of corporate plan or organizational idea and ask for input which he would use to make decisions. According to Campbell,

I generally make most of the organizational decisions around here. When we first started the company I did everything. I made all the decisions and didn't really explain to anybody why I made them. I was in a position though to have a very complete picture of the organization and was the only one in a position to make good decisions. Things have changed since the beginning though and there are just too many decisions to make. I've been adapting to our growing organization and trying to change. I let certain people make decisions but I don't feel right now that I can delegate all or even most of the decision making. I tend to be a bit of a perfectionist and expect an awful lot. I feel as though I'm a little ahead of the organization in terms of knowing or thinking about where we are going, where we ought to be, and what ought to be done. I have a tendency to figure things out, make assumptions, and make decisions. That confuses people sometimes but I think it's what we need right now. I use the information I'm given at executive meetings but really make final decisions mostly myself.

Following Monday staff meetings each V.P. met with his own department managers to communicate organizational plans, decisions, or discuss company or department activities. Such meetings gave managers the opportunity to formally meet with their area V.P. and communicate with him and with each other.

The monthly written report was another important communication tool used at Datavision. Each Vice President was responsible for preparing a monthly activity report for the President. Once he received all five reports he consolidated the information into one report for the Board of Directors and each Vice President. In order to best prepare such reports, Larry Campbell met with each V.P. and his managerial staff, for several hours, during the week before the reports were to be written.

The atmosphere at Datavision was friendly. Simultaneously a formality was emerging. In earlier days doors were always open. Managers felt comfortable dropping in to chat with V.P.s and the President. As the organization grew the atmosphere changed and, although managers usually met their V.P.s whenever necessary, Campbell was seen by appointment.

THE INTERVENTION

On September 16, 1977, approximately one month after completing their executive seminar, Campbell, Leona, and Personnel Manager Harold Wheeler had a luncheon meeting with Dave Brennan. Brennan was an organizational consultant recommended to Campbell and Leona by both a seminar faculty member and fellow participant. (See his personnel profile, *Exhibit 5*.) Larry Campbell explained,

We attended MOE generally because there was a feeling on the part of some people that our hang-ups (turnover, morale problems, people feeling overworked) were organizational and somehow we weren't managing the organization to be effective. As a result of our seminar experience, we decided to hire an organizational development (OD) consultant to come in, do some work, help us bridge the gap between many different parts of the organization. We expected he would do that by talking to different people, sensing feelings and attitudes, and bring them forth in a way that doesn't offend people. We had had a sense of this OD need before going to that program, about a year earlier, and in fact hired someone who came on for a day. Anyway, after the summer program we, Matt and I in particular, were really motivated to do some OD work. Brennan seemed like the right guy.

During their three-hour lunch Brennan explained himself and his ideas to Campbell, Leona, and Wheeler. He outlined a possible action strategy for Datavision. Dave Brennan recalled,

I spoke with the three of them back then and told them that I was interested in new and developing organizations. I've done a lot of work with high technology in rapid growth situations where there are very bright people, usually engineers. I thought that I could help the V.P. group work together more effectively. Larry and Matt referred to that as "team building."

As a result of that meeting Brennan was hired to help Campbell's staff work more effectively as a managerial team. Brennan planned to initiate the "team building" effort in three phases. To begin, he would interview each member of Campbell's staff individually. Next, on November 3 and 4, 1977, he planned to meet with Campbell and the staff at a resort in Rhode Island for an off-site session. Finally, Brennan suggested that after Rhode Island he hold a meeting with company managers reporting to the staff. Dave planned to meet with those managers, about 25 in all, by himself and then have Larry and the V.P.s join the session for a question and answer period.

Interviews with Top Management Group

On October 18, Dave Brennan spent the day at Datavision interviewing the top staff. These interviews served two major purposes: (1) By introducing himself to the staff, Dave was able to explain his goals, Larry's goals in hiring him, and his plans for carrying out the team building task. (2) In addition, by questioning each manager Brennan could learn more about the operating environment at Datavision. He reported,

I started all my interviews by saying, "I'm Dave Brennan. I'm here to interview you but before we can do that I need to know what kind of expectations you have and what you've heard about me." I got five different stories from those five different guys. The theme was basically that Larry had gotten a hold of me because he went to Harvard, he (Larry) thought I could help them work together better, and that they needed it. Although initially people were a bit formal and stiff I was received very well.

The idea of a consultant was not new to Datavision executives. Approximately a year before Dave Brennan was hired another O.D. consultant came to Datavision, interviewed executives and managers, and made some recommendations to Campbell. Datavision executives were also used to off-site two-day meetings. Characteristically each quarter, executives and their wives went to a resort for a combined business meeting and social gathering. One Vice President commented,

We were relieved to meet Dave. We all felt that Datavision needed something. We'd probably all mentioned our interest in having outside help to Larry independently. We hoped Dave would give us what we needed. I wasn't so sure that anything

would change, but I was willing to give it a try. If nothing else I was sure he could act as referee when we started yelling at each other at the off-site meeting. We were in the habit of getting pretty excited at those sessions.

After introducing himself, Dave asked questions about Datavision's strengths and weaknesses and about Larry and their fellow V.P.s. He was particularly interested in assessing problem areas which might be preventing the top management group from working together as a team. As a result of his interviews Brennan identified six recurrent and key issues.

1. Lack of trust among the top level people and across the organization
2. Confusion about company goals
3. Poor decision making policy and too much decision unmaking
4. Lack of clarity regarding organizational structure
5. "Cronyism"
6. Conflicting management styles at the executive level

Dave designed a flip chart presentation for the two-day session which included a list of the six problems and illustrative quotes gathered during the interviews. After laying the meeting's ground rules he planned to use the charts to introduce the issues and help promote discussion. His agenda for the off-site meeting included convening on Thursday, the 3rd, at 8 a.m., working until 12:00, and working again from 4 p.m. to 8 p.m. The first day would raise problem issues and "clear the air." On Friday, the 4th, Dave scheduled meetings from 8 a.m. to 12:00 and 3 p.m. to 6 p.m. Dave expected that on Friday the group would be ready to devise strategies for dealing with Datavision's weaknesses.

The Off-Site Meeting

On Thursday morning Dave began the session by explaining his agenda and the ground rules for the two-day meeting. According to one V.P.,

There were several rules Dave suggested we follow. First, he said that we should try to stay on the topic of conversation and not bring in other issues when we were concentrating on one issue. Next he suggested that if we were discussing or criticizing the behavior or style of a particular person then we had to look that person in the eye. Also, you had to give the person being discussed a chance to talk and respond. Finally, the receiver of criticism also had the power to control the flow of conversation. If he was upset, offended, or uncomfortable he had the option to say stop—I'd like to discuss something else.

As part of the ground rules Dave also described the role he would play at the meeting: an unbiased outsider whose primary function was to help people listen, talk, and hear each other more effectively. According to another V.P.,

To be honest, when we were beginning that meeting in Rhode Island I was thinking to myself, we've been trying to get along for years, we've had a consultant, we've met together at off-site gatherings. I was discouraged and didn't think it would work. I was also convinced, though, that I would try and because Dave had come across so straightforward and capable, I had a glimmer of hope. I trusted him and wanted this to work out for us. I felt willing to do what had to be done and even put myself on the line.

Another V.P. recalled,

I thought that we all really had a good feeling at the start of the session. Larry was behind the effort. I really thought it could work.

After setting up the rules, Dave unveiled his flip chart presentation. The first chart included a list of all six problems and quotations illustrating each issue. He focused on each problem one by one trying to elicit additional comments and discussion. Participants were hesitant initially, but began to contribute by clarifying their ideas.

Trust was a major concern around Datavision. Nearly each V.P. had criticized other executives. According to one V.P.,

We've developed strict territories around here, we stay out of each other's departments mostly because we don't trust or approve of what the other guy is doing. I'd like to question someone on their department's activities but I'd have to let them do it to me and I'm not sure I want that.

Apparently these feelings were particularly true between Marketing and Engineering. It was not unusual for Walter (V.P., Engineering) and Bob (V.P., Marketing) to argue and blame each other for missed deadlines. Bob was quite vocal in blaming the slippage in orders on the inadequacies of the Engineering Department. Each V.P. took great pride in his own department and seemed to feel that, "things are operating real well in my department. If everyone else took care of his area like I take care of mine things would be terrific around here."

Another problem related to trust was that no V.P. seemed to feel he could confront another V.P., or could discuss negative feelings about another V.P. or manager openly to Larry. In some ways they didn't feel that Larry would listen and in other ways they didn't want to diminish another man's reputation.

Confusion about company goals was a problem related to the trust issue but presented separately. One commonly held feeling was that no one around Datavision was skillful enough to plan for the company's future. Each Vice President had confidence in the organization's technical competence but felt that no one was really in touch with the marketplace and realistic enough to make some good planning decisions for the business. One V.P. explained at the meeting,

We are all, except Scott (V.P., Manufacturing) relatively new at managing. We are probably all experts in our own areas but because we don't really trust each other we don't pool our information. That kind of coordination isn't the norm around here. Another reason for the confusion is that the company may have outgrown whatever managerial skills and planning skills some of us had.

One major focus of planning criticism was the Marketing Department. One representative sentiment, participants recalled was,

There are many places our system can be used. We haven't figured out what's happening in the marketplace. Our competitors seem to know. We are, or have become very weak in that area. Our sales are dropping and we've been eating away at the backlog. There are some real doubts about the skills in that department. The V.P. in Marketing had made some particular blunders we all knew about, blunders that especially affected the Engineering and Manufacturing Departments. He'd talk to a customer, find out what the customer wanted and promise a system. That would have been a good move except sometimes the product wasn't designed or produced yet.

To a lesser extent the Engineering Department was criticized for not developing products quickly enough or not effectively designing a less costly product. During the session V.P.s initially became defensive when criticized this way, but learned, as the session went on, to listen to the criticism and try to deal with it constructively. Dave commented,

They were all putting a great deal of effort into working hard at listening and abiding by the ground rules. Bob Fowler, who took the most criticism tried especially hard to sit quietly and respond rationally.

Decision making and unmaking was related to the goal issue and a source of complaint. Several V.P.s commented to Dave, "It seems that no one is willing to take a stand on long range goals." Not only did V.P.s worry that no one, particularly Larry, was willing to take a stand on long range goals but sometimes when a stand was taken it would be reversed quickly. Several of the V.P.s had mentioned this during their interviews and again during the Thursday session.

Sometimes these Monday Staff meetings we had were more confusing than not having them at all. Sometimes we'd talk for eight hours straight and leave without having a real sense of what had gone on. Other times Larry outlined some very definite plans and ideas. We left the meeting assuming our policy was one way. You'd tell your managers and make sure the policy was understood. Soon you'd get a memo that the policy was changed. Larry did that all himself. That kind of change of plans was very confusing and irritating for Datavision employees. It was also pretty embarrassing for the V.P. who made a statement that was reversed or negated a week later.

Perhaps the decision-making problem attributed to Datavision executives by each other was, in part, related to the nature of a high technology business. During the meeting, several V.P.s were irritated as they recalled leaving a meeting committed to a marketing, engineering, or manufacturing course of action which would be changed when the Finance Department discovered a new piece of data. One V.P. commented, "It is apparent when Matt goes to Larry with some new information because we are all told to stop what we were doing and proceed a different way." The V.P.s felt that this type of situation was frustrating and costly. Engineers who had to stop one activity and get geared up for another lost valuable thinking time. Manufacturers also became angry when they set up shop to proceed one way and then had to close down to restructure activities.

During Thursday's meeting several V.P.s confronted Larry with comments like, "sometimes it seems you make decisions for reasons of your own, unmake them for reasons of your own, and don't bother to communicate to us why or what is going on. You make decisions without involving people who have a right to be involved."

Voices became raised during these

kinds of confrontations although participants consciously tried to control tempers. Dave contributed only to add a comment like "Well Larry, did you understand exactly what Bob was saying? Why don't you rephrase that." "Does anyone else feel the same way. How about you, Scott?" By questioning that way, Dave helped Larry, the V.P.s, and Tom better understand the criticism and avoid one-to-one hostile confrontations.

Lack of clarity was a problem related to organizational structure. Participants recall feeling angry as the group began to discuss this topic. The consensus among the V.P.s was that Larry made all the organizational decisions and in many ways they didn't make sense. "One day a certain service group is a member of one department and the next day it's been moved and reports to another department." One particular irritant to several V.P.s was the fact that Tom (Manager, Customer Service) reported to Larry. The V.P.s were angry because Tom had been elevated to an executive level and had managers reporting to him. During their interviews, several V.P.s told Dave that they felt Tom didn't have the title or experience to be a member of the top staff. At the meeting they confronted Tom with these feelings. Tom remembered that at the off-site meeting he,

Was really shocked to hear that people, Matt in particular, doubted my credibility. I had trouble relating to them, but I just thought that was because I was a friend of Larry's.

Cronyism was the fifth problem which Dave found to be recurrent. In thinking back about the meeting one V.P. expressed the sentiments of the rest when he reported, "Tom Sisco didn't belong there. We told him we tolerated him but didn't trust him in the company and didn't trust him to be there. He was a tennis buddy of Larry's which is why he was there in the first place."

Active discussion took place around the cronyism issue. The V.P.s felt that the friendship between Larry and Tom stood in the way of business because around the company, people felt that you got promoted if you were Larry's friend. Tom recalled,

Those kinds of feelings were surprising to me because I really thought we played down our friendship. It was good to get it out in the open though because I knew where I stood, we all did, and that was good.

When first discussing these five issues the group had been somewhat subdued. As the hours went by they grew more willing to participate. Matt, Walter, Bob, and Larry were the most vocal participants. Tom and Scott were fairly reserved. Dave attempted to include them and elicit their comments when they were "watchers" for too long. When introducing the sixth issue, however, Dave had a difficult time getting anyone to comment right away.

Conflicting management styles was an issue that each staff member discussed with Dave during their respective interviews. As a result Dave was keenly aware that Bob's (V.P. Marketing) management and decision-making style was completely different than each of the other V.P.s. Bob himself was aware that he had a different approach and a different philosophy than his peers. Bob described himself as "the kind of person who is caring, feeling, people oriented and intuitive. I have a gut feeling for a project or procedure and am often right. No one else around here feels that way. Larry and Matt in particular are logical and analytical, it is a very different style."

Dave Brennan remembered that after interviewing the staff,

It became obvious that Bob was perceived as the center of many other of Datavision's problems. Before the meeting on Thursday I had breakfast with Bob. I wanted him to be aware before the session that his management style was seen, not only as different but in conflict with the management styles characteristic of other Datavision executives. He was upset about that, didn't like it, but said that he wasn't surprised. When we got to the issue in the meeting, people started denying it. At that point I had to confront them and said, "Bullshit, these are your quotes right there. I said let's not monkey around, we've only got two days and there's a lot of hard work to do. I really need your help." After being straightforward in that way a couple of the guys admitted to their feelings and their quotes. After that point, for the rest of that day the discussion centered around Bob.

At this point Walter and Matt in particular, became vocal. Even Scott entered into this part of the discussion. Each perceived Bob as having a caustic, hostile, angry approach. Scott expressed the opinions of Walter and Matt when he commented, "We all felt that Bob was into winning and losing. He was confrontive and angry. He raised his voice and was very aggressive. That was just not necessary to get the job done. It wasn't our style here."

At the session Matt remembered expressing the idea that,

Bob and I had a very different approach to decision making, and I knew he was certainly aware of it. He just fought me on it all the time. I believe in reality; facing it, living with it, and making well thought out logical decisions based upon it. Bob couldn't give me data to back up his ideas, or wouldn't and that annoyed me and at the meeting I let him know how I felt.

Another serious criticism directed at Bob related to his "empire building" and salesmanship attitude. More specifically, Bob was seen as someone who needed to feel important and powerful and would approach customers as if he was in control of everything at Datavision. He promised customers products and then would ask Engineering to develop them. He'd promise customers deadlines which were impossible for Manufacturing to meet. Scott Palmer recalled,

It really boiled down to a lack of trust in Bob. At the meeting we all took turns and confronted him on these issues. He didn't seem to be getting the marketing job done. Our sales were down, we were eating away our backlog. He was probably feeling some pressure but as a result he'd take things out on Walter or, try to put blame somehow on Engineering or Manufacturing.

When issue number six came out into the open all subsequent discussion became focused on Bob. Every other issue was related back to Bob's inabilities and personality style. Although Dave helped maintain calm, and the criticism was delivered constructively, Bob was subjected to several hours of direct confrontation. Walter commented,

For a long time Bob and I had had problems. This was a forum for expressing my feelings about those problems and getting them out on the table. We all tried to explain ourselves pretty calmly. He may have perceived it as an attack.

Bob said later that he had perceived the session as an attack. At the time he did not react defensively or with hostility. Although he admitted feeling initially that the whole session was a setup to confront him he listened to everyone's comments and tried to understand them. He also redirected some of the criticism if he thought he was being unfairly blamed for something or that others could benefit from similar criticism.

Scott Palmer stated,

Because Dave was there, I guess we were able to voice complaints we had never voiced before. For the first time I was able to tell Bob that it really irritated me that he never listened. That kind of honesty caught on and Bob and Larry went back and forth about individual management styles and things about each other that bothered them. Bob said Larry always turned around his (Bob's) decisions. Larry expressed the feeling that Bob was too dogmatic. It was refreshing in a way because people had things buried for five years that they were able to express then. As positive as it was though, in some ways it was brutal. Bob sat there, through criticism that was mostly directed at him and maintained his cool. I give him a lot of credit, we all did. He was open and made no attempt to stop the flow of conversation. We all learned a lot about each other during that time. We all wanted this thing to work and all appreciated Bob's willingness to listen and take criticism pretty calmly.

Larry commented,

You could almost see the improvement. Bob was really trying. He did quiet down and acted much calmer. He tried not to raise his voice and seemed to really hear what everyone else was saying.

As the first day ended people were energetic and exhausted simultaneously. Participants remember having positive and negative sentiments about the day. They were relieved to get their feelings about problem issues, particularly Bob, out into the open. However, it was upsetting for most of them to imagine what Bob must have been going through during the day. All credited Dave Brennan for being an effective coach, moderator, and guide. They perceived Dave as helping keep decibels down, fists from flying, and the conversation flowing. When the meeting adjourned, the group went to dinner feeling that they worked hard and made some good progress.

Although the schedule for Thursday did include a four-hour break in the afternoon, the group stopped only two hours for lunch. They were as energetic Friday morning. Friday's meeting was to run from 8 a.m. to 6 p.m. with a quick break for lunch in the middle of the day. Larry and his staff agreed that corporate planning would be the topic of discussion for day two. The group discussed their planning methods, how to make efficient use of their meeting time, how to communicate individual department needs, and set up ground rules for meetings.

Larry ran most of the meeting on Friday and together the group developed a planning procedure for Datavision. The plan

excited every one because it seemed to integrate functional area needs. The session on Friday was characterized by energy and activity. Overall, Scott and Tom remained less vocal than the rest of the group but seemed as enthusiastic about what they were accomplishing. Walter recalled, "Our feelings were very different on Friday than they were on Thursday. We seemed more committed on Friday. Larry was listening more carefully and Bob was almost low key. He only spoke his fair share of the time."

The group worked steadily, all day, Friday. They seemed invested in preparing planning strategies together. Dave was less involved Friday than he had been Thursday but, apparently, his presence was a catalyst for discussion. One V.P. recalled,

On the second day Dave had the effect, even when he didn't say anything, of helping us talk without ignoring each other or becoming argumentative. He wasn't involved as an obvious leader but he did promote honesty and openness on our parts; the first day especially but even the second day. Even when he was quiet we did need him in the room. That became obvious when he left to make some phone calls in the afternoon on Friday. After a few minutes, I guess when we realized he was gone, no one said a word. Apparently, we needed him there to really help us communicate, team build, or whatever.

At about 5:00 in the afternoon Larry suggested cocktails, which had not been served Thursday or before 5:00 on Friday and initiated a feedback session. He wanted to hear perceptions of his meeting behavior and asked Matt, Walter, Bob, Tom, and Scott to take turns commenting. They mentioned strengths like "you seemed to be listening more," "you seemed to take our suggestions seriously," "you were trying hard to get our input." They also asked him to try to maintain some of these behaviors back at the office. Larry enjoyed the feedback process and suggested they continue to comment on each participant. On the whole, the feedback was positive and related to listening skills and the high levels of honesty. At least overtly, the group was proud of itself. At 6 p.m. the meeting ended and because he had plans Friday night Larry headed back to Boston. Those who stayed on had an informal post-meeting dinner.

After the session participants reflected about what had been accomplished and what might be accomplished as a result of their efforts. Feelings about the meeting ranged from very positive to very negative. Tim Sisco stated,

I came out of that meeting feeling very high. So many things came out in the open as a result of those two days I felt we could all be much more open and honest with each other and had a very good idea about who the Vice Presidents were and where they stood on certain issues. I learned a lot about Walter and Matt. I felt I could work with both guys much more efficiently as a result of those sessions.

Another positive, yet less enthusiastic opinion shared by several staff members was,

When we first heard about going to Newport we all had a certain amount of skepticism about being able to work together well and about our planning capabilities. We had consultants before that, we were used to off-site meetings. I wasn't convinced that this guy (Dave) on this time thing would be any different for us. The first day was very encouraging though. We didn't have fistfights and didn't yell too much. We had all been so open that there was a collective feeling that things might really change. We were all hoping for it anyway.

There were a couple of participants who, despite overt enthusiasm, were doubtful that the session had changed anything or would act as a catalyst for future change. Their comments were,

We have a pattern of leadership, decision making, and management style here that we are used to. We've had consultants before who pointed out the same problem issues to us that Dave did now. We didn't listen a year ago, why should we listen now?

Meeting with Next-Level-Down Managers

Dave scheduled a meeting with company managers who reported to session participants for the week following the session. The meeting would let the managers know what had taken place in Newport and would run for about an hour. For the first half, Dave would meet with the managers alone and after about 30 minutes the officers would join the session.

On Monday, November 7, 1977, Campbell sent a memo to the 25 managers that were to be included, announcing that a meeting would be held November 8, 1977, at 11:00 in the conference room of Datavision's main building. Dave Brennan stated,

I wanted to do three main things at that meeting. I wanted to present an overview of the idea of team building, gain credibility, and give a brief description of the Newport meeting. I didn't plan on describing comments or anything like that but I did want to explain the process, major issues raised, and the sense of excitement and commitment that came out of that meeting. I hoped that would promote questions that I could answer and that the officers could answer when they entered the room.

There was some confusion surrounding that November 8 meeting. Not all the managers were aware that any special off-site meeting had taken place. Some thought it was to be a typical managers meeting during which Larry would announce some kind of change in the organization. One manager recalled,

Some of us were blasé, others curious, others pissed off. No one really knew what was up. Those of us who knew that the meeting was about consulting were, for the most part, unimpressed. We had spoken to consultants before and hadn't seen any results. There was no reason to think this would be different.

Larry began that November 8 meeting. He explained briefly that the officers were "all fired up" about new corporate goals, strategies for planning, increasing market share, and profits. Next he pointed to Dave as the man who was going to help achieve those goals. Several managers remembered:

Dave began his presentation by saying something like, "Well I'm sure you're all curious about the weekend we spent in Newport." Someone spoke out at that point and said, "Frankly we don't give a damn about what happened in Newport because lots of us don't even know they went to Newport." At that point there was silence. Dave handled it well. He explained and proceeded as he had planned. He probably thought he had a better idea about what was going on than we did.

As the meeting progressed Dave talked mostly about organizational development and Newport specifically. He outlined general problem issues. Managers at that meeting agreed that Dave seemed credible, likeable, and genuinely committed to changing things at Datavision. They were less convinced that things could, in fact, be changed. They were hesitant to confront Dave with those feelings. As he spoke many managers felt doubtful and whispered among themselves. As reconstructed later by participants at that meeting, the ideas going through people's minds and being exchanged were:

We don't have a team work problem in the company. The only problem is at the top. The rest of us work together fine because we know we have to. The troops communicate across departmental lines. It's just the generals that don't.

We've heard all these promises before, nothing will change now.

If they'd get together and take a stand maybe something would get done. Larry sends a memo to go ahead and proceed a certain way on a product, or something. The next thing you know he sends another memo that says with more information the project stops.

It is going to take a lot for most of those guys to improve as managers because, first of all they are all engineers and second of all, they never had to manage anyone before they managed us. They just were never taught how to do it.

The officers go off to the woods for a couple of days and think they are a team now. Its just not true. It can't be. They can't be a team when they all have such strong personalities.

About 45 minutes into the meeting one manager asked Dave a question. In doing so, he raised a volatile issue, one that every manager reported remembering and worrying about. The question was "Don't you think that, at the top, there may be a couple of people who won't change because they don't really want to and, in fact don't have the capacity?" Dave responded with a flat "No." He explained that Newport convinced him that all the officers were committed to changing and were willing to work very hard at integrating, planning, and acting as a team. Until that point Dave was viewed as a competent ray of hope for Datavision. At that point, however, several managers became discouraged. They remembered,

Dave really lost credibility points. It was no secret that there were attitude, capability, and personality differences and problems at the top. Bob Fowler was very different from the rest of them and there were bad feelings about that filtering through the company. We couldn't believe that Dave hadn't picked up on that or wouldn't tell us. If he didn't figure that out then he wasn't so skillful or had been lied to.

A wave of cynicism and doubt spread through that conference room after Dave's response. Feelings of frustration, anger, and discomfort permeated the meeting. One manager commented,

We wanted things fixed very badly, we wanted Brennan to be able to give us solid evidence that things could improve. Instead his efforts seemed like they would almost have to be fruitless. It was almost like a joke after that. We were all very very skeptical.

Another manager reflected,

We all felt pretty awkward after that. When the officers came in it got worse. People asked a couple of questions trying to assess their (the officers) real commitment to organizational development, Dave Brennan, and team building, but the tone was disbelieving and doubtful. The people who were relatively new to the company were more hopeful than those who had been around for four years or so. Generally though even those of us who were new weren't convinced that it would change, I don't really think we expressed our doubts or questions very honestly during that meeting. We became even less open and honest, though, after the officers came in.

Campbell's Perspective

After the officers' session in Newport, Larry Campbell felt committed to O.D. work and team building in Datavision. He was enthusiastic and felt that his fellow officers were similarly excited. His spirits were dampened after the managers' meeting. He stated, "It was really the first time I was aware of such widespread skepticism. That disappointed me and discouraged me."

He became even more discouraged when, after the meeting, he approached several of the managers individually. Such discussions convinced Larry that many managers at Datavision were certain that the officers could never work together as an effective team and that, given who they were, no O.D. consultant could help change things.

Simultaneously, other events disturbed Larry. Financial results for the company's second quarter were in, and both revenue and income were well below prediction (see *Exhibit 6*). In addition, it was two weeks into November, sales were down, and the backlog was becoming smaller and smaller. Dave Brennan reported,

Larry called me with two major problems. He was very upset by the amount of skepticism felt by the managers. It seemed to him that they didn't believe anything the officers said. He also mentioned that he had approached a couple informally and, it seemed to him, that the whole team building and planning effort would fall by the wayside if he didn't come to grips with what he saw to be the major issue. He continued and reported that, he felt, there was no confidence in Bob. He was convinced that, if he didn't deal with that then "we can plan ourselves to death and nobody is going to believe the planning process."

Larry was distressed and discouraged. He was not sure how to proceed. He recalled,

It all of a sudden became obvious to me—Bob was an outsider in the organization—I don't think he was viewed as a competent marketing guy. His style was troublesome for some people too—I had a realization. Everyone was against Bob. Morale was very low. I wasn't 100% sure what to do. Whatever it was though, it had to be done quickly.

EXHIBIT 1 Datavision (A): Datavision Incorporated and Subsidiary Consolidated Statements of Income for the Years Ended April 30, 1973, 1974, 1975, 1976, 1977 ($000's)

	1973	1974	1975	1976	1977
Net Sales	$3,457	$7,265	$9,461	$10,183	$16,640
Cost of Sales	1,976	4,236	5,759	5,661	9,471
Gross Profit	$1,481	$3,029	$3,702	$ 4,522	$ 7,169
Operating Expenses					
Engineering, Marketing, General, Administrative & Other	$1,280	$2,609	$3,309	$ 4,254	$ 5,253
Income (Loss) from Operations	$ 201	$ 420	$ 393	$ 268	$ 1,916
Interest Expense, Net of Interest Income	12	87	230	302	265
Income (Loss) before Provision for Federal and State Income Taxes	189	333	163	(34)	1,651
Provision for Income Taxes					
Federal	$ 76	$ 123	$ 59	$ (12)	$ 860
State	17	21	4	–	–
Income (Loss) before Extraordinary Credit	$ 96	$ 189	$ 100	$ (22)	$ 791
Extraordinary Credit—Federal Income Tax Reduction Resulting from Net Operating Loss Carryforward	76	123	–	53	–
Net Income	$ 172	$ 312	$ 100	$ 31	$ 791
Net Income per Common Share					
Before Extraordinary Credit	$ .09	$ .15	$ .08	$ (.02)	$ .50
Extraordinary Credit	.07	.09	–	.05	–
Net Income (Primary)	$ .16	$ .24	$ .08	$ .03	$ .50

EXHIBIT 2 Datavision (A): Consolidated Operations Report, Quarterly Comparison

	First Quarter FY 1978			First Quarter FY 1977		
	Budget	Actual	Percent	Budget	Actual	Percent
Revenues						
System and Upgrade Shipments, Customer Funded Eng. Shipments, Less Discounts—Syst. & U/G Cust. Fund. Eng., Net Shipments, Customer Services, Application Development, & Other Revenue						
Total Revenue	$5,014,000	$4,721,764	100.0	$3,324,857	$3,397,296	100.0
Cost of Sales						
System and Upgrade at Standard, Manufacturing Variances, Color Plotter Development, Customer Funded Engineering, Customer Services, Application Development						
Total Cost of Sales	$2,797,932	$2,503,704	53.0	$2,019,429	$1,980,898	58.3
Gross Profit	$2,216,068	$2,218,060	47.0	$1,305,428	$1,416,398	41.7
Operating Expenses						
Engineering, Marketing, Corporate Administration, & Other	$1,621,770	$1,602,761	33.9	$1,115,161	$1,143,888	33.7
Income from Operations	$ 594,298	$ 615,299	13.0	$ 190,267	$ 272,510	8.0
Interest Expense	60,000	37,305	0.8	78,000	83,677	2.5
Foreign Currency Exchange	–	2,768	–	–	–	–
Income before Tax Provision	$ 534,298	$ 575,226	12.2	$ 112,267	$ 188,833	5.5
Provision for Income Taxes	283,000	335,000	7.1	60,000	85,000	2.5
Net Income	$ 251,298	$ 240,226	5.1	$ 52,267	$ 103,833	3.0
Net Income Per Share	$.14	$.14		$.04	$.08	

EXHIBIT 3 Datavision (A): Organization Chart

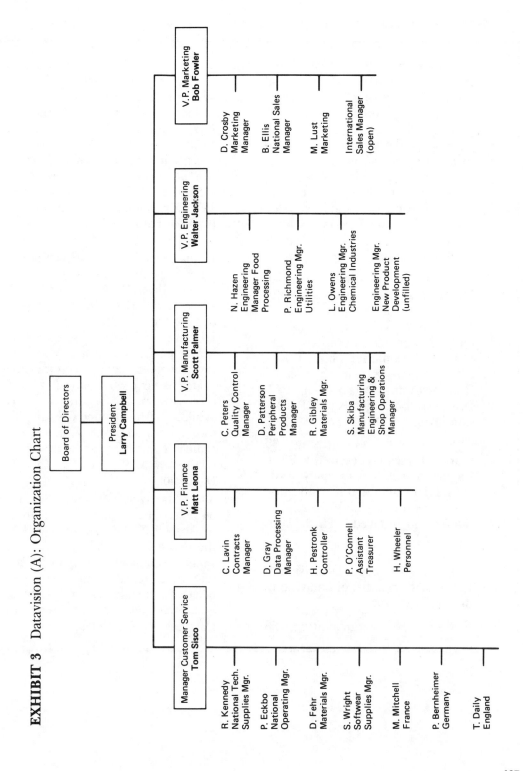

EXHIBIT 4   Datavision (A): Personnel Profiles

Larry Campbell: President, 38 years old. Dr. Campbell received a BS, MS, and Ph.D. in Engineering from Berkeley. During his graduate studies, Dr. Campbell consulted for several organizations in the area of process control. After a brief period as a professor at Berkeley he went to work in research at Lincoln Labs at MIT. He worked there for two years and founded Datavision in 1969. Dr. Campbell is a member of Datavision's Board of Directors.

Bob Fowler: V.P., Marketing, 37 years old. Mr. Fowler received an undergraduate degree from Fordham and an MBA from New York University. After his graduate education he went to work for Exxon, then Pitney Bowes in Sales. He was recruited by a search firm and came to Datavision in 1972. Fowler is also a member of Datavision's Board of Directors.

Walter Jackson: V.P., Engineering, 36 years old. Jackson received a BS in Engineering at the University of Arkansas. He continued his education in engineering at the University of Illinois and received a Ph.D. After finishing his doctorate Jackson went to work at MIT, stayed there for one year and left to begin Datavision in 1969. He is a member of Datavision's Board of Directors.

Scott Palmer: V.P., Manufacturing, 38 years old. Mr. Palmer received a BS in Engineering at the University of Rhode Island. He continued his education at Wharton and earned an MBA. After graduate school Mr. Palmer went to work for General Electric in manufacturing where he worked for 10 years, before being recruited and joining Datavision in 1973. Mr. Palmer is also a member of the Board of Directors.

Matt Leona: V.P., Finance, 39 years old. Leona earned a BS in Electrical Engineering from Case Western Reserve and an MBA from Harvard. He went to work for IBM directly out of Harvard, in finance and pricing. He stayed with IBM for several years before joining and working with an investment banking firm for one year. His next job involved venture capital work at General Electric. While at GE he invested GE's and his own money in Datavision. He became a member of the Board of Directors in 1975, left GE to join Datavision.

Tom Sisco: Manager, Customer Service, 34 years old. Sisco earned a BA from St. Anselm's College, went to work in the Peace Corps and then spent 8 years as a manager at the United Parcel Service Company. Sisco and Campbell were neighbors and friends. Sisco was personally recruited to Datavision by Campbell.

EXHIBIT 5 Datavision (A): Personnel Profile

R. David Brennan: 38 years old. Brennan received a BA in psychology at the College of Wooster, an MS, and a Ph.D. from Case Institute of Technology. His Ph.D. was in Organizational Behavior. In 1966 he began working as a self-employed consultant in the area of organizational training and development. He has worked in a variety of settings including large and small businesses, government and community agencies, and educational and health institutions. Simultaneously, since 1967, Brennan has been on the faculty of the Whittemore School of Business and Economics at the University of New Hampshire. He has taught a variety of courses in the organizational behavior area. In 1977 he was promoted to full professor. At that time he decided to work primarily as a consultant but is still affiliated with the University as an adjunct professor. Brennan has had additional business experience. Between 1973 and 1975, while on leave from UNH, Brennan was employed by Digital Equipment Corporation in Switzerland as the European Personnel Manager.

EXHIBIT 6 Datavision (A): Consolidated Operations Report, Quarterly Comparison

	Second Quarter FY 78			Second Quarter FY 77		
	Budget	Actual	Percent	Budget	Actual	Percent
Revenues						
System and Upgrade Revenue	$4,466,000	$3,986,298	90.4	$3,300,000	$3,294,611	89.6
Customer Funded Eng. Revenue	478,000	423,405	9.6	467,000	382,761	10.4
Total	4,944,000	4,409,703	100.0	3,767,000	3,677,372	100.0
Less Discounts—Syst. & U/G	401,000	224,445	4.9	343,500	319,006	8.2
—Cust. Fund. Eng.	43,000	21,659	.5			
Net AGS Revenue	4,500,000	4,163,599	82.8	3,423,500	3,358,366	86.9
Customer Services	774,000	800,249	15.9	434,000	438,160	11.3
Application Development	138,000	58,526	1.2	52,500	66,586	1.7
Color Plotter	37,000	-	-	-	-	-
Other Revenue	-	4,693	.1	-	4,584	.1
Total Revenue	5,449,000	5,027,067	100.0	3,910,000	3,867,696	100.0
Cost of Sales						
System and Upgrade at Standard	1,696,000	1,677,761	33.4	1,400,000	1,441,325	37.3
Manufacturing Variances	-	106,944	2.1	-	(53,933)	(1.4)
Customer Funded Engineering	304,000	257,798	5.1	231,000	254,251	6.6
Customer Services	810,568	764,647	15.2	423,918	422,995	10.9
Application Development	103,352	32,375	.7	52,987	57,562	1.5
Color Plotter	97,503	111,299	2.2	-	-	-
Total Cost of Sales	3,011,423	2,950,824	58.7	2,107,905	2,122,200	54.9
Gross Profit	2,437,577	2,076,243	41.3	1,802,095	1,745,496	45.1

Operating Expenses						
Engineering						8.1
Marketing						16.4
Corporate Administration						7.7
Other	1,797,620		1,829,601	36.4	1,223,754	1,246,904
						–
						32.2
Income from Operations	639,957		246,642	4.9	578,341	498,592	12.9
Interest Expense	79,600		41,059	.8	84,100	83,639	2.2
Foreign Currency Loss (Gain)	–		8,445	.2	–	(3,397)	(.1)
Income before Tax Provision	560,357		197,138	3.9	494,241	418,350	10.8
Provision for Income Taxes	297,000		135,000	2.7	243,000	209,000	5.4
Net Income	$ 263,357		$ 62,138	1.2	$ 251,241	$ 209,350	5.4
Net Income Per Share	$ .14		$ .03		$ .18	$ .15	

Wood Structures, Inc.

Late in the summer of 1988, owner-founder Bill Alcorn and his management group at Wood Structures, Inc. (WSI) were concerned about the turnover problem in WSI's manufacturing organization, and particularly in its Saco plant. It was the busiest period of the year for builders of prefabricated wood trusses, and despite a full production schedule with significant overtime hours at both WSI plants, the company was having trouble keeping up with sales and delivery schedules.

WSI's core product lines, stock (25%) and custom-designed (75%) prefabricated wood floor and roof trusses, were particularly vulnerable to the business cycle and to fluctuations (both seasonal and cyclical) in the construction industry. Given these conditions, Bill Alcorn considered it fortunate that WSI had rarely experienced a slump (other than the seasonal dips that occurred every year) in nearly twenty years of operations. By 1988 the Maine-based company with plants in Biddeford and Saco was recognized as one of the leading wood truss producers in the United States and was far bigger than its closest competitor in New England. At $20 million annually, sales had reached an all-time high. (*Exhibit 1* tracks the growth in WSI's sales during the 1980s. *Exhibit 2* gives comparative data on wood truss producers in New England and nationwide.)

Now, however, Alcorn was worried about WSI's ability to remain prosperous through the next wave of the economy. The manufacturing organization was having great difficulty meeting demand during the boom period of 1988, and management saw turnover as the most important cause of the problem. Unless they could get control over attrition on the shop floor, the management group feared increasingly severe delivery delays and quality slip-ups on the work that did get done. If that happened, it might jeopardize what Alcorn considered one of WSI's greatest advantages: the loyalty of lumberyard distributors who consistently recommended WSI products over the competition.

THE TURNOVER PROBLEM

Employment levels had always fluctuated during the year as WSI hired seasonal workers to meet the increase in demand during the summer construction period (*Exhibits 3* and *4*). Turnover had typically been higher in the busy peak months, when new hires and seasonal workers showed a tendency to leave before the season was over. But this year, the quit rate among production employees appeared to be even worse than in the past. WSI was now hiring three production people for every one who stayed. The personnel director had warned Alcorn that the company risked exhausting the local labor pool unless

Research Associate Colleen Kaftan prepared this case under the supervision of Professor Louis B. Barnes as the basis for class discussion rather than to illustrate either effective or ineffective handling of an administrative situation.

more of the new hires chose to stay through the busy season.

Almost a hundred people had left the manufacturing organization in the first six months of 1988, half of them within their first two to three weeks on the job. Some seemed to quit as soon as their first few paychecks gave them spending money for the summer. Others left—as some had every year—for outdoor construction jobs as soon as the weather made these available. Still others walked out when the work proved more strenuous and regimented than they had expected.

But the problem was not limited to new hires: 22 core, year-round employees had also resigned between November of 1987 and June of 1988. At least five of those had been lured away from WSI early in the production season by a newly established competitor that was offering slightly higher wages for similar jobs in a nearby town. Bill Alcorn was distressed to discover that some of those employees had been recruited by a former supervisor while the supervisor was still on WSI's payroll.

Several years earlier, Alcorn and the WSI management group had been caught completely unawares by a bitter—and successful—unionizing campaign that started during peak season. A certain animosity had colored the relationships between the shop floor and the office ever since, although most people agreed that the original force of the anger had subsided on both sides. Alcorn himself had maintained some distance from the plant, in part because he was trying to step back from day-to-day management of the company by delegating more responsibility to Vice President Frank Paul and his management team. (See *Exhibit 5* for an organization chart.)

Bill recognized his detachment was making it hard for him to figure out the cause—or a solution—for the turnover problem. He told the casewriter that he was open to any discoveries she might make in talking with employees throughout the company.

COMPANY BACKGROUND

Bill Alcorn spoke of WSI as his family. The company had its origins in Bill's 1963 decision to move to Maine, where he could live in beautiful surroundings while still applying his Masters degree from the Yale School of Forestry by working with a lumber company in Biddeford. (His previous employer had offered him a product research position in an East-coast industrial metropolis, and the young Alcorn family declined the move.)

Three years later, Bill and his new employer formed a partnership to market prefabricated homes being promoted by Weyerhauser Company. When Weyerhauser pulled out of that market after the recession of 1969–70, Alcorn and his partner decided to stay in business as WSI. Bill became sole proprietor in 1977, when he built the Biddeford plant and bought out his partner in an amicable separation.

Alcorn made two key strategic decisions in the early days of the company. First, WSI would concentrate on trusses as a single and developing aspect of the prefabricated housing industry. (In the early 1980s the company began distributing a fuller line of related products, but trusses remained its core manufacturing business.) Second, WSI trusses would be distributed solely through lumberyards. People close to the company thought both decisions had served WSI well, at least in the early stages. By concentrating on trusses, WSI had developed an expertise that its more diversified competitors took longer to achieve. And by resisting the temptation to sell directly in competition with lumberyards, WSI had cultivated loyalty in an extended, if informal, dealer network while avoiding the expense of an in-house marketing organization.

WSI's business environment grew more complex as the prefabricated truss industry developed. Rising job site labor costs and the scarcity of framers able to build complex structures encouraged contractors to choose prefabricated trusses over on-site construction. The continuous stiffening of building code requirements added to the importance of high-quality structural materials. At the same time, the availability of better trusses accelerated the move towards more complex and interesting floor, roof, and ceiling designs. Truss manufacturers were forced to follow the trend in order to stay competitive.

With the advent of the mini-computer in the late 1970s, much of the design, specification, and approval work could also be done in-house by truss manufacturers. WSI's own design department, established in 1981, soon gained a reputation for quality in the industry. By 1988 design work was one of the factors that differentiated WSI products in an otherwise commodity-like market.

Product quality and service responsiveness were other factors that differentiated WSI trusses from the competition. Lumber dealers cited the company's reputation for top-grade materials, quality assembly work, and quick on-site repairs when problems did occur in recommending that contractors choose WSI trusses even at slightly higher prices and occasionally longer delivery times than other suppliers'.

Along with the favorable reputation came growth. After a series of expansions brought the Biddeford plant to the maximum possible capacity for the site (and with no other land available nearby), a second plant was opened in Saco (some 10 minutes to the north) in May of 1986. The Biddeford

crews continued to build most of WSI's stock roof and floor trusses, while the new Saco plant housed the more complex custom roof truss fabrication and overflow stock work from Biddeford.

The Manufacturing Organization

The plants themselves were similar in design: large open-plan construction sheds—cold in the winter and hot in the summer—filled with an array of tables and machines on which the various trusses were prepared and built. Based on shop orders from the design department, the sawyers selected and cut wood (which was delivered by the forklift drivers from the yard) for the trusses to be built. A "catcher" retrieved the cut pieces as they came off the saw and, after a minimal inspection, sorted them by length and angle of cut. The forklift driver then assembled all the pieces required for a specific order (including cut lumber and metal fastening plates) and delivered them either to presplicers or to the tables and presses on which the trusses would be built. There, work crews of two or three builders set up the job and did the actual assembly work. When a truss was ready, the workers removed it from the machines either manually or using hydraulic lifters, and sent it out to the yard.

In the busy season the metallic sounds of saws whined over the pounding of hammers and hydraulic presses. Forklifts moved constantly around the plants. Work in process was piled near every station. Outside, the yard people sorted and stacked lumber, and bundled trusses for delivery as they came out of the plant. Every morning the WSI drivers lined up to load the day's deliveries.

Nonmanufacturing space at Saco was limited to a reception area in the foyer, a plant manager's cubicle with a window facing the shop floor, and a lounge/lunchroom that could also be used for employee meetings. At Biddeford, Production Manager John Applin sat in a glass-walled office that jutted out over the shop floor.

The Office Organization

The sales, design, quality control, and administrative functions were located in an elegant complex of offices superimposed on the Biddeford building. Bill Alcorn himself had chosen most of the striking collection of art—all done in wood and related materials—that adorned the office area. He had also planned the unusual office shapes and the ingeniously exposed roof trusses that reminded visitors of the work going on below.

In contrast to the shop workers, the "office people" had remarkably low turnover rates at WSI. The average length of employment among 65 staff and management personnel in 1988 was seven years. Office employees usually cited the beauty of their facility as one reason they liked their jobs. Most of them also mentioned the compensation and benefits (especially health insurance). Several said they appreciated the feeling of mutual respect they got from working closely with management within their own departments, but did not feel the same closeness with management or employees from other departments, even though their offices were fairly near each other.

Vulnerability and Planning

When New England's condominium boom started softening in 1988, WSI's sales mix again illustrated the company's vulnerability to changes in the construction industry. The shift to smaller projects with one-of-a-kind designs increased the design component in any given order, while shortening production runs, requiring more frequent production downtime for set-ups, and limiting the possibilities for long-range planning of delivery schedules.

The trend seemed to reinforce an already-existing tendency for strain between departments such as sales and design. In one common dispute, for example, designers resented salespeople taking orders without getting all the data necessary for the building code approval process. Salespeople, in turn, thought designers were being stubborn and/or disorganized with their repeated requests for further information, which forced the salespeople to make multiple calls to the customer even after the sale had been concluded. A few efforts at cross-training the sales representatives had not improved matters much, nor had a two-year shift that placed some designers directly in the sales department. The result was an uneasy truce (punctuated by occasional shouting matches) in which the departments usually steered clear of each other.

At the executive level, the difficulty of predicting such changes in the economy or their likely impact on WSI led Alcorn, Frank Paul, and others to see planning as an almost futile activity for WSI. They discussed popular approaches regularly in meetings of the Executive and Management Committees (committee membership is noted in *Exhibit 5*) but did not often find ways to apply them in their work. (One member of the Executive Committee suggested that finding applications was not a fruitful activity in committee meetings. In his candid assessment, the committees functioned more as honorific positions than as decision-making bodies.)

Management had undertaken a major strategic study with a consulting group in the early 1980s. Most executives kept a copy of that study in a desk drawer. They had adopted some of its findings (such as the addition of distributed products to smooth WSI's sales curve) but did not otherwise seem to think about strategy in their daily activities.

When the executive group did articulate a program, follow-through often fizzled after a few initial efforts. Many people—Bill Alcorn included—found it more appropriate to operate in reactive, "firefighting " mode, responding speedily to the demands of the market.

For example, they preferred to treat short-term shop scheduling as a way of avoiding inventory buildups in product lines that might not move in a downturn or if customer preferences changed. The most complex custom-designed trusses, of course, could never be kept in inventory; every order had to be scheduled as an exception.

Another consultant had designed a short-term shop scheduling and incentive compensation system in 1984. That program was still very much in evidence at both plants, and was the principal method for getting trusses built at WSI. All designs became detailed work orders through a system that occupied a substantial portion of the design staff's time. Despite these multiple efforts, employees at all levels of the organization agreed that scheduling problems had probably contributed to the breakdown of the WSI family in 1983.

THE UNION

In 1983, a unionizing campaign began with the firing of a second shift employee on a hot summer night. Faced with a large backlog of work to be completed for shipping the next morning, a night supervisor demanded that all the night assemblers work overtime until the order was completed. Rich Grant, a veteran assembler who had already been on the job for twelve hours, categorically refused. Tempers flared, the supervisor told Grant not to come back if he left, and the next morning Grant and his wife Bev (also an employee) started looking for ways of bringing in a union at WSI.

News of the campaign didn't reach management for a month. By that time Rick Grant had appealed his dismissal and was brought back on board with full pay for the two weeks he had been off. Production Manager John Applin attributed the incident to the difficulties of working under the pressure of fast delivery schedules, the heat, and a generally understandable overstepping of bounds by the supervisor on duty.

Bill Alcorn was shocked to see the first outside organizers at WSI's gate in early

September. He considered their intrusion to be a direct, personal affront and a violation of his "family" at WSI. Nevertheless, in talking personally with old-time employees, he realized that both he and his management team had, in fact, been out of touch and that supervisory practices might occasionally have gotten out of control. At one point he wondered if a union could help establish clarity, openness and a greater sense of routine in the plants.

Contact with outside union representatives soon eliminated that hope, however. Bill was left with a sense of outrage at what he perceived as the outside organizers' self-promoting exploitation of the problems at WSI. He hired the most combative labor lawyer available and vowed to stay personally involved in the fight. At one meeting in which workers were airing complaints about erratic and unfair supervisory practices, for example, Bill stood up and declared his full support for the supervisors at WSI.

When the certification vote passed by less than ten votes, Bill Alcorn resolved to get the toughest contract he and his lawyer could negotiate. By all reports, they succeeded. The lawyer himself contended it was the most strongly pro-management contract he had ever seen.

Years later, employees from both management and the shop floor still recalled Alcorn's bitterness at the appearance of the union. Several executives said he seemed to take the campaign even harder than he had his own divorce, some years earlier. Even supervisory and plant management personnel felt his anger over the incident, and some felt that he held them personally responsible for the union's presence at WSI.

Bev Grant, whose initial phone calls had brought the organizers in, still worked at WSI in 1988 and still claimed to feel a strong sense of loyalty for Bill Alcorn and for the company. However, she recalled:

I know they were promising us things would change, but how could we take a chance at that point? I like Bill Alcorn and I know he took it very personally—I felt like explaining it to him sometimes, like asking him, "What would you do in our place?" He came around and talked with us, said they'd been out of touch, but how could he promise us it wouldn't happen again?

The Situation in 1988

Despite the basic similarities of their operations, the Saco plant had played the role of "poor cousin" to the Biddeford shop almost from its opening. Several Biddeford-based managers admitted they simply did not travel to the Saco plant as often as they thought they should: "The six miles distance might just as well be six million miles." Fax machines, direct phone lines, and courier service had not sufficed to bridge the gap, in part because there were always more than enough fires to put out in Biddeford.

Saco's productivity and turnover records were consistently below those at Biddeford. Most people thought that drug and morale problems were worse at Saco too. Some employees, however, said they preferred working at Saco because they were free of management's "surveillance" there.

Second shift crews at both plants almost always underperformed their counterparts on the first shift. Shift rivalries often flared when one group (usually the second shift) was expected to finish up a work order left over from the previous shift. During the summer months in particular, this often meant that second shift workers would be expected to work overtime without advance notice to finish an order for early morning shipping. First shift workers sometimes arrived to discover their counterparts had not cleaned the work area before punching out the previous night. They retaliated, on occasion, by leaving incomplete set-ups or otherwise making life difficult for the second shift's return.

The broadly-understood "pecking order," then, put Biddeford first shift at the top and Saco second shift at the bottom. Within each shift there also seemed to be a hierarchy of jobs, with sawyers being at the top and yard/support people in last place. Workers rarely moved between shifts or jobs. Most groups claimed to prefer their own positions to any other in the company. Management wasn't quite sure why. The explanation most commonly heard among shop workers for Saco's "inferior" performance was the inherent difficulty of the manufacturing tasks there (even though the production sequences were the same).

Biddeford's stock roof and floor trusses entailed relatively straightforward assembly work on readily accessible tables. By contrast, the more complex and often larger custom trusses made at Saco required more sophisticated set-ups and, for the bigger pieces, a grueling regime of climbing on and off the three-foot high tables where the worker had to kneel while hammering the component parts together. The materials used for Saco's larger trusses were also heavier and clumsier to handle. In the words of one Saco assembler:

Why do people quit? Because the job *sucks*—it's repetitive, it's boring, and it's *hard*. But the benefits are pretty good and the pay's ok if you're willing to work hard. Some of the guys don't have that hardworking attitude but a lot of us here do.

WSI's processes were considered to be among the most automated in the industry, and management was always interested in new ways of making the job easier—provided they did not significantly increase what Bill Alcorn saw as an already comparatively heavy capital burden. Many small but effective changes had been introduced through an employee suggestion system, in which the author of a suggestion received $50 and a WSI jacket for proposing an easily-implemented improvement. The shop workers generally appreciated this, but many said that further improvements could and should take place. A few even stated that they would withhold an idea for a simple improvement until they were certain of receiving a reward for submitting it to the suggestion system. "We don't want to let them rip us off for our ideas," one Saco assembler put it, "so sometimes we wait until it's time for another reward, or split a suggestion into two parts, or figure out another way to make sure we get our due."

Hiring and Training

The annual hiring season usually began in late April or early May, as both plants geared up for the summer building season. Unfortunately, the Saco plant seemed to draw from the same labor pool as Biddeford, and both towns were experiencing hiring competition from nearby cities, including Portsmouth, only 30 miles away. WSI's typical new hire was between 18 and 23 years old, often with some construction or factory experience, but rarely both. Less than 5% of the applicants and about 1%–2% of those hired were women.

New hires learned about their jobs from their co-workers. A new assembly worker joined two more experienced members of an already existing team, who were then expected to train the new worker over his first two weeks on the job. The veteran workers received their incentive pay as usual and were not charged for the new hire's contribution during the first week. The new worker counted as half a crew member in the incentive calculation for the second week. (Incentive pay was available to the new hire himself only after 90 days on the job.)

With no standardized procedures or directives, the training system yielded varying degrees of success depending on the methods employed by the work crews to which new hires were introduced. Some assembly groups at either plant accused others of exploiting the new hires—using them as errand boys and offering virtually no real introduction to the job—in order to increase their own incentive pay during the first two weeks' grace period. (One supervisor called the training system "learning by your ordeal.") Existing crews often expressed resentment at being broken up to include trainees. And the fact that trainees often moved to other work crews after their first two weeks seemed further to limit some crews' interest in training good co-workers.

A number of veterans remembered their own training as more effective than the current practice. Some had spent a week in introductory classes; others had learned on the job after a cursory review of plant procedures. Still others believed that training by work crews could be more effective if practiced more uniformly. Indeed, some of the best-performing assemblers had received only on-the-job training under the current system. Comparisons were hard to make as there were no hard data showing that any one method produced better or more committed workers than others.

The Incentive/Compensation System

Shop orders and bonus pay Some employees loved the scheduling/incentive system. Others hated it. Almost all considered it a critical part of their weekly pay. In the right jobs, the fastest workers could earn as much as $150 per week or more in bonus pay.

Sawyers, catchers, and presplicers received bonus pay whenever they exceeded their scheduled production volume. Assemblers' incentive pay was based on quality as well as quantity. Indirect workers (including forklift drivers) got an average of the bonuses earned on the machines they served, to a maximum of one dollar per hour.

Most people on the shop floor were fully aware at virtually any time of the week where they stood in terms of bonus pay. Many enjoyed competing with co-workers and with their own previous records. A few assemblers claimed that an idle machine in summer meant workers had figured out they would earn more by doing jobs on other machines—even if those machines were slower or less efficient than the unused machines.

Almost all shop workers considered the cap on indirect workers' incentive unfair. The assembly crews also complained about the lack of a quality component to the sawyers' and presplicers' incentives. The sawyers countered that their greatest contribution came from constant use of the saws, and that the catchers' initial quality check *should* be subject to the work crews' further inspection, even if it slowed the assemblers down.

Many assemblers resented the random quality control inspections and observed that catching problems after the fact was unproductive. Some also argued that the random checks were used to discriminate against crews and shifts that management wanted to harass. The quality control people attributed the suspicions to the inspectors' unpredictable routines as well as their independence from either plant.

A new manager of quality control hoped to change the defensive relationship between his department and the shop floor:

It's an untenable situation, adversarial to the highest degree. They see quality control as trying to reach into their back pockets, so their attitude is, "We'll get them before they get us." I would scrap the short-term piece rate system completely. It's no longer an incentive anyway, because they see it as a given part of their income.

Asked what they thought would happen if the incentive system was dismantled, however, most of the plant employees gave variations of the same answer: "The pace would slow down. We wouldn't work as hard. We'd build fewer trusses."

Hourly wages The hourly pay scales also made some people happy and irritated others. Recent hires often appreciated the chance to move rapidly up the wage scale. On the other hand, longer term workers sometimes complained that they had reached the peak of their earning power and could no longer expect advancement after about three and a half years on the job. (Starting pay was $6.35/hour and the maximum was $9.03/hour.) Older employees and those with family obligations thought WSI's relatively liberal benefits (including comprehensive health insurance) compensated somewhat for the narrow wage range, but the majority of young, single workers were less interested in the "intangible" benefits.

The overall compensation package was part of the union contract, now in its second three-year iteration. By mid-1988 even Bill Alcorn was beginning to think the favorable contract wage levels might be pricing WSI out of the Biddeford-Saco labor market. His concerns were underscored by the discovery that several of the former employees who had left WSI for the new competitor claimed to have done so for the slightly higher hourly rates the new company was offering.

THE UPSTAIRS-DOWNSTAIRS SCHISM

When asked to explain WSI's high turnover rate, one assembler suggested that the distance between "upstairs" management and the "downstairs" shop floor workers was to blame:

I've often wondered why people aren't proud to say they work at WSI when you run into them on the street. We're hard workers and we usually try to do our best. But I guess we sort of resent management in a lot of ways, and they don't like us very much either. A long time ago, I overheard a conversation between two managers, and they called the people downstairs "the animals." Now I guess it's almost the other way around—we end up feeling the same way about the supervisors and the people upstairs.

Laborers often accused supervisors of inconsistency and favoritism. A commonly heard remark on the shop floor was that "it's rare to get two supervisors to agree on anything." Perhaps as a result, according to one shop steward, both workers and supervisors tended to stick too literally to the terms of the contract:

Some of the supervisors take things too seriously. They manage by the book—they'll fire you the first time you do anything wrong. The contract makes it very clear when you can do this, and I guess they're afraid if they let anything slide then everybody's going to take advantage. But they also use the contract to make themselves look better—they'll keep a guy in the yard because they like his performance there, even though the guy might want to move inside and make a little more money. Technically they have the right to do that, but it sure doesn't make the guy feel good about his job.

Another steward insisted that the contract was still entirely necessary, if only to combat some supervisors' tendency to manage by exception:

They can always work around the rules, make exceptions for their favorites. Like the perfect attendance award—you get $500 for a perfect record. One guy used a sick day last year but his supervisor fudged the records so he'd get the money. Everybody knew about it, but in order for the union to take action you have to be able to prove it.

One supervisor admitted that workers might perceive her decisions as arbitrary and/or inconsistent. However, she went on to describe the communications gap from the supervisors' perspective:

As a laborer I thought the plant manager was a snot, but when I got to be a supervisor I realized he has his own problems too. I feel a little closer to management now but I can still see how people on the floor imagine things and get mad when they think we're being unfair. We need more communication. The people upstairs are working together and most of the people downstairs are working together. But the people upstairs aren't working with the people downstairs.

When "upstairs people" did come down to the shop floor, they were not always appreciated by supervisors nor by the workers themselves. One supervisor noted:

I hate it when somebody from upstairs comes in and changes the rules just to be nice—like they changed the whole floor layout just to help one guy, and then as supervisor, I had to try and explain it to everybody else. They think they're being responsive but they're really just being inconsistent.

A sawyer from Biddeford seemed to concur:

I wish more things were focused on the business itself. They spend too much time trying to win the humanitarian of the year award—they fluff you up so much—but I want to focus on making money. I just want to get to work.

A second supervisor had difficulty finding a common thread in management's frequent shifts of emphasis in the manufacturing organization:

There's no sense of continuity—we don't have any real job description as supervisors and they keep changing what they want us to look at. In summer it's production, production, production. Then they want us to talk about quality for a few months, and after that it'll be reducing indirect costs, so we cut out preventive maintenance—but that'll affect our capacity to produce the following summer. Or they get on a kick about housekeeping or safety. I once gave a huge lecture on safety and the next day they had one of my guys up on a ladder on the forklift to put a radio antenna on the office roof.

Still another supervisor attributed WSI's problems chiefly to the failings of upper management:

I think upper management's job is to set the direction for the future. But upper management has so many problems here that they never have time to set the course. Most of them have no prior executive experience, they just moved up from the shop floor. Nobody procrastinates like they do on big decisions. They're too busy just trying to run the place.

MANAGEMENT AT WSI

If WSI was a family for Bill Alcorn, it was also among his favorite hobbies. His attempts at stepping back from daily management masked a profound degree of caring about the company, its obligations to employees and customers, and its chances for survival when threatened by a fluctuating economy. Several executives said that Bill's personal style and the "home grown" nature of the business set the tone for relationships throughout the management organization. Except for a few more recent outside professional hires, most of senior management had spent the majority of their careers at WSI.

Frank Paul, for example, took a summer job as a driver in 1970 and then worked part time in the plant while attending accounting classes at the University of Maine during the school year. Later he moved into the office one day a week to do bookkeeping, continuing to work on the shop floor and make deliveries on other days. By 1978, Frank was named Vice President and second in command to Bill Alcorn. That arrangement was still in place a decade later.

Both Bill and Frank described the communication system that had evolved between them as unusually close—albeit largely limited to business matters. Frank tended to be blunt and occasionally caustic in encounters with his own subordinates, while Bill seemed at times almost inscrutable to everyone but Frank. The ability to "read Bill" was particularly important to Frank:

I've always been a little confused as to why Bill put up with my way of doing things. It's impossible to imagine we could be alike, given how varied our backgrounds are. I grew up in a tenement here in Biddeford and he's from a wealthy St. Louis family. When his main concern was finding a place to board his horse, mine was finding a place to play football out of the street.

Probably it works because I've learned how to read him so well. I feel I can even interpret his body movements—know from his smallest comments what's important to him. I decide I'm going to satisfy him but then I have my own way of accomplishing what he wants.

Bill, too, commented on Frank's ability to pick up the smallest signals, from dress and hair length to more substantive issues affecting the company:

In many ways Frank is the antithesis of me, although he has tried to emulate me around some things. He's a street fighter, very smart and quick to learn, and he has no trouble talking about money or other things I feel very reticent about. He's extremely sensitive in picking up my signals and he usually gets it right. Maybe that has hampered my development—if he were denser I'd have been forced to be more direct in communicating.

Bill thought that Frank's and the other managers' career patterns meant they knew the organization inside out and had long-standing experience in dealing with each other. At the same time, he sometimes wondered whether more outside experience would have given them greater confidence in their abilities on the job and more opportunities for personal growth. As Frank put it, they were comfortable but not always challenged, and not entirely sure they could "make it on the outside." Another veteran said his colleagues were so averse to long-term or strategic thinking that they sometimes "started fires" just to have something immediate to do. Several employees at all levels commented that the executive group at WSI seemed to function as a collection of separate departments rather than a unified company.

A few managers claimed that a "leadership gap" was responsible for the lack of a strong common focus among WSI manage-

ment. Some thought this arose from the tradition of "doing whatever needed to be done" without regard for job descriptions or divisions of responsibility during the early days at the company. Others suggested that Bill Alcorn's own management style allowed people to avoid taking initiative or following through on most significant projects. For example, no one seemed to feel directly accountable for a $200,000 electronic saw that had been ordered for Saco almost two years earlier but that was still not functioning properly in 1988.

Frank Paul described other aspects of his boss's "familial" approach to managing WSI:

On the one hand, we know he's not likely to fire anyone unless we do something extremely wrong or immoral. On the other hand, we resent having to go to him for approval of what seem to be minor things. If we have an inner fire about something, we sometimes go around him to avoid having to justify the details. A long time ago, for instance, I forged his signature on a check for an office party he didn't really want to have. Six months later he finally mentioned it to me, almost in passing, saying he didn't like my doing that.

I probably should have been fired on the spot, but I knew even then you could go a long way before he'd let you go.

We also use Bill as an excuse sometimes. If he questions a small part of somebody's proposal, that person may just drop the whole idea, and nothing will get implemented. It's like the President asking for a line item veto, and the Congress insisting on all-or-nothing acceptance of a whole budget package.

Or we use him as a crutch, sharing the blame for our delays and failures if he's been involved in the decision. In that sense he tends to enable people not to be successful: if we can't fail, then how can we succeed?

Some saw Alcorn as unwilling to surrender control to the management group but also—perhaps paradoxically—uncomfortable about imposing a strong sense of direction. That description seemed at least partially accurate to Bill. In recent years he had sent Frank Paul, John Applin, and other executives to management development programs to help alleviate the gap. He had also forced himself to leave for extended vacations, putting Frank solely in charge during the busiest season. And he had attended a program at Harvard Business School that took him away for three weeks in May, three years in a row. Still, he was not yet entirely comfortable passing the baton. One critical question remained open in his mind: whether Frank and the other members of management were simply trying to understand and follow his directives, or whether they actually had the same "deep down concern" and sense of responsibility for the company that he had.

WHAT NEXT?

Looking back in 1988, Bill Alcorn talked of 1983 as a year of "union and reunion." He had attended his 30th high school and 25th college reunions, "lost" his WSI family to the union and, on the last day of the year, also lost his father to a long battle with cancer. Five years later he was marking the twenty-second anniversary of the company, and wondering what the next 5—or 20—years would bring.

Casewriter conversations with workers suggested that there was still a sense of loyalty among many production workers. Most claimed to like their jobs and immediate work groups best of those available in the company, despite the underdog label that many positions carried. Even the relatively low pay levels did not seem to be a major deterrent. One worker said:

They keep trying to blame everything on the money. I don't think it's the buck—it's respect and dignity. They need to make it so the people want to come in here every day.

From another:

WSI could be performing at least 50% better if people could work better together. And all that would take would be for management to pay a little more attention to us. They have a hurry up attitude for customer orders but nobody's hurrying to take care of us.

Some complaints were aimed at the union rather than at management, and there was even talk of a possible decertification campaign. A number of workers in both plants said that the union did little more than collect its dues (the agency shop agreement required employees to pay dues whether they actually joined the union or not). "We'd vote the union out in a minute if we had guarantees we wouldn't get screwed again," declared one veteran assembler. Nevertheless, the shop stewards still believed they were performing a valuable service. Some claimed to be helping ease the strains between management and the workers. According to one:

The company could solve a lot more of this upstairs-downstairs split if they worked at it. Most of the potential grievances we have can be worked out just by sitting down and talking the problem through. Usually it's not a lot more than a case of hurt feelings. I've had four grievances so far this year, and none of them went through because I get people together and solve them. Whether you like the union or not, nobody can deny that this place has come a long way. It was a jungle when I started six years ago. At least now we don't have supervisors screaming at people, or throwing hammers at the guys.

If some of the negative circumstances had been eliminated over the years, some more positive aspects seemed to have been lost as well. A few workers recalled almost wistfully the days when WSI had been a smaller, more closely-knit organization. In the words of one:

Bill used to say he thought of WSI as his family. I really wish it could go back to being more that way. It would be good if we could find ways for everybody to get to know each other better, to mix more. Even a volley ball game where we mix up all the teams would be a way to bring people together. One banquet a year just doesn't seem to be enough.

A member of the executive group put it more darkly:

I keep wanting to believe we're going to do things differently, but we've said so many times before that things were going to be better, and then we always slip back into the old ways. When that happens, I imagine getting an eighteen year calendar and putting it up in my office, so I can just cross off the days one by one until my retirement.

All of these voices echoed in the case-writer's ears as she sat in Bill Alcorn's office late one September afternoon. To their chorus, Bill added a question of his own: "So, what do you think we should do about our turnover problem?"

EXHIBIT 1   WSI Sales History, 1980–1988

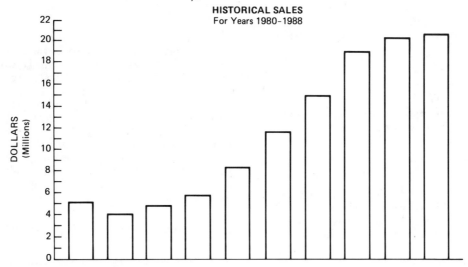

EXHIBIT 2   Comparative Data on Wood Truss Manufacturers: *Automated Builder*'s Top 50 Component Manufacturers (Ranked by Gross Component Sales Dollar Volume)

Rank	Company Name	Sales / Employees / Do you have in-house CAD? If not, do you plan to buy next year? / What is the biggest problem you see inhibiting component sales?	Plants	Roof	Floor	Wall Panels	Doors	Other
				Production for New Res./Cmmcl. Uses; Remodel Res./Cmmcl. Uses				
1	Shelter Systems Group Hainesport, NJ	$49.6 / 500 / Yes / SF contractors unwilling to allow credit for cmpt. labor savings	5	45%	30%	20%	0%	5%
		88%/10% new; 2% commercial remodel						
2	Trussway Houston, TX	$47.3 / 450 / Yes / Improved exposure to available markets	5	43%	33%	2%	0%	22%
		80%/20% new						
3	Carolina Components Corp. Raleigh, NC	$42.8 / 375 / Yes / No comment	9	15%	5%	10%	40%	30%
		80%/10% new; 10% res. remodel						
4	Kimtruss Corp./AMCIL Irvine, CA	$31.0 / 300 / Yes / No comment	5	85%	10%	0%	0%	5%
		70%/25% new; 5% res. remodel						
5	Stark Truss Co. Inc. Canton, OH	$28.0 / 500 / Yes / Education for user	7	94%	5%	1%	0%	0%
		60%/40% new						
6	Shuck Component Systems Inc. Glendale, AZ	$24.0 / 217 / Yes / No comment	1	20%	13%	0%	25%	42%
		84%/14% new; 1%/1% remodel						
7	Automated Bldg. Components Long Lake, MN	$24.0 / 175 / Yes / Lack of component knowledge by framing contractors	3	30%	10%	0%	60%	0%
		55%/43% new; 1%/1% remodel						
8	Latham Lumber & Truss Roseville, CA	$24.0 / 350 / Yes / Hiring and training personnel	N/R	44%	19%	6%	25%	6%
		80%/10% new; 5%/5% remodel						
9	Miron Truss & Comp. Corp. Kingston, NY	$22.0 / 175 / Yes / No comment	3	25%	15%	30%	30%	0%
		70%/20% new; 5%/5% remodel						
10	**Wood Structures Inc. Biddeford, ME**	**$20.0** / **225** / **Yes** / **No comment**	**2**	**75%**	**25%**	**0%**	**0%**	**0%**
		60%/35% new; 2.5%/2.5% remodel						

EXHIBIT 2 *Continued*

Rank	Company Name	Sales Employees / Plants / Do you have in-house CAD? If not, do you plan to buy next year? / What is the biggest problem you see inhibiting component sales?	Plants	Roof	Floor	Wall Panels	Doors	Other
				Production for New Res./Cmmcl. Uses; Remodel Res./Cmmcl. Uses				
11	Century Truss Co. Brighton, MI	$15.5 96 Yes Lack of wood technology awareness by architects	1	81%	19%	0%	0%	0%
		68%/27% new; 4%/1% remodel						
12	Marquette Fabricators Sparta, MI	$15.5 No response No response No comment	2	88%	8%	0%	0%	4%
		83%/15% new; 2% res. remodel						
13	W. Kost Inc. South Elgin, IL	$15.0 175 Yes Increasing our production capability to satisfy demand	3	74%	6%	0%	0%	20%
		95%/4% new; 1% res. remodel						
14	Truss-Com North Highlands, CA	$14.5 250 Yes Increasing degree of difficulty of jobs	3	80%	20%	0%	0%	
		80%/20% new						
15	Blue Ox Industries Inc. Kernersville, NC	$14.2 Yes Inexperienced or inability of builders/contractors to maximize the value and contribution available by using components	4	80%	15%	0%	0%	5%
		70%/20% new; 8%/2% remodel						
16	Causeway Lumber Co. Fort Lauderdale, FL	$14.0 160 Yes Engineering trusses	4	55%	5%	0%	40%	0%
		85%/5% new; 8%/2% remodel						
17	Rigidply Rafters Inc. Richland, PA	$13.0 105 No, plan next year Bad economic news; delivery time; poor quality trusses	2	90%	10%	0%	0%	0%
		20%/30% new; 5%/20% remodel; 25% ag.						
18	Dolan Building Materials Sacramento, CA	$12.5 100 Yes Ability to meet demand; space, machinery limits and skilled labor	1	75%	20%	0%	5%	0%
		95%/4% new; 1% res. remodel						
19	Fagen's Inc. Verona, PA	$11.5 120 Yes Sales; customer knowledge of component advantages	9	35%	10%	15%	35%	5%
		75%/15% new; 5%/5% remodel						
20	Littfin Lumber Co. Winsted, MN	$11.0 120 Yes No response	1	80%	18%	0%	0%	2%
		85%/5% new; 10% res. remodel						
21	Automated Bldg. Cmpts. Inc. North Baltimore, OH	$11.0 170 Yes Contractors can't accurately evaluate component values	3	70%	10%	15%	0%	5%
		50%/50% new						

EXHIBIT 2 *Continued*

Rank	Company Name	Sales Employees Do you have in-house CAD? If not, do you plan to buy next year? What is the biggest problem you see inhibiting component sales?	Plants	Roof	Floor	Wall Panels	Doors	Other
					Production for New Res./Cmmcl. Uses; Remodel Res./Cmmcl. Uses			
22	Raymond Building Supply North Ford Myers, FL	$10.5 185 Yes Lack of knowledge by design professionals	3	59%	10%	0% 80%/10% new; 5%/5% remodel	31%	0%
23	J. C. Snavely & Sons Inc. Landisville, PA	$10.0 250 Yes Attitudes held by design professionals	2	50%	5%	15% 75%/20% new; 3%/2% remodel	10%	15%
24	Nelson Lumber Co. Ltd. Lloydminster, Alberta	$10.0 100 Yes No comment	1	48%	2%	10% 75%/18% new; 6% res. remodel	6%	34%
25	Gang-Nail Components Fontana, CA	$9.5 130 Yes No comment	1	90%	10%	0% 80%/20% new	0%	0%
26	Trusco Inc. Doylestown, OH	$9.1 80 Yes No comment	2	91%	7%	0% 50%/50% new	0%	2%
27	Powell Truss & Door Co. Powell, OH	$9.0 105 Yes No comment	3	64%	3%	0% 70%/23% new; 4%/3% remodel	20%	0%
28	Kent Trusses Ltd. Sundridge, Ontario	$7.5 120 Yes Long delivery times; can't find additional help	1	90%	10%	0% 70%/20% new; 10% res. remodel	0%	0%
29	All-Fab Bldg. Cmpnts. Inc. Winnipeg, MA, Canada	$7.3 120 Yes Code inequities between stick-built and engineered roof systems	2	60%	15%	15% 55%/45% new	0%	10%
30	Allied Bldg. Components Inc. Buckner, KY	$7.2 65 Yes No comment	1	35%	15%	50% 100% new commercial	0%	0%
31	B. & H. Truss Systems Inc. Hesperia, CA	$7.2 100 No, no plans Keeping up with demand	1	95%	5%	0% 90%/10% new	0%	0%
32	Consolidated Lumber & Truss Co. Santa Maria, CA	$7.0 50 Yes No big problems; price competition but can handle	1	95%	5%	0% 90%/5% new; 3%/2% remodel	0%	0%

EXHIBIT 2 *Continued*

Rank	Company Name	Sales Employees / Do you have in-house CAD? If not, do you plan to buy next year? / What is the biggest problem you see inhibiting component sales?	Plants	Roof	Floor	Wall Panels	Doors	Other
				Production for New Res./Cmmcl. Uses; Remodel Res./Cmmcl. Uses				
33	Roberts & Dybdahl Des Moines, IA	$7.0 68 Yes No comment	6	80% 65%/22% new; 5%/8% remodel	20%	0%	0%	0%
34	Porter Building Products Bear, DE	$6.19 0 Yes No comment	1	50% 85%/15% new	25%	12%	0%	13%
35	Lena Builders Inc. Eleroy, IL	$6.11 175 No Lack of contractor acceptance of wall panels	2	35% 90%/10% new	9%	57%	0%	0%
36	Truss Span Corp. Auburn, WA	$6.0 70 Yes No comment	1	75% 50%/50% new	25%	0%	0%	0%
37	Linton Roof Truss Inc. Delray Beach, FL	$6.0 75 Yes Poor cost accounting by truss cos. brings down price structure	1	90% 90%/3% new; 7% res. remodel	10%	0%	0%	0%
38	Atlas Roof Truss Div. Jacksonville, FL	$6.0 100 Yes No comment	3	80% 90%/5% new; 5% res. remodel	15%	0%	0%	5%
39	Southern Bldg. Products Inc. Lake Worth, FL	$6.0 90 Yes No comment	1	80% 90%/10% new	20%	0%	0%	0%
40	O'Connor Lumber Co. Westfield, MA	$6.0 50 Yes Scheduling production to meet customer needs	1	42% 90%/10% new	25%	16.5%	16.5%	0%
41	Villaume Industries Inc. St. Paul, MN	$6.0 90 Yes Plant capacity and man hours	1	90% 100% new res.	10%	0%	0%	0%
42	A. C. Houston Texas North Las Vegas, NV	$6.0 100 Yes Lack of knowledge by design professionals about wood trusses	1	60% 65%/25% new; 5%/5% remodel	30%	0%	0%	10%
43	Associated Truss Co. Mesquite, TX	$5.8 35 Yes Type and design of residential construction	1	80% 20%/73% new; 5%/2% remodel	10%	10%	0%	0%

EXHIBIT 2 *Continued*

Rank	Company Name	Sales / Employees / Do you have in-house CAD? If not, do you plan to buy next year? / What is the biggest problem you see inhibiting component sales?	Plants	Roof	Floor	Wall Panels	Doors	Other
				Production for New Res./Cmmcl. Uses; Remodel Res./Cmmcl. Uses				
44	Idaho/Reno Truss & Component Co. Meridian, ID	$5.6 / 100 / Yes / Competition from steel or laminated wood	2	80%	20%	0%	0%	0%
		55%/35% new; 5%/5% remodel						
45	Madera Component Systems, Inc. Phoenix, AZ	$5.2 / 70 / Yes / No comment	1	75%	25%	0%	0%	0%
		65%/35% new						
46	Wickes Components Mansfield, OH	$5.2 / 45 / Yes / No comment	1	40%	2%	2%	56%	0%
		95% new res.; 5% res. model						
47	Hughes Roof Truss Co. Ltd. Ajax, Ontario	$5.1 / 30 / Yes / Design variety and complexity	1	90%	2%	0%	0%	8%
		40%/30% new; 10%/20% remodel						
48	Universal Builders Corp. Branford, CT	$5.0 / 24 / Yes / No comment	1	40%	60%	0%	0%	0%
		40%/60% new						
49	A-1 Roof Trusses Inc. West Palm Beach, FL	$5.0 / 100 / Yes / No comment	2	85%	15%	0%	0%	0%
		90%/10% new						
50	Comtech Inc. Fayetteville, NC	$5.0 / N/R / Yes / Building plans without adequate structural solutions	N/R	40%	10%	0%	30%	20%
		70%/15% new; 10%/5% remodel						

Source: Automated Builder, September 1988.

EXHIBIT 3 Average Monthly Sales as a Percent of Average Annual Sales

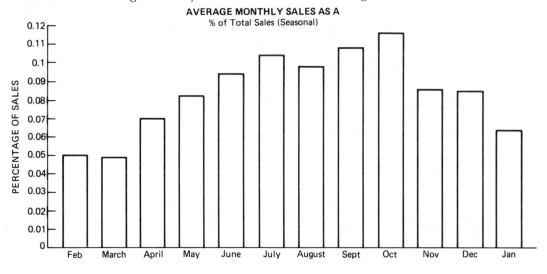

EXHIBIT 4 Monthly Employment Figures, 1987

Month	Total Number of Employees	Women Employees	Production Workers	Production Worker Hours	Production Worker Overtime Hours
January 1987	223	32	147	5,757	349
February	231	34	150	5,587	270
March	228	30	152	5,741	214
April	251	36	169	5,989	241
May	265	41	179	7,436	782
June	275	40	191	7,900	759
July	273	44	185	7,213	747
August	279	49	194	7,922	978
September	276	39	208	8,185	847
October	247	35	182	7,198	691
November	239	36	175	5,806	371
December	199	27	136	5,180	394

EXHIBIT 5 Organization Chart, 1988

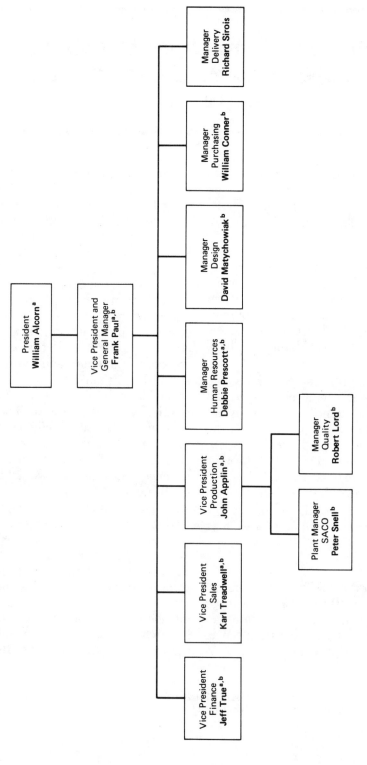

ᵃ Member, Executive Committee
ᵇ Member, Management Committee

Incongruent Hierarchies: Daughters and Younger Sons as Company CEOs

LOUIS B. BARNES

The daughter or younger son who becomes head of the family business must struggle with both self-identity and changing family role expectations. How do they do this?

FATHER CEO: My oldest son is the nicest guy in the world and expects to become president of the company. But, my second son would be better. I also have a younger daughter in the business. I don't know what to do. I've told the kids they may have to decide.

DAUGHTER CEO: From the time I became president eleven years after I joined the company, I was competing with my father—not from my side but from his side. Then the family struggle really started, particularly when my older brother wanted to join the business.

YOUNGER BROTHER CEO: I can't replace him, because he's my older brother, and I have to think my way out of it, or we may have a confrontation.

The three remarks come from three different chief executive officers (CEOs) of three different companies. Each had a painful decision to make from a different perspective. Yet, each was also struggling with the issue of having a daughter or younger son take over as head of the family firm. All three knew that daughters and younger sons do not typically take over family businesses. All three were also learning that special problems face such CEOs. Parental ambivalence was one obstacle. Sibling rivalry was another. Self-esteem was a third.

In a sense, these problems of ambivalence, rivalry, and self-esteem arise because of two incongruent hierarchies. One hierarchy reflects the individual's position within the family. Daughters and younger sons tend to rank lower than older and eldest sons. The other hierarchy represents the individual's position within the business. The higher the position, the better it is. When for one reason or another a daughter or younger son becomes the chief executive officer, the incongruence is obvious. The two status structures conflict.

This hierarchical incongruence can lead to family stress that becomes even more painful when older siblings are actively involved in the business. Although the patterns for daughters differ somewhat from the patterns of younger sons, confusion and ambivalence can reign in both cases. Family members and outsiders do not know which hierarchy to respond to or to rank higher. Is the daughter or the younger son to be treated

Louis B. Barnes, "Incongruent Hierarchies: Daughters and Younger Sons as Company CEOs." In Family Business Review, Vol. 1, No. 1, Spring 1988 (San Francisco: Jossey-Bass Inc.), pp. 9–21.

as the head of the business or as the lesser of family members?

In this paper, I want to explore the tensions that arise from these incongruent hierarchies and the ways in which daughters and younger sons try to reshape their own identities and force the reshaping of other people's expectations. In order to do this, I shall use some of Erik Erikson's (1950) life cycle concepts as a metaphor for the restructuring of family relationships. The data come from taped interviews, group discussions, and teaching cases involving several hundred participants in the Owner/President Management Program, an executive program at the Harvard Business School that I teach.

TRADITIONAL SUCCESSION PATTERNS

Throughout human history, parents have traditionally used hierarchy and primogeniture to set the rules for younger generation succession. The prevailing assumption is that the eldest or only sons are first in line. They should take on the major family obligations and responsibilities. This assumption tends to hold true in both kingdoms and commerce. As one younger son CEO put it: "My older brother's involvement in the business originated when my father died. As we grew up, my brother was the dominant character. He was an all-state football player with a scholarship to the state university. His size was always the conclusion to solving problems as we grew up. The only way I was able to gain anything or progress with anything was to be three or four steps in front of him thinkingwise. Then I never had to confront him or have that obligation of confrontation. When my father died, he left an ongoing construction business with about $10 million of work in progress. We children had to decide what to do with the business. At the meeting after my father's funeral, everybody looked to me to help solve the problems— always directing the questions to me. I felt somewhat out of place, because my older brother, who had only been a field superintendent, was sitting at the head of the table, and I was sitting at the side but always being

confronted with the questions. . . . At that time, the banks were drawing money out of the company at the rate of several hundred thousand dollars a month. Nothing was selling, and so our income was zero. We were bleeding cash phenomenally, and I knew that my brother didn't know how to deal with this problem. And yet, I knew that by his sitting at the head of the table at his house after he had conducted all the funeral arrangements and everything, I would not be able to take control of the company. My uncle suggested at the meeting that we had to have someone in authority. Somebody had to make the decisions. Everybody there agreed, including my brother, that maybe it was okay for me to participate in making the decisions. But, he was going to be the president and CEO."

However, such assumptions do not always work out, nor did they in this company. Eldest sons do not necessarily succeed as CEOs. Sometimes they cannot even assume the CEO position until a dominant father dies. Father-son rivalries and tensions can run high. The failure stories usually involve a father who is unable or unwilling to give up power and an eldest son who is unable to take power. The son's continuing dependency damages his own sense of self-esteem. But, his frustrated struggles to become his own man may also threaten the father. The son's succession may spell the father's obsolescence and irrelevance. Such struggles often end in the son's abandoning the family business until after the dominant father dies. It seems little wonder that only 30 percent of first-generation family businesses remain under family control during the second generation. One poignant comment came from a company president who said, in a study we did some years ago (Barnes and Hershon, 1976, p. 105): "Fortunately, my father died one year after I joined the firm."

DAUGHTERS AND YOUNGER SON CEOs

Powerful as these eldest son cases are, they differ somewhat from the problems that daughters and younger sons face when they become CEOs of a family business. Daughters seem to face the most complex challenges. They may find doubt and skepticism coming both from parents and from siblings. Doubting fathers seem to give a daughter a much harder time when she accedes to power than they do to younger sons. Another male sibling may create difficult obstacles for either his sister or his younger brother. The younger son CEOs with whom I talked often had fathers who were finally ready to yield control, sometimes because they had already had enough fighting with an older son. However, both daughters and younger sons usually encounter a network of rival siblings, not to mention senior business associates, who think they know the business better.

In recent years, primogeniture has become less automatic than it once was. The presence of a favored child may challenge old primogeniture assumptions. Sometimes, the issue is perceived competence. We can see this at work in the comments of the father CEO that head this article. Sometimes, family politics is blamed for unseating an elder son as CEO, as in the Bingham newspaper family of Louisville or the Sebastiani and Mondavi wine families of California.

Today, the choice for CEO in smaller companies may go increasingly to daughters as more managerial women enter the workplace. Some women who hit so-called glass ceilings in large corporations where high-level promotions go only to men head for smaller firms to become first- or second-generation entrepreneurs. On still other occasions, daughters or younger sons start a business and hire an older brother or parents as subordinates.

Under these conditions, family dynamics and hierarchies are upset. The lower-status sibling may appear simultaneously at the top of the company hierarchy and at the bottom of the family hierarchy. Such incongruent structures create tension among family members. The typical response to such tensions is to want the hierarchies to align with each other. Either the daughter or son CEO must gain top dog respect and status from family members, thus upsetting the family hierarchy, or he or she must assume a subservience that ill suits the CEO role in the business hierarchy. A good example of the problem is shown in a now classic teaching case involving the Henry Manufacturing Company (Hershon, 1974).

In the Henry Manufacturing Company, the youngest son became CEO of a second-generation family business in 1970. The company was founded in 1953 by his father. The new CEO was the youngest of ten children and the only one with an M.B.A. degree. Two older brothers had worked for the company, but they left in 1958 when they could not get along with their father. In 1959, the father sought his youngest son's help as general manager and an older son's help as a salesman. The youngest son also had difficulties with his father but became president when his father's health began to fail. At that time, the new CEO also began acquiring majority stock control of the company from his parents at a premium price.

Meanwhile, the older son had become the company's best salesman. His commissions typically reached well into six figures each year—far higher than his youngest brother's salary—as company products grew in value and volume. Still another brother of the new CEO, the oldest son, served as the company lawyer. Both older brothers held seats on the company's board of directors and were minority stockholders.

In 1975, the key managers of the firm strongly urged the CEO to introduce a five-year growth plan. The plan required new investments, overseas expansion, and lower sales commissions once the current salesman contracts expired. Both older brothers opposed the plan, arguing that the company should consolidate its present gains, not expand. The salesman brother then resigned from the board, though not from the sales force. Several months later, he led what was later called the "revolt of the sales force" when he and several other key salesmen threatened to resign unless the present sales commissions remained. The youngest brother CEO refused. The salesmen backed down.

A few months later, during a marathon three-day board meeting, the CEO bought out all the other stockholders. He then fired his oldest brother as company lawyer on conflict-of-interest grounds and began to implement the five-year plan. The salesman brother retired several years later when his sales contract expired. Tensions remained very high between the brothers' families for some time.

The youngest son CEO described this period as one of the hardest times of his life. His managers wanted him to act like an assertive company president. His brothers wanted him to play the submissive younger brother. The decision to expand the business and cut the lopsided sales commissions led to a period of prolonged family stress. Reflecting on the conflict with his brothers, the youngest brother recalled, "It was very, very hard. They're the ones who used to take me to the circus and buy me ice cream cones when I was a kid."

The major revolt in this case was not the one led by the sales force but the one within the youngest son, who faced the role conflict posed by incongruent hierarchies and who, after his father died, challenged his older brothers to a fight that he could win. In a sense, he was struggling to build a new identity both in the eyes of those around him and in his own eyes.

RESTRUCTURING IDENTITY

This restructuring of identity seems to be a pervasive pattern in almost all the cases that I have followed. The daughter or younger son faces a major perceived dilemma. He or she must either move psychologically above his or her lower-status role position in the family hierarchy, or his or her CEO status suffers. It becomes a time either of major transition or of failure. It also involves bringing the incongruent hierarchies into line with each other by gaining new prestige and respect, primarily from the family. That in turn means a shift of behavior and perceptions on the part of the individual, family members, and often outsiders as well.

These evolving struggles fit easily into the pioneering psychosocial concepts of Erik Erikson (1950). Erikson divided the human life cycle into eight phases. As *Figure 1* shows, each phase features a major developmental crisis and tentative resolution into basic strengths and action capabilities. In combination, the developmental phases give us a useful way of thinking about the human life cycle.

According to Erikson, the life cycle begins for the infant with the conflict between trust and mistrust as the infant enters a totally new world. This first crisis evolves into a beginning resolution and strength of hope and a sense of future. The second phase concerns the early childhood crisis that pits autonomy against shame and doubt. Its resolution sets the stage for our patterns of self-control. The third phase involves moving into play age and a crisis of initiative and guilt. The fundamental strength gained during this period is a sense of purpose from which an individual moves on to the school age crisis of industry versus inferiority. The resolution here involves the strength of competence.

But no early crisis is forever resolved. Later critical events in adolescence and adulthood lead us into recurring doubts. We reopen issues that we seem to have resolved and seek new resolutions. Old values and strengths come into question and become new turning points, particularly during and after times of major stress. These are the times when our sense of identity is retested. Given the tensions caused by their incongruent positions, daughter and younger son CEOs try as adults to renegotiate earlier resolutions with parents and siblings. If they do not, they fall back onto the lower rungs of the family hierarchy.

The transition is not easy, and although the data are soft, there are some clear patterns. As I noted earlier, younger sons typically find that their chief adversaries are older brothers unless the older brothers were immobilized early in life by the father's dominance. Both siblings and fathers pose major problems for daughters. Mothers seem to be facilitating for the younger sons and a potential obstacle for the daughter unless the mother herself has had an active career. One CEO daughter talked about the transition struggle with her father in this way: "When I took over the business, it was because my father had no one else to turn to. My mother had died when I was very small. He needed me to take over. He couldn't run the business, and he was getting physically ill worrying about it. Then when I was successful, he felt that it was because he was incapable. He resented that, too. It's like he wanted to say, "I'm still alive. I'm still strong. I'm still daddy." "

All the basic strengths tentatively put to rest during earlier phases of the life cycle are shaken and retested during times like these. Even as an adult, a daughter or younger son CEO finds old resolutions of love, identity, competence, initiative, autonomy, and trust all challenged. These resolutions get most publicly tested in daily business and family interactions. As the CEO demonstrates successful competence, other members of the family hierarchy feel increasingly threatened. In effect, the daughter or younger son is struggling with growing up anew. The peak crisis for our purposes is what Erikson calls industry versus inferiority, which resolves as a sense of competence. But, it is not quite that simple. Daughter and younger son CEOs have to rework still earlier Eriksonian dilemmas with parents and siblings. They struggle with initiative versus guilt, its consequent sense of redefined purpose, and with the even earlier crisis of autonomy versus shame and doubt, in which one's sense of self-control is at stake. Underlying all these is the issue of trust versus mistrust. For the youngest brother CEO described earlier, this meant losing family love and trust in order to gain his managers' trust and their hopes for company growth. His newer identity lay in the autonomy of becoming his own man, defining new purposes like the five-year plan, running a growing business, and acting more like the CEO boss and less like the little brother. He built new patterns of trust, self-control, purpose, and competence with his managers at the heavy cost of family love and affection.

For the daughter or younger son CEO, building a new identity means getting out from under one's low-status role in the family hierarchy. It also means that the expectations, perceptions, and behavior of family members, friends, and even business colleagues must change (Sampson, 1963). The problem becomes one of how to increase congruence for members of the two hierarchies. The secret lies in making behavior patterns feel more congruent to those in both hierarchies. Revised family patterns are the hardest to modify, sometimes because they are so historically entrenched and sometimes because outside friends and associates do not help in the reconfiguration. These outside forces are important. When outsiders simply reinforce old memories and expectations of the family hierarchy, the consequences can be discouraging. One woman CEO put it this way: "I started the company and brought in my mother and my brother as part owners. But my roots come from a grandmother who wheeled and dealed. She bought all this land and was really a business person. My mother inherited that risk-taking ability and passed it on to me. It's interesting, because my brother is a college professor in another city and is a very low risk taker. He was home last month. We talked about the business, and there was a lot of conflict, because he'll never take risks. It puts a lot of strain on the family. Last month, my brother also went to the bank with me, and who do you think the bankers looked to? It's like I'm not even there."

ACTION PATTERNS IN A LEARNING PROCESS

Renegotiating identities involves a family learning process. Self-initiative is the starting point for such a process, but it is not enough by itself. The expectations and behavior of others must also change. That sometimes happens voluntarily, sometimes under duress. Such changes in expectation were shown one day during an intense discussion held by a group of company presidents. One father worried aloud about the day when his daughter might marry an incompetent son-in-law who wanted to manage the family business. The speaker was challenged by other male CEOs, who asked why his capable daughter should not take precedence over her husband in that job. He thought about it and agreed with a great sigh of relief. One of the other men went on to say: "The position of women is changing greatly. I have a father and two brothers in the business with me. My daughter is twelve, and maybe more than anything else because I'm daddy, she says that someday she wants to come in and be president of the company. And I say, 'That's right.' Then she turns around and points to me and says, 'But you're not going to be around when I'm president.' I think that she's got it right all the way."

The difference between the woman CEO and the men was that she was describing expectations and behavior in an ongoing situation, and they were speaking more hypothetically of their expectations for the future. But, the message is clear in both cases. Once the daughter or younger son initiates the struggle to be recognized as competent, something has to give. Sometimes, this comes only after daughters or younger sons "prove" their competence publicly and loudly, thus forcing family members to accept the new status relationship after a prolonged struggle. Such self-initiative demonstrates autonomy, purpose, and competence. CEOs often do this under pressure from their key managers. Sometimes, the transition comes more quietly, although it is still initiated by the daughter or younger son CEO. Sometimes it is the "right" time for such transitions, as when a father's health, age, or increasing wisdom helps the emerging initiative. One woman CEO said, after long years of difficulty with her father, "Things have suddenly changed. In fact, I got my first compliment from him recently. We were in litigation, and I was placed on the stand. When I got off the stand, my father said—the first compliment in my life—'You were terrific. You were really good.' He's never said anything like that to me, no matter what I've accomplished. Everything he's said before was that, 'If you don't do it my way, it won't work. You're not accomplishing anything.'" Six months later, the father was privately giving his daughter increasing responsibility as his health continued to decline, but both maintained the family hierarchy roles in public.

In another case where an older brother was already in the business, a younger son initially perceived a father's withdrawal from the business as weakness. Later on, it seemed more like wisdom: "As the business started to grow, my father very wisely, though I didn't know it at the time, started to step aside so I wouldn't have a conflict with him. In fact, at that time I looked down upon him as a very mediocre man. I thought he wasn't very capable, and indeed he wasn't capable of building the business. My brother, who was five and half years older than I was, became my figurehead father, a rival and a motivator to me. I had to prove that I could be myself and that I could be better than he was. I probably outworked him because of that."

Sometimes, family perceptions change only with time, accomplishment, and outside recognition. The younger son quoted earlier in this article whose brother insisted on being company president after the father's death later noted, "My brother came to me privately about two and one half years ago and asked, 'Why am I the president?' I reminded him of our earlier family meeting and of the fact that he was very adamant about being the president. He said, 'Well, that's silly, and we don't need to do that.' It took two and a half years to get him to that point, though."

However, the relationship between the brothers remained difficult, because they could not agree on the distribution of rewards. The younger brother took more responsibility, brought in the new business orders, and wanted more money for his work than the older brother felt was appropriate. They were headed for the confrontation that the younger brother had never initiated before.

THE ROLE OF HIGH-STATUS FRIENDS

Although help in restructuring hierarchies sometimes comes from within the family, as when a mother mediates on behalf of a younger son or a father voluntarily withdraws, help more often comes from the outside. In a number of cases, a high-status friend from outside the family has helped to smooth the transition (Freilich, 1964). Sometimes, it was a business partner. Sometimes, it was a company director or advisor. Occasionally, it was a friend who could see both sides of the picture and, most important, had the confidence of both parents and siblings. Here is one case where a business partner helped a father to gain perspective on both his sons: In a sales and service company, the father recognized that his younger son was much like himself and had more energy and flair for the business than did an older son who preferred back office administration. The older son was very shy. The father took over the grooming of the younger son, while his partner took on a mentoring role for both boys but paid particular attention to the older son.

Or, take another case where the daughter quoted at the beginning of this article would have given up without the help of a high-status friend who was trusted by all family members. The youngest daughter went from treasurer to president after eleven years in a high-tech business. She was promoted after her father fired a nonfamily heir apparent—something he had done before. Neither an older brother engineer nor two older sisters had ever expressed interest in working for the company. After the youngest daughter became CEO, she felt that her father and his chief technical officer would not let her take any major responsibility. They also became increasingly critical of her actions in early 1986 after her older brother said that he would like to join the business. The father was delighted, but the daughter was not. The father suggested that she might like to change jobs. Soon after that, he called a family meeting to discuss the family business but did not invite her. She asked why but got no information. Soon after that, she resigned from the company, blaming her siblings and mother for lack of support. A month later, her father died. Much to her surprise, the daughter found that she had inherited most of the company stock. Even then, she would not rejoin the company until a new board of directors took office about six months later. The new chairman, an old family friend, asked her to come back to help her brother as comanaging director, stressing the need for the two of them to work together. Her brother also asked her to return. She did.

In this case, the daughter felt unable to gain further autonomy and competence at her own initiative, particularly after being excluded from the family meeting. She felt that both family and company hierarchies weighed too heavily against her. Only after her ownership and absent competence immobilized both the board and her brother did the family decide to set up a board that would try to work with her. In this case, the high-status friend built a mediating bridge between her family, her brother, and herself but only after the brother became more dependent on her than she was on him.

In a third case, another woman CEO was supported by a high-status family friend who was also an officer of the bank that held the company's loans. The daughter CEO was the purchasing agent in a failing family business until the consulting firm that her father had hired made a report to the father and to the loan committee of the bank. The bank officers were stunned by the consulting firm's recommendation that the family sell the business to them at a low price so that the consulting firm could take over and run the business. The father was inclined to go along with the sale, but the bankers were not. The consulting firm was fired. The banker and his associates insisted that the daughter be made president. Her father reluctantly agreed. The company began to turn around economically and became quite successful under the daughter's direction.

In each of these three cases, the helpful high-status friends were acceptable to parents, to the younger CEO, and to the siblings. They had no personal axes to grind. More important, they had built up trust over a period of time. That was something the short-term consultants did not do in the case just cited. It is something that, in general, hired consultants are often unable to do. Psychologist Harry Levinson (1983, p. 76) makes an interesting point about consulting with family businesses when he notes, "Usually a consultant is sought by one of the younger sons to help alleviate the chronic pain of [several warring sons]. . . . Usually the consultation is sought by a person of lesser power in the system—one who is experiencing pain and seeking to reach the entrepreneurial power of the person of greatest authority. The authoritative person ordinarily sees no problem, or feels that he can manage it, or resents the intrusion of the outsider and the brashness of the family member who invited the consultation."

The active effort by the lower-status person to reduce pain and seek help holds true in my experience also. Levinson (1983) is not optimistic that such efforts can succeed. However, there are times when they can if the outside high-status friend—often not a consultant—has won the respect of those fathers, mothers, or siblings who possess the greater family power. Consultants often fail to build such credibility with all family members, sometimes because their billing rates do not permit that kind of involvement, sometimes because they fail to take the larger family system into account. Furthermore, consultants are often suspect because they are perceived as being out to perpetuate their own role and income.

This critical point of self-interest sometimes makes it difficult either for consultants or for family members to serve in the high-status friend role. The role works best when the outsider is seen not as indulging in self-gain but as honestly seeking what is best for all family members and their business. Parents or older siblings agree to such help only after they feel forced to do so by a loss of control, as in the two cases involving daughter CEOs cited earlier. In both cases, the family members needed the daughter's help more than she needed them at that point. In each case, the daughter CEO had established her own self-control, separate purpose, and competence. She had become her own person, and the high-status friends recognized this. Family recognition came only when other family members felt enough pain and dependency to call on the daughter or younger son CEO for help. At those times, the older parent or sibling became more willing to renegotiate identities and dependencies.

CONCLUSION

Daughters and younger sons who become CEOs cannot easily shake off their family ties to the bottom levels of the family hierarchy. As CEOs, they then become key figures in incongruent hierarchies. Their positions in the two hierarchies are out of line with each other. This incongruence can lead to discomfort, tension, and agony for all members of the family. Outsiders who see this pain are often at a loss to know how to deal with family members as the problems become public and sometimes tragic.

But, whereas the origins of the problem are structural to begin with, only day-to-day actions and behaviors serve to bring the two hierarchies into line with each other and to change expectations and perceptions. For the daughter or younger son CEO, this means getting family recognition as a grown-up, authority figure, and competent adult. It means a new, or at least a modified, identity and a reworking of old relationships. Sometimes, the process is traumatic as the new CEO establishes trust, autonomy, initiative, and competence among business associates while abandoning family ties. Occasionally, the daughter or younger son CEO gets a helping hand from older family members, but this is not as often as we might like. The threat and rivalries are too high until a cooperative climate is established. That can sometimes be done by acts of independence or competence by the daughter or younger son. It can also involve outside high-status friends who help to bridge the gap between business and family. Such friends play a delicate role. They must be trusted by all parties, and that often depends on prior long-term relationships.

None of these processes is easy. The temptation is for one or more family members to get discouraged, sell the business, abandon it, or give up. The fact that they cannot always solve these problems from within the family hierarchy system is the crux of the problem for daughters and younger son CEOs. What can solve the problem is recognition that the problem has structural origins and some behaviors that help to restructure the family hierarchy so as to make the perceptions of family members more congruent with the business hierarchy.

REFERENCES

BARNES, L. B., and HERSHON, S.A. "Transferring Power in the Family Business." *Harvard Business Review*, 1976, *54* (4), 105–114.

ERIKSON, E. *Childhood and Society*. New York: Norton, 1950.

FREILICH, M. "The National Triad in Kinship and Complex Systems." *American Sociological Review*, 1964, *29* (4), 529–540.

HERSHON, S. A. "Meeting of the Board of Directors, Henry Manufacturing Company, Inc."

Harvard Business School Case Services, 475-031, 1974, 1–12.

LEVINSON, H. "Consulting with Family Businesses: What to Look for, What to Look Out For." *Organizational Dynamics*, Summer 1983, pp. 71–80.

SAMPSON, E. E. "Status Congruence and Cognitive Consistency." *Sociometry*, 1963, *26*, 146–162.

FIGURE 1 The Eight Phases of the Human Life Cycle

Phase	Life Cycle Crisis	Resolution
Old age	Integrity versus despair	Wisdom
Adulthood	Generativity versus stagnation	Care
Young adulthood	Intimacy versus isolation	Love
Adolescence	Identity versus identity confusion	Fidelity
School age	Industry versus inferiority	Competence
Play age	Initiative versus guilt	Purpose
Early childhood	Autonomy versus shame and doubt	Self-control
Infancy	Trust versus mistrust	Hope

Source: Erikson, 1950.

Transferring Power in the Family Business

LOUIS B. BARNES and SIMON A. HERSHON

One of the most agonizing experiences that any business faces is the moving from one generation of top management to the next. The problem is often most acute in family businesses, where the original entrepreneur hangs on as he watches others try to help manage or take over his business, while at the same time, his heirs feel overshadowed and frustrated. Paralleling the stages of family power are stages of company growth or of stagnation, and the smoothness with which one kind of transition is made often has a direct effect on the success of the other.

Sons or subordinates of first generation entrepreneurs tell of patient and impatient waiting in the wings for their time to take over the running of the company. When the time comes, it usually comes because the "old man" has died or is too ill to actively take part in management, even though still holding tightly to the reins of the family business. Often this means years of tension and conflict as older and younger generations pretend to coexist in top management.

As one second generation manager put it, speaking of these problems: "Fortunately, my father died one year after I joined the firm." Concerning another company, a prospective buyer said: "The old man is running the company downhill so fast that we'll pick it up for nothing before the kids can build it back up."

The transition problem affects both family and non-family members. Brokers and bankers, professional managers, employees, competitors, outside directors, wives, friends, and potential stock investors all have more than passing interest as a company moves from one generation to the next. Some of these transitions seem orderly. Most, however, do not. Management becomes racked with strife and indecision. Sons, heirs, key employees, and directors resign in protest. Families are torn with conflict. The president-father is deposed. Buyers who want to merge with or acquire the business change their minds. And often the company dies or becomes stagnant.

The frequency of such accounts and the pain reflected in describing the transfer of power from one generation to the next led us to begin a more formal research inquiry into what happens as a family business, or more accurately, a family *and* its business grow and develop over generations. Specifically, what happens in the family and company between those periods when one generation or another is clearly in control but both are "around"? In addition, how do some managements go through or hurdle the family transition without impeding company growth? And can or must family and company transitions be kept separate?

The research project on these questions

Authors' note: The authors gratefully acknowledge the help and sponsorship they received from the Smaller Company Management Programs at the Harvard Business School.

Reprinted by permission of Harvard Business Review. "Transferring Power in the Family Business," by Louis B. Barnes and Simon A. Hershon, vol. 54, no. 4, July-August 1976.

began in June 1974 and is still continuing. It has included interviews with over 200 men and women and multiple interviews in over 35 companies, not all of which went beyond the first crucial transition test. This article contains some of the initial findings and conclusions.

PROFESSIONAL OR FAMILY MANAGEMENT?

Some observers and commentators on family business believe that the sooner the family management is replaced by professional management in growing companies, the better. The problems just described can lead to disruption or destruction of either the family or the business, sometimes both, in the long run. Furthermore, the argument goes, an objective, professional management will focus on what is good for the business and its growth without getting lost in the emotions and confusions of family politics.

This rational argument for professional management in growing companies has many strong advocates. It has even been suggested that the family members should form a trust, taking all the relatives out of business operations, thus enabling them to act in concert as a family.[1]

Like any argument for objectivity, the plea for professionalism has logic on its side. It makes good business sense, and in a way, good family sense as well. It guides a business away from mixing personal lives with business practices, and it helps to avoid the evils of nepotism and weak family successors who appear so often to cause transition crises.

Historically, the main problem with this rational argument is that most companies lean more heavily on family and personal psychology than they do on such business logic. The evidence is overwhelming. There are more than one million businesses in the United States. Of these, about 980,000 are family dominated, including many of the largest. Yet most of us have the opposite impression. We tend to believe that, after a generation or so, family businesses fade into widely held public companies managed by outside managers with professional backgrounds. The myth comes partly from a landmark study of big business by Adolph Perle and Gardner Means, who maintained that ownership of major U.S. companies was becoming widely diffused and that operating control was passing into the hands of professional managers who owned only a small fraction of their corporation's stock. This widely publicized "fact" was further used by John Kenneth Galbraith to build a concept which he called the "technostructure" of industry, based in large part on the alleged separation of corporate ownership from management control.[2]

There is evidence to the contrary, though. A study reported in *Fortune* by Robert Sheehan examined the 500 largest corporations on this question. Sheehan reported that family ownership and control in the largest companies was still significant and that in about 150 companies controlling ownership rested in the hands of an individual or of the members of a single family. Significantly, these owners were not just the remnants of the nineteenth century dynasties that once ruled American business. Many of them were relatively fresh faces.[3]

The myth is even more severely chal-

[1]   Harry Levinson, "Conflicts That Plague the Family Business," HBR March–April 1971, p. 90.
[2]   Adolph A. Berle and Gardner C. Means, *The Modern Corporation and Private Property* (New York: Harcourt Brace & World, 1968) and John Kenneth Galbraith, *The New Industrial State* (Boston: Houghton Mifflin, 1967.)
[3]   Robert Sheehan, "Proprietors in the World of Big Business," *Fortune*, June 1967, p. 178.

lenged in a study of 450 large companies done by Philip Burch and published in 1972. By his calculations, over 42% of the largest *publicly* held corporations are controlled by one person or a family, and another 17% are placed in the "possible family control" category. Then there is one other major category of large "privately" owned companies—companies with fewer than 500 shareholders, which are not required to disclose their financial figures. Some well-known corporate names are included in this category: Cargill, Bechtel Corporation, Hearst Corporation, Hallmark Cards, and Hughes Aircraft, among others. Burch notes that contrary to what one might expect, the rather pervasive family control exercised is, for the most part, very direct and enduring. It is exercised through significant stock ownership and outside representation on the board of directors, and also, in many cases, through a considerable amount of actual family management.[4]

When one thinks more closely about families in big as well as small businesses, some well-known succession examples also come to mind, suggesting that family transition and corporate growth occur together even though there may be strain in the process. For example:

- H.J. Heinz was founded by Henry J. Heinz to bottle and sell horseradish, and today H.J. Heinz II, a grandson, heads the billion dollar concern.
- Triangle Publications owns the *Morning Telegraph*, *TV Guide*, and *Seventeen*. It was founded by Moses Annenberg. He was succeeded by his son, Walter, and a daughter, Enid, is now editor-in-chief of *Seventeen*.
- The Bechtel Corporation was begun by Warren A. Bechtel, for building railroads. His son, Steve Sr., directed the firm into construction of pipelines and nuclear power plants. Today, Steve Jr. heads the $2 billion company, which is now further diversified.
- Kaiser Industries, built by Henry J. Kaiser, includes Kaiser Steel, Kaiser Aluminum and Chemical, Kaiser Cement and Gypsum, Kaiser Broadcasting, Kaiser Engineering, and Kaiser Resources. The present industrial giant is headed by Henry's son, Edgar, now over 65 years old. An obvious successor is Edgar Jr., president of Kaiser Resources Ltd.

Should a family business stay in the family? The question now seems almost academic. It is apparent that families *do* stay in their businesses, and the businesses stay in the family. Thus there is something more deeply rooted in transfers of power than impersonal business interests. The human tradition of passing on heritage, possessions, and name from one generation to the next leads both parents and children to seek continuity in the family business. In this light, the question whether a business should stay in the family seems less important, we suspect, than learning more about how these businesses and their family owners make the transition from one generation to the next.

INSIDE AND OUTSIDE PERSPECTIVES

What are the implications when the transition from one generation to the next includes both business and family change, and what are the consequences also if business and family, though separate, remain tied together in plans, arguments, and emotions? In considering these questions, it might help to examine two perspectives in addition to

[4] Philip H. Burch, Jr., *The Managerial Revolution Reassessed* (Lexington, Mass.: D.C. Heath, 1972.)

age difference. One is the family, the other is the business, point of view. Both of these can be viewed from either the inside or the outside.

Exhibit 1 shows these four different vantage points from which to observe family and business members. One viewpoint is that of the "family managers" (inside the family and inside the business) as seen by both old and young generations. When they forget or ignore the other three perspectives, they can easily get boxed into their own concerns. This kind of compulsion includes hanging onto power for the older generation and getting hold of it for the younger. To both generations, it implies the selection, inclusion, and perpetuation of family managers.

A second perspective comes from "the employees," again older and younger, who work inside the business but who are outside the family. Understandably, they face different pressures and concerns from those of the family managers, even though many are treated as part of the larger corporate family. The older employees want rewards for loyalty, sharing of equity, and security, and they want to please the boss. Younger employees generally want professionalism, opportunities for growth, equity, and reasons for staying. Both age groups worry about bridging the family transition.

A third perspective comes from "the relatives," those family members who are not in the active management of the business. The older relatives worry about income, family conflicts, dividend policies, and a place in the business for their own children. The younger, often disillusioned brothers and cousins feel varying degrees of pressure to join the business. Both generations may be interested, interfering, involved, and sometimes helpful, as we shall see later on.

Finally, the fourth perspective comes from "the outsiders." These are persons who are competitors, R & D interests, creditors, customers, government regulators, vendors, consultants, and others who are connected to the business and its practices from the outside. They have various private interests in the company which range from constructive to destructive in intention and effect.

A curious irony is that the more "outside" the family the perspective is, as shown in *Exhibit 1,* the more legitimate it seems as a "real" management problem. Yet the concerns in the left column boxes are typically just as important as, and more time consuming than, the outside-the-family problems on the right. These inside-the-family problems tend to be ignored in management books, consultant's reports, and business school courses. Ignoring these realities can be disastrous for both the family and the company.

Our studies show that the transfer of power from first to second generation rarely takes place while the founder is alive and on the scene. What occurs instead during this time is a transition period of great difficulty for both older and younger generations. For the founder, giving up the company is like signing his own death warrant. For the son or successor, the strain may be comparable. As one of these said:

"I drew up the acquisition papers to buy my father out, because for a long time he has been saying he did not care about the business anymore. However, when it was all taken care of, and we presented him with the papers, he started to renege. Everything was done the way he would like it. Yet he would not sign. He finally told me he did not think he could do it. He felt it awfully hard to actually lose the company. He said he felt he still had something to give."

And another commented:

"I can't change things as fast as I would like to. It is absolutely clear to me that things need to be changed. However, it is not easy. First of all there is the function of age and experience as well as being the boss's son. Every other officer in the company is in his fifties. What I am talking about now are deep sources of dissatisfaction. I would like more ownership. Now I have only 7%, my father has 80% and my family another 13%. In my position, I just cannot move the company fast enough. We argue a lot, but nothing seems to change. I have set a goal for myself. If I cannot run the company within two years, I am leaving. I'll do something else."

THE COMPANY TRANSITION

While family managers feel the multiple strains as the generations overlap during periods of transition, another related process is occurring as the company grows and develops. Various authors have tried to describe this process.[5] But, where one describes a smooth procedural development, another sees a series of difficult crises. For some, a series of growth stages is important. For others, it is the merging of functions with processes that count. Most writers do not tie business growth or decline to family transitions. However, the following points stand out for us in relation to company transitions.

1. Organizational growth tends to be nonlinear. Organizations grow in discrete stages, with varying growth rates in each stage.
2. Periods of profound organizational development often occur *between* periods of growth. These slower periods often are viewed with alarm, but they force managers to examine what the company has grown toward or into. These periods of development are the transition periods which appear less dramatic (i.e., there is less growth) but may be most crucial to a company's preparations for its own future.[6] The apparent floundering can provoke useful learning once management begins to adopt and encourage new practices and procedures.
3. A typical management response to transitional strains is a total or partial reorganization of the company. This sometimes helps shake up old habits but rarely resolves a transition crisis.

What is needed is time for the social and political systems of the company to realign themselves into new norms and relationships.

Exhibit 2 shows how a later growth stage differs from and builds on the earlier ones. The first stage is characteristic of an entrepreneurial company with direct management. The second is typified by a rapidly growing product line and market situation with second-level management set up in specialized functions. The third stage has divisional operations with a diverse line of product and markets. Whereas the management style of the first stage is highly personal and direct, the second tends to become the more collaborative style of a boss and specialized peers. The third stage typically involves a looser, impersonal, collective style, with the chief executive managing generalists as well as functional specialists. Under the patterns of the first stage, the core problem for a small company is survival. The patterns of the roughly defined second stage show a size and scope requiring such specialized functions as finance, production, marketing, and engineering.

As the company's size continues to increase, it is likely to evolve toward third-stage patterns of growth: At this point, different product lines become separate companies or divisions, while, in multinational firms, the

[5] George Strauss, "Adolescence in Organization Growth: Problems, Pains, Possibilities," *Organizational Dynamics*, Spring 1974, p. 3; Robert B. Buchele, *Business Policy in Growing Firms* (San Francisco: Chandler Publishing Co., 1965); Theodore Cohn and Roy A. Lindberg, *Survival and Growth: Management Strategies for the Small Firm* (New York: AMACOM, 1974); Lawrence L. Steinmetz, "Critical Stages of Small Business Growth," *Business Horizons*, February 1969, p. 29; Bruce L. Scott, "Stages of Corporate Development—Part I," Harvard Business School Note 9:371–294, BP 798.

[6] Larry E. Greiner, "Evolution and Revolution as Organizations Grow," HBR July–August 1972, p. 37.

separation may also be on an area basis (e.g., Europe, North America, Latin America, Middle East, Far East) as well.

In between the box-like stages of growth shown in *Exhibit 2* appear the transition phases which help to prepare an organization for its next stage. To cross the broken lines separating one growth stage from another in *Exhibit 2* requires time, new interaction patterns, and an awkward period of overlap. In effect, the broken vertical lines of *Exhibit 2* represent widened time zones of varying and irregular width.

As we have seen, family transitions and company transitions can occur separately and at different times. However, we found that they usually occur together. As a company moves from the problem of survival to one of managing rapid growth, it must develop new control, motivation, and reward systems. It also requires a management style that can integrate specialists and their functions. This development cannot occur without a top management that wants to take the extra step beyond survival thinking. That is where an eager younger generation comes in. He, she, or they are more likely to want to go beyond traditional practices. This pent-up energy seemed to be a major factor in getting beyond company transitions in 27 out of 32 businesses we studied where the company had gone beyond the first growth stage.

Another kind of transition occurs between the second and the third growth stages. Company and division units in stage three had general managers in both the head office and the decentralized units who had learned to work with both other general managers and functional specialists. This meant that they had to have or develop a sense of the complex interdependence that characterizes most major companies today.

These dual transitions seemed best catalyzed when the old management forces somehow helped to pave the way for the new. The following case is a good example[7]: When Max Krisch came to America in 1851, he brought an expertise in baking and an old family recipe for bread. Soon after settling, he established a small bakery. The business grew, and Max got help from his three sons as soon as they were old enough to operate the ovens after school and on weekends. When Martin, the oldest, graduated from college in 1890, he joined the business and soon started suggesting changes which he was convinced were good for the company's growth. His father refused, and the two men would often end up in disagreement. Sometimes the arguments were long and bitter.

Eventually, Max's wife abandoned her role of neutrality and intervened on Martin's behalf. She begged Max to give Martin a chance to implement his ideas. Reluctantly, Max agreed and let Martin take the first step.

Martin's idea was to sell bread to milk peddlers who would offer it for sale to their milk customers. It was a new concept at the time, and it worked. The demand for Krisch's Bread increased sharply.

At this time, too, the second brother, Peter, was ready to join the company. Martin realized that the company's production capability would soon be unable to keep up with the increasing sales. He hoped that Peter could take over, modernize, and expand production, but again Max reacted strongly. He argued that the baking of Krisch's Bread could not be done in volume without ruining the quality. Martin and Peter eventually promised their father that if the new methods harmed the bread's quality they would discontinue them. Over time, Max again agreed to go along with the change, and Peter worked closely with his father to increase production while still maintaining quality. Again, too, the mother was behind the scenes trying to keep peace in the family.

---

[7]   This and all following cases are based on real circumstances, but fictitious names and industries are used.

When the third brother, Kurt, joined the firm, Martin gave him the responsibility for bookkeeping and financial affairs. Fortunately, Kurt had a good head for figures and did the job well.

As Max became less active in the business, Martin was in charge, with Peter heading production, while Kurt handled the financial end of the business. The business flourished. Occasionally, the three sons felt hampered by Max's continuing strong opinions on some aspects of the business. At these times, the boys' mother would often referee the disagreements. Partly because she was a sensitive person and a good listener, she was usually able to help the father and sons arrive at some mutually satisfactory solution to their problems.

Our studies show that when the familial and organizational transitions occurred together, as in the Krisch case, they typically took place in an atmosphere of strain and uncertainty. Quite often, a mother was a behind-the-scenes influence. More often, though, the transitions were not managed well either inside the family or inside the business. In the Krisch case, Martin guided the company into its second growth stage. But it was his mother's sensitive management of the family relationships that eased that process and eventually permitted the brothers to achieve an outstanding growth record for the firm. Although Max's time-tested ways and methods fell by the wayside as his sons took over, he became a useful adviser once both he and his sons accepted Martin as head of the business though not head of the family. The transfer of power inside the business took place when Max moved into a new working relationship with his wife. With Martin managing the business transition and his mother helping to hold the family together, Krisch's Bakeries made both transitions.

The second transition period for Krisch Bakeries is also instructive. After an impressive growth record over a 30-year period, Martin Krisch and his brothers set the wheels in motion for the transition to the third generation. Martin's son, Max Krisch II, was the most obvious successor.

By 1925, the company had established an executive committee of both family and nonfamily managers who made decisions by consensus. The brothers believed that such an arrangement helped keep the family together and provided valuable inputs from nonfamily members on the executive committee.

In preparation for the transition, Martin, who was then 55, hired an outsider who suggested that a new role of coordinator be set up for the committee which he took on initially and then passed on to Max II, who had just been brought onto the committee as a member. Soon after, Martin was advised by the outsider that he should get off the committee and out of the company as much as possible.

Thus Martin began to spend more and more of his time away from the company in civic, volunteer, outside boards, and other business activities. At times, he was frustrated and unhappy over not being in the mainstream of the business, but he gained some satisfaction in watching Max II develop into a manager who set new wheels in motion for the company's expansion and diversification into new areas of business. New product lines were developed, the company was broken into divisions and a chain of other businesses was started. All seemed to be going well until the company was hit by an antitrust suit which restricted and delayed some of its most ambitious plans.

Though the Krisch Bakeries' plans for wider ownership, diversification, and expansion were stalled for a number of years, it seemed to again make the dual transition on both the family and the business levels.

THE SINGLE TRANSITION

Even though most of the companies we studied changed top management and growth stages together, other companies showed one transitional change at a time. A stagnant company can get that way when the older generation gives way to the younger without any company transition. The Quinn Company was one of these.

In the Quinn family business harmony had been difficult to achieve. The founder, Josiah Quinn, established his industrial supply company in 1911. He began the business with a partner, and it grew steadily. As business improved, the partner took a less active role, and Quinn soon began to resent the partner's equal salary and taking of the profits.

When his wife suddenly died, Quinn impulsively sold the business to his partner and took his five children West. After several years there, he returned home and began a new business, remarried, and had two children by his second wife.

Eventually, Quinn's oldest children joined the firm. They worked well together, and the company prospered. When his second set of children also joined the company, however, jealousy and resentment increased. Conflict began to disrupt operations daily. The problems flowed over into family life, where his wife took the side of "her" children against "his." Finally, Quinn decided to set up a separate company for his wife's children. He founded it under another name, brought customers from the other company, and enjoyed helping it get started.

When World War II broke out, Quinn's most capable son in the first company was drafted. He was sent out West, married, and eventually set up his own company in San Francisco. This left the first company without a really capable successor, though the departed son's brothers and brothers-in-law

worked to keep the company going. Again, dissension increased. While the company continued to operate after Quinn died, its performance levels never rose over the next 30 years.

The Quinn Company's transition from first to second generation was influenced by a major split within the family, by the loss of its key young successor, and the divisive role taken by Quinn's second wife. The family conflicts seemed to keep Quinn and his heirs from dealing with company transition problems, since all their energies were spent on inside-the-family problems. The result was a family transition without a simultaneous company transition. Such single transitions were even harder for those inside the family and the company than when the two transitions occurred together. Today the Quinn Company is heading painfully into another transition, its second generation having apparently suffered much, but having learned little from the first one. The older family managers find it hard to let go as the 66-year-old president steps aside uneasily, only to be replaced by a 68-year-old in-law whose sons wait impatiently and sometimes irresponsibly for their turn. Meanwhile, the company suffers.

Another type of single transition occurs when a company moves from one growth stage to the next within one management generation. Such growth occurs rarely, it seems, in the first generation, partly because entrepreneurs tend not to be reorganizers, and growth requires reorganization along with a shift in management styles. We found these company transitions without a family transition to occur more often during the second generation. Whereas first generation entrepreneurs had trouble shifting to high growth strategies and more collaborative styles; the sons were more flexible, possibly because the shift from a second to a third stage growth pattern involves letting go of less personal ties or possibly because they had more help in making the shift. Here is an example of such a transition: When Wells Thomas died, his hardware supply business passed on to his two sons, Paul and Bing. Paul handled production, and Bing worked in sales. The two brothers built the family firm into a major hardware supply house. Paul became chief executive officer, and he and Bing eventually diversified the business into retail hardware stores, medium equipment companies, an electrical manufacturing company, and several unrelated businesses. Along the way, they brought in six third-generation members of their own and their sister's families. But these younger family members never quite made the grade. Paul, with Bing's approval, fired five of the six and handed the presidency of the corporation over to a man who had been president of one of the acquired companies.

His justification for discharging his sons, nephews, and sons-in-law was the good of the family business, and therefore in the long run the interests of all family members. Nevertheless, he had created a split in the family that never healed. Meanwhile, the new company president admitted that Paul had become like a father to him, and it was apparent that the father-son parallel was very strong for both of them. There was still one nephew in the company, and although he had an important position, it was clear that he had no inside track on succession plans.

Thomas Enterprises moved faster than most companies do in its growth cycle, possibly because Paul Thomas was willing to sacrifice family harmony for what seemed to be business efficiency. Ironically, though, the fired family members each went on to successful careers in outside jobs, most of them pleased in retrospect to get out from under Paul's reign. Whether any one of them could have taken over the sprawling company is hard to judge at this stage. What is clear is that Paul found another "son" who became heir apparent. In an artificial way, the "succession" transition actually came along only slightly behind the company transition.

The three patterns shown in the Krisch, Quinn, and Thomas cases suggest some overall advantages of family and business transitions occurring at the same time. The Quinn and Thomas cases also show what happens when family managers, relatives, employees, and outsiders cannot form a power coalition to protect either the family or the business transition, whichever is jeopardized by family conflicts. In the Quinn case, the family managers withdrew in the face of destructive family pressures typified by Quinn's second wife. She not only divided the family but had a strong hand in dividing the company into two separate enterprises, each also competing with the other. In effect, the microcosm of family conflict became replicated in the macrocosm of the two companies. Without capable second generation managers, the original Quinn business never got beyond the first growth stage.

In the Thomas case, the opposite occurred. The relatives retreated "for the good of the family business" as Paul Thomas put it. They helped to destroy the family by abdicating in favor of the dominant older family managers, Paul and Bing Thomas. In the process, some competent family managers were lost. However, the point is not whether Paul and Bing were right or wrong, it is only that they made sure that they were never really tested or questioned by the intimidated relatives. Neither employees nor outsiders found a way to help either.

Under the distorted dominance of either family managers or relatives, not only crippled transitions but regression can set in. Consider one more case: In the Brindle Company, a father had handed the business over to a son-in-law, did not like the results, and reclaimed the company, even though the son-in-law had done an impressive job of managing the company in terms of growth and expansion. Several years later, with the son-in-law out of the business, but still with a small ownership stake, Mr. Brindle sold the company at a fraction of the price that the same buyer had offered while the son-in-law was running the business. The business' growth had stalled and declined. The company had gone from second generation back to first generation, and the family was shattered to the extent that the two youngest grandchildren born to the son-in-law and his wife had never been permitted to meet their grandparents.

MANAGING THE TWO TRANSITIONS

If, as in the Brindle case, a single dominant power force tends to cause lopsided transitions or regression, how can a constructive pattern be built for creating and managing both transitions? The answer seems to lie in a power balancing setup that prevents polarized conflict. Only in the Krisch case, of those described earlier, was this power balancing done effectively. Yet it also happened in at least some of the other companies we studied. It may help to look at some of the assumptions and mechanisms that were used to encourage and manage the two transitions.

The Company Will Live, but I Won't

The key assumption for growth was an almost explicit decision by senior managers that "the company will live, but I won't." This assumption, so often avoided by older family managers, is almost built into the forced retirement programs of established companies. But an entrepreneur or even his sons, as they get older, must somehow consciously face and make the decision that, even though they will die, the company will live. Often, that decision occurs not because they are pushed into it, or out of the company by the younger family managers, but because of the intervention of relatives, noncompeting employees, or trusted outsiders, who may find a way of helping to pull the old family manager into a new set of activities.

At some point, a critical network of family managers, employees, relatives, and outsiders must begin to focus upon the duality of both family and business transitions. Such talks should, in our opinion, begin at least 7 to 8 years before the president is supposed to retire. Even though the specific plans may change, the important assumptions behind those plans will not.

Mediation vs. Confrontation

Time after time we saw cases in which an entrepreneur's wife played an important role in bridging the growing gap between father and sons, as happened in the Krisch case. It also happened that an entrepreneur's widow would step in as a peacemaker for the younger generation. But when it came to helping make both transitions occur, the wife was more important than the widow. As in the Krisch case, she would help or persuade her husband to look toward the (children's) future instead of his own past. In effect, she provided a relative's outside-the-business perspective. Such outside perspectives turned out to be crucial in transition management, because they helped to heal and avoid the wounds of family conflict.

In some management circles over recent years, a cult of confrontation has been built. Confrontation is regarded as calling a spade a spade, not in anger, but as a way to move beyond conflict toward problem solving. The approach is reasonable and works in many business situations.

As we pointed out earlier, though, families and their businesses are not necessarily reasonable. The primary emotions tend to be close to the surface, so that conflicts erupt almost without reason. Attempts at confrontation by one party often fail, because they are seen as open or continuing attacks by the other.

When such nerve ends are raw, partly because of family jealousies and partly because of historical sensitivities, a third party or outside perspective can provide mediation and help to soften hardened positions. Relatives, outside directors, friends, and key employees all take this role in family companies. But they do something else that is equally important. They can help to begin a practice of open dialogue that cuts not only across age levels, but across the different perspectives of family managers, relatives, employees, and outsiders. The dialogues can aid in manpower planning and in managing the transitions. The question is how to develop such dialogues so as to include all the relevant perspectives.

Mechanisms for Dialogue

None of the dialogue mechanisms we observed or heard of is a cure-all. But each brought different important combinations of people together. One company management had periodic family meetings for family managers and relatives. Another combined family managers and employees into project teams and task forces. Outside boards of directors, executive committees, and non-family stock ownership (to be sold back to the company at the owner's death or departure) brought together family managers, employees, and outsider consultants on major policy problems in a number of companies. One family company had in-company management development programs, but invited outside participants and also gave periodic progress reports to the financial and civic community for comment and review. At one extreme, family managers and key employees did set up a series of confrontation sessions, but only after detailed planning. The ground rules were carefully worked out and over the years both family and company transitions made good progress. At the other extreme, companies would hold various lunches or social events where the open dialogue opportunities were limited but sometimes possible in an informal setting.

Future Role Building

Unwillingness to face the future stalls both family and business transitions, since in one sense the future can only mean death for an older family manager. But in a more limited sense it implies new but separate lives for the manager and his company. If some of the above assumptions and mechanisms begin to take hold, they will lead to the building of new roles. The older managers learn how to advise and teach rather than to control and dominate. The younger managers learn how to use their new power potential as bosses. Family managers take steps to learn new roles outside the business as directors, office holders, and advisers. Employees learn new functional management skills as well as new general management skills. Relatives learn how to take third party roles to provide an outside perspective.

BEGINNING NEAR THE END

We have been describing one of the most difficult and deep-rooted problems faced by human organizations. Family owned and managed concerns include some of the largest as well as most of the smallest companies in the United States and possibly the world. It seems pointless to talk about separating families from their businesses, at least in our society. Families are in business to stay.

However, as one management generation comes near its end, the life of the business is also jeopardized. Meanwhile, critics, scholars, and managers like to pretend that the "real" business problems lie outside of the family's involvement. This may be true in some cases, but it can also lead to and perpetuate four sets of tunnel vision. Family managers, relatives, employees, and outsiders adopt separate perspectives and separate paths.

Our studies, however, suggest that the healthiest transitions are those old-versus-young struggles in which both the family managers and the business change patterns. For this to happen, "the old man" must face the decision of helping the company live even though he must die. If he can do this, the management of transitions can begin. In effect, a successful family transition can mean a new beginning for the company.

Writers like to think that their work and words will have a lasting impact upon the reader. However, the history of the topic we are discussing provides little cause for such optimism. In fact, a truly lasting solution may come only from experience such as that described by an entrepreneur, who said:

"I left my own father's company and swore I'd never subject my own children to what I had to face. Now my son is getting good experience in another company in our industry before coming in to take over this one. Within five years of the day he walks in that door, I walk out. And everyone knows it—even me."

EXHIBIT 1   Pressures and Interests in a Family Business

	Inside the family	Outside the family
Inside the business	The family managers Hanging onto or getting hold of company control Selection of family members as managers Continuity of family investment and involvement Building a dynasty Rivalry	The employees Rewards for loyalty Sharing of equity, growth, and successes Professionalism Bridging family transitions Stake in the company
Outside the business	The relatives Income and inheritance Family conflicts and alliances Degree of involvement in the business	The outsiders Competition Market, product, supply and technology influences Tax laws Regulatory agencies Trends in management practices

EXHIBIT 2 Characteristics of Company Growth

Organizational Characteristic	Patterns of the First Stage	Patterns of the Second Stage	Patterns of the Third Stage
Core problem	Survival	Management of growth	Managerial control and allocation of resources
Central function	Fusion of diverse talents and purposes into a unified company	Fission of general authority into specialized functions	Fusion of independent units into an inter-dependent union of companies
Control systems	Personal (inside); survival in marketplace (outside)	Cost centers and policy formulation (inside); growth potential (outside)	Profit centers and abstract performance criteria (inside); capital expansion potential (outside)
Reward and motivation	Ownership membership in the family	Salary, opportunities and problems of growth	Salary, performance bonus, stock options, peer prestige
Management style	Individualistic; direct management	Integrating specialists; collaborative management	Integrating generalists; collective management
Organization: Structure	Informal	Functional specialists	Division organizations
CEO's primary task	Direct supervision of employees	Managing specialized managers	Managing generalist managers
Levels of management	Two	At least three	At least four

Managing Interpersonal Feedback

LOUIS B. BARNES

With the emergence of the "information age" in the 1970s and 1980s, it became clear that how managers dealt with information systems would be crucial to business success and even survival. It became equally clear, however, that information comes in many forms: there are quantitative "facts" and qualitative opinions, historical records and future speculations. Above all, there are the differing perspectives of individuals at all levels of the organization. These individuals not only know the facts about a situation; they also develop feelings about those facts—feelings that can emerge as new "facts" when they become subjects of discussion.

These feelings-facts provide the basis for many organizational disagreements and misunderstandings. Yet managers often discount the importance of people's feelings, including their own; in trying to resolve problems, they focus on what they see as the hard facts. Particularly when it comes to giving feedback to superiors, subordinates, and colleagues about their behavior at work, managers often fail to acknowledge to themselves and to others how their feelings affect their appraisals of another person's behavior. Often they express these feelings only obliquely. For all involved, the result is usually an awkward and uncomfortable exchange, and the opportunity to learn and improve working relationships is lost. The chances are that we have all been in such situations.

During the 1960s and early 1970s, companies tried to incorporate interpersonal feedback into organization development programs—T-groups, sensitivity training, encounter groups, and other variations on a theme that all too often stressed "letting it all hang out" as the way to convey feedback. More restrained approaches tended to be overshadowed. By the mid-1970s, however, most organizations recognized that interpersonal feedback had to be carefully managed in order to serve the company and its employees most effectively.

The purpose of this note is to help you think about the issues involved in talking with other people about how you and they feel about each other's work-related behavior; I will discuss the perspectives of both the sender and receiver of feedback. Opportunities to exchange these feelings may arise during performance reviews, informal conversations, team-building exercises, company training programs, critiques of meetings, or planning sessions. The discussions may involve only two people, or they may involve a group of people. They offer the chance to learn, to build trust and improve working relationships, and to ultimately increase organizational effectiveness. For these results to occur, however, an unusual level of candor is required. Unfortunately, many people believe that candor between co-workers cannot be beneficial, for two reasons. John Anderson's paper, "Giving and

Professor Louis B. Barnes prepared this note as the basis for class discussion.

Note: This discussion draws heavily upon an internal company document by John Anderson, "Giving and Receiving Feedback." Quotes from the document are used with the author's permission.

Receiving Feedback," describes these reasons as follows:

1. People who work together would not be open and candid with each other. The result, therefore, would be a superficial and useless experience.
2. If people *were* open and candid with each other, it would disrupt working relationships and escalate old grievances into further ill feelings. It would be too dangerous.

Like many fears, these may, of course, prove to be self-fulfilling prophecies; people who believe them help to make them happen. But the experience of many companies shows that we can manage interpersonal feedback so that it is rewarding to the individuals involved as well as to the organization as a whole.

BUILDING NORMS

The process of managing interpersonal feedback first requires norm building. By norm building, we mean an implicit or explicit agreement on ground rules for discussion, feedback, and behavior. As Anderson notes:

In general, people seem to be both concerned enough for one another, and trusting enough of one another, that they are able to be *appropriately* open in exchanging feedback. It is my belief that instances in which people have only hurt or confused one another in exchanges of this kind have been the result not so much of motivational problems, as of problems of skill in giving feedback—that is, knowing how to do it well and what kinds of pitfalls to watch out for.

In this note, I shall focus on describing those skills that help us to be appropriately open while avoiding the pitfalls. But first, one critical motivational problem must be mentioned. That is the issue of one's intentions. As Anderson observes:

The first, most general, and most significant criterion that "helpful feedback" must meet is simply that it be *intended* to be helpful to the recipient. . . . The sender of the message should ask himself or herself beforehand, "Do I really feel that what I am about to say is likely to be helpful to this person? Do I unload a burden of hostility . . . for my own personal benefit, regardless of the expected effect on the receiver?" Otherwise, the sender of the message may imagine that the only obligation is to be open and honest—that the

name of the game is "candor"—and that as long as he or she is truly and completely "level," the only obligation has been fulfilled.

The desire to genuinely help the other person as well as the working relationship is the foundation of managing interpersonal feedback. Realistically, however, in giving and receiving feedback, we also want to help ourselves. To help ourselves, the other person, and the relationship, the norm of helpfulness has to be created. Senders, receivers, or even participating observers of feedback can help establish this norm. How? Anderson suggests three necessary conditions:

1. Each person must understand what has been said. This has behavioral implications for both senders and receivers as they start to test the relationship.
2. Each person must be willing and able to accept the feedback that he or she receives. Sometimes that is the hardest part. We don't always want to hear what others are trying to say.
3. A person must be able to do something about the feedback if he or she chooses to do so.

Before we explore these three conditions, it is worth thinking about *who* should be involved in these understanding, acceptance, and action exchanges. We said before that the settings can vary from two-person performance appraisals or discussions to team-building sessions involving small or large groups. Each approach has advantages. The two-person exchange permits privacy and can encourage a constructive honesty that may be harder to achieve in a more public setting. Two-person trust is often easier to build than multi-person trust. On the other hand, the additional perspectives found in a group setting offer the higher level of objectivity and credibility and can thus provide a stronger basis for supporting behavioral change. The more that the understanding, acceptance, and action norms can be supported and reinforced, the more likely that interpersonal feedback will be useful. The group setting is usually best if managers are trying to develop a wider culture of effectiveness, or if superiors are hoping to get valid feedback from subordinates. As Anderson notes:

One of the advantages of entering into this sort of thing in a group, as opposed to doing so only in a one-on-one relationship, is that feedback that each person gives another can be checked around the group to see whether anyone else has common experience of this kind which would clarify the meaning of what has been said. This should be done whenever possible, both as a check on the validity of the observation as well as to be sure that the recipient receives as many examples as are available to help him or her understand what has been said.

Understanding

How do you help another person understand the feedback you are trying to give him or her? And how do you go about trying to understand what other people are trying to tell you—especially when their feedback is unfavorable? Anderson has several suggestions:

- The feedback should be specific rather than general. If the person being given feedback can be cited specific examples of instances

in which he or she behaved in the way described, it will be much easier to understand what has been said than if the message is given only in terms of generalizations. For example, if the person is told that he or she talks too much, or doesn't express thoughts very clearly, this is likely to be *less* helpful than if a particular instance can be cited, related to time and place, where this behavior was exhibited. If you can recall vividly to a person's mind a particular instance in which he or she rambled on long after having gotten an idea across, either to an individual or to a group, then the person is more likely to be able to grasp the meaning of what is being said. At the very least, an area will have been opened up that can then be further explored. . . . The key here is: Don't just generalize about what kind of person the individual is—give clear examples.

- Recent examples of behavior are better than old ones. . . . What took place two minutes ago will be more vividly recalled than what took place an hour ago—which in turn will be more easily remembered than that which took place yesterday, last week, last year, five years ago, etc.

These suggestions can aid both the donors and receivers of feedback. Of course, being on the receiving end can be especially difficult if there is much discrepancy between what we believe and what are are hearing from others. How can we handle the dissonance? The most natural response is to become defensive, a posture that can impede understanding and set a bad example for others. Anderson has several suggestions for avoiding defensiveness:

- If you have trouble understanding what has been said to you, and the giver(s) of the feedback is unable to come up with examples that clarify things for you, you should begin to seek and speculate on possible examples yourself with the group—to say, for example, "Remember the time we met last Friday, and I did such and so. Is that the kind of thing you are talking about?"
- To be certain you understand, it is a good idea to try to summarize briefly for the

group what you understand them to be saying. This gives a final opportunity to check misunderstandings that might have occurred.

Finally, A's understanding of B depends partly on B's efforts to understand A. Like all norms, norms of understanding are built upon exchange and reciprocity. To give feedback effectively, we must try to understand it when it comes our own way. Reciprocity begins only when one party or the other takes the lead in trying to understand the feelings being delivered.

Acceptance

Even when we understand the feedback being given to us, we may still not want to accept it, partly because we don't trust the motives or intentions of those giving us the feedback. Furthermore, there is always the danger that we may accept feedback as valid when, in fact, it is *not* valid. That's when other trusted opinions should be sought. Again, Anderson has some suggestions to help A understand when B's motives are not merely self-serving:

- If B's tone of voice, facial expressions, choice of words, and everything else about B communicates directly to A the impression that "I value you, and I really would like to help you, and that is the only reason I am telling you this," then A is more likely to attend to the message with an open mind than if B merely rattles off a list of observations about A's behavior, perhaps without even looking directly at A while doing so.
- [The receiver of negative feedback] will . . . be more likely to respond in an accepting frame of mind if the message is descriptive rather than evaluative—that is, if the sender describes what happened and communicates the *personal* effect it had, as opposed to evaluating its goodness or badness, rightness or wrongness, in more general terms. For example, if B were to tell A that: "This may not be your problem—it may be mine. However, I want you to know that when you

act toward me the way you do sometimes (describe a situation in time and place), it is very difficult for me to (think straight, keep from getting angry, keep my mind on what we're talking about—whatever fits the situation)," it is much more likely for the message to be accepted in an open frame of mind than if B were to tell A that "I think it is just awful when you act toward people that way. You really shouldn't do that. That's a senseless way to behave, why don't you grow up, etc."

The latter point, on being descriptive rather than evaluative, can be difficult to grasp. After all, giving feedback *means* evaluating another person's behavior. But it is one thing to blame the other person for the problem and another to describe the impact of that behavior on you while recognizing that the problem may be partly you and *your* sensitivities. After all, it's *your* perception that defines the other person's behavior as a problem. Sometimes, too, even when other people change their behavior after constructive feedback, we refuse to change our perceptions of them ("You can't turn a sow's ear into a silk purse"; "You can't teach an old dog new tricks"; "Once a scoundrel, always a scoundrel."). It thus becomes very important to to describe accurately both what you observe in the other person's behavior and what you feel going on within yourself (e.g., annoyance with your own inability to cope with the situation, frustration at not making more progress on the task, a desire to blame the other person but knowing that there may be another side to the story, and so on). Both parties need to work at clarifying and expressing their real feelings beyond defensiveness. Anderson comments:

It can be very helpful to an individual and to a group if the recipient (and we would add the donor) of feedback is allowed and encouraged to share his or her feelings with the group about the particular behaviors that have been discussed. The risk of defensiveness is one that all involved should be alert to. However, if people can openly explore some of their feelings about why they may tend to behave in particular ways at particular times, two things can happen. First, people may arrive at a better understanding themselves of why they behave in the way they do . . . and thereby be in a better position to consider what they might do about it. Second . . . if they have genuinely shared . . . some of their concerns and some of the internal struggles they have in these situations, [others] may at least find it a little easier to understand and accept them as they are in the future.

In other words, if a useful norm of acceptance is to be worked out and implemented, both the receiver and sender of feedback must struggle to examine their own role in creating the particular problem.

There is one last important consideration when it comes to the acceptance of feedback—the readiness of the recipient, which depends to some extent upon how dissatisfied a person is with his or her own role and responsibility for a situation. People are usually more ready to seek feedback once they recognize the discrepancy between the situation they want and the situation they have helped to create. However, when dissatisfaction leads them to blame external events or parties, they will likely resist feedback unless they trust the source as being both objective and helpful. Such factors as timing, the setting of the discussion (e.g., away from the stress and pressures of work), who's involved, the stated agenda, careful listening, and some agreement as to the *existence* of problems are important. Once we accept some responsibility for having helped to create the problem, we can begin to struggle toward understanding and accepting what we can do to solve the problem.

Action

It is useless to give someone feedback suggesting that they should do something if, in fact, there is nothing they can do. Anderson describes the issue this way:

- Suppose you feel that a particular person does not present his or her ideas as forcefully and persuasively as he or she ought to . . . and you decide you want to tell them about this. This is still a pretty general feeling, and before saying anything [you should consider] what there is *specifically* about his or her delivery that prompts your feeling. You may think, for example, that the person doesn't organize his or her thoughts as well under some specific circumstances as you know he or she is capable of from other shared experiences. . . . On the other hand, suppose that you feel that the only thing that interferes with his or her ability to persuade . . . is that he or she is physically a very small person with a high squeaky voice or an even more pronounced speech impediment. If you are really trying to be helpful, there obviously is no point in calling attention to these kinds of things. . . . So by this criterion, you might or might not decide that it would be helpful to tell the other person that you felt he or she did not project ideas as forcefully or persuasively as he or she might. Whether you choose to do so or not would depend upon your best estimate of the receiver's ability to do something about the particular obstacle you saw.
- Sometimes when people are exchanging their views and feelings about one another, there may be a tendency to feel that you haven't really done justice unless you have told people "everything that bothers you" about them. It is not necessarily desirable, however, to be "complete" in the negative feedback you might give a person. It may be quite a large enough task, for example, for anyone to understand, accept, and consider doing something about . . . behaving in two or three key areas. . . . Other things being equal, the more you unload, the more threatening the experience is liable to be and the more difficulty the receiver is likely to have in accepting any of it in an open frame of mind.

In addition to giving feedback that is appropriate for realistic action, it is important to view the corrective actions as a mutual task responsibility, not just something the recipient has to solve by himself or herself. Certain questions need to be considered: How does a recipient get future feedback that signals progress or regression in the eyes of others? What actions will both parties be watching for? In what form does the recipient want future feedback? What can we do that will genuinely help another person to make progress? Possibly, we need to change some of our own time-honored patterns of behavior, such as giving advice on how *we*

once solved a similar problem. That's not as useful as helping the recipient to explore ways of dealing with his or her problems in the here and now.

Shortcut signals, such as glances, code words, humor, brief encouragement, or nonverbal cues, can help provide on-the-job feedback. The important thing again is that these signals be intended as helpful to the recipient and the relationship as well as to the sender.

TOO MUCH CAUTION, TOO LITTLE CONSIDERATION

Despite the care that we have tried to take in describing useful processes for managing interpersonal feedback, the biggest problem usually found in organizations is the problem of excess caution. All too often people are *not* told things that would help them behave more effectively because of our fear of "not wanting to hurt them." As a result, the problem is perpetuated, and people get hurt later when—often after years of loyal, ineffective service—they are fired, demoted, or suddenly told that they are worth far less to the organization that they had thought. In this sense, "kindness" can often be the cruelest feedback that we can give, particularly if we could really help someone by being constructively honest sooner. Unfortunately, organizations are littered with the burned-out and broken careers of thousands who never had the opportunity to learn from honest feedback that was intended to help, no matter how clumsily and awkwardly it may have been delivered.

If too much caution is the greatest problem, then too little respect for the indi-

vidual is the next greatest. Some managers get so carried away with giving large doses of feedback that they fail to take account of each person as a separate individual. John Anderson addresses this point well, and we shall give him the last word:

Finally, some people react negatively to the very idea of doing this sort of thing—meeting as a work team, for example, and exchanging views openly of how people see each other, positively or negatively. The feeling may be that, "I am what I am, and I have the right to be that. And no group of people has a right to dictate to me what I should be like." My feeling is that this is exactly right. It remains, and should remain, the right of every individual to evaluate what he or she hears, decide what to believe, and decide in what respects, if any, it is personally worthwhile to make an effort to change. The purpose of a learning experience of the kind described here . . . is simply to give individuals better and clearer information than would ordinarily be received on which to make their own judgment of their personal effectiveness in working with others, and of how or whether they wish to further develop that effectiveness.

3

Organizational Transitions

Introduction

Our last section focuses on changes permeating the entire organization. Just as individuals, families, and work groups go through transition, so do companies. We can picture a form of "life cycle" for firms, a life cycle which evolves and spirals into the future. Firms move from planning stages through start-ups (or restarts) into early or later-stage development. Firms experience successive periods of growth and decline. Some companies fade into decline, are acquired by others, or die. Some adapt to new environments and enter stages of renewal and growth.

None of this happens without individual, family, or work group involvement in varying degrees. The cases in this section typically show that involvement, but, more important, they try to show how the parts relate to and affect the whole—and vice versa. One basic question is, what management attitudes and actions help some firms to survive and grow? This question has perplexed organizational theorists for many years. Our own biases are reflected in the selection of cases we have chosen for this section.

Each of the cases describes a company whose senior management wanted to move along a "different," nontraditional path. A few of the CEOs might be classified as dreamers or visionaries. Several knew that they were gambling not only with their own future but with the organization's as well. They still pursued the vision in quest of their own values as realities. In several cases too, values and reality seemed to clash. The company and the people within it weren't behaving the way that senior management wanted. But why? And what role was management itself playing in hindering the organization's progress?

Sometimes the line between existing visions and off-target management may seem very thin. Some readers of each case in this section will see an avant garde organization in the making. Others will see false hopes, absurd actions, and disastrous idealism. Such perspectives probably say more about the reader's values and visions than they do about the protagonists in each case.

Most of the companies described in this section are relatively small with sales of less than $100 million a year. Somerset Tire, Sun Hydraulics, and Modern Advanced Concrete are still in their first generation of management. Two others, Specialty Packaging and Johnsonville Sausage are second-generation companies. And John Hancock Mutual Life Insurance Company, of course, is not only much larger but much older.

A recurring theme in each case is that individual people and work groups at all levels and different parts of the firm can choose to act in ways that make a difference—however large or small—in the life of the organization. The potential for initiative lies not only at the top of the hierarchy but throughout the interactive parts of the firm. In that sense, this section on organizational transitions is also about individuals—each one of us—who spend significant parts of our lives as members of organizations.

Sun Hydraulics Corporation (A)

Bob Koski tended to think like an engineer. He enjoyed developing innovative solutions for complicated problems. His creativity and his skill in avoiding predictable difficulties had contributed to his success at every stage of his career. In ten years with Dynamic Controls, Inc. (from 1959 to 1969, a decade during which Dynamic Controls' annual sales grew from $600,000 to $5 million) he had risen through the ranks from product engineering to industrial sales, marketing, product development and top management. By 1969, as V.P.–Director of Corporate Development, he held the second highest position in the company, behind the company founder.

In early 1970, however, Bob decided to focus his energy on a different category of problem. Throughout his working life he had seen countless instances in which business organizations seemed to hamper, deflect, or even crush the human contributions they were designed to harness. He believed there were systematic, identifiable forces at work in this counterproductive process. With careful analysis and painstaking determination, he thought, the negative patterns could be uncovered and eliminated to free up the human energy that was so often lost in organizational politics.

At age 40, he left Dynamic Controls. His goal was to design and create a new company that would avoid the human relations problems he had observed virtually everywhere he looked in the world of organizations.

Bob gave himself three years to get his new business on its feet. He assumed it would take at least five years of operations to gain a reputation with distributors and at least three years to begin showing a positive cash flow. He intended to spend a full year planning and preparing every aspect of the new operation. The new firm would be called Sun Hydraulics Corporation.

While he expected to stay in the design, manufacture, and sales of fluid power products, Bob was not sure yet just what Sun Hydraulics' product line would be. Industry growth and his own product development capabilities seemed to indicate that there was room for Sun Hydraulics in the marketplace. Bob believed the new company, if successful, could eventually grow at least as fast as the company he was leaving. (*Exhibit 1* gives 10-year growth projections for Sun Hydraulics under pessimistic, realistic, and optimistic assumptions about the new company's business environment.)

By preference, Bob expected to exercise some control over the pace of growth. Moreover, he did not want the organization itself to grow beyond 200 to 250 employees in any one location. Of more immediate interest to him were the interrelations between his strategic choices and his primary goal of designing a dignified working environment for technical, manufacturing, and clerical personnel alike.

This case was prepared by Research Associate Colleen Kaftan, under the supervision of Professor Louis B. Barnes, as the basis for class discussion rather than to illustrate either effective or ineffective handling of an administrative situation.

THE PROBLEM AND ITS MANIFESTATIONS

According to Bob Koski, the single most obvious culprit in the "standard" organizations he knew was the organization chart. The mere existence of a formally designed hierarchy tended to force individuals into defensive, unproductive and damaging behavior patterns and ultimately to prevent the organization from responding to changing business requirements. Problems he associated with rigid organizational structure all too frequently caused key employees to leave the company or, at a minimum, they "took the fire out of people's eyes."

For example:

Every key individual in the company I helped to build (with one exception, and he was physically located elsewhere) left the organization. I think they were driven out by pride caused by organization charts. Organizational restructuring, for them, represented above all a series of demotions.

These people were quite competent, but unfortunately they were given titles, like vice president of something, or manager of something. As the company outgrew their capabilities and needed to hire or promote more talented people who would appear on the organization chart as their superiors, there was no place the old-timers could go that would satisfy their egos. They had to leave. They could not stay and save face with all the other employees. They had to leave.

So, if that was the effect of having an organization chart, then it really was a tragedy because they lost all the talent, all the know-how, all the accumulated experience those people represented.

Another problem Bob associated with typical business organizations was the process he called "ossification"—an exaggerated focus on prescribed procedures as they "congealed" over time in the minds of employees:

I think ossification takes place when, for promotion, it becomes more important that a person know how the business works internally than anything about the external activities of the company. At that point in time, it's like a cancer has taken over that is very difficult to stop. By not having an organization chart that people look at sideways and by not having job descriptions and titles, it might be possible to defer that process of ossification.

Now, all of the management thinking I've read in the past says that the way to get things done efficiently is to start with a process of describing jobs clearly. But if you do that, it almost always seems that you go through a life cycle. On a month-to-month basis, you can follow a sequence of predictable events which have tragic consequences down the road.

"Articulate" people rise in power and assume control. "Knowledgeable" people, if not also articulate, become discouraged and either leave the organization or settle into middle management positions as passive obstructionists. The process takes about eighteen months.

ELEMENTS OF A NEW DESIGN

The first measure of Bob Koski's success with Sun Hydraulics would be the new company's record in attracting and keeping talented engineers. Their contributions would be critical to Sun Hydraulics' performance in the fluid power industry. In addition, the quality of their relationships with shop and other employees would determine Sun Hydraulics' ability to develop, manufacture and market quality products. This in turn would shape Sun Hydraulics' reputation with distributors, customers, bankers, suppliers, and others on whom the fledgling company would be depending as it carved its place in the market.

Bob expected Sun Hydraulics to develop a personality of its own based on its employees' contributions over time. From the outset, however, he intended to emphasize several specific ways in which Sun Hydraulics would differ from other more typical organizations.

Horizontal Management

There would be no hierarchy, no titles, no formal job descriptions, no special benefits, no reporting relationships, and no close supervision in Sun Hydraulics. People would be expected to decide for themselves, based on widely shared information on operations, how best to contribute to the company's objectives. Both manufacturing and office personnel would be expected to work with others in the organization whenever they deemed it necessary to accomplish their tasks. "Horizontal management" would encourage the formation of "natural clusters" or groups to achieve whatever work had to be done.

Bob characterized the essential differences between "horizontal" and "hierarchical" management in terms of a popular approach to understanding human relationships. This framework would classify many typical working relationships as "parent-child" interactions. Bob hoped that horizontal management would create an "adult-adult" environment at Sun Hydraulics.[1]

Some functions, such as salary setting and performance reviews, would be difficult to perform in an entirely horizontal organization. To the extent it was possible, Bob expected the organization to develop new ways of approaching these functions within the framework of horizontal management. In every case the driving value was to be one of mutual respect.

Eliminating Intimidation

Critical to promoting mutual respect was the elimination of what Bob called "intimidation functions" in the organization. For example, Sun Hydraulics would have no purchasing agent, a job Bob described as "intimidating suppliers." Instead the company would strive to build solid working relationships with suppliers who would be trained to understand Sun Hydraulics' needs and be motivated to respect them out of shared long-term interests.

Likewise, there would be no quality inspectors in the plant. Each shop employee would be responsible for the quality of his or her own work. The importance of high standards for Sun Hydraulics' precision products would be understood and emphasized by all. Whenever quality problems arose, the person discovering them would be expected to initiate corrective action rather than merely point out the error to someone else. This might entail reworking, scrapping, or joint problem-solving with other individuals or departments as required to eliminate the flaw. Each and every product would be subjected to an extensive functional test before shipment to assure consistent product quality and to catch any errors.

Operational Communications

The foundation for Sun Hydraulics' unorthodox climate would be a wide-open system of operational communications. By that term, Bob Koski meant that all information pertinent to the company's operational activities would be made available to all employees.

---

[1] The references to "parent-child" and "adult-adult" relationships were developed by Eric Berne in his book *Games People Play: The Psychology of Human Relationships* (New York, Grove Press, 1964).

If we want to encourage self-management, we have to figure out a way to give people the information they need to decide what they want to do. This is predicated on the notion that people have a hard time doing nothing. If they're going to do something, they would rather do something useful than something nonuseful, and given an opportunity to figure out what's most useful, that they might just do that.

So the first task of horizontal management, to me, is to dismantle the power structure that controls operational communications, making sure that everybody has equal access to whatever information they need to do their jobs.

Ideally these open communications would allow shop employees to schedule their own work. Scheduling was a particularly important problem in manufacturing the kinds of products Sun Hydraulics would make. For one thing, the production processes were complicated and lengthy. Typically it took several weeks longer to manufacture a set of hydraulic valve parts than the lead time the customers were willing to give for their purchases.

It was also very difficult to forecast sales within acceptable ranges of accuracy. As a result, most companies in the industry experienced problems with inventory control and/or with chronic stress in meeting short delivery deadlines.

These "hassle factors" represented an area in which shop employees in typical hierarchies could tend to lose respect for the decision makers in management. It was also an area in which Bob expected Sun Hydraulics to outperform the competition with its emphasis on open communications and self-direction. If each employee were encouraged to work at reducing the production scheduling problem from his or her own perspective, the collective solutions would be more comprehensive and easier to implement:

My understanding is that hierarchies were originally developed because workers were unwilling, uneducated and uninformed. There were very limited capabilities for passing information. So it was a very efficient system for that time.

Today people aren't threatened any more by anything and you have great potential for communications. I think horizontal management is first made possible by universal information. The more we develop it, the more it will enhance self-management.

Group Self-Management

As an outgrowth of horizontal management and open communications, Bob expected that natural clusters would emerge among employees according to their work locations and tasks. Many natural clusters would include both office and plant people working together, for example, to develop new products or processes.

Where necessary, these groups would perform the control functions that were usually built into the hierarchy in other companies. In matters such as job-related behavior, Sun Hydraulics' employees would feel responsible to their peers rather than to a superior imposing an externally derived set of rules. For example, shop safety rules would be written by the workers involved who afterwards would be responsible for their implementation.

Most training would also occur within these work groups and with minimal formal structure. New employees would be brought into the group and given basic orientation by their peers. They would then be encouraged to ask any group member for help whenever needed.

Contrary to industrywide practices there would be no standard production times or procedures and no piece rate pay incentives at Sun Hydraulics. The work groups themselves would be free to adopt whatever methods seemed best to them. The focus would be on the group's contribution rather than on any individual's performance record.

The Decision-Making Process

Decision making was another vital area in which Bob Koski wanted Sun Hydraulics to be different from other companies. Many "people problems" he'd seen seemed to arise from the power dynamics embedded in typical decision processes. In analyzing the problem, Bob had identified four recurrent roles in decision making:

- The "author"—the discoverer of the need for a decision (who usually assumed proprietary rights to the decision)
- The "executive" on the formal or informal organization chart, who most people believe should make the decision (who would regard other decision makers as encroaching on his prerogative)
- The "expert"—the party most knowledgeable about the subject of the decision (who could be expected to defend this position)
- The "soldiers"—the person(s) most affected by the decision on a day-to-day basis

First, each of these role participants should be identified in what Bob called the "decision discovery process." In Sun Hydraulics Bob hoped to instill the understanding that all four parties should work together to arrive at joint decisions. "Authors," "experts," and "executives" should be encouraged to subordinate themselves and to serve as consultants to the "soldier(s)" who would either make the decision or, at a minimum, be comfortable with a consensus decision. He expected the decision discovery process to enhance both the quality and the implementation rate of the decisions that resulted.

The Ideal Employee

One quality in particular seemed more important than any other in the kind of people Bob sought to join him in creating Sun Hydraulics. That was the person's ability to be an accurate judge of his or her own competencies. Even beyond skills and intellectual capacity, Bob planned to focus on accurate self-assessment as a critical asset for prospective employees and colleagues.

It seemed to Bob that high proportions of most managers' day-to-day activities were actually spent resolving problems created by people who were not good judges of their own competencies and that without these problems there would be little need for managers as a separate class of employees.

Using self-knowledge as a hiring filter, he expected to be able to put together enough skilled and talented people, from Sarasota, Fla. and elsewhere, to make Sun Hydraulics a reality.

THE FORMAL PLAN

Bob Koski set down his ideas in a 34-page document entitled, "Sun Hydraulics Corporation: Plans and Objectives." Early in 1970, he circulated the handwritten report to four local bankers and a number of other people likely to be interested in the start-up.

His plans and objectives included detailed 10-year projections about sales, number of employees, space requirements, and the development and construction of Sun Hydraulics' first plant. There were also pro forma financial statements under three alternative sets of assumptions (see *Exhibit 1*). These in turn were supported by a series of descriptive statements about the fluid power components business and Sun Hydraulics' product, manufacturing, and distribution policies.

In Bob's mind, though, his overriding purpose was most accurately stated in the sections on Sun Hydraulics' corporate creed and philosophy:

CORPORATE CREED

The creed (or philosophy) of a company when clearly expressed and enthusiastically used creates the foundation of a corporation's internal and external personality.

For this new corporation to quickly establish itself and maintain a high product standard while growing rapidly it will be important to develop an ethical, aggressive, responsive and stable impression on customers, distributors, employees and vendors as soon as possible.

Perhaps most importantly, the ultimate quality of a corporation is largely determined by the character of its employees who are attracted into employment and develop because of the corporation's environment.

THE PHILOSOPHY OF SUN HYDRAULICS CORPORATION

To obey the "golden rule" in all relations both within and without the company no matter how difficult this may seem at the time.

To respect the dignity of every individual and to be courteous at all times.

To honestly and fairly make and meet our commitments with customers, distributors, employees and suppliers and to establish stable relationships with them.

To be a leader in our chosen fields of activity and in the development of our industry and community.

To be a growing company so that employees are continually provided an opportunity for additional responsibilities.

To constantly improve our products and services so that they are worth more to our customers and to constantly improve our operational methods so that we can afford higher than average wages.

To provide steady and continuous employment for persons hired with reasonable working hours and safe working conditions.

To encourage employee self-improvement and to promote from within whenever possible.

To keep employees and stockholders informed of company policies, procedures and plans.

From Plan to Reality

Having distributed the pre-incorporation prospectus to a number of interested parties, Bob Koski continued to think about Sun Hydraulics as he awaited their feedback about his ideas and objectives. For one thing, he was concerned about the reactions he might get from potential investors and other key individuals whose help he would need to make Sun Hydraulics a reality.

Beyond that, he wondered whether he would ever be able to breathe life into the organization as he now imagined it, and whether the reality would bear out his "unorthodox" beliefs.

Finally, even if all signals pointed in the direction of a successful start-up, he realized that Sun Hydraulics would then take on an existence of its own. At that point, his plans and convictions would develop into specific forms and behavior patterns as the organization came to life. He wondered what those specific forms would be, and how they would fit together when Sun Hydraulics grew to be a full-fledged business organization.

EXHIBIT 1 Sun Hydraulics Corporation (A): Growth Projections

Year	Pessimistic Sales			Realistic Sales			Optimistic Sales		
	Sales ($)	Employees (no.)	Floor Space (sq. ft.)	Sales ($)	Employees (no.)	Floor Space (sq. ft.)	Sales ($)	Employees (no.)	Floor Space (sq. ft.)
1970	10,000	5	3,000	25,000	5	3,000	35,000	6	3,000
1971	75,000	6	3,000	125,000	9	3,000	140,000	8	3,000
1972	185,000	11	5,000	250,000	15	5,000	270,000	16	5,000
1973	300,000	18	5,000	370,000	19	5,000	390,000	22	5,000
1974	425,000	22	5,000	520,000	26	5,000	570,000	29	10,000
1975	575,000	30	10,000	690,000	34	10,000	800,000	41	10,000
1976	750,000	38	10,000	900,000	46	10,000	1,125,000	56	15,000
1977	950,000	49	10,000	1,175,000	59	15,000	1,500,000	73	15,000
1978	1,150,000	59	15,000	1,500,000	75	15,000	2,000,000	95	25,000
1979	1,450,000	75	15,000	1,900,000	95	25,000	2,600,000	120	25,000
1980	1,800,000	95	25,000	2,350,000	115	25,000	3,400,000	165	40,000
1981	2,150,000	110	25,000	3,000,000	150	40,000	4,300,000	200	40,000

Note: Considerable data exist to support the proportions of sales, employees and space.

Source: "Sun Hydraulics Corporation: Plans and Objectives," internal document prepared by Bob Koski in 1969.

Sun Hydraulics Corporation (B)

In 1985 Bob Koski described Sun Hydraulics' actual performance record for the casewriters:

We followed our pre-incorporation plan so closely that 10 years later we were within a percentage point—correcting for inflation—of our most optimistic projections.

Sun Hydraulics' business results were positive by any standards. The company's sales had grown by 30–35% annually, some 25% beyond the National Fluid Power Association's industry average (see *Exhibit 1*). The growth had been orderly and controlled according to the original plan. Profits were usually twice the industry average, while many products were priced up to 10% below comparable offerings from the competition. During an industrywide slump in 1982 and 1983, Sun Hydraulics had been able to remain modestly profitable by scaling back production and reducing inventories, and had done so early enough to avoid employee layoffs.

Even more important for Bob was the employment record: other than a senior designer's reluctant departure in 1985 for health reasons, the company had not lost a single key individual in 15 years of operations. Among the 10–12 people generally recognized as the most creative hydraulics engineers in the U.S., four had chosen to come to Sun Hydraulics. Although compensation was not appreciably higher at Sun Hydraulics than at other similar companies, virtually all Sun Hydraulics employees agreed that the company was an extraordinary place to work.

Moreover, Sun Hydraulics had achieved widespread recognition in the industry for its innovative design, its quality products, and its highly ethical standards for business dealings. Bob believed that many of the positive results stemmed from the philosophy and practices he called "horizontal management." It was this nonstandard approach to management that had provided the foundation for the company when he established it in 1970.

THE ORGANIZATION

By 1985, Sun Hydraulics' uniquely integrated product line included a 200-page catalogue of hydraulic system components. The company counted some 170 employees in Sarasota, Fla. as well as six others employed in small marketing and warehousing operations in the U.K. and Switzerland.

The main facility had been built in 1980 on a beautiful site bordering a bird sanctuary. It was five times as large as the previous factory, originally built in 1970 and expanded in 1975 to accommodate the company's early development.

There were glass partitions between the

This case was prepared by Research Associate Colleen Kaftan, under the supervision of Professor Louis B. Barnes, as the basis for class discussion rather than to illustrate either effective or ineffective handling of an administrative situation.

plant and the open-plan office space, but both office and shop people could frequently be observed "crossing over" to the other part of the building. All employees shared a common lunchroom facility, which included several outdoor picnic benches overlooking a pond in the bird sanctuary.

About 20% of Sun Hydraulics' outstanding stock had been made available to a few highly competent employees whose contributions were critical in shaping the company's future in the marketplace. These stock options were offered only to key employees who were already contributing valuable input, as an incentive to stay with Sun Hydraulics. They were never used as an incentive for individuals considering joining the company.

Beyond this, there were no perquisites or special benefits for anyone in the company. There were no formal job descriptions, no organization charts, and no prescribed reporting relationships. Nor were there official titles aside from two that seemed indispensable for interactions with the "outside world" (Bob Koski was president and one of his close colleagues was controller). No correspondence and no business cards included titles. Furthermore, in the words of one executive:

There are hardly any heroes in our organization. When something good happens, we try to suppress the hype. When something bad happens, we try to suppress the "down."

The Office

About 25 "office people" took care of the administration, product design, marketing, and computer programming functions at Sun Hydraulics. The group Bob Koski called the "management team" tended to be closely involved in each others' activities and to "get things done collectively." The idea of collec-

tive responsibilities had led to an organizational concept Bob Koski called "shared offices." A "shared office" included several people commonly identified with the activities that might normally be assigned to a single person as department head in a more typical organization. *Exhibit 2* shows Bob's graphic representation of the "shared office" arrangement at Sun Hydraulics. The drawing was his first attempt ever to prepare anything resembling an organization chart for the company.

Hiring and responsibilities Most of the office people had been hired after long discussions about Sun Hydraulics' unusual philosophy and practices, and about the areas in which the prospective new hire might be able to "fill a vacuum" in the company's activities. In hiring decisions, however, there was invariably greater emphasis on the qualities of the person and his or her fit with the organization than on the "vacuum" or the job to be done.

For example, a vacuum might go unfilled for months until the "right" person was found. On the other hand, a good person might be hired long before he or she was actually needed in the company. And even when people were brought in with specific "vacuums" in mind, their own choices about job activities might take them into entirely different areas. One engineer, who had been hired with a product development function in mind, had "become intrigued with the computer" in his first days on the job, and since had concentrated entirely on creating new programming applications.

Another market-oriented engineer hired from outside the company had not yet moved to Sarasota some 9 months after joining Sun Hydraulics. According to several of his new colleagues in Sarasota, this man had decided to spend time "wandering around" learning more about the market. They were certain that one way or another his wanderings would be of benefit to the company. No one had fixed ideas about whether or when he would join them in the Sarasota office.

Each individual was expected to choose the range of activities in which he or she could best contribute to the organization. Frequently, these choices led to a natural expansion in the individual's responsibilities. For example, one person whose activities initially consisted largely of administrative and clerical work began slowly to use her considerable interpersonal skills in her everyday interactions. Both plant and office people tended to approach her with questions and problems about working relationships and other "personnel" issues. After a few years with Sun Hydraulics she was broadly recognized as the person most responsible for "human resources" and related matters in the company.

Office architecture The controller and his assistant had the only enclosed offices in the building. The others, including Bob Koski, used workplaces separated from each other only by waist-high sectional dividers. A small glass-walled library and a larger conference room were available for use by plant and office employees alike.

Some people had found it difficult to adjust to working in the open office plan. One engineer temporarily decided to change his working hours in order to have "quiet time" in the evenings to finish preparing the new catalogue. Another had set up a provisional work space in a storage area to which he retreated occasionally to work on special projects.

Interactions For the most part, however, the new office design had been successful. Bob Koski thought the arrangement was helpful for communications in the absence of scheduled meetings:

There are no formal meetings at Sun Hydraulics. Meetings are generally impromptu and people vote themselves in or out based on their interests. Typically two people will begin a discussion and discover they need some information. They'll go together as a pair to see another person. That frequently draws a small crowd until people see whether they're interested or not, and the problem almost always gets taken care of on the spot.

The same flexibility was apparent in interactions with people from outside the company. Bob Koski believed the absence of titles, while confusing to outsiders, contributed to getting things done at Sun Hydraulics:

If a salesman were to walk in the door, the first thing he'd say is, "I want to talk to the VP of so and so." We ask what he wants to talk about and then send him to the right person. If he asks what that person's title is we tell him there aren't any titles. They're usually looking for someone who can make a decision. Since I always refuse to, they give up on me. I think I could sabotage the system simply by making decisions. I just don't.

Many of the "office people" interacted regularly with people in the plant. Some thought that despite the casual atmosphere, shop personnel still might feel intimidated and reluctant to come into the office area. A few of the shop workers did come into the office to meet with colleagues there, and some had switched to office jobs when there were openings that suited their interests and skills. Office workers went out to the plant floor whenever they thought it was necessary.

The Plant

Like the office area, the shop was clean, airy, and generously adorned with green plants. Work benches and heavy equipment were arrayed in an extended horseshoe around the main door, according to the production sequence. Production floor space had increased fivefold with the move to the new facility in 1980. A number of "old-timers" remarked that the increased size and the addition of 50 new shop workers since the move had limited the opportunities for close, friendly relationships they remembered from the previous facility. Others thought the new plant had simply enlarged and enhanced the area in which the friendships with fellow employees could develop.

One recurring comment was that with 170 people now working at Sun Hydraulics, "It takes a lot longer to get to know everybody's name." Another common remark was that the enlarged space "makes it much harder to sing rounds with the people in the next department."

"Family groups" and lead persons

There were 12 departments or family groups in the plant, from the lathe group, to drilling, tool making, machining, deburring, stamping, and packing. A test bench served as a worktable for trying out new product ideas in conjunction with the design and development process so that production workers could provide input and gain familiarity with new products before they entered the production phase.

Family groups worked closely together with little formal division of individual roles. One benefit of the "family" relationships that developed over time was a natural tendency to find better ways of working. The resulting productivity increases were impressive: Bob Koski pointed out that several departments had developed new methods that increased their productivity by 400% over a period of 4–6 years, without resorting to any unusual equipment.

Each group included at least one informally-designated "lead person." The lead people (also called "supervisors" although the use of such "standard" terms was not encouraged) were generally people with long tenure, the most experience, or broad skills in the department.

Leaders tended to emerge naturally from within the groups. They often took the initiative in training new people to do the various tasks in the group. Beyond that, their role usually also included other activities such as introducing new employees to the group, taking responsibility when the group needed to resolve a problem jointly with another group, and coordinating the department's overtime schedule.

Plant supervision There was a single official supervisory level in the plant. Two foremen and their assistants were available to oversee daily production and materials management activities. Their only formally planned supervisory task was to conduct individual wage and performance reviews semiannually with each of the workers in their departments. In addition, the two foremen worked closely with managerial and clerical people in a "shared office" for other decisions regarding the production function.

The leader of the "shared office" group was Bob Devereaux, who had come to Sun Hydraulics in 1979 after accomplishing a series of successful plant turnarounds in a high-level manufacturing position for a much larger company. He shared a small glass-walled office adjacent to the plant with Bob Voorhees, a 14-year veteran whose responsibilities Bob Koski described as "a sort of roving superintendent." Directly across from their work space was another glass-walled enclosure in which two schedulers monitored and coordinated shop activities with a battery of eight computer terminals. Together the members of this "shared office" group accomplished many of the tasks that would have been called "production and operations management" in a more typical hydraulic components plant.

In fact, while all of them acknowledged the tremendous difference between Sun Hydraulics and other, more hierarchical organizations, some had difficulty describing their collective work activities without using the "standard" terms and titles familiar to the other companies. According to Bob Voorhees:

I joined Sun Hydraulics about a year after it was founded. In those days I had a hard time getting Bob Koski to let us use words like "foreman," "supervisor," and "manager." We know our ways of getting things done are different from other places, but we still have to use their words because people have to know where to go for help. They need to know who's running the shop. Otherwise it just gets too confusing, especially for the ones who come here from other companies.

Even though people sometimes used "standard" terms to talk about their work at Sun Hydraulics, Bob Koski maintained that the working relationships they described were more "horizontal" than "vertical" in nature. Bob Devereaux clarified the conscious mechanisms by which Sun Hydraulics' people enacted the more egalitarian environment:

One of the things we've been doing—and we've tried to build it in to every part of the organization—is to keep pushing decisions and responsibilities down so they're at the lowest possible level. We've consciously avoided creating any elite groups or formalizing any structure. We knew that once we built it in we wouldn't be able to get it out.

For example, when a new and complicated generation of computerized flexible machining centers was brought into the plant, the operators themselves were sent to the vendor's factory to be trained for the programming functions. This unique approach (no other company had ever asked the vendor to train relatively unsophisticated shop workers to program these highly advanced machines) avoided the usual practice of forming a specialized "elite" program-

ming group. At the same time it ensured that the skills needed to run and maintain the machines remained "right down at the people level." An added benefit of Sun Hydraulics' approach was a better acceptance rate and a faster start-up time than the machine tool vendor had ever seen in any other installation of the machines.

Production scheduling Another area in which responsibilities were pushed to the lowest possible level was the scheduling of each group's daily activities in the plant. Groups received regular updates on the parts that were needed, and were expected to plan their own activities to accomplish as many of the tasks on their lists as possible.

In 1985, this self-scheduling procedure was in the process of being fully automated. After an extended search, Bob Koski had concluded that no externally available computerized scheduling system could meet Sun Hydraulics' needs. As a result, a sophisticated new system had been developed internally beginning in 1976. The new programs, when fully applied, would provide "live" data (based on known immediate and computer projected orders rather than on staff-generated sales forecasts) about parts to be produced, delivery dates, and order priorities for anyone in the plant who wanted it.

Within this framework of "universal information" shop workers would be encouraged to make their own decisions about what to produce and when. The system would help reduce inventories while affording greater flexibility in responding to customers' orders.

A few departments had already switched over to the computerized system. They had experienced some difficulty with the change, even though the computers affected only the way they received and recorded information, not the way they made decisions or carried out the work. After a few months' training and actual use of the programs, however, there seemed to be better understanding and increasing acceptance of them among the departments in which they had been introduced.

Overtime and cross-training Shop workers followed a four-day, ten-hour schedule, and could choose to come in for overtime on Fridays and Saturdays at their own discretion. They could also choose to do overtime in areas other than their own, and departments frequently "helped each other" in this way when the personnel were cross-trained.

Cross-training occurred naturally when people showed an interest in switching departments or in "helping out" in busy areas. The same mechanisms operated even more strongly within the "family groups" so that many employees were capable of doing most or all of the jobs within their department groups.

Circle groups In 1983 a new kind of group activity was initiated at Sun Hydraulics. Each department (including office as well as shop workers) was invited to form a voluntary "circle group" to identify and work on ways of improving the overall quality of working life at Sun Hydraulics.

Circles could meet for an hour each week on company time. Employees who chose to join a circle received training in communication skills and in joint problem-solving procedures. Circle leaders also learned about group processes and tech-niques for managing meetings. In addition, two elected "facilitators" from the plant trained extensively and participated in all circle start-up activities.

A year and a half later the groups could take credit for dozens of small interventions that helped improve product quality, production processes, and the company environment in general. They had also set up classes, training programs, and field trips to enhance their understanding of Sun Hydraulics' overall activities.

Several groups had stopped meeting because "there weren't any problems in the department." In fact, there was some question about the next steps to be taken by the ongoing groups. A few group members reported a rising resentment from lead persons or among their coworkers in the shop about the time they spent in circle meetings.

The circle members did, however, believe their activities were important to the company as a whole. One suggested that despite any controversy that might surround the circles' activities, their informal benefits had gone far beyond the list of concrete accomplishments:

Even people who are profoundly against quality circles—and I have trouble understanding how you can be against them—are starting to behave in a "quality circle way." They start to talk about a problem and I think, "Hey, that was a quality circle thing you said!" And they don't even realize it.

CURRENT CONCERNS

There were a number of issues being discussed in various parts of the organization in early 1985. One had to do with Sun Hydraulics' lack of formal structure or standard procedures. While the management group had always resisted the risk of rigidity they associated with formalizing any organizational arrangement, they wondered if some official structure was necessary now that the company had grown.

In particular, the question of formalization came up in discussions about hiring and firing, training, performance and salary reviews, the "policing function," and communications in general. The problem was to find a way of instituting some procedures in these areas without damaging Sun Hydraulics' unique organizational climate.

For example, there seemed to be some confusion about the appropriate roles and behavior for lead people in the plant. Some discord seemed evident in the emerging negative sentiment regarding circle group activities.

Another illustration of possible malaise was an incident in which a lead person had been asked to leave the company. After nearly ten years with Sun Hydraulics, the person had begun behaving in ways that caused discomfort, embarrassment, and even fear in some members of his work group. The difficulties remained unknown to management for almost a year and then persisted after a warning and reevaluation period. The dismissal was remembered as a painful event by people from all parts of the company. Bob Koski was especially concerned about the extended time it had taken for the employee's unacceptable behavior to come to the attention of anyone in the office group.

Other questions revolved around the stand-alone viability of the nonstandard approach to management. What were the critical elements contributing to Sun Hydraulics' success in human as well as business outcomes? Could a similar climate be "transported" to the new manufacturing operation that was to be set up in the United Kingdom? How should the new British company be developed?

A final focus of concern was Bob Koski's role in maintaining the integrity of Sun Hydraulics' approach. Bob's colleagues in the management group were convinced that his contributions had made the company what it was. Bill Clendenin, the controller, observed that:

Bob is the visionary; he's the one who doesn't let himself get detoured from the long-term goals. We do the detail work but he's the visionary.

He and I differ in that he doesn't think he's that important. Unless we find a way to make him personally not too important, we may end up looking much more like a conventional company as time goes on.

The task of the future, as Bill saw it, was to incorporate Bob's personal imprint into the organization:

Now we have to find a way to keep this same feeling of being involved in a total operation, being part of a total whole, at the same time we're spreading geographically and becoming much broader as an organization. How do we clone Bob Koski and spread his philosophy while retaining this sense of belonging to a total unit?

Bob himself wanted to believe the organization would retain its personality and climate even without his immediate presence. He felt a personal need to explore the issue further, to find out whether the "Sun Hydraulics approach" had any validity outside the company as he had created it.

If the approach *did* have merit beyond its applications in Sun Hydraulics, he thought it should be communicated to a larger population. On the other hand, if the organization could be expected to regress or collapse without his personal input, he proposed that the "collapsing" should be done purposely and should be undertaken soon in order to avoid a more painful, unplanned transition at a later date.

On April 2, 1985, Bob Koski stood before Sun Hydraulics' assembled employees on the 15th anniversary of the company's founding to recognize a new milestone. March 1985 had been the first month in which a million dollars worth of products were shipped. Bob wondered how to proceed.

EXHIBIT 1 Sun Hydraulics Corporation (B). Sun Hydraulics vs. Industry Average: Monthly Sales, 1972–1985; Company/Industry Comparison. *Source:* Company records.

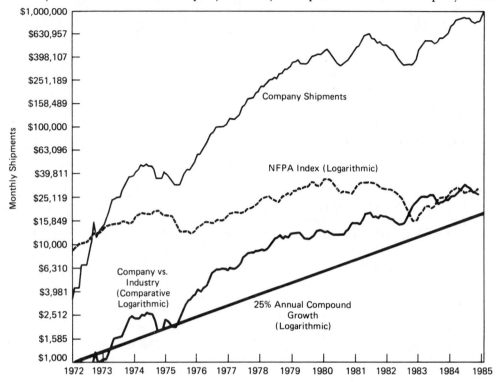

EXHIBIT 2 Sun Hydraulics Corporation (B). "Shared Office" Organization at Sun Hydraulics.

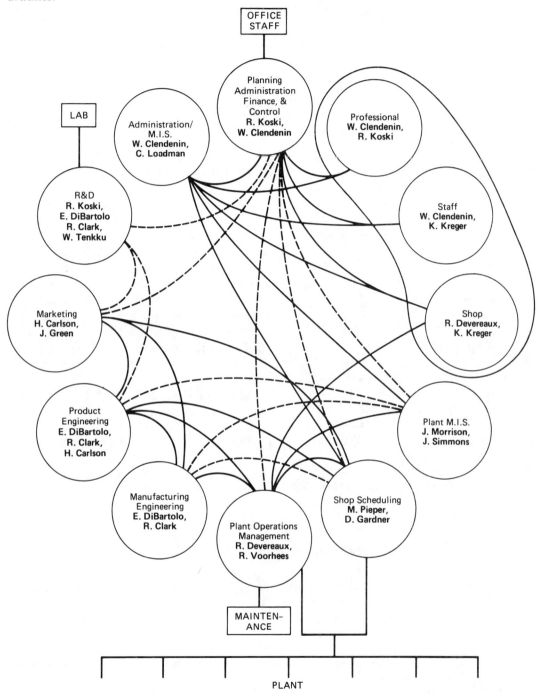

Somerset Tire Service (A)

People have accused us of instituting something that smacks of socialism. Our answer to that is, "Socialism, hell! We're just making capitalists out of people who might otherwise have *become* socialists!" We started our employee ownership system because we needed money—it was that simple. But it's turned out to have some pretty good effects that go way beyond the money.

The speaker was Jack Apgar, president of New Jersey-based STS (Somerset Tire Service). Jack had started the company in 1958 by purchasing a small retread shop in Bound Brook, New Jersey, with a total capitalization of $20,000. By 1985, STS operations included wholesale and retail tire outlets, 29 auto service centers in a three-state area, and a parts warehousing and distributorship operation in addition to the greatly expanded retread business. (An informal organization chart sketched for the casewriter is shown in *Exhibit 1*.) Overall sales in 1984 had exceeded $35 million. STS had averaged 30% annual growth for the first 15 years of its existence and some 20% annually since then.

Late in 1984, Apgar and his associates opened merger and/or acquisitions negotiations with STS's largest New Jersey competitor, Tire Warehouse. The potential expansion would be substantial even by STS standards: overnight, the company would add almost 100 employees and 11 branches. Retail tire sales volume would double.

STS had run into trouble in the early 1970s when it acquired a large forklift dealership. The venture had turned sour in part because of differences in organizational style ("they were a different breed of cat") and a union organizing campaign in the forklift operation. The arrangement had been terminated—at considerable cost to STS—within a few years. This time, however, Jack Apgar and his top management team believed they had much better chances for success. In recent years, branch acquisitions had become a routine occurrence, but continuous expansion had never been allowed to dilute STS's unique system of shared responsibilities and rewards. In short, STS's managers seemed unconcerned about the group's ability to "swallow the whale" while maintaining the qualities that had contributed to the company's success. Their chief concern seemed to be *how* to manage the assimilation if and when the deal could be satisfactorily closed.

MANAGEMENT AT STS

According to Jack Apgar, one of Somerset's key success factors lay in the company's stock ownership and profit-sharing systems. But even beyond the financial incentives, there were several other ways in which STS differed from other companies, and from its

This case was prepared by Research Associate Colleen Kaftan, based in part on an earlier case written by Marilyn Taylor, under the supervision of Professor Louis B. Barnes, as the basis for classroom discussion rather than to illustrate either effective or ineffective handling of an administrative situation.

competitors in the tire industry in particular. Very few of those differences had been formalized or even expressed in writing. For example, there were no formal job descriptions and no formal organization charts. Management at Bound Brook talked instead about broad "areas of concentration" in individuals' work.

The top five or six executives knew each other's "areas" so well that they could cover for each other during absences. They consulted with each other on most important area decisions and often undertook joint research efforts to determine appropriate activities for the company. Many of their discussions took place outside normal business hours. Such impromptu meetings were called by any one or two managers whenever they felt a need for group discussion. Occasionally the meetings went on late into the night for several evenings in a row. The group generally tried to achieve consensus on all major issues before moving to implement decisions.

In the branches, the managers were given almost complete liberty to "run the business" the way they thought was best. The head office people saw their role as providing support to help implement store managers' decisions.

The record in 1985 seemed to bear out many of Jack's beliefs about human motivation and management. STS prided itself on high customer loyalty, low employee turnover, and extremely low pilferage rates in an industry plagued by expensive inventory losses.

Hiring and Training

Educational background was not a big factor in a hiring decision at STS. Instead, the company looked for enthusiastic people who had the interests and aptitudes needed in the tire industry. "Training" mainly consisted of individually planned rotations through several different areas in the company. These "assignments" could vary in time from a few days to several years, depending on the individual and the positions available. They served as opportunities for employees to expand their capabilities while performing jobs they liked:

You hire a kid who's crazy about cars and let him work on cars all day. Then over time you give him other experiences so he can move into other responsibilities if he wants to. Or you get an entrepreneurial type and work with him 'til he's able to run his own business.

Another source of employees came from sole proprietors whose tire or service businesses were in jeopardy, or who were nearing retirement but had found no successors. Over the years Jack Apgar had issued standing offers to acquire a number of businesses this way. Every once in a while someone called to take him up on the offer.

New hires, regardless of previous experience or expectations, almost always started in the central tire warehouse at Bound Brook, where the head office and the retread shop were located in the same building. The new employees began to make acquaintances among the top management team there. Deliveries to the various branch stores also exposed them to other aspects of the business. Often a recent hire would suggest his own next assignment.

At the same time, some new hires seemed to be dissatisfied with this first assignment. Warehouse work was strenuous, unglamorous, and lacking in regular opportunities to interact with customers or with fellow employees. Turnover rates were higher in the warehouse than in any other part of the company. Management did not seem to be bothered by this high turnover.

Branch–Head Office Relationships

The path toward greater responsibility varied with the individual's interests and aptitudes. Occasionally management would suggest an advancement to a store manager's position before the individual felt ready for the change. Other times an employee might ask for added responsibilities before management expected him to be ready, or before there was an apparent opening. In both cases the differences of opinion would be brought into the open and discussed until the parties reached a resolution satisfactory to both.

Once managers were in place, the goal of head office was to "get rid of the drudgery for them, so they can spend 100% of their time doing what they like and do best." The key to this was STS's "record-keeping system."

Each manager spent no more than 20 minutes per day reporting on sales and expenditures. The accounting department processed all information and provided regular feedback on profits to each manager. A quarterly review of profitability by branch and by product gave managers the chance to compare their own performance with that of other branches within the company.

The head office also took care of any collection problems the branch might have. While a bad check would affect the store's bottom line, collection responsibilities were handled by the head office.

The Bound Brook head office also served a sort of "clearing house" role, finding and supplying needed inventory, shifting extra help from one branch to another to cover busy periods, and so on. Purchasing and advertising were centralized functions at STS. All other decisions were subject to Jack Apgar's rule of "pushing the responsibility down to the lowest level possible."

Like the top management group, store managers were expected to spend time after hours to attend group meetings for new product introductions and other issues of concern to the whole company. While the managers were free to set their own working hours, these extra responsibilities sometimes made for a long working week. Jack Apgar thought that such a time commitment was normal among highly motivated people: "I never saw anybody make any money by working only 40 hours a week."

Financial Incentive Systems

Employee ownership With one or two exceptions, all of STS stock was owned by current employees of the company. Any employee who had worked a year or more for STS could purchase stock at the current price. The first purchase was to be in the amount of $1,000 (increased from $500 in 1979). Thereafter, the employee could purchase any number of shares. Upon separation from the company, the employee's holdings had to be sold back as treasury stock at the current price, which was established yearly by a CPA firm the company had retained since 1958.

Somerset's growth record made the stock option an attractive benefit for some employees. According to one supervisor from the retread shop, it meant that "We're all going to be millionaires by the time we're sixty-five."

The profit-sharing program A second feature of the financial incentive system was the company bonus system. STS's plan was adapted from one pioneered by the Lincoln Electric Company in Cleveland, Ohio.[1] Apgar remembered:

---

[1] James F. Lincoln, *Incentive Management.* Cleveland, Ohio: The Lincoln Electric Company, 1951.

Before I read Lincoln's book, I could see myself running a sales company. But after I read *Incentive Management*, I knew I had found the key to running a manufacturing concern. The first year we were in operation, we put in the profit-sharing plan. We still have it today.

Each year, 20% of STS's estimated after-tax profit was set aside in a profit-sharing program for all employees. This total amount of $30,000 in 1974 had grown to $290,000 by 1984.

The employee allocation within each unit was a function of the number of employees at the unit, the unit's contribution to total sales, and the unit's contribution to overall profit. The manner of determining the amount to be distributed to individual employees differed from one unit to another. Some managers made the allocation themselves. Others asked an assistant and perhaps a senior employee to make the decision. Still others delegated the decision to a committee of employees selected by the manager or by the employees.

To allocate the managerial share for both the head office in Bound Brook and the branches, managers were divided into support people and operating managers. The president, executive vice president and controller, vice president of retail sales, vice president of wholesale sales, and managers from distribution as well as real estate and construction, formed the support group. The managers of the retail and wholesale stores and the heads of the subsidiary corporations were the operating managers. Each operating manager evaluated and ranked the support managers and vice versa. The individual profit share was allocated to each participant on the basis of his average ranking.

Every employee, regardless of length of service, participated in profit-sharing. During the first year of service, however, the bonus size was prorated to date of hire.

Branch incentive programs Two other incentive systems were also in operation in 1984. They were the store manager's share of his store's profit and an incentive program designed by each store manager for his employees. The store manager's annual salary was equal to 40% of the store's profit for that year. His monthly paychecks were a fixed-amount draw on the total amount. The end-of-year adjustment gave him extra cash at the time the final figures were calculated. (According to the head office group, draws were guaranteed and if a manager was not hitting his incentive goals, the head office would explore ways of maximizing other strengths of the manager. This might include a job change if necessary.)

Some managers at larger branches had recently begun to delegate 5–10% of their personal profit earnings to particularly helpful assistant managers. They felt that it provided additional incentives for the best assistant managers and gave the managers a feeling of shared responsibilities with a "partner."

Sales promotion incentives for other employees posed a more delicate problem. According to Jack Apgar, bonuses based on sales were a tricky business:

If you pay too much, the customer will get things he doesn't need, but if you pay too little, the employee won't go to the extra bother of bringing the need to the attention of the customer or the store manager.

The New ESOP

About 25% of Somerset's 250 employees had taken advantage of the stock purchase option by 1984. This figure was five times the percentage of stock owners in the national population, but it still fell short of the goal at STS. Some believed that the $1,000 minimum initial purchase prohibited broader participation in the ownership program.

As a result, the management group decided to institute a companywide ESOP (Employee Stock Ownership Plan) at the end of 1984. Instead of being distributed as a cash bonus for all employees, the annual profit-sharing fund would be used to purchase treasury stock in the employees' names.

The new system was partially implemented in 1984, using half the usual bonus pool. Beginning with 1985, the entire pool would be used for the ESOP. Legally there could be no preferential schemes (other than a percent of annual compensation) in allocating ESOP benefits to individual employees. As a result, the merit-ranking system would disappear entirely beginning in 1985, when all employees would receive shares according to their relative income levels.

The accumulated benefits would be vested on a progressive schedule. Individuals would own 30% of their ESOP rights after three years in the program. Each additional year increased their free holdings by 10%. At the end of ten years in the ESOP, the individual's rights were fully vested.

The ESOP was to be administered by a five-member committee and a trustee appointed by the STS board of directors. ESOP shares carried common stock voting rights and individuals could instruct the committee who, in turn, instructed the trustee to vote according to their wishes. They could, for example, vote on the appointment of senior corporate officers through the election of directors. (In 1985, the board of directors included most "support group" managers as well as two retail store managers. There were no outside directors.)

Despite a series of meetings and presentations on the subject, not all employees seemed to understand in early 1985 the complex workings of the ESOP. Nor were they all aware of the fact that the entire bonus pool would go to the ESOP from 1985 onward. Nevertheless, management expected that by extending ownership to all employees, the new ESOP would concretize the STS philosophy of placing control in the hands of the people closest to the job.

A former Marine with an avowed propensity for action, Jack Apgar claimed he had never worried much about controlling people at STS:

Some outside executives just don't understand this kind of program. They ask me how I keep control over the company. The answer is I don't! With employee ownership, you don't have to. Everybody in the company knows he's got to work to earn his job.

Take the example of security: if a guy here steals a tire, he knows he is stealing from himself and from the guy who works with him all day long. So he doesn't do it, or if he does we can be pretty sure we'll known about it before too long.

The company's executive vice president explained it a different way:

If you possess the qualities that Jack has—especially strong effective leadership—you don't *need* control.

The Theory of Sponsorship

Management at STS put a high premium on relationships: customers, competitors, suppliers, and the community at large were considered to be valuable partners, as were employees both past and present. Jack Apgar described the philosophy:

It's a basic premise: we are going to maintain our relationships. We call it the theory of sponsorship. We want to make everyone who comes into contact with us a sponsor. Once in a while it means we lose money dealing with unreasonable people, but that really doesn't happen very often. We want everyone who knows us to come away respecting our integrity. If you push for it, it happens.

Some thought the "theory of sponsorship" might have been behind the opportunity to acquire Tire Warehouse, since Apgar and his management team were trusted and well respected in the industry, even by rival companies like Tire Warehouse.

TIRE WAREHOUSE

From a single-location wholesale tire distributor, Tire Warehouse had grown to be an 11-outlet chain of tire sales and auto service centers by 1985. Now in its second generation of family management, the company was closely governed by the founder's son and the original controller. A single general manager was responsible for communicating and implementing his two senior colleagues' directives at all 11 branches. Reporting to him were a manager and one or more assistant managers at each outlet.

Not all the details about the business were easily available to the potential acquirers at STS. Much could be inferred, however, from the long years during which the rival companies had operated and grown up together in the same geographical territory.

Unlike the STS stores, many Tire Warehouse branches had been placed in out-of-the-way locations off the main thoroughfares. Tire Warehouse ads sometimes included maps to help customers find the location nearest them. Moreover, the branches did not have a distinctive "look" as did the STS stores. They *did* carry a "warehouse image," part of management's attempt to position the chain as a low-price provider of many different kinds of tires, accessories, and services.

While STS customers seemed to come from the middle class and up, Tire Warehouse targeted customers from the middle class and below. STS executives estimated that there was about a 50% overlap in customer base. By STS estimates, Tire Warehouse was selling some 47 units/location/day as compared with the STS average of 27 units/location/day. No comparable information was available regarding the auto service business.

The percentage of college graduates was far higher among "front room people" (managers, assistant managers, and sales personnel) at Tire Warehouse than at STS. In keeping with industry practice (but unlike STS), the managers and assistant managers spent most of their time on sales and administrative functions. Extensive records were gathered for analysis by the two top executives and the general manager. These three executives developed standard operating directives for all branches. These directives included headcount, hours, pricing, special promotions and the like, which were sent on to the 11 branches. The "front room people" at Tire Warehouse wore different colored shirts than employees in the service bays. They rarely crossed over to the service area other than to seek information from the mechanics.

Tire Warehouse managers were paid on a percent of their store sales volume. Other store personnel (including mechanics) received commissions on their own sales as well as on overall store volume. This system apparently placed Tire Warehouse employees above average compensation levels for the industry. In addition, at senior management's discretion some employees received end of year bonuses to reward good performance. According to Jack Apgar, however, the most successful Tire Warehouse managers made less money than the best performing managers at STS. Other benefits were equal, if not better, at STS than at Tire Warehouse.

STS managers seemed eager to take on the challenges of a "quantum leap" in their company's operations. The tire business had decreased about 10% nationally (although STS tire sales had actually increased by 6%) during the previous year. The trend was expected to continue as enhanced quality reduced the need for replacement purchases. Noting a "shakeout in the industry," Jack professed to be "tickled to death to take advantage of it."

With the downturn in the tire business, the more successful competitors were developing broader capabilities as auto service centers. Both STS and Tire Warehouse had embarked successfully on this path. Changes in auto servicing procedures were requiring more sophisticated equipment and mechanics, and (according to STS executives) even more attention to motivation and "personal chemistry" in the branches.

Unlike some of the other acquisition possibilities that had come to Somerset, Tire Warehouse was both large and relatively profitable in 1985. The question of size was an interesting one. According to Jack, any company with over $2 million in sales was considered "huge" by local industry standards. By taking STS "beyond the scale of sole proprietorship," management had brought the company into a new realm of organizational practices.

These practices would continue even with a major increase in size, in the opinion of most head office people at STS. Their plans for managing Tire Warehouse started with "pushing decisions down to the lowest level," just as was the practice at STS.

There were, however, some indications that other organizations had suffered from such increases beyond a certain (unknown) size. At least four star managers from a neighboring state tire and auto service chain had recently approached STS seeking jobs. One of them claimed their dissatisfaction with the old employer arose from a new, impersonal management style in the 70-outlet organization:

We got very big and then the founder died. His wife had to bring in somebody else to run the business. That's when we started losing the personal character. Now they run everything by the numbers. It seems like the more you do, the more they're after you to double it in the next year. It becomes a task to go to work in the morning.

At STS there was not much worry about a similar erosion as the company grew bigger. The management group believed that STS was home grown and robust enough to make outside recruitment of new managers unnecessary. Furthermore, as one executive commented:

What are we going to do about growth? The whole system will work the same way. We'll just keep pyramiding our branch structure. We can change the chemistry of a store simply by putting one of our guys in it, and he doesn't have to be the manager, either.

Jack Apgar continued:

We've been doing this for 26 years. The increase from one branch to two was more traumatic for STS than it'll be to go from 29 profit centers to 41.

Asked about his responsibilities as CEO of a larger company, Jack responded:

I don't mount tires. I don't even think about tires. I think about moving this company forward and keeping 250 employees happy.

Every week somebody asks me where we get our guys. I hate to tell them, but we get them the same place they get theirs! They think we pay our people more but I don't know that we do. Our policies are not humanitarianism or utopia; they're just good business.

So why don't our competitors do what we do? I don't know. We eat up competitors every day.

Reacting with some amusement to the case-writers' queries about size, one of Jack's closest colleagues asked a question of his own: "You don't think we could outgrow this, do you?"

EXHIBIT 1 Somerset Tire Service (A). Informal Organization Chart. February 1985.

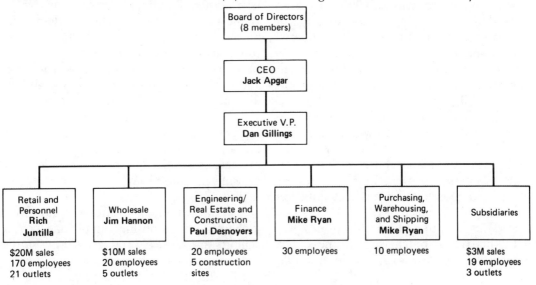

Note: The individuals named on this chart constituted the "support group" for the pre-1985 profit-sharing allocation system.

The board of directors was composed of the six executives named on this chart in addition to two retail store managers.

The Johnsonville Sausage Co.

Ralph Stayer hung up the phone and leaned back in his chair, deep in thought. One of Johnsonville Sausage's private label customers—Palmer Sausage—was considering increasing its purchases from Johnsonville by a huge amount. In fact, the company was talking about placing an order that, if accepted, would account for 25% of Johnsonville's annual sales volume. Ralph wondered how he should react.

OVERVIEW

The Johnsonville Sausage Co. was purchased in 1945 by Ralph's parents and was located in Johnsonville, Wisconsin, a small town about 60 miles north of Milwaukee. The company was a rural meat market—a family home with a storefront, a sausage kitchen, and a slaughter shed and smokehouse out back.

At the time it was purchased, the business was small—roughly $50,000 per year in sales—but quite profitable: the shortage of meat and consequent rationing had inflated price. Soon after the Stayers purchased the business, however, the U.S. government eliminated the rationing system, and profits began to fall.

In order to survive, the Stayers opened a retail food store in 1946 with a local man who sold groceries. The Stayers supplied all of the meat, and managed the meat counter. This business did well, and the Stayers opened two more retail stores in conjunction with this grocery business in 1948 and 1952.

Thus, for quite a time, the business was a full-line retail butchering business. Mr. Stayer would buy livestock from local suppliers, slaughter the animals, and sell meat in the three retail stores. Mr. Stayer also made fresh sausage, which had acquired an excellent reputation in the area. He managed these stores, and Mrs. Stayer kept the books for the business.

Ralph was clearly interested in running the business with his father and worked with him summers during high school and college. When Ralph graduated from Notre Dame in 1965 with a bachelor's degree in business, he and his father took a hard look at Johnsonville's operations. Essentially, there were two aspects of the business—wholesale and retail. They concluded that it would be difficult to grow the retail meat business without opening grocery stores as well. The Stayers had no interest in getting involved in this aspect of the business, and retail supermarkets had evolved to the point where they typically had their own full-line meat departments.

The wholesale business, however, looked more promising. Ralph had begun selling some sausage products to other stores in the area (but not local establishments competing directly with the Stayers' retail busi-

This case was prepared by Assistant Professor Michael J. Roberts as the basis for class discussion rather than to illustrate either effective or ineffective handling of an administrative situation.

ness). The product had been well-received, and Ralph was confident that he could increase sales. The Stayers decided to focus their efforts on building this segment of the business.

Ralph built the wholesale business to the point where it accounted for $4 million in sales in 1975; $15 million in 1980; and $50 million in 1985. The company had been transformed from a small family of workers to a business of well over 500 employees. Ralph was officially named president in 1978, but had assumed most of the day-to-day decision-making authority for the wholesale business in the early 1970s.

The remainder of this case describes the business in more detail and the changes that transpired as the company grew.

THE BUSINESS

Products

Johnsonville Sausage's product line consisted of three types of sausage, which in total accounted for approximately 120 SKUs:

Fresh sausage: Made from freshly butchered pork and beef cuts. Popular fresh sausage products included bratwurst, Italian sausage, breakfast links and patties, and kielbasa. Fresh products had a shelf life of approximately three weeks.

Smoked sausage: A sausage made in the same manner as a fresh sausage, but to which nitrates and nitrites are added as a "cure"; this preserves the meat and gives it a characteristic red/brown color. The sausage is then cooked for 2–4 hours in a hot oven with smoldering wood chips to impart a characteristic flavor. Smoked sausage had a shelf life of approximately two months.

Semi-dry sausage: Semi-dry or "summer" or "slicing" sausage was made like a smoked sausage, but was cooked for 3 or 4 days. This removed most of the moisture, and preserved the sausage while giving it a strong flavor. Semi-dry sausage was typically much larger than an average sausage, and could be sliced like a salami. Semi-dry sausage had a long shelf life of at least four months.

Product varieties within each category were created by the use of different spices and by varying "link length" and the sausage casing.

The Production Process

All sausage began as a combination of beef and pork cuts. Johnsonville slaughtered its own hogs and its own beef up until 1973, when it decided to purchase these cuts from local suppliers. Then, in 1980, the company purchased a slaughtering operation in order to provide fresh pork. Live hogs were purchased weekly, and slaughtered daily at the company's slaughterhouse in Watertown, Wisconsin, 80 miles south of Sheboygan. The butchered pork was shipped daily in 2000-pound bins to the Johnsonville plants.

The processing plants ran on a two-shift basis, so that the fresh meat could be turned into sausage on a continuous basis. Fresh meat was delivered to the plant by 10:00 p.m. when the first shift began to turn this meat into sausage filler: meat was ground, and spices and flavorings added.

At 6:00 a.m., the second shift would arrive and begin stuffing sausage with this mixture:

- The sausage meat was emptied into a large hopper, and was extruded into the casing.
- For fresh sausage, the links were then placed on styrofoam trays, flash frozen, wrapped in cellophane packages, and packed to create boxes that could be shipped.

- For smoked or semi-dry sausage, the links were placed in the smokehouse, and cooked/smoked for a time with a seasoned wood.

USDA inspections were also a part of the manufacturing process. Workers had to test samples of each product for fat, protein, and moisture content, and report the results to the USDA.

This entire process was carried out in large refrigerated rooms. Sausage production was typically finished by 3:00 or 4:00 p.m., a scant 24 hours after the hog had been butchered.

Fresh sausage was stored in large refrigerated rooms. Because of its relatively short shelf life, and Johnsonville's desire to sell a fresh product, inventory was kept at a minimum—two days or so—and all products were made in response to customer orders.

During the summer months, fresh sausage was extremely popular, particularly the bratwurst for which the company was famous in Wisconsin. Johnsonville had the ability to produce on a two-shift basis if required during these summer months.

All of the company's production had originally been produced in the plant that was attached to the original Stayer home. The Stayers had moved out while Ralph was a youngster, but he still pointed out his old bedroom, which was now used as the purchasing office.

Johnsonville built a new plant in 1978, which was now used only for fresh products; the old factory was used strictly for smoked and semi-dry products.

Sales and Distribution

The company relied on a combination of brokers and its own direct sales force to sell its product. The firm employed 25 salesmen in 1985. Food brokers were used outside of Wisconsin. Part-time "demonstrators" were used by the company to cook and distribute free samples of product in retail stores. The product was initially sold primarily by word of mouth. The company did its first print advertising in 1975. Johnsonville also worked with stores to develop promotions, which typically included a discount on the price of certain products as well as co-op advertising.

Fresh bratwurst has been the product most responsible for Johnsonville's growth; "brats" were sold at Milwaukee Brewers' Stadium and were extremely popular. In fact, several annual polls of sportswriters and broadcasters revealed that the bratwurst was the favorite "Stadium food" available anywhere:

Bratwurst is one of the passions that consumes, and is consumed by, Costas [NBS sportscaster]. Name a ballpark, and Costas will tell you the best item on the menu.... And when it comes to ballpark food, no other stadium occupies a more hallowed spot in Costas' heart, on his palate or in his stomach, than Milwaukee's County Stadium. "The single best ballpark item anywhere, at any ballpark, hands down, is the bratwurst with the sauerkraut and red sauce, at County Stadium," he said, "It's not even close."[1]

In addition to publicity like this, the firm inaugurated a TV ad campaign in 1981 that focused on the "brat fry" as a social event. The commercials feature uninvited guests overwhelming a man who is cooking Johnsonville brats. The brat fry had become a popular Milwaukee area social event, and local papers described the phenomenon:

In east central Wisconsin, spring is marked not by returning robins or budding willows, but by frying bratwurst.... Brat fries are prevalent in this four-county area year round. . . .[2]

---

[1] *The Milwaukee Journal,* July 21, 1985, p. 6.
[2] *Chicago Tribune,* April 8, 1984.

Sausage was distributed by a fleet of 10 company-owned trucks, which left the Johnsonville plant each morning. The trucking business was separately incorporated and run as a distinct business. In order to permit the carrying of full loads, the company carried non-Johnsonville products to some neighboring states.

Markets

The company initially began serving only the Sheboygan market through its retail outlet there. Several more retail outlets were added in that area in 1948–52, and the firm did not start wholesaling until Ralph began selling to other stores in 1965. Some other jobbers were added between 1968 and 1972. Initially, only Ralph sold the products; he worked first with small retailers and then local chains to convince them to carry the products. Once they had been signed on as an account, jobbers took weekly orders for the products.

By 1975, Johnsonville was serving two of the largest grocery chains in Wisconsin, as well as a host of other, smaller accounts in the greater Milwaukee area. Still, the company operated solely within that state. In order to sell outside of Wisconsin, Johnsonville would have to comply with stricter federal inspection standards, which would require the opening of a new plant. In 1978, Johnsonville decided to open a new plant, and began serving the state of Indiana; Ralph's sister Launa was the sales rep for that state.

As time went on, the company continued to expand its distribution both within and out of the state. Johnsonville expanded to Iowa, Indiana, Illinois, and Minnesota, and several other neighboring states. Meanwhile, the firm's market position in Wisconsin continued to strengthen. Their share of the bratwurst market in the greater Milwaukee market rose from 7% in 1978 to 46% in 1985. The company's Italian sausage was number two in this market, and its breakfast sausage ranked number four.

THE ENTREPRENEUR

As the company grew, it underwent a series of changes, both in its structure and in its philosophy.

Ralph's Early Style

Ralph described his early style of managing the business:

I ran the business from the sausage stuffer. I made all the decisions about purchasing, production scheduling, pricing, and advertising. I called on our major accounts. We had some office help to handle the payroll and receivables and payables. But I made all the decisions. As the company grew, I did hire a financial person and a sales manager. I still made all the decisions and let them handle the implementation details.

1980: The Seeds of Change

In 1980, Ralph began to feel uncomfortable with the business and the manner in which he was managing it:

I was fed up with the business. The quality of our product was slipping and no one seemed to care. I had always been proud of the fact that people seemed to enjoy their jobs, and took pride in their work. But that seemed to change. People were careless—equipment was being poorly cared for, a bad product was making its way into the market.

We did an attitude survey, and general morale was just even with the national average.

One incident particularly sticks in my mind. I'd hired someone early on, who was very competent. Then one day it struck me that he was just a soldier, carrying out my orders. I tried to get him to take more responsibility, but he couldn't; I'd ruined him. A few years of my style had beat the independence out of him. I vowed I'd never do that again to a man.

During the time that Ralph was attempting to work through his thoughts and feelings about the business, he happened to hear a lecture by a professor from the University of Wisconsin. Dr. Lee Thayer was addressing the issue of how managers could change their philosophy and style of management. Dr. Thayer taught and did research in the organizational behavior field, and had training in the psychology area as well. Thayer began working with Ralph to change Johnsonville. He described the process:

The philosophy that we were trying to implement had several dimensions.

- First, performance is key. And in a well-developed system, there is no conflict between what is best for the company and what's best for the individual. If there is, there is a problem with the way things are being defined, or the way the system is set up.
- The second element is the idea that people do need help to accomplish their objectives, and that *this* is the job of management. The way we can help them is to define very carefully what their job is, define explicitly what the performance standards are and then give them the resources they need to accomplish their objectives.

The first task was to develop a new model of managerial performance in Ralph Stayer's mind. There were several elements to the process. First, he participated in several seminars where we reviewed the new philosophy. Next, he would call me frequently with questions regarding particular decisions that had to be made. We discussed how these issues should be handled if we wanted to be true to the philosophy we were trying to implement.

Ralph described the role that Lee Thayer played in the process:

Lee Thayer played a vital role in this organizational transition. First, he was a touchstone for me personally. We talked at least several times a week. He helped me understand my own role as a leader, and the importance of that role to the organization. Even more importantly, he was a sounding board for working through specific issues and problems.

He was there at the inception of the program, and encouraged the entire company and kept the process going. He was an objective voice that could help us see when we were making progress, and when we were slipping back toward our old ways. We wouldn't be where we are today without him.

Ralph spoke about how he had come to view his job:

The most important step was developing the understanding that if I was dissatisfied with the way people in the company were performing, it was my fault, not theirs.

My first task is a developer of people: our organizations "members." I spend a lot of time with people in the organization just talking things through. I don't tell them what to do anymore; I send them out to make their own decisions. If two people come to me—say manufacturing and marketing—to resolve a dispute, I send them back out; I'm not paying them to push tough decisions up to me; I'm paying them to think.

My job is as a coach, a supporter, a resource. I'm here to help them do their jobs better. I've figured out the few key things I need to know, and don't bother with the rest. I'm proud of the fact that there are a lot of details about the business that I just don't know—advertising and promotion plans, for example.

We have a motto here that "Your job is to eliminate your job!" By that, we mean that a manager should delegate so much of his responsibility, and develop the capability of his people to work together to such an extent that his existing job virtually disappears—it has been delegated to those who work with him/her. Of course, that person's job continues to evolve as the people they work with delegate new responsibilities to them.

Whenever I see a problem, I look at myself, not "them." First, I assume that if people aren't achieving the performance results we've decided upon, that some of the problem is my fault—I'm not creating the right environment or giving them the kind of support they need. I need to figure out what part of the problem I am, and how I can change to eliminate it.

It's my job to ask questions, to surface and describe issues, and to create an environment where all of the relevant parties can discuss these issues.

THE ORGANIZATION

The Johnsonville Philosophy

Ralph firmly believed that the change in philosophy was the most important thing that was happening at Johnsonville. The root of that philosophy was a deep moral commitment to the individual. Change at Johnsonville was initiated in an effort to make *people* feel better, not to make the business better. Ralph spoke about this philosophy and the impact it has had on the business:

We have gone from a company where I made all of the decisions to one in which responsibility for decisions is distributed to the area best suited to make them. Rather than having one entrepreneur on top, we are trying to have an organization where everyone is an entrepreneur. We want each person to see him or herself as the instrument of their own destiny.

Instead of looking outward for more and more business, I am looking inward at our organization and the people that comprise it. We are on the leading edge of developing a far better way for our people to live and work together. The beauty of the system is that it builds on itself. As people grow, opportunities for sales and profits grow, which in turn provides more opportunities for people to grow.

The key to this philosophy is that *people see Johnsonville as a means to their ends, not vice-versa.* We are not the means to the end of profit. It's the other way around: profit is the means to our ends. It is not that profit is unimportant. It is the seed corn that makes everything else work. Our increase in profits has allowed us to increase our investments in the business and increase the compensation for our people at the same time. This has all occurred in a mature, consolidating industry where both profit margins and compensation have been declining overall.

The first step in implementing our philosophy, then, is getting together and deciding what our ends are.

We begin at a fairly high level of abstraction: clearly, what we all want is job security, increasing compensation, and a job that's rewarding. We have attacked each of these objectives and spent a lot of time thinking about each one in more detail, understanding how we can achieve it.

Job security comes from having customers who value the product. We can all work at this by keeping our eye on the customer. It is everyone's responsibility to make a quality product, to innovate and to think about the future. The key here is performance. We need to be clear about what our performance objectives are and how we are meeting them.

Compensation is the bottom line in this company, not profit. We will work to make this as big as we can. The smarter we work, the better we become at making customers, the bigger the payoff will be. As we each become more skilled, the performance of the whole company improves. Job security and compensation will both increase.

Finally, the job should be rewarding. Work is a very large part of our lives—all of our lives. It provides the things we want for ourselves and our families. But if we cannot make our lives more fulfilling, more challenging, more rewarding—more fun—then we're all losers in the game of life. We've got to put life back into our work. We've got to put meaning and worthwhileness and purpose back into the one thing we do most with our lives—our jobs. We spend more of our waking hours in our jobs than in any other single thing in life. If all we had to show for it was a paycheck, we would be poor indeed.

We believe that the objective is to develop a non-adversarial company—where everyone's best interest is served by the whole. Whenever we encounter a conflict, we analyze it to determine what changes should be made to resolve it.

The beauty of this philosophy and our objectives is that they all fit together—there is no conflict in achieving these goals. Working toward one is working toward them all. That is because they all revolve around performance. With good people, who have the tools and help they need, working toward superior performance improves job security, improves compensation, and most importantly, makes for rewarding work.

Structure

As the organization structure evolved, there was a great deal of emphasis placed on allocating responsibility properly, or, to use Ralph Stayer's phrase, "deciding who owns the problem." As an example, customer letters of complaints or praise were typically sent to direct line workers. If a letter complained about too much salt or a "flavor pocket" (i.e., all the spices in one bite of sausage), the letter was routed to the employees in the meat-grinding room who added the spices. If the complaint was relative to a tough or split casing, the letter went to the sausage stuffers. They wrote a letter explaining the cause of the problem, the steps that were taken to avoid it, and apologized for the inconvenience. Employees were able to send out coupons for a free product to such customers.

During the early stages of the organization's transition, Ralph attempted to delegate responsibility to the people he had in place below him, but found that some of these individuals were unable to accept the kind of responsibility that Johnsonville's new philosophy required. In response, Ralph brought in new people to the three key positions that reported to him. All of these individuals had a great deal of experience in their respective functions. Moreover, Ralph screened them carefully to be sure that they would enthusiastically embrace the firm's philosophy.

- Bob Salzwedel, director of Information and Financial Services, was brought in to Johnsonville in late 1981. He had been with a CPA firm.
- Russ Wiverstad joined Johnsonville in mid-1982 as its director of Product Acquisition and Manufacturing.
- Mike Roller, director of Sales and Marketing Services, joined Johnsonville in mid-1984.

The following sections describe how each area of the organization evolved.

Manufacturing

In the late 1960s, the manufacturing operation had been carried out by Ralph and three or four workers who performed all operations, from slaughtering to stuffing and smoking the sausage. This operation was entirely contained within the original Stayer home/factory. See *Exhibit 1*.

When Ralph began working at Johnsonville in 1965, his father supervised production. Ralph gradually took on more responsibility, and was responsible for most operations by 1973. Ralph took the president's position in 1978. Then there were 70 to 80 individuals working at Johnsonville, organized as shown in *Exhibit 1*.

When the second plant was opened in late 1978, Jim Gebler was elevated to the position of plant manager for this facility; Jim had begun working at Johnsonville as a truck driver, and had worked making sausage with Ralph for ten years. Ralph continued to manage the old plant. Then, in 1980, Ralph hired Pat Weiss to supervise both plants. He formalized the manufacturing organization, developing supervisor positions which had previously not existed.

In response to Ralph's attempts to delegate more responsibility, and his dissatisfaction with the way in which Weiss was managing the manufacturing organization,

Ralph hired Russ Wiverstad in May of 1982. Pat Weiss was let go.

Russ had been with Oscar Mayer for 30 years, rising to a plant manager position where he was responsible for 700 employees. Russ talked about the reasons he had left Oscar Mayer and joined Johnsonville:

My job at Oscar Mayer was essentially the enforcement of company policy—policy doesn't exist unless it's enforced. They had standards based on time and motion studies, and if a group wasn't up to par, it was my job to yell at the supervisor. I got sick of it.

Russ talked about the changes that had transpired since he joined Johnsonville:

When I joined the company, Ralph was making all of the day-to-day operating decisions in the manufacturing area: ordering, scheduling and the like. It took a little while for Ralph to develop trust and confidence in my abilities, but once he did, he delegated a lot of responsibility to me. Over the years, he's become even less involved in the day-to-day operations. Our relationship works on the principle that it's my job to keep him informed, not his job to ask me the right questions to find out what he needs to know. I think one of the factors that allowed our working relationship to evolve so well was that Ralph didn't *have* to delegate. He was doing it out of choice, not necessity. So, it could happen slowly, at a pace he was comfortable with, and that let him develop confidence in me. As Ralph delegated to me, I delegated to my subordinates. Where all the budgeting and planning used to be done by the vice president, Manufacturing, those numbers now come from the shop floor.

Originally Russ had been responsible for Plant 1 (old), Plant 2 (new) and the slaughtering operation. Over the years, as new functions in the organization had been articulated, Russ assumed responsibility for:

- Engineering—developing plans for new plant and equipment
- Research and Development—including USDA testing, packaging, product and process development

- Purchasing—buying meat, spices and packaging
- Personnel Development—education and training

The supervisor position in the manufacturing area had been eliminated. Each function—grinding, packing, stuffing, etc., had a designated "lead person." Within a given function, workers worked as a team—they would alternate specific jobs, i.e., a worker who picked sausages off a conveyor belt and placed them on a styrofoam tray would switch jobs with a person who wrapped the sausage or who packed the wrapped trays in boxes. This was something that the workers themselves had proposed, and that helped eliminate the routine of some of the jobs. This fit with the company's philosophy in a number of ways. If the workers had true responsibility for performance, then it was up to them to organize the line how they saw fit. Doing so increased their own enjoyment of their jobs, and improved performance. By broadening the scope of their knowledge and skills, workers had come up with new ideas for organizing the work and for new equipment that would make them more productive.

The lead person's responsibilities were not to supervise the other workers, but to collect data, help train new workers, and get information to workers.

A group of workers met each morning to taste a sample of the previous day's production, and discuss any ideas on how the product could be improved. Recently, the firm had begun an effort to break jobs up even further, and the lead people were disappearing. Their responsibilities were spread over all of the workers.

Manufacturing workers were evaluated in comparison to budget. On an annual basis, beginning each fall, two or three people from each of the main areas within the manufacturing area would become part of a budget team, together with people from sales and accounting. Working with the sales force, the line workers would develop a sales forecast for the coming 12 months, by product line. They would then develop budgets, and set goals for certain key measures, including:

- Labor efficiency: pounds of sausage per man-hour
- Yield: pounds of meat used per pound of sausage produced
- Labor cost: dollars of labor per pound of sausage

Workers collected the data required to measure their progress towards these goals, and analyzed and posted results versus budget on a monthly basis. Daily figures for yield, efficiency and cost were produced. Again, all of these steps were taken to ensure that workers had all of the information and help that they needed to understand and improve their own performance.

The capital budgeting process was part of this cycle as well. Line workers developed proposals for new capital equipment. They justified qualitatively why the purchase of the equipment is warranted, and then performed a more complex financial analysis, estimating return on assets. Income-producing projects were judged against a 25% ROA (pretax) hurdle rate, while safety and quality-oriented investments were evaluated in a less quantitative measure.

During this process, the finance area was viewed as a resource to be used; they were not managing the budgeting process, but were providing service as needed to the line workers.

Sales and Marketing

Ralph performed the retail sales function during the first several years of the company's attempts to expand sales in this area.

Following success locally, two of the state's largest chains began distributing Johnsonville products.

In 1975, Ralph hired Dick Gustafson from one of Johnsonville's meat suppliers to help build sales to retail accounts. By 1978, Gustafson was managing two other salesmen: the number grew to five in 1980.

As Ralph began to delegate more responsibility, however, Gustafson was unable to grow into the job; Ralph replaced him in 1981 with Paul Brandon, who began to shift the firm away from direct store sales and delivery to a focus on grocery warehouses. The effect of this shift was an immediate volume surge, followed by a reduction in items carried by retailers and a consequent increase in promotion and related marketing expenses. The effect of this policy error was still being felt when Brandon resigned in late 1983.

Ralph hired Mike Roller in mid-1984 to supervise the sales force, and to take on the responsibility for marketing, which Ralph himself had been managing. It fell upon Roller to reorganize sales and marketing operations in order to set the stage for further growth and development. During his first year, he concentrated on rebuilding distressed customer relations; building a management team with well-defined responsibilities, adding performance measures and accountability; putting a marketing and administrative structure in place, building internal and external information systems; and initiating an entry-level training program. Roller also developed the product line in response to suggestions from retailers and the sales force, and significantly reduced operating expenses.

Roller's second-year efforts focused on improving the caliber of individuals in the sales organization and expanding marketing operations to new geographic areas and product segments. The company's first formal marketing plan was developed, including volume and expense budgets that had been developed by the line managers. Timely information systems were developed to allow the monitoring of actual results against this plan.

Staff was added to address operating problems and/or pave the way for further expansion:

- Sales coordinator: added in early 1986 to eliminate coordination problems between sales and manufacturing
- Food service director: added in late 1985 to spearhead the company's expansion into food service institutions, a lucrative market
- Marketing coordinator: to coordinate the implementation of the company's promotional activity—couponing, demonstrations, and the like
- National account manager: added to begin to develop Johnsonville's business with major national accounts

Roller had divided the sales force into three groups: food service (restaurants and ballparks) retail and food processors. Each of these three groups reported to him, as did the marketing, sales administration, trucking/distribution and internal operations staff. Roller also managed the sales coordinator. Each Tuesday the sales force would send in its sales projections for the coming week. The sales coordinator would get inventory data from the manufacturing department. He would also look at the details of promotions and advertising planned for the next 90 days. Based on this data, the sales coordinator would develop:

- A 90-day rolling forecast of sales to give manufacturing and purchasing a "best guess view"
- Production requirements for the following week
- Estimates of production requirements for each day

This information would then be sent to each of the two plant coordinators who would develop a production schedule for the week, based on the requirements developed above as well as their own knowledge of manufacturing efficiencies. This information was then used by the purchasing area to make arrangements for purchasing the necessary hogs and beef.

Individual salespeople developed their own plans and budgets, and received monthly data—broken down by account and expense item (i.e., travel and entertainment, promotions, advertising).

Finance and Administration

Richard Bassuener was hired to work for Mrs. Stayer as a bookkeeper in 1976. The job consisted primarily of general ledger work, as well as payables and receivables. As Ralph began delegating more responsibility, he felt the company needed to develop financial information systems to collect profitability and return-on-asset data by product line. In addition, he wanted to develop more detailed budgets, and timely status reports.

Bob Salzwedel was hired in 1981 to manage the finance function. His responsibilities included acquisitions, cost and financial accounting, as well as accounts credit and collections, and data processing. Richard Bassuener remained in charge of the accounting functions.

Bob felt that the job of the finance area was to provide people with the information that they needed to run the operation themselves.

Several of the traditional accounting functions were in the process of being transferred to sales or manufacturing:

- Billing and credit were being placed under the sales function.
- Cost accounting was part of manufacturing.

In Ralph Stayer's words, "We do two things here—make sausage and sell it. They are the two line functions, and as close as possible to 100% of what we do should fall under one of these two areas. All support functions—including me—are here to serve these two functions. We work for them."

Personnel

The personnel function had undergone a dramatic shift over the years. In 1980, Donna Schwefel, a secretary, had started the personnel department. This department kept salary records and did the hiring for most of the direct labor jobs. The department also administered the performance review that was used as a basis for hourly wage increases and promotions. This department was also responsible for administering the benefit programs and maintaining the other personnel records that were required by law.

As the organization developed, and as Johnsonville placed more emphasis on individual acceptance of responsibility, the nature of the personnel function changed dramatically. Ralph felt that the personnel function was too important to be delegated to a staff area—it was a line function: "The only difference between Johnsonville and its competitors is our people."

First, many of the typical personnel functions left the personnel department and became the responsibility of "the line."

- Lori Lehmann, who was a packer on the bratwurst line, expressed a frustration shared by many of her fellow workers: new workers were typically thrown on to the production line with no training or orientation. Lori suggested developing a training/ orientation program for new hires. She was encouraged to do so, and developed a training/orientation guide for all the manufacturing workers in the new plant, as well as specific training for the direct positions.

Lori presented this program to all new employees.
- Following success with this project, Lori suggested that people on the line have the opportunity to interview prospective hires. This effort was a success and, in early 1986, plans were under way to dismantle the role of personnel in the hiring functions.

The performance review process was also removed from the personnel area. The new process worked as follows:

- Each individual worker was responsible for developing his/her own job description. This listed responsibilities, the performance objectives for each responsibility, and the standard measures along which performance would be judged.
- Individuals were responsible for updating their job descriptions whenever their responsibilities changed.
- Individuals were also responsible for measuring their own performance and analyzing any deficiencies that they found, and for suggesting ways in which they will improve in these areas.
- At least semi-annually, individual workers met with their leader and reviewed these results, and agreed on the performance evaluation. This was supplemented with almost daily discussion regarding objectives and performance.
- Based on a semi-annual review, workers were assigned points, from 1 to 100, for their performance. The total number of points was then totalled on a companywide basis, and the bonus pool ("company performance share") was allocated in proportion to points earned.

The personnel function had shifted its focus to the human development area. Terri Case, a local high school teacher, had been hired in mid-1985 in response to a Johnsonville ad seeking an individual "committed to life-long learning."

Terri reported to two individuals:

- Bob Salzwedel, Finance and Administration, for compensation and personnel issues, such as group insurance, benefits, and profit sharing

- Russ Wiverstad, Manufacturing, for personnel development

Ralph Stayer, as part of his emphasis on "people development," wanted Johnsonville to be a vehicle through which individuals could accomplish their own personal goals, whatever they may be. Every individual in the company was given an $80 educational allowance, to be spent in whatever manner they wished. Some took cooking or sewing classes; others signed up for flying lessons. Magazine subscriptions were another popular use for these funds. This policy fit with the philosophy that Johnsonville should serve as a means to the individual's own ends.

Ralph had also arranged for all workers to receive a free economics course, taught on plant premises by a local professor. The course covered basic micro- and macro-economic theory, as well as looking at the United States in an international competitive perspective. Ralph Stayer commented on this:

It's important for people to understand where they fit into our economy, and how Johnsonville fits into the picture. If we want to create job security, we need to know what our competitors are up to, and understand how international competition has hurt so many other U.S. industries.

Individuals were paid for the time they spent attending the first lecture. After that, the course was free, but they would have to attend on their own time.

The hiring process was also unusual. In addition to the typical questions about prior experience, potential hires were asked:

- Why do you want to work for Johnsonville?
- How do you spend your leisure time?
- What would you like to be doing in five years?
- How do you define cooperation?

- How do your friends describe you?
- What do you have to offer a group?

In Terri's words, "If someone isn't sharp enough to write a well-thought-out paragraph on why they want to work here, they are probably not qualified to handle the kind of responsibility we give people."

Compensation

Prior to the transition, workers had been paid strictly on an hourly basis, which was about equal to the local average. Hourly increases were typically granted once a year. In 1979, a profit-sharing plan was introduced that contributed toward a worker's pension fund. Management viewed it as unsuccessful, because it did not tie compensation to individual performance; it seemed not to affect worker motivation, perhaps because its effect was not immediate.

In 1982, the company instituted a policy of no across-the-board wage increases. Increases would only be given for an increase in responsibilities. This was tracked via the workers' job descriptions, which were formally reviewed twice a year.

In addition to wages, workers received a company performance share, which was a function of both the firm's and the individual's performance.

There were three "pools" to which a share of the company's profits was added semiannually:

- Hourly workers
- Salaried workers
- The three senior-level managers (did not include Ralph Stayer)

Ralph described the philosophy behind the compensation system:

Nothing happens without necessity. To get great performance, it is necessary to build a system where only great performers can survive. Our compensation system is a good example. In the executive group, Russ, Bob and Mike split their bonus completely upon the basis of what they did to build people during the year. This same percentage is used to compute their share of a net worth incentive—they can each get an additional bonus of up to 15% of the company's annual increase in net worth.

Everyone's performance was reviewed, based on their own job descriptions and performance targets, and that performance was rated on a scale of 0 to 100. Each pool was then assigned a number of points which equaled the sum of every worker's point rating. Each worker then received a share of the pool that was equal to their point rating divided by the total number of points in the pool. Since the plan was introduced, average payments to production workers had been:

1982–$200
1983–$700
1984–$350
1985–$800

This represented between 5–6% of the workers' annual wage. Management hoped to increase this percentage to 25% over the next several years.

Some workers were very enthusiastic about the company performance share (CPS). Typically, they had increased their responsibilities over the years, and received hourly increases as well, so they viewed the CPS as a true "bonus." Other workers, however, complained that they had not received any wage increase over the past 3–4 years. They felt that the CPS was a poor substitute for the annual wage increase that they had formerly enjoyed. In addition, workers seemed to think that there was not much variation between the best and worst performers. The compensation system did seem to have broadened individuals' perspective on the company, however. People ques-

tioned Ralph Stayer on the impact of acquisitions and capital investments on the company's performance and the CPS.

Research and Development

Prior to the transition, the research and development area was not formally delineated in the organization. Ralph would work on his own ideas. Now R&D was viewed as the responsibility of everyone in the organization. One of the company's recent, and successful, new products "Beer 'n Bratwurst," was developed by a team within the company. The product consisted of a bratwurst that was made with beer, instead of water, to replicate the flavor that many brat fans achieved by soaking the product in beer.

The idea for the product came out of a brain-storming session held during the summer of 1984. Together with individuals from the sales and research area, this team tested and refined the product, which was introduced six months later.

A similar process resulted in the company's ham and cheese sausage, a mild bratwurst containing bits of ham and cheese. Ralph Stayer wasn't even aware that the product was under development until he was presented with samples.

Systems and Controls

There was an emphasis at Johnsonville on "self-control." In Ralph Stayer's words, "The notion of control systems is an illusion; the only real control is when people control themselves." In line with the company's philosophy, individual performance was key to the achievement of both the individual's and the firm's goals. Thus, the system began with a great deal of emphasis on describing responsibilities and performance targets at an individual level:

- Individual salespeople developed the budgets and forecasts for which they were willing to be held accountable.
- Manufacturing employees used these forecasts to develop budgets and production targets for which they agreed to be held accountable.

Out of these individual commitments, firmwide projections and budgets were developed. These budgets were used as a yardstick against actual performance, and as a control on spending. Nonbudgeted items over $500 had to be approved at the vice president level.

Employees wrote their own job descriptions, set their own performance objectives, and described the measures that would be used to evaluate performance against these objectives. It was the subordinate's responsibility to demonstrate his/her own performance to their superior, not vice-versa. There was a great deal of emphasis on monitoring one's own performance:

- Manufacturing workers collected the data to evaluate their own performance daily.
- Salesmen received weekly and monthly reports on their performance versus budget.

It was viewed as the individual employee's job to analyze these data and understand them. If there was a shortfall compared with expectations, what was the cause? If plans were being exceeded, what could be learned from this?

Through this approach, individuals could improve their own performance and better their own skills and abilities; it was their responsibility to keep their supervisor informed of any problems.

Workers did punch a time clock, but they didn't punch out for lunch, and their hours were no longer tallied by accounting. It was each individual employee's responsibility to total his hours weekly.

Ralph described the issues the firm faced on developing its systems:

Traditional flows of information are totally inappropriate for what we are trying to accomplish. Traditional information systems transfer the problems away from those individuals that are best-suited to deal with them effectively. The key is to develop systems to push problems back to where they belong. We divide information into two types—history and control. Control data are developed to help each person or group control their own operations. They are generated and kept at the operational level. Historical information shows trends and overall performance, and flows to whoever is interested.

One example of the manner in which Johnsonville worked was a specific problem which the firm had with "leakers"—vacuum-packed plastic packages of sausages which "leaked" air back into the package, thereby shortening shelf life. One worker described how the problem would have been handled in the days prior to the transition:

Someone from Quality Assurance would have been measuring the total quantity of leakers, and when it reached a certain point, they would yell at the foreman and tell him to reduce the number of leakers and the guy wouldn't have a clue what to do about it, so he'd just yell at the people who worked for him. That's the whole reason you need a foreman, so you have someone to yell at when there's a problem.

The problem, however, was handled very differently. A "Pride Team" of volunteers was formed around the leaker problem. This team of first-line workers, with the help of a manufacturing specialist, investigated the leakers and discovered four possible sources:

- The die, which punches out the plastic package
- The plastic film, which is used for the plastic packages
- The packaging machine, which actually shrink-wraps the sausage

- The operation of placing the sausage in the wrapper

Only this last cause was a "man-made" source of leakers, the rest were machine- or materials-related. The workers developed a set of priorities for attacking these problems, based on their analysis of the frequency with which each of these causes contributed to the leaker problem.

They attacked each problem, working with materials suppliers, making adjustments to equipment or the manner in which it was used. Within two months, the machine/materials problems, which accounted for over 80% of the leakers, had been completely eliminated.

Some new practices were developed for the direct laborers, and this solved the "man-made" leaker problems as well. As a final step in the program, some representatives from the Pride Team visited retail outlets to educate them on how to handle and store the product once it had left the plant, in order to decrease problems which were caused at the store level.

During this process, the workers themselves collected and analyzed the data every day to determine how they were progressing on the leaker problem, and these results were posted daily, by the workers themselves.

Summary

Each of these elements of Johnsonville's organization was carefully thought out to be sure that it was consistent with the firm's philosophy. When new situations arose, Ralph would get all of the affected individuals together and discuss the issues, drawing out opinions from all concerned.

Most found the environment stimulating. They enjoyed their new responsibilities and their changing nature. It was these stories of personal accomplishment that Ralph Stayer was most proud of.

The greatest joy for me has been watching people take the program and run with it. Seeing people's expectations of themselves and of what they might become being lifted to levels that would not have been possible any other way.

THE PALMER SAUSAGE DECISION

The employees of Palmer Sausage had gone out on strike in mid-1985, and the company had farmed out its production of sausage items to a number of subcontractors. Johnsonville had produced ring bologna and wieners for Palmer, and the products had sold so well that Palmer asked Johnsonville to continue making the product even after the strike was settled. Palmer sold these products outside of the geographic regions in which Johnsonville competed.

In mid-1986, Ralph Stayer received a phone call from Palmer's vice president of manufacturing, informing him of the fact that Palmer was thinking of closing one of its

midwestern plants, and would consider giving the lion's share of the business to Johnsonville. As per standard practice in the industry, any contract for private label production would permit cancellation of the business with 30 days' notice.

Ralph described the thoughts that raced through his mind:

On one hand, we would love to have the business. We make a 25% ROA on this private label business—it is profitable for us. But in our last business plan, we decided that we did not want to push private label business over 15%; after that point, it would begin to compete for capital with the rest of our business. This order alone is for a dollar volume that will represent 25% of our sales.

We are running at a very high capacity utilization now. In order to process this business, we will have to run 2 long shifts, 6 or 7 days a week. (Johnsonville could not operate more than 18 hours per day because it is necessary to break down the equipment and clean it on a daily basis.) This will really push us to our limits. It could have a demoralizing impact on our own people, and cause the quality of our own products to suffer.

Longer term, it will force us to build another plant much sooner than we had anticipated. Suppose we build for this business and then they cancel our contract? Our return on that investment will drop dramatically, and we will have to lay off the workers we hired for this business.

Ralph wondered what he should do.

EXHIBIT 1 The Johnsonville Sausage Co. Johnsonville Organization in Early 1960s, in 1978, and in 1985

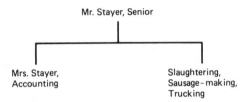

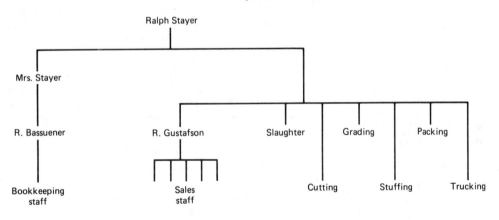

Specialty Packaging, Inc.

Beth Hayes relished the signs of spring as she set out on the forty-minute drive home from her office outside Minneapolis. The commute to St. Cloud was a pretty one, and Beth liked to drive—especially after a satisfying day spent tackling the challenges of her new job. A Certified Financial Planner, Beth had risen through the ranks in the financial services company for which she worked, and had recently been promoted to a new management position following her company's merger with another, larger group. Combining the two operations was proving to be a delicate task, and Beth felt gratified to be part of the transition team. Being the youngest vice president in the group and the only woman on the transition team did not seem to inhibit Beth's ability to contribute. Her boss had recently told her that her responsibilities would continue to expand as the merger took hold. If all went well, there appeared to be no limit to Beth's opportunities for advancement in the new organization.

Unfortunately, life was not quite as rosy for Beth's husband of three years. As CEO and treasurer of Specialty Packaging, Inc., Bill Hayes had encountered a nearly continuous series of problems over the last several months. Notwithstanding Bill's strenuous efforts to instill a spirit of teamwork in his top management group, the winter of 1986–87 had been fraught with arguments and mutual distrust. Specialty Packaging was also suffering a competitive onslaught from offshore producers in its main product line, the plastic holiday packaging business. To make matters worse, the past few days had seen a resurgence of union campaign activity on the company's day shift. Bill was not sure whether the event was an isolated incident, as his production manager described it, or a signal of deeper troubles in the plant.

Beth and Bill had always been very supportive of each other in their careers. Beth thought their mutual respect and their commitment to sharing difficult problems contributed to the strength of their marriage. The openness was especially important to Bill, whose first marriage had not been as successful a partnership. Bill had told Beth how much he appreciated her serving as sounding board and—at times—as devil's advocate by offering her own perspective about the situations he described. On his side, he always tried to help her by playing a similar role. Now, as other drivers started to switch on their headlights in the mid-April dusk, Beth felt almost grateful for the interlude the travel time afforded. She used it as an opportunity to sort through her thoughts about her own day, and to focus on the ways in which she could be helpful to Bill.

This case was prepared by Research Associate Colleen Kaftan, under the supervision of Professor Louis B. Barnes, as the basis for class discussion rather than to illustrate either effective or ineffective handling of an administrative situation.

BACKGROUND ON SPECIALTY PACKAGING, INC.

Founded just forty years earlier by Bill's father, Robert Hayes, and his college friend Nils Olmsted, Specialty Packaging had always been at least moderately profitable and was considered to be a stable part of the St. Cloud community. Rob Hayes and Olmsted had chosen St. Cloud for its natural beauty and because of the cultural climate created by the town's two college campuses. In 1946, the two partners had set up their original manufacturing shop in a small warehouse, using a reconditioned rubber extruder to produce their first vinyl stretch closure products. Each partner manned the "plant" for an eight-hour shift daily, and their sole employee took the third shift to keep the extruder running 24 hours. In addition, Nils Olmsted (who had converted the extruder himself) took charge of the constant tinkering that was necessary to keep the extruder running, while Rob Hayes handled administrative activities and scoured the markets for raw materials. Both men were continually on the lookout for opportunities with customers. Their early division of labor persisted informally throughout the partners' careers, and according to Rob Hayes, it always served them well.

In forty years of operations, the company's product line expanded to include some 3000 unique items of specialty plastic packaging for commercial as well as ornamental use. A plant built in 1962 required expanding just three years later, and successive construction programs added a warehouse in 1975 as well as a product laboratory in 1978. Finally, in 1982, a $1.2 million project brought another major expansion and an upgrading of the entire plant site.

The company's core business, a holiday packaging line, consisted of plastic boxes, bags, and special closures for use in retail stores. Holiday packaging products had grown to account for as much as 60% of the company's unit volume and 50% of profits in the late 1970s, but in the face of severe competition from off-shore producers the line had dropped to 50% of unit volume and 30% of profits by the mid-1980s. Over the same period the company's employee population had dropped from a high of 200 to the current level of 180. Sales in recent years had hovered around $13 and $14 million per year.

The atmosphere at Specialty Products' 40th anniversary celebration during the summer of 1986 reflected the traditional, family-oriented culture Rob Hayes and Nils Olmsted had cultivated: relatives came to tour the plant, the under-thirty group competed against the "oldtimers" in an annual softball challenge, and a late-afternoon picnic gave way to dancing on the softball field. Bill Hayes was particularly pleased with the way Beth had won the respect and affection of employees at all levels in the organization. Both Beth and Bill remarked later that the pleasant "down home" feeling of the party made it seem unlikely that the company could ever go through the kind of tensions that had surfaced over the winter.

Bill Hayes' Career

Bill and his sister Amy had grown up feeling they were part of a "Specialty Packaging family" in St. Cloud. The Hayeses and the Olmsteds were close personal friends, and Bill considered Nils to be his "honorary uncle." Both Bill and Amy went East for their education, and Bill joined a Chicago-based multinational after receiving his master's degree in chemical engineering in 1966. Neither Amy Hayes nor the Olmsteds' daughters showed an interest in working at Specialty Packaging or even in returning to live in St.

Cloud. By contrast, Bill always assumed he might come back to the company some day.

After seven successful years with his first employer, Bill received an urgent call from his father late in 1973. Nils Olmsted had died unexpectedly. Rob Hayes was struggling to come up with a plan for carrying on without his partner and closest friend. If Bill were interested in joining the company, now would be the time to make the move. Rob thought they could figure out a way to buy Nils' share and to keep the company going.

In relatively short order Bill moved his young family to St. Cloud. He started at Specialty Packaging as a process engineer, and spent the next several years rebuilding most of the operating equipment to increase productivity. In so doing, he discovered one of the less favorable aspects of Nils Olmsted's legacy: most of the impetus for technical enhancements had flowed directly from Nils, and the employees had never developed a sense of responsibility for suggesting ways to improve the manufacturing processes. In fact, Nils had actively discouraged employees from reading trade journals, for example, saying he didn't want the literature to be "putting ideas into their heads."

By 1976, Bill was promoted to vice president of the company, and his father retained the presidency and chairmanship. Specialty Packaging's business had been relatively flat throughout the early 1970s, and sales began to dip with the weakened economy at the end of the decade. The picture brightened in the early eighties, and 1982 was the company's best year ever. In 1983, however, foreign competition took a severe toll on the holiday packaging business. The repercussions were felt inside the plant even though a 20-person payroll reduction was handled mostly through attrition. Before the year was over Rob and Bill had a unionizing campaign on their hands.

With much effort and controversy, the management group was able to convince a majority of shopworkers to vote the union down. Bill credited their success to the loyalty many oldtimers (over 20% of the employees were members of the company's twenty-five year club) felt personally towards Rob Hayes.

The year 1984 was also eventful for Bill, both personally and at Specialty Packaging. After a two-year courtship, he and Beth were married and Beth moved from Wisconsin to join him in St. Cloud. At about the same time, Bill's parents decided to retire and move to the home they'd bought in Arizona. Bill took over as CEO and began the transition to the "post Nils and Rob" era. To make the transition complete, the whole family agreed that Bill should buy his parents out.

The Buyout

In order to free up his parents' investment in the company and to insure adequate long-term income for them as well as for his sister, Bill arranged a leveraged buyout with several special features. The plant and other property were placed in a family real estate partnership, so that rental income paid by the company would accrue to family members. In addition, Bill took control of 100% of the voting shares. Bill's sister Amy maintained ownership of the special class of preferred nonvoting stock that had been created for her when the Hayses bought Nils Olmsted's shares after his death.

Bill thought the arrangement served everybody's needs quite well. At times since the buyout, however, he had been aware of the heavy responsibility the real estate partnership left him for keeping the buildings fully occupied. Added to Bill's personal commitment to carry on his father's tradition of being a respected employer in the community, the real estate partnership made it all the more critical for Specialty Packaging to fight the threat of foreign competition.

Bill also occasionally considered alternate structures for Amy's holdings. One plan they had discussed was to convert her non-voting stock to long-term notes with a 15-year maturity. No principal would have to be paid during the life of the notes, but Amy would receive regular interest payments and, since the interest expense would be tax deductible, the company would be able to pay up to 30% more with the same financial effect. And Amy could look forward to receiving her principal at a time when she might need it for her children's education.

Such questions were put on the back burner to be addressed as part of a long-term strategy for the company. In the meantime, Bill turned to the more urgent problems of taking charge at Specialty Packaging. His goal was to establish a new era of professional management without sacrificing the loyalty the employees felt for the company as it had been.

THE NEW MANAGEMENT GROUP

Between 1984 and mid-year of 1986, Bill added a new layer of top management to the Specialty Packaging organization. (*Exhibit 1* shows the organization chart as of July 1986.) As Bill conceived it, the new team's tasks included firming up the old organization, getting a better grasp on costs and margins of existing business, and setting a more market-driven strategic agenda for the company's future. Bill considered himself to be a member of the team, and—at least at first—he was quite enthusiastic about their chances for success.

Outside Hires

All three new top executives came from outside the company, although one of them knew the organization fairly well through his consulting work. Bill convinced systems consultant John Peterson to join the company full time as manager of finance and administration in 1984. Late that same year, he hired Terry Reed as operations manager. Finally, with encouragement from both John and Terry, Bill undertook an executive search for a top-notch marketing specialist. Ted Abado came on board as director of marketing/sales in July of 1986.

John Peterson A CPA with extensive experience in corporate accounting, administration and computer system design, John had also spent several years as marketing manager for a mini-computer company. After years of working in larger companies, he had struck out on his own in his mid-thirties and had been successfully self-employed as a management consultant since 1981. In that capacity he had been working with Bill for several years, most recently for the design and implementation of new computer systems for the whole company. John's presence had been especially helpful to Bill through the buyout period, and Bill was glad to see him come on board full time.

According to John, some things about the "old way" of doing business would have to change for Specialty Packaging to remain profitable in the long run. For one, the "good guy" image Nils Olmsted and Rob Hayes had developed for their company would have to be sacrificed in light of the fierce new competition from abroad. With the strong web of relationships they had developed over the years, Nils and Rob had been able to "sit back and take orders" without worrying too much about costs or profitability. In the tougher environment, John thought Bill would have to work harder at getting the best possible deals from suppliers (raw materials represented a large component of Specialty Packaging's product cost).

The company would also need to "get more out of the existing customer base," which, to John's mind, meant rethinking the traditional customer service orientation. For example, it might be necessary to cut down on some low-margin single-customer products, or to reduce the number of short-run special order sales. Such steps could help improve the contribution from manufacturing, esecially until a new direction for the company was chosen and the now somewhat out-of-date equipment could be upgraded.

Terry Reed   At 56 years of age, Terry Reed had amassed considerable production management experience before coming to St. Cloud. Bill had been most impressed by his accomplishments in cost-cutting and equipment upgrade programs. Terry had also worked in several unionized plants, which Bill thought might be an advantage given the recent unrest in Specialty Packaging's work force. At Terry's request, Bill agreed to include a deferred compensation plan in Terry's contract in order to provide Terry with some pension income from Specialty Packaging. The specifics of the arrangement were to be worked out at the conclusion of Terry's impending divorce.

Terry's mandate was to begin a new round of upgrading equipment while at the same time getting the maximum possible production from the existing machines. John Peterson estimated that Specialty Packaging's technology lagged that of its closest domestic competitor by nearly five years. Both John and Bill expected Terry to steer the company through a few difficult years of operations while the management group as a whole forged and implemented a new, more "market-driven" strategy.

Terry and John soon started pressing Bill to hire a marketing professional who would bring in the expertise the company needed. Bill took some time coming to grips with the higher salary scale he would have to consider to attract the right caliber of person. Finally, though, he accepted the idea, and all three men agreed that Ted Abado was the best of the available candidates.

Ted Abado   Ted's résumé showed an impressive list of accomplishments in his fifteen years out of college. He had held half a dozen different jobs in four well-known companies, starting with sales and sales management, working his way up to have responsibility for generating and implementing marketing programs, and later being a general manager of a plastics product division. Most recently he had served as president of a foreign precision tool manufacturer's new U.S. subsidiary.

Ted had grown disillusioned with that job when the parent company seemed to lose interest in the U.S. operation simply because exchange rate fluctuations made it harder to tap the American market. According to the headhunter, Ted's objective for a new position was "a marketing management opportunity where broad experience in strategic business operations–including P&L responsibility—would be valuable." Ted came on board shortly after the anniversary celebration in July of 1986. Having finally put his whole management team in place, Bill felt full of enthusiasm about Specialty Plastics' "second forty years." Unfortunately, by midwinter his high spirits had already started to sag.

Inside Hassles

The new management group had yet to grow into the cohesive "team" Bill had envisaged. The three top executives seemed more interested in meeting one-on-one with each other and with Bill than in solving problems together. Ted and John found it easy to agree on strategic issues, in part because Ted had a great respect for the financial data John had developed. ("It's as good as any information I've had in bigger companies," claimed Ted.) On his side, Terry was mostly threatened by John's cost figures. Whenever there was a discussion about the margin contributions of specific operations in the plant, Terry reverted to the argument that John's numbers were wrong. Oftentimes the old-guard foremen bolstered Terry's position, and Bill had trouble deciding which "faction" was closer to the truth. As a result, progress towards defining a new strategic plan was slow and halting at best.

All three new executives placed the onus on Bill to lead them out of the impasse. Yet Bill believed that if they were to act as a group, they should probably try to arrive at joint solutions. Furthermore, even though they wanted Bill to "be a leader," both Terry and Ted rejected any "interference" by Bill in what each one called his own "sandbox." Their protective attitudes made it difficult for Bill to find out what was going on in each department without appearing to step on his managers' toes.

For example, Terry seemed to get upset every time he heard that Bill had been out on the shop floor. On one occasion, one of the older production employees mentioned to Bill in the parking lot that the previous night's shift had run off "a pile of junk" that would be shipped out that day to a long-standing customer. The employee grumbled that such quality problems would never have happened in the "old days under Nils and Rob." Bill's response had been to investigate directly and then to take the matter up with Terry. The incident angered Terry, who had already heard about the problem and was working on a solution.

According to Terry, Bill's reaction undermined Terry's own standing in the plant, since it gave the employees the impression that Bill lacked confidence in Terry. On the other hand, Bill thought he might have given an equally negative impression by failing to respond to the employee's complaint. He worried that the shopworkers might think he was unconcerned about problems in the plant, and that older employees in particular might start feeling a sense of alienation.

Bill thought that the conflict with Terry was somewhat exacerbated by Bill's decision to change his stance towards Terry after Terry's divorce became final in the autumn of 1986. During the proceedings, Bill had tried to be helpful and understanding of Terry's difficulties, and to provide a friendly ear whenever Terry needed to talk. Pressure for improved plant performance was not part of their conversations. Once the divorce was final, though, Bill wanted to shift their relationship back to a more professional plane. In order to do so, Bill consistently brought their discussion back to business issues whenever Terry started to talk about personal problems. Bill also started emphasizing the need for performance even in the face of problems.

One of Terry's biggest concerns after his divorce was negotiating the deferred compensation package Bill had approved on hiring him. The two men were now having difficulty agreeing on the structure and funding for the package, and the delay was extremely unsettling for Terry. Bill finally asked a human relations consultant to join in their negotiations. The new input seemed to be helping, and Bill expected the differences to be resolved to Terry's satisfaction fairly soon. The consultant suggested that a resolution would help Terry's performance immediately, pointing out that "if Terry puts as much energy into his work as he's using in these negotiations, there'll be no stopping him in the plant."

To make the tensions worse, the competitive situation turned out to be even more unstable than the management group had expected. In mid-November, the single largest customer for the core holiday packaging line called to say that he had an offer from a Taiwanese producer interested in providing 100% of that customer's product needs. The customer gave Specialty Packaging the opportunity to compete with the offer. Bill, Ted, John and Terry all agreed that the company had to pursue the business, even though it meant adding a fourth shift and running at full capacity with virtually no profit margin throughout the winter months. The business would be critical to Specialty Packaging during the two- to three year transition to a higher-margin product line, and everyone agreed they had to do whatever it took to keep it.

Thus Terry called the customer, and made an offer for their total business at a price lower than that of the previous year. Several days later the customer called Terry back telling him he recognized the pressure this full capacity commitment would put on Terry. He said the Taiwanese were so anxious not to be shut out that they had offered to underwrite the cost increase that would result from a lower volume for Specialty Packaging. The customer invited Terry to quote some new numbers for a smaller portion of the volume.

Terry was excited by this prospect of taking some pressure off his plant, and he got Bill to agree to a 50% proposal for a higher price than the original quote. Unfortunately, the Taiwanese then used this initial inroad to reopen their offer for the entire volume at a much lower price. In the end, Specialty Packaging was forced to take a 50% supply contract at a price 5% lower than the one in their original full capacity offer. Naturally, the incident left Terry feeling even more defensive. It also gave Ted and John additional material to use in their criticism of Terry and Bill alike.

On his side, Ted was insisting that Bill stay out of the marketing sandbox. Ted resisted any questions Bill had for him about his early market analysis, saying it was too soon for him to give answers "off the top of the head." He preferred to work with "real numbers" and did not want to discuss possible outcomes until he could substantiate his opinions with the data he was gathering. His usual response to Bill's queries was, "You hired me to do a job, so just let me do it and don't tell me *how* to do it." In fact, Ted was so confident of his own abilities that he believed Bill would want to give him an equity position in the company once the success of the new marketing plan started to become apparent.

In the meantime, Ted was also quite protective of his turf in the new sales organization he was building. He had filled both of the new territorial sales positions with recent college graduates, and planned to train them personally in sales and sales management techniques. His own track record out of college qualified him to train others, according to Ted: "I can train anybody to be a salesman, provided he has enough ambition and the right kind of personality."

Like Terry, Ted resented any attempt by Bill to talk directly with the salespeople without going through Ted first. For instance, Ted took strong exception to Bill's request that he be put through to one of the new salesmen who had called to report on his visit to an old, valued customer. Ted saw Bill's conversation as "interference" in his relationship with the salesman. Bill found himself explaining that he had only wanted to congratulate the salesman for a job well done.

Ted also wanted to keep his new sales staff away from the influence of the "old guard" in the organization. Despite Ted's professed respect for Pete Williams, the former technical sales manager (and a 27-year veteran of the company), he insisted on separating Pete from the new sales organization. First, he changed Pete's title to technical service manager. Later, he told Bill categorically to "keep Pete away from my salesmen."

Bill realized that Ted and John Peterson might be correct in their claim that Specialty Packaging had to have a new perspective and a new set of attitudes to be effective in the more stringent competitive environment. He also understood that the oldtimers might relay habits and opinions that were no longer appropriate. Nevertheless, he wondered if there might be a way to make the transition without alienating people like Pete Williams, who was obviously upset by the changes.

Pete had always been a cheerful, hardworking manager whose contributions were greatly appreciated by customers. These days, though, he seemed so disgruntled that he was beginning to have a negative influence on most of the people around him. Many of the other older mid-level managers seemed to be having trouble with the new marketing focus, too.

The Latest Incident

Early in April of 1987, Bill had been startled to notice a stranger handing out union cards at the factory gate between the day and evening shifts. Reluctant to investigate directly, he nevertheless learned from Production Manager Ralph Gibson that the event probably stemmed from the dismissal for cause of a single line worker a few days earlier. The former employee had vowed to "get Terry" for the action, but most of the other workers who had been present agreed that the firing was appropriate. As a side remark, Ralph told Bill that things were going much better with Terry, and pointed out that "we *need* Terry in this plant."

Heartened by Ralph's comment, Bill was still worried by the thought of another union campaign. His concerns were heightened a few days later when he received a letter typed on the company's in-house communication system letterhead but sent by mail "because we don't want [Terry] Reed to get it. . . ." (*Exhibit 2* is a copy of the letter.) The incident seemed to have blown over when the stranger stopped coming to the gate, but Bill was inclined to take any union threat seriously.

PROBLEM-SOLVING

By the time she saw the sign for the St. Cloud exit, Beth was feeling eager to hear about Bill's day. Bill, John, Terry, and Ted had planned to spend two days away from the office with a team-building consultant. Beth wondered how Bill would react to the workshop, and whether the first day's session had produced any positive results.

Most likely Bill would have stopped at the office on his way home to see if there had been any new developments on the union issue. Beth and Bill liked to push each other for concrete solutions to the problems they discussed at home, but neither of them was sure of the best way for Bill to react to this one—or even whether he should react at all.

Above all, Beth hoped there would be some resolution to the series of problems Bill had been experiencing over the winter. The previous night, Bill had talked somewhat dispiritedly about his hopes for Specialty Packaging. He was having trouble reconciling the demands from Terry and Ted that he "be a real leader" with their complaints whenever he tried to get a handle on operations. He wondered whether he'd ever be able to see the executive group function as a team—even with the help of a consultant—and whether they would be able to get the company on the right strategic track within the next few years.

Candidly, John Peterson had told him it was a matter of "focusing his attention"—a skill John thought Bill would have to work at developing. Bill was willing to admit that his attention had been "divided" during the period preceding his divorce in 1979 and again—more happily so—after he met Beth in the early 1980s. More recently, he had been working on a project for a new joint venture that had fallen apart over the winter.

Bill also acknowledged his tendency to react immediately whenever somebody hit one of his "hot buttons"—for example, when one executive came to complain about another's activities or when a mid-level manager claimed there was a "crisis" for Bill to handle. This "instant action" syndrome was partly a carry-over from his early days with the company, when the whole organization reflected more the personalities of Nils Olmsted and his father than the professional management style he now wanted to encourage.

News from Bill's Day

Bill was on the phone when Beth arrived home. He whispered that there was nothing new on the union front, and then handed her a list of "trust and teamwork issues" that the management group had identified in a brainstorming session at the team-building workshop during the day. (See *Exhibit 3*.)

Beth settled on the sofa to read the list. Many of the items were familiar from her discussions with Bill and with various company executives. Still, she thought it must have been hard for Bill to hear the negative messages. She hoped he hadn't found the day too discouraging. Just the night before, he had confided to her:

Sometimes I think, hey, maybe it's *me*! Maybe *I'm* the one—I've got to bring somebody else in here to *run* this joint—get out of here and let them do it . . . but my *people* like me, and I like them. I know they're good. I have a lot of faith in them. If I can only get this organization working so that they can do what they can do.

Beth was convinced that careful consideration and sustained effort would allow Bill to achieve his goal. She wondered what steps they could make in the right direction.

EXHIBIT 1 Specialty Packaging, Inc. Organization Chart, July 1986. *Source:* Company records.

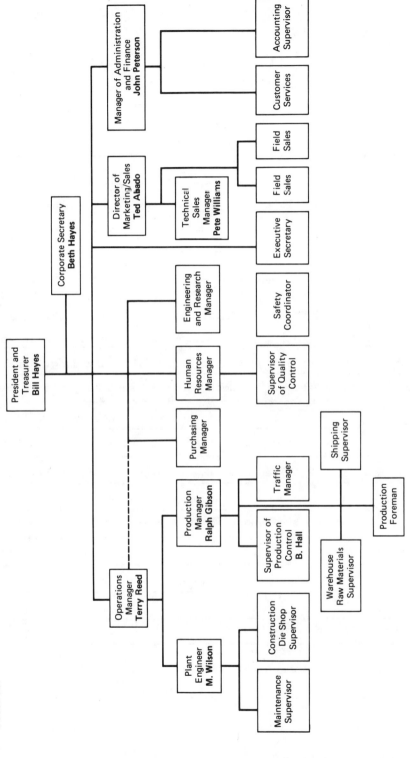

EXHIBIT 2 Specialty Packaging, Inc. Internal Correspondence Mailed to Bill Hayes.

STRAIGHT TALK
Honest communication from person to person

Date — Apr. 15, 1987

Bill

We are sending this by mail because we dont want Reed to get it out of the Straight Talk box. We want you to know that the union thing is not just a passing thing, and until you do something about Reed we will push. this letter is being mailed to most of the shop along with sign up cards. we want you to now tht terry is an

airogent bastard who only has one right opion, his. He tells the workers to but out and uses m. wilson [a day shift foreman] as a fool. We are smart enough not to tell wilson anything. What terry needs is a union stewert to nock him down when he jumps on people.

We didnt want to go this far but even the foremen will not stand up for us. Also we have asked that the windows be opened for air and |Plant Engineer] Hall keeps making excuses. He is just like terry. He never gets things we need on the machines done. He is terry's <u>yes</u>-man.

We wil be watching and talking among ourselfs and waiting --------

the men

Source: Bill Hayes' personal file.

TRUST AND TEAMWORK ISSUES

1. There is a need to delegate and *stick to it*.

2. There is a fear of the family and its historic omnipotence.

3. The St. Cloud community has a tendency to be nosy and jealous and everybody knows everybody's business.

4. Specialty Packaging has a history of being somewhat feudalistic but the knights don't have any power.

5. The "old timers" really manage a lot and fill the power vacuum. They have an undue influence on the organization.

6. There is a lot of blaming others as against doing each individual's job.

7. People in the organization are good at pushing other people's buttons, especially Bill's, which leads to panic, which leads to lack of credibility.

8. I've been trained here to work one on one.

9. In fact, in a company that is owner managed, we have to realize that whatever really happens is to Bill's personal benefit.

10. A lot of one to one dealing and very little dealing directly with the management team as a group. The one to one often gets in the way.

11. There is a lot of selective communication.

12. There is a good deal of avoiding adversity and confrontation. The problem just stays there. It never gets resolved. We avoid conflict and also avoid resolution.

13. Bill doesn't want to hurt anyone.

14. We need to make decisions and stick to them.

15. In the plant there is a feeling of *inconsistency* of direction *and* a feeling of opportunism so that we're jumping from one direction to another.

16. "Bill will do what he wants" so it doesn't matter what we think.

17. We all wait to see what Bill tells us.

18. Only Bill has authority.

19. Bill doesn't show the organization that he really backs his management.

20. Long-term employees have a personal loyalty to Bill and have a direct link to him behind our backs.

21. The process should make the decision—Bill shouldn't.

22. There is a sense, inherited from Rob Hayes, that "it's my plant" versus the team.

23. Bill elicits opinions on management from lower levels.

24. Regarding decisions, everybody is good at pushing Bill's button.

25. Priorities then tend to shift a lot. We have overreactive behavior and inconsistency.

26. There is a history of spokes in a wheel with all power leading back to Olmsted or Rob Hayes. R&D, production, and marketing are all separated. It's an atmosphere that is friendly, but autocratic.

27. There's no new blood. The place is still filled with Nils Olmsted's people.

28. There is a great resistance to outsiders and change.

29. Promotions are based on tenure and loyalty as against professionalism, education and performance. The "mustangs" (old-line middle managers) aren't clearly professionals and have a hard time working with the "outsiders."

30. There is confusion on what the company is doing—people say: "Am I involved?" There is less confusion in the manufacturing/production area than in the rest of the company.

31. There is confusion as to who is my boss.

32. Within management, there is a lack of clarity on functional goals. In fact, we don't really have goals. There's very little clarity on what the company's goals are.

33. The organization is very sensitive to "back checking." Any discussion by Bill with others below top management communicates that Bill doesn't trust his top people.

34. A better way would be to learn what is going on through written reports and observations.

35. There is a lot of confusion about executive compensation and security of management roles that Bill needs to clear up.

John Hancock Mutual Life Insurance Co.: The Inflation Strategy Task Force (A)

I have never worked in an effort that was more frustrating. It isn't that Paul Murphy isn't an intelligent person. He just doesn't know how to manage something like this. Senior management needs to step in. After all, you set this whole thing up. Can't you do something, Jack?

Vice President Sam Hendricks was unhappy and thought John Hancock President John G. McElwee should know it. In Sam's judgment, the Inflation Strategy Task Force, established by the powerful eight-person executive committee, was stuck. Hendricks felt that the stakes were very high, and that senior management should be aware of the problems. The task force was created on October 30, 1980 with Sam as one of its members. It was now early February of 1981.

The Inflation Strategy Task Force was made up mainly of third- and fourth-level managers. It had been set up by the executive committee which said that it wanted new ideas and visions on future strategic directions for the John Hancock Company. Sam liked the idea, but felt that it was also time for senior management to take more active leadership in the company's future.

At first, Hendricks couldn't pinpoint the problem. The task force's assignment was a complex and tough one: what should the company's future strategy be assuming that the runaway inflation of the 1970s would continue along with, (1) soaring interest rates, and (2) the consequent falling sales of standard life insurance products as customers sought higher investment returns? Cash flow problems had become so severe in the spring of 1980 that John Hancock had been forced to borrow ($300 million) from the banks for the first time in its 120-year history. By 1980, there was also a dramatic increase in competition within what was coming to be called the financial services industry. In addition, several members of the executive committee were new along with Jack McElwee and Jim Morton who were to take office as CEO/chairman and COO/president at the end of the year. McElwee and Morton said that they wanted to shape the executive committee into a different and less fragmented force in the company. The executive committee had a history of often being a corporate battleground. Hendricks had heard that McElwee had even said that members would be asked to resign from the committee if they couldn't work effectively together. Hendricks wondered if the task force's problems were just a case of poor delegation and follow-up by the executive committee. Or maybe it was simply the people on the task force. Here were seven aggressive mid-career vice presidents, each seeking change in a conservative company under a conservative task force chairman who was a senior vice president. Despite talk of freed-up time, most members had taken on the task force duties on top of their regular work. Each member also came from a different area of the company and was backed up by several

Professor Louis B. Barnes prepared this case as the basis for class discussion rather than to illustrate either effective or ineffective handling of an administration situation.

Copyright © 1988 by the President and Fellows of Harvard College. Harvard Business School case 9-488-049.

eager junior staff people who were supposed to do the initial research and staff work.

These might all be contributing factors, but after thinking it over, Sam Hendricks had decided that the crux of the issue lay in another direction. He concluded that task force chairman Paul Murphy's style of leadership was a major problem. Murphy seemed too slow to act and possibly in over his head. In Hendricks' judgment, Paul Murphy just hadn't moved the task force or gotten it organized to get the job done. Furthermore,

task force member Jim Thompson seemed to agree with Hendricks. Sam finally decided that he should go to company president and CEO designate, Jack McElwee with his concerns. He had talked informally with McElwee about his concerns on a number of other occasions. Sam knew that the task force was very important to McElwee, to retiring CEO/Chairman J. Edwin Matz, and to operations vice president, and president designate, E. James Morton. Now, as he faced Jack McElwee, he wondered how to proceed further.

BACKGROUND

The John Hancock Mutual Life Insurance Company was the nation's sixth largest insurance firm with total assets of $18.8 billion under management in 1980. The company was founded in 1860 and had a work force of over 20,000 people. Over 5,000 of these employees worked in the head offices in Boston, Massachusetts, many in the famous glass tower in Copley Square. Historically, the company had built its early reputation on sales of individual life insurance policies. As recently as 1974, 92% of individual sales had been whole life insurance products. Using prudent investment policies, the company had become a leader in its own sector of the industry.

By the late 1970s, however, much of this traditional leadership seemed to be eroding under pressure from inflation, high interest rates, competition, alternative investment opportunities, deregulated institutions, high costs, and obsolete products. Similar problems faced the whole life insurance industry. Indeed, the major mutual insurance companies had been losing market share of discretionary spending for three decades. The combination of forces seemed to particularly threaten and reduce John Hancock's time-honored position as an industry leader. Although the company had

long since branched into other insurance product lines, its overall business had become highly competitive. By 1980, there were some 40,000 firms competing in what was being called the financial services industry. Some competitors, critics, and even Hancock employees felt that the company's best days were over. With a senior management that included six executive vice presidents, 20 senior vice presidents, and over 40 vice presidents, the company had become known in some circles as a top-down, conservative, and somewhat ponderous bureaucracy. Turf battles and dissension had become part of the company's history (see *Exhibit 1* for a partial organization chart), and there seemed to be no clear sense of strategic direction. As one observer noted, "It's like rejuvenating an old elephant." Yet, according to the company's 1980 Annual Report:

John Hancock's 119-year history is one of adapting to meet new needs—with new or refined products, appropriate technologies and, where called for, organizational change. We began our corporate existence offering life insurance protection to individuals; vastly broadened that market with the introduction of small debit policies; extended the group business in the 1920s; and played an active role in the great expansion in pension and employer-paid health coverages in the postwar era.

Since the late 1960s, we have evolved from a relatively simple organization offering individual and group coverages into a complex structure of subsidiaries offering a much extended range of financial services. The evolution continued in 1980 with the formation of a holding company, John Hancock Subsidiaries, Inc., to coordinate more effectively the policies and operation of our subsidiaries.

Nevertheless, behind the scenes, some members of senior management were concerned about the company's future. Mssrs. Matz, McElwee, and Morton had been talking about the issue for several years. With J.E. Matz retiring at the end of 1981, both Jack McElwee and Jim Morton were determined to define a new corporate sense of direction with less departmental self interest and factionalism. In addition, Matz, McElwee, and Morton all believed that something specific had to be done to help John Hancock get out of its bureaucratic posture and new strategic directions. But as Jack McElwee noted:

Nobody *really* knows what the financial services industry will be in the future. We all admit to that. We are all trying to be flexible. We know we all are not doing everything right, and the jury is still out as to which companies will have the right combination and the wisdom and courage to remedy the situation as it evolves. When will this happen? When will the paradigm of the new FSI be in place? In my view, it won't be before 1990.

THE TASK FORCE

After considerable debate, discussion, and several position papers written by members of the executive committee, the Inflation Strategy Task Force was set up by the executive committee which chose the task force members to represent a broad cross section of the company. Excerpts from the task force's assignment read:

Under the assumptions of continued high inflation, intensified consumer and regulatory pressures, and new nontraditional competition, the task force is to determine: (a) the best eventual configuration for our product organization, both Home Office and Field; (b) the main outlines of the products that this organization will most likely sell and administer; (c) the principles of an appropriate compensation profile for such products. Finally the task force is to devise the best strategy for transition from our present organization and product lines to those formulated by actions described in the paragraph above.

The eight men assigned to the task force represented different special areas of interest and expertise. The only senior vice president on the task force was the chairman,

Paul Murphy, who at 51, had an MBA, an LLB, had worked mainly in the administrative side of Field Sales, and had served on many corporate committees. Some employees wondered why McElwee and Morton had chosen Paul Murphy to head the task force. One manager recalled that Murphy had chaired one task force some years earlier which had been "torn apart" by a previous executive committee when the task force made its recommendations. Murphy was considered bright, thoughtful, doggedly determined, and sometimes reticent to push his own views. The youngest member assigned to the task force was Jim Thompson, who had a PhD in physics and at 30 years old, was described by one manager as, "If not the finest mind on the committee, at least the most creative. He's very junior when it comes to corporate tenure, but he's generated respect at all levels." The other six members were:

Sam Hendricks. Age 45. Bright, articulate, sometimes needling. A passionate advocate for his own positions. Hendricks had a PhD in Economics and served as corporate economist. He had sometimes spoken of his desire for line responsibility.

Joe Brown. Age 37. Described as ambitious, articulate, a workaholic, and an occasional, abrasive devil's advocate. Brown had broad company networking experience as a key member of the firm's legal office.

Al Crosby. Age 46. From marketing. Wide experience in large-scale management functions. A Wharton MBA, he had recently managed a highly successful, cross-corporate cost reduction program. Hard driving and highly respected.

Don Dorman. Age 54. Worked in a pivotal position in marketing research. Articulate, witty, and considered a burr under the saddle of every boss he's worked for, yet highly respected for his ideas.

Frank Welch. Age 48. Described by one executive as "a quiet catalyst and an exceptional resource because of his grasp of comprehensive corporate issues—an actuary-philosopher." He sometimes irritated senior managers with his advocacy of "enlightened change." Currently head of the corporate planning office.

Gerald Long. Age 46. A bright, thoughtful, actuary who sometimes hesitated to present his own ideas. Highly respected for his quality of mind, Long had a national reputation in his own sphere of investment-related insurance products.

During November, the task force members tried to identify the topic areas to be covered in their assignment. As one member said, "The executive committee gave us the charge, and then they walked away." On November 21, the task force submitted an *Initial Report of the Inflation Strategy Task Force* to the executive committee outlining their future plans. The November 21 report said that the task force would submit its work in three additional phases. Phase I would consist of a report on: "certain factors/subjects which are material to our task (and) have been identified." Each topic area was assigned to a Task Force Member as follows:

1. Today's Purchaser of Financial Products and Services. Project Leader—Sam Hendricks.
2. The Purchaser Demographically Defined. Project Leader—Frank Welch.
3. Financial Products and Services Used by Tomorrow's Purchaser. Project Leader—Frank Welch.
4. Tomorrow's Customers' Attitudes toward Financial Products/Services Especially as Influenced by Persistent High Inflation. Project Leader—Don Dorman.
5. Government Involvement in Financial Sectors. Project Leader—Joe Brown.
6. How Will Competition in Consumer Financial Markets Be Different 5–10 Years Hence from the Present. Project Leader—Gerald Long.
7. How Will Technological Developments of the Present and Future Affect Financial Products, Distribution Systems, and the Like in the Mid and Late 1980s. Project Leader—Al Crosby.
8. Other Companies' Approaches to Preparing for the Future. Project Leader—Jim Thompson.

The November 21 report went on to say:

In Phase I, each project leader will draw upon his department's resources and other Task Force members to develop preliminary answers to: (1) a more complete definition of the subject, (2) an estimate of available source data and outside resources that are needed, and (3) a target conclusion date for that segment of the study.

During Phase I, project leaders will make interim progress reports on each factor to the task force for purposes of communication and advice. The Task Force will then attempt to synthesize the various presentations in order to develop an overview for marketing our products.

In Phase II, the Task Force will attempt to define what markets and products seem most advantageous for John Hancock in the late 1980s. This involves two kinds of considerations: a forecast derived from Phase I of future markets, and a selection for John Hancock from among these. The selection process will involve applying to various products the criteria which have been developed. In the course of Phase II, the Task Force plans to work as an entity rather than in subgroups.

. . . We would propose making this report on or about April 15, 1981.

Finally, Phase III was to provide an outline for implementing the steps recommended in Phase II.

By early February of 1981, each topic leader working with his own department's staff members had completed the individual project assignments and circulated a considerable mass of information to the other members. Some debate occurred within the project teams as junior staff members presented their own ideas for change. Task force members met 21 times during this period. One of Sam Hendricks' key staff members sat in on a number of these early meetings when Hendricks did not attend. She recalled that the task force got off to a poor start and noted that:

It was a group management problem. The issues were all there, but nobody was directing anyone to face up to them. There were three or four people who had a list of issues, and then all the people whose departments were affected—I suppose you could think of it as staff vs. line, but it wasn't quite that clear. To some extent, the people who had the major questions tended to be the more junior people, although that wasn't 100% true either. Then there was a chairman who, from my perspective, didn't ever force or structure things so that there was ever a resolution. Things were brought up, and then other things were brought up, and it was all kind of left hanging. I felt that the chairman needed to bring things up for a vote or a resolution. Instead, it just kept going and going and going in agonizing detail with strong opinions on all sides.

Member frustrations continued to grow. One observer commented that each project leader sometimes seemed caught between his own department's traditional interests, the desires of his staff member subordinates, and the task force directives. Another noted that:

The staff members were on the average 10 to 12 years younger in age and tenure than the task force members. This pattern produced an effect wherein the younger tigers inundated the task force members with data and recommendations which were in many cases quite radical. The task force members, who saw themselves as "radical" vis-à-vis the executive committee members, were in an interesting position. They had to moderate without emasculating the work of their respective aides and still incorporate the end product into the overall report.

Chairman Paul Murphy also commented upon some of the task force's problems:

We began to run into difficulty in preparing the Phase I report in late January. The members of the task force completed their assignments but had difficulty in collectively synthesizing all of the material and relating it to our charge. The turmoil in the task force troubled me considerably, because I was not particularly sympathetic to the methodological difficulties experienced by some of the younger task force staff members.

By early February, Sam Hendricks knew that not only he but several other members of the task force were worried about lack of progress. His meeting with Jack McElwee was his own response to that frustration. He was encouraged to learn that Jim Thompson apparently had similar concerns. Thompson showed Hendricks a memo which Thompson planned to circulate at the meeting on February 6, 1981. The memo said:

We do not have a problem with what we are trying to do as much as we have a problem with how we are trying to do it.
    We have a *process* problem. There is no mechanism for
1. Identifying the 5, 10, 15, or 20 issues *vital* to our study.
2. Bringing such issues before the task force in an orderly fashion for effective discussion.
3. Polling *all* members for their options to determine the extent of consensus or polarization.
4. Recording the status of each issue.

Without such a mechanism, we
1. Cannot locate inconsistencies in individual members' or the entire group's views.

2. Cannot identify the *significant* differences of opinion that lead to multiple scenarios.
3. Cannot proceed effectively to fleshing out the issues and synthesizing them into a written effort.

Sam Hendricks knew that Paul Murphy had received a copy of Thompson's memo. He wondered what Murphy would do with it, if anything. He also hoped that his and Thompson's concerns would encourage Jack McElwee, Jim Morton, and the executive committee to step in. He wondered what else he should say, or how he should pursue these concerns with Jack McElwee at the moment.

EXHIBIT 1 John Hancock Mutual Life Insurance Co. The Inflation Strategy Task Force (A). Organization Chart Effective April, 1983.

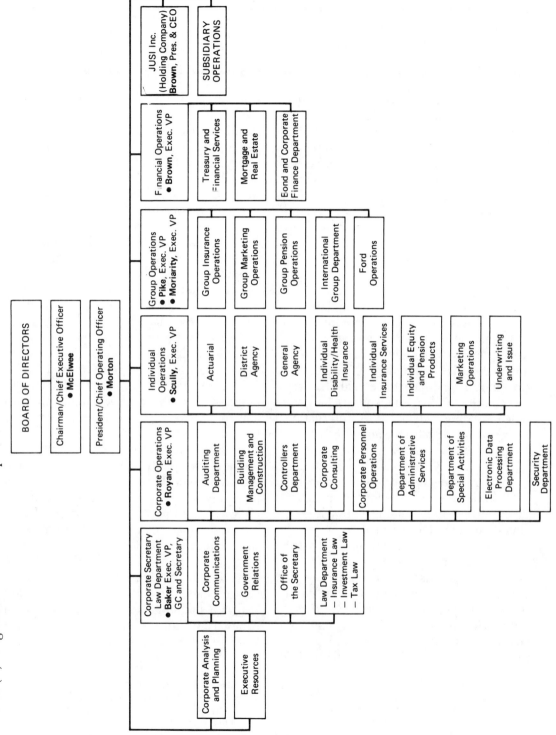

Modern Advanced Concrete (A)

Filiberto Crespi faced the beginning of 1977 with considerable trepidation. The coming year would mark an important transition for MAC, the 50-50 joint venture company of which Dottore Crespi was Executive Vice President and principal Italian shareholder. Crespi's American partner, International Constructors (a wholly-owned subsidiary of a major MNC conglomerate's chemical division) had recently informed him they wished to withdraw from the 18 year old partnership. Crespi had been invited to buy out International Constructors' half of MAC, which entailed about LIT 150 million (US$ 180,000[*]) in equity capital. In addition, International Constructors had guaranteed bank overdrafts of eight to nine times that amount, and without their guarantee, the overdrafts would have to be paid off. Crespi and another Italian (his cousin) had combined holdings identical to International Constructors. (*Exhibit 1* shows MAC's 1976 balance sheet.)

In 1958, Crespi and his cousin had founded *Mediterranea Additivi Cemento* S.p.A., a Milan-based company that produced and distributed various building materials for the Italian market. The original company also imported and sold International Constructors' line of grouts, flooring products, and admixtures for use in the preparation of concrete and mortars. MAC-I.C. was formed in 1961 as a joint venture between the original Italian company and International Constructors. At the same time, MAC began manufacturing grouts and admixtures locally under license from the U.S. partner. Under the partnership agreement, MAC paid International Constructors a percentage royalty on all sales of International Constructors' products.

By the early 1970s, MAC had grown to be the largest admixture distributor in Italy. Admixtures (or additives, as they were sometimes called) were used along with cement, water, and sand, gravel or other natural aggregates in order to produce a malleable blend which later hardened into concrete or mortar. The type and relative proportion of admixtures in the "mix design" varied according to such factors as architectural and strength specifications, placement procedures, atmospheric conditions, and the qualities of the other materials to be used. MAC-I.C.'s early line of admixtures included both liquid and powder products that were suitable for a wide range of concrete and mortar uses.

The Italian company's direct sales territory also included Austria, Greece, and Yugoslavia. Some foreign income came from joint-venture manufacturing and/or distribution operations with local partners. In addition, products manufactured in Italy were sold to International Constructors' other distributors throughout Europe and in a few more distant markets. MAC's overall sales volume had reached some LIT 4.4 billion (US$ 7.5 million) by 1972. (See *Exhibit 2* for a summary of growth and performance data from 1959 through 1975.)

However, despite technological devel-

---

[*]Financial data have been translated from Italian lire into U.S. dollars using exchange rates in effect at the time of the events described. A history of exchange rates and deflator indexes is provided in the Appendix.

The case was prepared by Colleen Kaftan Research Assistant, under the supervision of Prof. William J. Bruns, Jr., as a basis for class discussion rather than to illustrate either effective or ineffective handling or an administrative situation.

Copyright © 1983 by the President and Fellows of Harvard College. Harvard Business School case 9-383-132.

opments and increasing customer interest in using admixtures, MAC's performance had been dismal since 1973. The 1975 reports showed a loss of LIT 268 million ($410,500) on LIT 5.672 billion ($ 8.7 million) in sales. Crespi thought the poor results reflected both a cause and an outcome of MAC's problems with International Constructors. He had been disappointed by the American partner's failure to keep pace with the significant advances in concrete admixture technology that had occurred since 1973. Smaller companies without MAC's technical overhead and royalty costs were beginning to encroach on its traditional markets. Crespi believed MAC should take advantage of the new technology to introduce a more sophisticated product line, but International Constructors had not been contributing its technical expertise to the product development effort.

In 1975, Crespi had finally taken steps to develop MAC's own ability to innovate with admixtures, and eighteen months later he believed the added research and development costs were about to start paying off. The slide in performance had been stopped; 1976 was expected to be a break-even year. The improvement came in part from an increase in sales revenue for the first of the new generation of higher-technology admixtures developed in MAC's own new laboratories. MAC had registered the new product under the trade name of Rheomac. Most of the early users were purchasing Rheomac as a higher-priced substitute for traditional admixtures they might also have bought from MAC. However, since Rheomac was not subject to the original royalty agreement between MAC and International Constructors, the Italian company was saving on payments to the U.S. partner by promoting Rheomac instead of International Constructors' older products.

The future opportunities for Rheomac and other advanced products appeared tremendous to Crespi. He had suggested that International Constructors consider marketing Rheomac in other territories under license for MAC. The returns from the additional sales could then be used for further product development in MAC's new laboratories.

When International Constructors' new CEO requested a meeting with him in November 1976, Crespi had expected to discuss licensing conditions and royalty agreements for Rheomac and other new products to be developed by MAC. Instead, he was surprised to hear that International Constructors wanted to end the partnership. Under the partnership agreement, either could withdraw by selling to the other, and International Constructors offered to sell out to Crespi. He had accepted the offer immediately, because he believed that both he and MAC would benefit if he could carry out the purchase.

International Constructors was asking LIT 150 million (US$ 180,000), or roughly the book value of its equity shares. The price seemed reasonable to Crespi. Unfortunately, other aspects of the takeover presented financing problems that seemed almost insurmountable. First, the loss of International Constructors' guarantee would make it impossible to continue operating the firm unless Crespi could find another way to fund the overdrafts. The most powerful Italian banks were becoming skeptical about MAC's viability, especially since its prestigious U.S. partner had decided to pull out.

Crespi thought of bringing in another Italian partner. Negotiations were begun with the cement division of a large Italian group which was considering the purchase of International Constructors' share. Several other individuals and companies were interested in keeping MAC afloat, but none of them had the amount of capital that would be necessary to do so.

In order to protect his own investment,

Crespi also considered finding a buyer for his half of the business. This solution seemed the least attractive, though, since he was unlikely to get much more than relief from his bank guarantees in return. In Crespi's opinion, MAC was headed for a future that warranted a much higher price. Nevertheless, his personal fortune would be at stake if he failed to save the company.

BACKGROUND ON MAC AND THE CONCRETE ADMIXTURES INDUSTRY

In 1965, some seven years after the original company's founding in Milan, MAC moved its headquarters east to Treviso near the Adriatic coast. A new admixtures blending plant was built there on a site that would allow for expansion as markets grew. The principal admixture users were suppliers of premixed concrete, who could improve their control over hardening time and overall performance by including admixtures in the concrete mix. As the ready-mix industry developed throughout Europe, MAC's sales expanded along with it. MAC also adopted a "teaching policy" to promote the use of admixtures by informing architects, designers, building contractors and cement manufacturers how its products contributed to the quality of the finished concrete structure.

The MAC Organization

By the early 1970s, the company employed some 180 people in a relatively simple functional organization, as shown in *Exhibit 3*.

Manufacturing MAC's traditional products were of two basic types. Grouts and flooring products were dry powders sold in 25 to 50 kg bags. Admixtures were liquids delivered in drums or in bulk. The manufacturing process for both types of product used relatively simple blending techniques to mix small numbers of ingredients in roughly similar proportions. The raw materials were essentially waste substances, such as lignine from paper pulp waste, produced by and purchased from chemical companies as by-products of their own operations.

The quality control function was handled in the plant by line workers who reported to the plant manager. Like the manufacturing processes, the QC requirements were also quite simple for the traditional products. Since they were made from waste materials rather than from substances that were specifically tailored for use in concrete mix, the presence of some impurities was considered normal and inevitable. The admixtures were used in such small proportions (generally no more than 0.2%) in the overall mix that the impurities were not likely to cause problems in the finished concrete structure.

Labs and technology MAC's chief technical activity prior to 1975 was providing customers with service and advice about the use of admixtures and other MAC products for their building projects. The Technical Services laboratory had been set up with the founding of the MAC-IC partnership. The laboratory personnel worked closely with sales people on technical questions, and could request assistance from International Constructors' central research and laboratory units in the U.S. for specific problems beyond their competence.

Sales and marketing The sales task for traditional admixtures entailed working with the customer to produce a "mix design" for each job. The "mix design" specified the quantities and ratios of cement, sand, gravel and admixture necessary to achieve the desired strength and quality of concrete as a function of building conditions (e.g. temperature and humidity) and the structural design of the project. For traditional admixtures, creating the "mix design" was a relatively straightforward task, although it did require an engineering background for MAC's sales people and the assistance of the Technical Service laboratory.

According to Dott. Crespi, MAC's customers had never shown much interest in admixtures *per se*. They were more interested in construction processes in general and in the characteristics of concrete as a final product. For this reason, MAC had always based much of its marketing strategy on the technical assistance the company could provide for admixture users. In addition, MAC regularly sponsored seminars on advances in concrete technology, so that its customers and sales force alike could stay well informed of basic applications and new developments.

The strategy proved quite successful throughout MAC's first fifteen years of operations. However, by the early 1970s, the overhead cost for technical assistance began to be more of a burden than a positive contribution. Crespi described the problem as follows:

Since our manufacturing processes were fairly simple, smaller competitors—including some former employees—could produce similar products with far less overhead. They were telling customers to keep a small contact with us in order to get free technical assistance, but to buy most of their admixtures at cut rates from them.

Crespi believed that the best way to combat the new competition would be to upgrade the technological value of MAC's offer. Scientists and industrial laboratories in Germany and Japan had begun making discoveries that could significantly alter admix-

ture technology in the years to come. Related research was also being carried out in Italian universities. Crespi saw in these developments the avenue of the future for MAC and the concrete construction industry.

Superplasticizer Technology

A prominent scientist conducting research on the characteristics of poured concrete made the following observation about the breakthroughs in his field beginning in 1974.

We've been using concrete—working and building with it—for a very long time. We've also studied it at the universities for a long time and we have a good idea of what happens when you mix cement and water. But only now are we really beginning to understand *why* the mixture hardens, and to be able to influence that process.

The new understanding of how concrete was formed led to the development of superplasticizers, or synthetic polymer additives that made it possible to lower the water/cement ratio in the concrete mix without decreasing the fluidity of the wet concrete. A lower water/cement ratio yielded stronger, more cohesive, more durable, and less permeable concrete. However, until the advent of superplasticizer technology, contractors had needed to add water and use expensive vibrating equipment in order to ensure that the mix was workable enough to spread evenly throughout the structural frames. Superplasticizers served as a lubricant in the concrete mixture, so that water content could be kept at a minimum without sacrificing fluidity and ease of pouring.

Synthetic polymers had been used in other industries, such as textiles and leather, for some time before the superplasticizer applications began to be developed. Most of the major industrial chemical firms had the technical capacity to synthesize the polymers, but until 1974 they had never pursued large scale commercial applications for concrete production. At that time the combination of rising construction costs and advances in polymerization technology began to make it appear worthwhile to develop the potential new market outlet. Large chemical firms in Germany and Japan started focusing research and development resources on superplasticizer products. A Japanese company was first to begin selling superplasticizers. The German firm was attempting to devise a marketing strategy to introduce the new, more sophisticated and more expensive synthetic additives in the European concrete industry.

Dott. Crespi thought that a small, vigorous company with a detailed knowledge of concrete markets, such as MAC, should be well placed to compete with the larger, less specialized chemical companies. He believed MAC could put International Constructors' financial and technical resources to work to develop a lucrative new superplasticizer business throughout its existing sales territory and beyond. Naturally, he was somewhat surprised and frustrated to realize that International Constructors did not share his enthusiasm for pursuing the commercial applications of superplasticizer technology.

International Constructors' "Blind Spots"

Crespi suspected there might be several reasons behind International Constructors' reluctance to follow up on superplasticizer technology in spite of his insistent urging. First, admixtures represented a relatively minor portion of International Constructors' overall activities, and the company might have been slow to realize the true impact of the new discoveries. Second, MAC's performance since 1973 had probably diminished International Constructors' interest in the partnership in general. A third reason had to

do with the fact that International Constructors was an American company. It almost seemed to Crespi that the U.S. based executives were less readily convinced about the immediate value of innovations that came from outside their own country. Fortunately for MAC, the other major American competitor in Italy lacked the commercial organization for taking advantage of the new market, even though it had the necessary synthesizing capabilities to produce the polymers in Italy.

By 1975, Crespi felt that MAC was being "left behind by the market" as a result of International Constructors' lack of interest and unwillingness to support superplasticizer product development. Moreover, sophisticated customers in Germany and Switzerland were beginning to ask technical questions that MAC was unable to answer. Nor were there acceptable responses forthcoming from International Constructors' central laboratories in the U.S. The assistance MAC needed for the commercial-technical problems in question finally came from an unexpected source. Professor Mario Collepardi, who had long been a consultant and instructor for MAC's seminars, was able to provide answers in areas where International Constructors could give none. In Crespi's words:

Professor Collepardi has the ability to explain very complex technical concepts even to ignorant people like me. That's why his seminars are always so successful. Then in 1975 he helped us solve a product quality problem for some difficult, highly sophisticated Swiss and German customers. After that we decided to have a closer collaboration with him.

Professor Collepardi

His involvement in laboratory research at the University of Ancona had brought Prof. Collepardi to the forefront of the developing field of superplasticizer technology. However, he had never been convinced that his theoretical work would find practical applications:

University research is conducted under a philosophy which is completely different from the one that drives business research. I find it very interesting to work with theory, but in the long run I was becoming dissatisfied with the University environment. I wanted to see if it would be possible to have some of my ideas applied. For that I knew I had to approach the business people.

Early in 1975, Prof. Collepardi had written to five different enterprises to suggest a cooperative arrangement. Dott. Crespi had received one of the five letters, and had responded almost immediately. An agreement was reached under which Prof. Collepardi would spend one day a week as a consultant creating and directing a new research department within MAC. Collepardi would also retain his teaching and laboratory responsibilities at the University and would continue contributing papers and articles to the growing body of published work on superplasticizers.

THE NEW PRODUCT LINE

By late 1975, the new research department had already taken the initial steps toward developing a marketable line of superplasticizers and establishing a comprehensive strategy for opening the new market. Professor Collepardi had patented a formula which was put into production at one of MAC's chemical suppliers. He also introduced a set of concepts that would help customers see the value of using the more sophisticated additives rather than the older, cheaper products.

First, he coined the term "rheoplastic" (from rheo = fluid and plastic = cohesive) to describe the qualities of concrete prepared with the new polymer additives. The first product was called Rheomac, and both terms were registered as official trade names. Rheomac was brought to market early in 1976 by sales engineers who emphasized the concept of total cost per cubic meter of "*placed*" concrete (i.e. poured and dried in its final location). Customers had previously considered only the raw materials cost per cubic meter of concrete. The new approach allowed sales engineers to show how Rheomac's potential advantages in terms of structural quality and ease of construction (including transport, machinery usage, and labor) could justify the higher-priced admixture in the final cost of "placed" concrete.

For example, while traditional admixtures represented only about 3% of the cost of a cubic meter according to the traditional measure of raw materials cost, the new superplasticizers were about 20% of costs if calculated by the same measure. However, since the cost per cubic meter of "placed" concrete was 3–5 times as high as the other measure, the relative weight of superplasticizer cost for "placed" concrete was reduced to an average of 5%. In some cases there was an actual savings where superplasticizers helped simplify construction methods or reduced the need for skilled labor and costly vibrating equipment.

The initial marketing effort for Rheomac focused on the precast concrete industry, where the new customers had the technical expertise to understand the advantages of rheoplastic concrete. A further reason for choosing the pre-cast industry was the relative concentration of buyers, which made it easier to keep track of the new product's performance.

Initial sales were very encouraging. After four months on the market, Rheomac was bringing in revenues equal to 28% of International Constructors' most popular traditional admixture. International Constructors still seemed unconvinced about the value of the innovation. In particular, they were unwilling to support further development by paying royalties on Rheomac sales as MAC had requested.

Nevertheless, Dott. Crespi encouraged Prof. Collepardi to continue the developmental work. In April 1976, construction was begun on a new laboratory and library facility. Another expert in concrete and chemical technology, Dott. Corradi, was brought in to head the research and development laboratory.

Prof. Collepardi concentrated on instructing sales engineers and potential new customers about superplasticizers. A special program was put together for industrial designers and architects, who were also favorably disposed toward the new products. They were particularly interested in structural quality and strength specifications for finished concrete. The rheoplastic characteristics of superplasticizer-treated concrete contributed to a designer's sense of confidence by ensuring that the concrete would be properly mixed and placed, and that contractors would not be tempted to increase workability by adding water. The positive response from such an influential group

further convinced Crespi of the potential for Rheomac and other specialized polymers in the concrete construction industry.

The Transition

Dott. Crespi realized that the transition to superplasticizer products was presenting great challenges to the MAC organization. MAC did not have the manfacturing capacity to synthesize the new products in-house. As a result, the new technology team had to furnish exact formulas and specifications to an outside supplier, and then pay strict attention to quality control for the externally prepared product.

Moreover, the sales task would also be affected by the addition of more advanced products. The sales engineer's "teaching" role could be expected to be even more important than previously. Difficult new technical information would have to be mastered and transmitted by the sales force to the customers, and the seminars would have to focus carefully on superplasticizer applications as perceived by the various user groups. Yet Crespi believed that the higher value-added contribution and the growth potential of superplasticizer markets were the only things that could pull MAC out of the slump it had been experiencing since the early 1970s. MAC had already secured patents for a number of Prof. Collepardi's formulations and Crespi was eager to exploit them for their full commercial value.

DOTT. CRESPI'S CHALLENGE

Early in 1977, the cement division of a major Italian group was considering a takeover of International Constructors' interest in MAC. A positive decision from them might resolve many of the problems Dott. Crespi was facing. Unfortunately, however, it was far from evident that they would in fact choose to buy out International Constructors, and Crespi found it necessary to plan an alternative approach.

Working together with Dott. Alfonso Benedetti, MAC's Director of Finance, Dott. Crespi was exploring "every imaginable avenue" for financing the company. Having met with resistance from the larger national banks, they began approaching smaller local banks with requests for funds. Dott. Benedetti also tightened his control over working capital, collecting receivables as quickly as possible and stretching out payables. Several suppliers of raw materials and services, including the polymer synthesis company and a transport agent as well as some distributors were aware of MAC's difficulties and wanted to be as supportive as possible. They believed their own interest was tied up with MAC's and wanted to encourage the company's survival since its potential for future growth would contribute to their own.

Moreover, each of the functional department heads was strongly committed to getting MAC through the transition period successfully. Prof. Collepardi, Dott. Benedetti from the Finance Department, and their colleagues, Dott. Corradi from the new Research and Development Department and Ing. Tacchini from the Commercial Department had all told Dott. Crespi he could count on their complete loyalty. Their renewed efforts as a management team were already beginning to be rewarded in MAC's performance: the January 1977 figures showed further improvements over the 1976 breakeven results, and the positive trend was expected to continue.

In Treviso, the small northeastern Italian city where MAC was headquartered, the business community was buzzing with talk about MAC's serious troubles. It appeared next to impossible for Dott. Crespi to come up with enough capital to save the company if the single prospective buyer decided against the purchase. There would be very little time to act if the deal fell through. Dott. Crespi felt increasingly anxious and found it difficult to sleep as the February 1977 deadline for their decision drew near. He had taken advantage of their deliberation period in order to "stall" International Constructors as he sought alternative ways to absorb the other half of MAC. With no firm offers in his hands, he realized that time might be running out while he and Dott. Benedetti were desperately "stabbing at chances."

On the other hand, Dott. Crespi was concerned that International Constructors might be sufficiently impressed with the recent results to reconsider its decision to withdraw. Crespi was by now convinced that MAC would be better off without the U.S. partner. He had no desire to share rewards that International Constructors had not, in his opinion, merited. As a result, Crespi also found himself torn between two conflicting desires. First, he wanted to downplay MAC's newly developing superplasticizer business in order to avoid a late awakening of International Constructors' interest. At the same time, he wanted to convince the Italian banks, or potential investors, that MAC's future was indeed worthy of an extra push to get the company through the transition.

EXHIBIT 1 Modern Advanced Concrete (A): MAC Balance Sheet as of December 31, 1976 (LIT 000's)

Assets	Official	Adjustments	Total	Liabilities and Stockholders' Equity	Official	Adjustments	Total
Current Assets:				Current Liabilities:			
Cash	18,608	–	18,608	Bank overdrafts (Note 6)	1,311,665	(245,862)	1,065,803
Receivables				Accounts payable	890,446	–	890,446
Notes	583,846	–	583,846	Due to affiliated companies (Note 7)	131,143	315,270	446,413
Trade accounts	1,145,813	–	1,145,813	Miscellaneous payables and accrued liabilities	796,828	70,000	866,828
Affiliated companies (Note 7)	217,104	–	217,104	Accrued taxes on income (Note 3)	65,342	–	65,342
Other (Note 4)	166,045	–	166,045	Total current liabilities	3,195,424	139,408	3,334,832
	2,112,808	–	2,112,808				
Less reserve for losses on collection	(142,153)	–	(142,153)				
	1,970,655	–	1,970,655				
Inventories, net of a reserve for slow-moving and obsolete items (Note 1)							
Raw materials and supplies	149,235	–	149,235				
Finished products	246,846	–	246,846				
	396,081	–	396,081				
Prepayments	65,294	–	65,294	Reserve for Severance Indemnities	825,115	–	825,115
Total current assets	2,450,638	–	2,450,638				

Assets (continued)

Investments in Affiliates (Note 5)	374,489	(194,159)	180,330
Plant and Equipment:			
Land and buildings	631,679	(121,818)	509,861
Leasehold improvements	88,851	-	88,851
Machinery and Equipment	898,289	(287,681)	610,608
Office furniture and equipment	308,892	(82,504)	226,388
Vehicles	221,601	(32,453)	189,148
Construction in progress	31,348	-	31,348
	2,180,660	(524,456)	1,656,204
Less—Accumulated depreciation	(1,070,874)	280,447	(794,427)
	1,105,786	(244,009)	861,777
Other Assets:			
Deferred expenses, being amortized	4,580	-	4,580
Guarantee deposits	20,089	-	20,089
	24,669	-	24,669
	3,955,582	(438,168)	3,517,414

Liabilities and Stockholders' Equity (continued)

Less portion funded with an insurance company	(323,399)	-	(323,899)
	501,216	-	501,216
Stockholders' Equity:			
Capital stock, par value Lire 1,000, authorized and outstanding—800,000 shares	800,000	-	800,000
Legal reserve (Note 8)	37,866	-	37,866
Accumulated deficit (Note 11)	(578,924)	(577,576)	(1,156,500)
	258,942	(577,576)	(318,634)
	3,955,582	(438,168)	3,517,414

EXHIBIT 2 Modern Advanced Concrete (A): Summary of Growth and Performance Data, 1959–1975

	1959	1960	1961	1962	1963	1964	1965	1966	1967	1968	1969	1970	1971	1972	1973	1974	1975
Sales (LIT millions)	142	196	388	476	520	956	647	934	1198	1568	2020	3040	3372	4389	5342	7463	5672
Italy															4551	6626	4993
Exports															791	837	679
Sales (in millions of KG/Litres)															5	6.3	6.2
Net Income after Taxes* (LIT millions)			8.5	16.9	24.7	50.5	37.8	46.9	59.6	78.0	80.2	99.5	96.8	117.4	86.9	151.1	(1,127.5)
Adjusted Net Income*														252.1	189.7	298.1	(268.6)
Royalties Paid to International Constructors (LIT millions)														98.2	106.8	120.5	85.4
Total Employees						43	107	99	100	147	168	180	179	195			245

*The first figure gives net income as calculated according to official Italian accounting standards. The second figure includes adjustments.
Source: Company records. (Spaces have been left blank where data is unavailable.)

EXHIBIT 3 Modern Advanced Concept (A): MAC Organization Chart, circa 1974

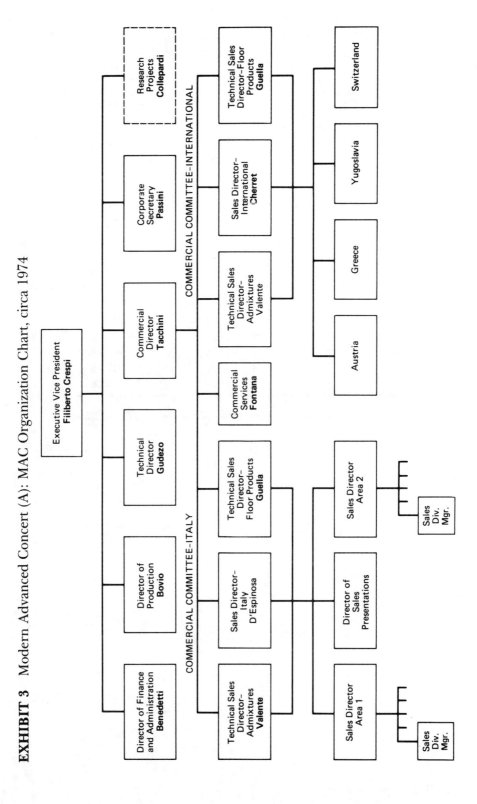

APPENDIX Modern Advanced Concrete (A): Average
LIT/US$ Exchange Rates and Exchange Rate
Index, 1960–1976

	Lire per U.S.$: End of Year	Lire per U.S.$: Average over Year	Index of Exchange Rate (1975 = 100)
1960	620.60	620.89	105.0
1961	620.60	621.09	105.0
1962	620.60	620.83	105.0
1963	622.38	621.60	104.9
1964	624.80	624.48	104.4
1965	624.70	624.90	104.3
1966	624.45	624.48	104.4
1967	623.86	624.13	104.4
1968	623.50	623.40	104.6
1969	625.50	627.32	103.9
1970	623.00	627.16	104.0
1971	594.00	618.36	105.4
1972	582.50	583.22	111.8
1973	607.92	583.00	111.9
1974	649.43	650.34	100.0
1975	683.55	652.85	100.0
1976	875.00	832.28	78.6

Source: IMF, *International Financial Statistics Yearbook, 1981, Vol. XXXIV.*

The Hidden Side of Organizational Leadership

LOUIS B. BARNES AND MARK P. KRIGER

I'll be damned if I understand how we make some of our most important decisions around here.
   —CEO of a Fortune 500 company
"The (Mustang) model (of 1964) was totally completed by the time Lee (Iacocca) saw it," says (Gene) Bordinat, now retired. "We conceived the car, and he pimped it after it was born."
   —*Time*, April 1, 1985
Leadership is one of the most observed and least understood phenomena on earth.
   —James MacGregor Burns

Let's start with the premise that no one has a good all-purpose definition of leadership. For most of us, the word conjures up an image of one leader with followers. However, the quotes above suggest that understanding—and assigning credit for—leadership can be confusing and highly emotional. James MacGregor Burns's recent book, *Leadership*, cites one study with 130 definitions of the term.[1] Another book notes over 5,000 research studies and monographs on the subject. The editor concludes that there is no common set of factors, traits, or processes that identifies the qualities of effective leadership.[2] Most of these books equate leadership with *the* leader who is a hero-person. That is one extreme. The other extreme is found in studies that view leadership as a set of personal attributes such as energy, cha-risma, or style. In between are the contingency theorists who argue that leadership depends upon anything from task conditions to subordinate expectations.

In a sense, all of these approaches are correct, but none is sufficient. All deal more with the single leader and multi-follower concept than with organizational leadership in a pluralistic sense.[3] None deals very well with the complexities that arise from the fact that managers are both leaders and followers, because of the very nature of organizational hierarchies. All bosses, including CEOs, are also subordinate to other people or pressures.

Nor do any of these approaches deal effectively with another fact of organizational life—that informal social networks exert an immense influence which sometimes overrides the formal hierarchy. A boss in one context may be a subordinate, relative, friend, or colleague in other company settings. A person's formal job status may be clear in the hierarchy, but that is only one part of an organization's network of relationships. Less formal network ties often dominate a person's or group's role behavior.

All of this reminds us of what we often forget. Leadership goes beyond a person's formal position into realms of informal, hid-

[1]   J.M. Burns, *Leadership* (New York: Harper & Row, 1978), p. 2.
[2]   B.M. Bass, *Stogdill's Handbook of Leadership: A Survey of Theory and Research*, rev. ed. (New York: The Free Press, 1981).
[3]   There are a few valiant efforts to break out of those constraints. See E.H. Schein, *Organizational Culture and Leadership: A Dynamic View* (San Francisco: Jossey-Bass, 1985); M.W. McCall, Jr., and M.M. Lombardo, *Leadership: Where Else Can We Go?* (Durham, NC: Duke University Press, 1978).

den, or unauthorized influence. Moreover, we need to remember that leadership, or the lack of it, is usually better recognized by the so-called followers than by the formal leaders. To some extent, these perceptions depend upon a person's formal status, but they also depend upon the roles that a person is assigned, chooses, or is allowed to take by others.

Yet studies of organizational leadership still focus mostly upon the *formal* leader who symbolizes all leadership, whether he or she is the CEO, Lee Iacocca, or Ronald Reagan. Such people not only get the public spotlight, but they also are placed on pedestals as heroes or scapegoats. Their associates become followers or lesser adversaries almost by default. Only rarely, sometimes in historical accounts written years later, do we learn of a formal leader's dependence on followers, spouses, or friends and of *their* critical leadership roles at strategic times. Sometimes we learn later of revised leader/follower combinations brought on by external crises, as in the case of Richard Nixon, Henry Kissinger, and Alexander Haig after Watergate. More often, though, the myth of the hero prevails.

In our experience, hero-leaders were only one small part of organizational leadership. We felt there was a need for leadership concepts that go beyond the notion of a formal leader with many followers. We had in mind a more wholistic organizational picture, where leader roles overlapped, complemented each other, and shifted from time to time and from person to person.[4]

We began to look for ways in which this more inclusive concept of leadership (as opposed to the concept of leader) worked in large organizations. We wanted to see if leadership changed depending upon time, place, situation, and people. As we shall see, our perspective on organizational leadership made us feel like theater critics; we observed everyone from executives to workers as though they were producers, directors, actors, and audience at different times in a complex decision drama.

DECISION DRAMAS

We began our study by focusing on decision making in large organizations, because we believed that effective decision making is part of effective leadership. As with leadership, our concept of decision making differed from some prevailing views. We defined it as the entire "decision process" surrounding a complex issue. This definition includes follow up actions and implementations, not just the actual decisions themselves. We wanted to understand how people formally and informally transformed decision ingredients into decision actions in pursuit of agreed upon or competing goals. This process resembled complex spirals of formulation and implementation. It took time, was difficult to measure, and often involved hundreds of organizational procedures, directors, actors, and audiences. We came to think of the process as an extended decision drama that involved a multitude of shifting roles.[5]

We knew we could encompass only a small part of this vast subject area in our study. However, sacrificing rigor for rele-

---

[4]   Even the newer studies tend to be guilty of this assumption that leadership behavior goes most naturally with one person, usually in a formal position. Most studies pursue the single leader and multi-follower concept, though occasionally shifting from one perspective to another. In addition to Burns's book noted above, see M. Maccoby, *The Leader: A New Face for American Management* (New York: Simon & Schuster, 1981); Schein (1985); W. Bennis and B. Nanus, *Leaders: The Strategies of Taking Charge* (New York: Harper & Row, 1985).

[5]   A.P. Hare, *Social Interaction as Drama* (Beverly Hills: Sage Publications, 1985).

vance, we struggled to broaden and deepen our understanding of how organizational leadership *really* worked in crucial decision dramas.

To begin our field study, we asked CEOs and other senior managers in several very large companies to suggest critical decision issues for study. They did. We also sought out some smaller firms in the same industries. Over a three-year period, we examined thirty major decision dramas in twelve different companies.[6] Since then, we have closely studied another half dozen situations and reviewed over one hundred specific company decisions drawn from teaching case files. All of the examples came from companies in heavy manufacturing, high technology, or financial services.

In all of the companies we studied closely, the CEOs and other executives were generous with their time, often giving us far more than the designated few hours that had been requested for interviews. Of the original thirty examples we studied, twenty-two involved multiple interviews; in these cases we also had access to archives, could attend meetings, and interviewed retired as well as current employees. The other eight studies were based on interviews of five or six hours each with one or two key executives.

In each company, we asked senior executives to focus on the roles of key actors and to evaluate a decision process, not just its outcome, as a relative success or failure. This proved difficult. Simpler decision processes tended to be more clear cut, outcomes or products dominated perceptions of the process. Sometimes the perceptions changed. In one case, a decision drama perceived by most managers to be a disaster in 1963 looked like a smashing success by 1980 because of changing market conditions in the industry. Nevertheless, opinions on success or failure were strong in some cases, and we shall refer to them when one consistent opinion seemed to prevail. The thirty original decision processes fell into seven major topic areas:

- Expanding into new world markets.
- Bringing new products into current markets.
- Major acquisition efforts.
- Developing a new manufacturing process.
- Reorganization and restructuring at the top.
- Executive rivalries, upheavals, and replacements.
- The rise and fall of international joint ventures.

Let us summarize and briefly state the "theory" we brought to this study. In retrospect, it seems consistent with our major findings. Our theory of organizational leadership involved: (1) many potential "leaders" in changing role relationships who, (2) moved from often vague concepts of purpose and vision into, (3) struggles with perceived certainty and uncertainty, and (4) reached patched-together decision actions in, (5) a spiraling process involving higher and lower, newer and older producers, actors, and audiences.[7] This concept of organizational leadership included *both* formal hierarchy and informal or quasi-formal networks.

The inclusion of these social networks was an important part of this study.[8] Effective organizational leadership involved hierarchical and social network leaderships working in complementary tension patterns

---

[6] The initial field work was done by the authors along with Doctors L. Wallace and J. Jaferian.

[7] For a somewhat similar approach, see J.B. Quinn, *Strategies for Change: Logical Incrementalism* (Homewood, IL: Richard D. Irwin, 1980; D. Gladstein and J.B. Quinn, "A Commentary on Janis' Sources of Error in Strategic Decision Making," in *Strategic Decision Making*, ed. H. Hennings (San Francisco: Jossey-Bass, 1985).

[8] J.A. Pearce II and F.R. David, "A Social Network Approach to Organizational Design Performance," *Academy of Management Review* 8 (1983), pp. 436–444.

over time. Multiple leaderships and their tensions came from competing hierarchies and networks.

The drama metaphor helps to suggest why these complex relationships often failed to work effectively. The producer-directors, stars, supporting cast, and audiences often change roles, disappear, and reappear during a decision drama, but sometimes individuals cannot handle the ambiguity and tensions that arise from those changing roles. Each drama had its ongoing dialogues, multiple settings, and changing plots. Each had backstage tensions, emotions, and power struggles as well as more politic behavior on stage. The tensions often swung from perceived ambiguity to polarized conflict, sometimes useful, sometimes not. Bridges of multiple and complementary leadership actions were sometimes built. Sometimes they weren't. Sometimes the enemy was an individual's limited perspective on the potential sources of leadership.

It might help to take several examples of clear failure, then look at some more successful cases. The first failure example comes from a multi-billion dollar heavy manufacturing company. This decision process was seen by almost all of the company's senior management as a failure. It involved new manufacturing techniques which might have revolutionized the entire industry had they worked. The drama began slowly in the late 1940s and built up for over twenty years; the project cost more than $30 million before it was abandoned. The executive who sponsored the project was a vice president for research and development (R&D) and a member of the company's board of directors. He was perceived as a strong leader by many employees. Neither this vice president nor his immediate subordinate, who became the new technology project director, ever saw the project's failure as a failure to add network patterns of leadership to their own hierarchical controls and formal authority. As we will show, they relied upon hierarchical position almost exclusively.

NEW TECHNOLOGY PROCESS

Act I

This heavy manufacturing company purchased several new patents abroad shortly after World War II, when it appeared that the competition might gain control of a *new technology process*. The major force behind the purchase was the vice president of R&D. He persuaded a new president/CEO and other senior managers to adopt his vision of what the patents could mean. The vice president's task was made easier, others said, because the company's top management was separated into a set of autonomous fiefdoms loosely coordinated by the president. Each vice president dominated his own functional territory. The norm was to run your own operation and not interfere with other territories. The R&D vice president rigidly subscribed to this hierarchical principle. As he noted in an interview in 1983:

I firmly believe that each person should have only one boss and know exactly what his responsibilities are. Debates are good if the two parties are equally informed and competent to judge, but if they're not, it's a waste of time.

That kind of wall building soon led to isolated thinking within R&D as well as tensions between R&D and other parts of the company. The tensions became conflicts when two functional areas laid claim to an issue. Manufacturing people saw the project evolving exclusively within R&D, and wanted to become involved, but the R&D project director did not want outside interference. As one R&D manager observed:

We were trying to move too fast then . . . one reason for this was that we had heard that our major competition and a European firm were about to announce a new process. In addition, the manufacturing and R&D people had polarized on the whole issue. Manufacturing felt squeezed out. They had the feeling that R&D was operating in secrecy, and that was absolutely true. At one point, the project director refused to let the plant manager of our largest plant even visit our pilot operation. That really made people in manufacturing mad. Some of them set out to destroy R&D.

Act II

The pilot plant never did get up to speed or meet its goals. Meanwhile, the project had assumed top priority within R&D, often to the chagrin of other project engineers. The vice president of corporate manufacturing became highly critical of the project. He felt that his people should take charge of the new project once it left the laboratory and moved into pilot plant operations. He finally wrote an unsolicited "Review of the New Technology Project" and gave copies to the president and to the vice president of R&D. The latter reacted angrily. He demanded that the manufacturing vice president stay away from the project. That did happen for a period of time, but the situation continued to degenerate and increased conflict developed both inside and outside of R&D. The project fell further and further behind.

Act III

About the time the vice president of R&D was due to retire, other board of director members and the president became greatly concerned about the non-producing pilot plant and continual cost overruns. After considerable activity behind the scenes, they set up a Project Appraisal Committee. The committee chairman was the vice president of manufacturing. The vice president of R&D, his new successor, and one other manufacturing executive were also on the committee. Several months later, the appraisal committee delivered two conflicting reports. One favored continuing the project. The other argued for termination. The board of directors voted for termination.

Within a few years, the entire R&D organization had been placed under manufacturing. The new corporate emphasis was on applied research. An R&D manager of that time stated:

Many R&D people got pushed out (of the company) and there were some pretty sad human situations. The worst thing was that senior management watched the whole thing go on. They didn't have to. The problems were on the horizon long before the R&D vice president retired, but they waited for his successor to come on. They could have asked the R&D vice president for the same kind of accounting five years earlier.

And the new vice president of R&D later said:

The decision to divisionalize the laboratories was the only one that was tougher than the one to abandon the New Technology project. It broke up the research labs for all practical purposes, and R&D suffered mightily for the next ten years. During that time, I never could get the CEO's ear on technical matters.

What Went Wrong?

Over the many years that the new technology drama went on, hundreds of people made thousands of decisions, many of them crucial. To be sure, the project was a technical failure. Possibly that could not have been helped. However, the human pain and crippled research efforts in this drama also raise questions of leadership. For example:

1. What should have been the role of the president and the board of directors? One could argue that this was a case of failed leadership at the very top. According to the president, he was trying to give his vice presidents the autonomy they needed to run their operations. However, neither he nor the board seemed to be aware of the rifts within R&D as a result of the R&D vice president's rigid control of the project. One senior laboratory manager of that time said, "Board members kept assuring us that they were behind the project. If they had only asked me for *my* opinion they would have felt different." In this case, there seemed to be too much laissez-faire ambiguity at the very top of the organization and too much conflict down below.

2. Why couldn't the vice president of manufacturing and R&D bridge their separate hierarchies and work together? There is considerable evidence that their conflict fueled the schism between R&D and manufacturing. Certainly the lack of lateral networking helped intensify those antagonisms.

3. Who was responsible for getting valid information to the president and the board of directors? There was much they never knew during this period. Should the dissenting managers within R&D have jumped over their own superiors with their opinions? Several of them felt that their vice president was pushing the project too fast and recklessly. They also felt powerless to argue their case above the project director or the vice president. Chains of command and hierarchy were considered too sacred.

Altogether, hierarchical leadership prevailed. The assumption was that someone in the right formal position should take care of things. However, in this case nobody did, at least not for some time. Meanwhile, less formal networks failed to tie hierarchies together across formal lines. There was no hierarchical call for them, nor were they volunteered. If they had been built, the information exchange upward, sideways, and diagonally might have made a vast difference. Unfortunately, assumptions of strong hierarchy like the R&D vice president's created defensive island domains. This isolation led to contempt, which led to destructive conflicts, and these conflicts multiplied.

These island antagonisms seem to go on when hierarchies operate without complementary networking across formal lines. As in the new technology case, one "leader" becomes the hero for some people while another "outside" leader becomes the villain. Territorialism takes over. Biased supporters identify themselves with one side or the other. A crisis mentality emerges. Some form of conflict or purge often follows unless a crisscrossing network is established to ease the tensions. Sometimes this can be a truly neutral third party like a fact-finding task force, a strong mediator, negotiations, or more senior executives resolving the conflict from above as the president and the board of directors eventually did in this case. They did so, however, only after the vice president of R&D had retired. The power struggle between the two vice presidents and their subordinates had already done its damage.

THE DANGERS OF DICHOTOMY

In our study, ineffective decision processes seemed to result not from conflict per se but from: (1) tension avoidance and unclear problem definition by formal hierarchical leaders, and (2) when those tensions became conflicts that polarized people and issues into what we saw as false and dangerous dichotomies. In the first instance, people at the top of the hierarchy did not get network acceptance of their own perspectives or transcend their own confusion with a sense of vision or mission. In the second instance, they and others failed to build bridges across escalating conflicts between different hierarchies. In both cases, hierarchies and networks failed to complement each other.

Of the two, the polarized conflicts are more dangerous, because all the elements get exaggerated and seem much clearer. Simplistic dichotomies can hurt people, delay needed cooperative efforts, and ultimately lead to internal warfare. That often happened during the less effective decision dramas we studied. Players became convinced of their inherent separateness and superiority. Leaders like the vice president of R&D above differentiated themselves from perceived rival leaders and their followers. People in formal roles differentiated themselves from those lower down or in "less" legitimate roles. As decision producers, they differentiated themselves from mere actors and each group differentiated itself from other groups. Such differences might seem very natural and necessary. In fact, however, noses went out of joint, actors became polarized antagonists, and the dangerous dichotomies emerged. It was a fairly common pattern. Take another example. This one occurred between the board of directors and the CEO.

In one company we studied, the founding entrepreneur was fired by the board of directors fifteen years after he and several others started the company. The board decision evolved after its outside members concluded that the CEO would never share decision-making authority with either them or his senior managers after the company grew in size and had gone public. His unilateral hirings and firings, endless problems with litigation, temper tantrums, condescending behavior, and erratic use of product development resources alienated all parties. This spiraled into a mass exodus by members of one project group and a palace revolution led by two of the other founding senior executives. Things went from bad to worse until the CEO was removed by the board.

In this case, the qualities that helped the CEO to stand out as an entrepreneur worked against him as others challenged his hierarchical authority. He had never learned to build work-related social networks and could accept no network challenges from inside or outside a company which was beginning to require multiple leaderships.

Some recent writers on leadership have contributed to the false mythology of the individual leader, thus increasing the dichotomy problem. Discussions of the difference between leaders and managers—a variation on the leader-follower distinction—have recently become popular. Note the following comments from one article on those differences:

Managers relate to people according to the role that they play in a sequence of events in a decision making process, while leaders, who are concerned with ideas, relate in more intuitive and empathic ways. The manager's orientation to people as actors, in a sequence of events, deflects his or her attention away from the substance of other people's concerns and toward their roles in a process. The distinction is simply between a manager's attention to *how* things are done and a leader's to *what* the events and decisions mean to participants.[9]

The writer found that some executives resisted his distinction between leaders and managers. They saw themselves as both—leaders in some situations and managers or audience in others. In a more recent article, the same author wrote:

Executives often reject the view that managers and leaders are different. Because uncertainty makes their jobs so extremely difficult, they feel that being a top manager takes more talent and ability than I appreciate.[10]

We would add that it isn't only uncertainty that causes the resistance. It is also the reluctance of executives to set up another dichotomy: a first and second class citizenry dividing leaders from (follower) managers. It doesn't take long for the leader-manager distinction to become a dangerous, counterproductive dichotomy. The CEO of one large, fast-changing company in our sample put it a little differently. He not only denied the difference but went on to stress the importance of multiple leaderships:

I've seen many recent articles which ask me to separate managers from leaders. That's too simple and naive. I think that I'm both at different times. Our major changes around here reflect a lot more leadership than is represented by me alone or what I've done.

FORMULA FOR FAILURE: ONE-SIDED LEADERSHIP

What can we learn from the elements of failure in these decision dramas? The tentative conclusions may seem strange at first. They all hinge upon an assumed complementarity of hierarchies and networks. Effective organizational leadership needs *both* hierarchical and network leadership. We must learn to advocate two seemingly different and sometimes opposite perspectives. The two are hard for one person to assume simultaneously without living a paradox and, at times, advocating almost the opposite of what he or she may represent publicly. It means two very different roles. One endorses and advocates hierarchy. The other builds and supports network leadership. Only this double perspective helps managers to sponsor and champion such apparent contradictions as the dependent boss, actors in the audience, and followers who lead. Several hypotheses then emerge with regard to effective organizational leadership:

- A major purpose for those with hierarchical status should be to create and strengthen independent but complementary network leaderships. These should include networks in which these sponsors are not directly involved.
- A major purpose for those in network roles should be to create and strengthen independent but complementary hierarchical leaderships. These should include hierarchies in which these sponsors are not directly involved.

[9] A. Zaleznik, "Managers and Leaders: Are They Different?" *Harvard Business Review*, May–June 1977, pp. 67–78; For more of the same, see N.M. Tichy and D.O. Ulrich, "The Leadership Challenge—A Call for the Transformational Leader," *Sloan Management Review*, Fall 1984, pp. 59–68.

[10] A. Zaleznik, "The Leadership Gap," *Washington Quarterly*, Winter 1983, pp. 32–39.

The basic notion of complementarity is elusive but important. It is critical to modern physics. It has even deeper roots in the world's major philosophies and religions. It came to physics in 1927 when Niels Bohr, a close reader of the Danish philosopher Kierkegaard, introduced it as a way of thinking about the physics of light.[11] Scientists had recently struggled with two totally different perspectives known as wave theory and particle theory. Both seemed important and useful, but the differences seemed irreconcilable. Gary Zukav describes the double perspective in a recent book on the new physics, *The Dancing Wu Li Masters*.[12]

Complementarity is the concept developed by Niels Bohr to explain the wave-particle density of light. No one has thought of a better one yet. Wave-like characteristics and particle-like characteristics, the theory goes, are mutually exclusive, or complementary aspects of light. Although one of them always excludes the other, *both* of them are necessary to understand light. One of them always excludes the other because light, or anything else, cannot be both wave-like and particle-like at the same time.

How can mutually exclusive wave-like and particle-like behaviors both be properties of one and the same light? They are not properties of light. They are properties of our interaction with light. Depending upon our choice of experiment, we can cause light to manifest either particle-like properties or wave-like properties.[13]

With apologies to Zukav, we want to paraphrase and emphasize several parts of this passage. Take the same words and make a few changes and emphases:

Hierarchies and networks, the theory goes, are mutually exclusive, or complementary aspects of leadership. Although one of them always excludes

the other, *both of them are necessary to understand leadership*. One of them always excludes the other, because leadership, or anything else, cannot be both hierarchy-like and network-like at the same time.

How can mutually exclusive hierarchies and networks both be properties of one and the same leadership? *They are not properties of leadership. They are properties of our interaction with leadership. Depending upon our choice of behavior, we can cause leadership to manifest either hierarchical or network properties.*

These paraphrased passages pose a tough assignment for both superior and subordinate managers. Yet we did find decision dramas where managers adopted such a double perspective. In one 1979 case study the CEO consciously blurred his role in the hierarchy and became an organization network builder among his subordinates. He practiced MBWA (Management By Wandering Around) long before the concept became popular. He consciously sponsored networks among other people in different parts of the company. As he noted:

I spend a fair amount of my time trying to reduce contempt in the organization. It is absolutely deadly. Not conflict but contempt. It is the ultimate in desecrating people's self image. Contempt, for example, can easily develop in an organization like ours between the production and the marketing people. It is essential to keep a dialogue going between them. Many companies fail because they do not. . . . The general manager's role is making sure the dialogue happens.[14]

We saw other examples of complementarity approaches at work. In one smaller successful manufacturing company, the president wrote a business plan in 1969 before the company began. He wanted no job descrip-

[11]   G. Holton, *Thematic Origins of Scientific Thought: Kepler to Einstein* (Cambridge: Harvard University Press, 1973), pp. 144–149.

[12]   G. Zukav, *The Dancing Wu Li Masters. An Overview of the New Physics* (New York: Bantam Books, 1979).

[13]   Ibid., p. 33.

[14]   *Renn Zaphiropoulos* (Boston: Harvard Business School Case No. 480-044).

tions, organization charts, formal titles, or formal hierarchies within the company. Most readers of the business plan conclude, even today, that it will never work.

As of 1985, the company had achieved an impressive growth record, was the most profitable in its field, paid only competitive salaries, had attracted almost half of the key technical experts in its field, had lost not one critical person in fifteen years except for a retirement due to health problems, and was on target with its ambitious business plan. There were still no job descriptions, organization charts, formal titles, or official hierarchies in the company, *but everyone knew* who did what or belonged where in the informal hierarchies and networks. The "president" said that he spent most of his time passing decision issues on to others and building cooperative networks. During the year of our study, he spent over five months away from the company exploring other technical and non-technical issues relevant to it. Yet according to other employees, the founder's beliefs and philosophy were crucial to the company's spirit and success even when he was not there.

The new business example was another decision drama which we will examine more closely in order to see these complementarity principles at work. It occurred in a large insurance company which made some pioneer moves into overall financial services by developing completely new product lines and businesses. It was a period of successful and radical transition; people in the firm referred to it as a major turnaround.

NEW BUSINESS

Act I

The president of a multi-billion dollar insurance firm became chairman and CEO when the old chief executive retired. At that time, a senior vice president became president and chief operating officer. According to the new chairman/CEO:

There is the perception around here that, since the new president and I came in, things have really turned around. But that's wrong. Some of the change started some time back when the two of us began needling our predecessors from below. But the main thing was the pressure from outside which we helped the former CEO to translate and articulate. Several of us, including the old CEO, expressed concern to each other about the effects of economic inflation on our business as early as the mid-1970s.

The transition thus began when company executives first saw critical problems in the business environment and because the two new officers pushed their concerns upward. The old CEO, close to retirement, began to build a new leadership network by closely involving his two subordinates, who had very distinct skills. The new chairman had come up through the administrative side of the company. The new president had an actuarial background. As the chairman noted, leadership at this stage came from a triad of people. They operated more as a problem-solving network than a hierarchy.

Act II

Several months before officially taking office, the new chairman made a list of candidates for several vacant executive committee jobs. Before this time, the executive committee had a reputation as a battleground for special interests. It was described by one member as "a body of competing gladiators."

The new chairman visited each candidate and spelled out his requirements: no territorialism, a strong concern for total company interests, a sustained effort to trust the other members, a willingness to experiment with change, and a desire to build complementary team interests with other members. He said that failure to contribute to such a climate would not be tolerated and could result in discharge. He asked each person to consider whether these rules were acceptable and to let him know. The eventual result was an executive committee with high commitment to these values and norms of behavior. According to one executive:

I'm terribly high on our present executive committee.... We now have an executive committee which can take both an analytical approach and also has a sense of the whole. They've developed a really good knack of knowing when the time is right for something. My understanding is that they know that they've got to work together with none of the historical turf battles.

Act III

A major test for the new executive committee came in early 1980 when it became clear that increased inflation rates were forcing the company into a perilous financial condition. The new president described how networking leadership really emerged at this time.

The three or four of us who were ultimately responsible for the safety and the future of the company began holding a series of very informal meetings. We found that we were in agreement on two points which I might paraphrase as follows. "First, things ain't never going to be the same again. Second, but, we don't know *how* they ain't never going to be the same again."
We approached this dilemma by forming a new committee, but we genuinely wanted this committee to be different. So, rather than follow-

ing our traditional course of collecting our most senior executives and having them produce over a two year period a three volume report . . . we collected what we felt were a group of the best and brightest younger people. We told them we wanted them to look ten years into the future and tell us what was in store for the business and what steps we should take to ensure that at the end of that time we were a prominent presence in the radically new and rapidly evolving financial sector.

This was a new approach for the company. With little relief from their regular jobs, and given only this vague assignment, the task force struggled to organize itself. According to interviews with members, its early days were filled with tension and frustration. Members searched blindly for direction and clarity. They worked through that phase. In the second phase, tremendous enthusiasm developed. One member said that the committee had gone from being clearly the worst one he had ever served on to being the best by far. Recommendations came together and were presented to the executive committee on schedule. Another member added:

I don't feel even now that I can talk about that task force easily. I was there and it was a mess at times. The chairman of the task force provided integration, but at the time it felt like a lot of wheel spinning. A number of members were pretty frustrated. What were we to study? Everybody was sending around copies of speeches, analyses of different data, etc. It all ended up with an astronomical amount of paper—seven full notebooks.
However, all of that may have been a necessary and desirable part of the process. Eventually we knew that it was not just the spinning of wheels. We were learning about points such as *how* inflation had a differential effect on different parts of society. Another realization was that the world really was changing on us and that, *even though inflation was to go away*, we should make the changes we were proposing.

The task force then provided what the president later called "a bewildering list" of goals and challenges to pursue if the firm was to compete effectively in the future. Implementing even a few of these ideas would lead to major changes in the company. The president's honesty is impressive. As he noted:

Well, we gulped and essentially said, OK. We said that we think your version of the future is credible and while your laundry list of projects is formidable, it fits the vision, so let's get on with it. . . . At first, the process was dreadfully confusing . . . the confusion and apprehension of those early days was not confined to the troops. Those of us managing the undertaking—or being managed by it, if you will—were also concerned and uncertain. We were putting an enormous amount of pressure on the company.
　　Our uneasiness was not helped by the rumblings that soon came to our ears. . . . We found that it wasn't much comfort to anyone when we told them—we sure do know where we're going— it's over there somewhere.

Radical Success

The results were impressive. Two years after the executive committee received the "bewildering list," twenty-two new task forces were at work. They, in turn, set in motion seventeen major product modifications, new business lines, and company acquisitions. The whole effort involved thousands of new executive decisions, hundreds of new roles, and millions of dollars. Despite the tension and uncertainty, the results were regarded as highly successful.

　　But what about the leadership patterns? There were a number of them. Top management began as producers, directors, and authors in this drama with only a vague idea of what the script and scenery would look like. They became the key actors during Act II. The chairman had set the stage by using hierarchical authority to set up an executive committee network based on team principles. This group ended up during later

scenes in supporting cast, audience, and backer roles for the new ventures. New hierarchies were built as new businesses evolved, but the organization took on more network-like characteristics overall. There are several other points of interest we should note.

1. Outside economic tensions initially led top management to conclude that: "Things ain't never going to be the same again." They took those words seriously. By turning that script over to a group of subordinate authors, they avoided creating a future that would simply mirror their old images of the past. During those early days, the executive committee had neither the data nor the direction to create specific goals, but they knew that things had to change. Their initial version was unclear, and their initial steps were unclear even to themselves. Their early joint decisions thus became tentative markers on new paths. The emphasis was on creating a wobbly but continuing process. It was the process more than any products that held management's attention during this phase since there were few early products. It was a time for flexible and exploring networks.

2. Top management resisted the temptation to pretend that everything was under their control. Instead of centralizing or taking direct responsibility for action among themselves, the chairman, the president, and the executive committee created their own supportive network and then sponsored new networks below them. These subordinate networks went on to create their own new decision dramas as authors and actors.

3. These network leaderships combined the energy and ideas of more junior staff members with executive committee guidance, vision, and approval. It was not a question of one group formulating and the other implementing. Each was doing both. The higher and lower level networks provided balance and perspective for each other. The chairman and president both made important decisions, but so did others. The critical process involved getting complementary implementation agreements which could work effectively across different functions and lines and vertically up and down the hierarchy.

Most of the leadership patterns described resembled other effective decision dramas we studied in one important respect. People ended up feeling good about working with each other and about their own leadership contributions. We found only one other generalization with specific regard to the formal leaders. Each used his hierarchical leadership in order to sponsor leadership networks among other people. Otherwise, the formal leaders we interviewed had little in common when it came to energy, charisma, intelligence, and sensitivity.

In the more effective decision dramas, the subordinates of these CEOs, while below them in the executive hierarchy, contributed greatly to the organization's leadership through their own networking and hierarchical actions. As actors, authors, or producer-directors they operated within and beyond the immediate top management. What is interesting is that relative success in one decision-making effort served as no guarantee for success the next time. The networks had to be reestablished each time around the new drama.

Since organizations will inevitably have informal networks and formal hierarchies, management must constantly develop new leadership patterns in each. The danger is that if each does not get active sponsorship from the other, they will simply perpetuate themselves, which leads to isolation, polarization, and contempt. In addition, hierarchy will always dominate, since it controls the most rewards. Without sponsorship, networks will go underground or remain passive. That is what happened in the new technology drama, unbeknownst to an isolated top management. It happened in other situations we studied as well.

Breaking these dichotomy patterns seems to require an almost exaggerated act of trust, the taking on of new roles, and creating new interdependent patterns. Both formal management and the "best and the brightest" group did this initially in the new businesses situation. As the new president of the insurance company noted above: "We genuinely wanted this committee to be different." Top management moved into new roles and created network patterns upward, laterally, and diagonally. It required the networking task forces to find their own sharper vision and to take leadership into the new areas they wished to explore. Each group had to live a high tension paradox, going well beyond its traditional role.

THE SHOELACE THEORY

One other metaphor may help to clarify what we mean. By assuming complementarity rather than isolation or antagonism between hierarchies and networks, we create a "shoelace" assumption or theory which *in the minds and behavior of the actors* holds potentially opposite or isolated sides together in a changing but constructive tension. These separate "sides" may represent different hierarchies or hierarchies competing with networks. We saw the new chairman and president use this shoelace theory in several ways during the new businesses example. Each had his separate strengths, which could either complement or compare with the other man's. Each was strong in certain areas, but was organizationally stronger with the other's sponsorship and support. Hierarchy rarely prevailed in their working relationship, and yet it was always there. The two men used their hierarchical positions to expand their own complementary networking within the executive committee. The executive committee, in turn, also shoelaced lower levels of network leadership into existence. The shoelace assumption permitted a constructive tension between separate hierarchies by setting up network forms of leadership. It tied different leaders in with each other in a nonpolarized, nonisolated fashion.

The "best and the brightest" planning group was another example of the shoelace theory at work. Its members were potential rivals for promotion coming from separate hierarchies. Rivalries surfaced as members tried to create a working task force. But the group began to to succeed as the chairman helped pull individuals together, as members gained respect for, and contributed to, each other's work, and as deadline pressures increased. In this sense, the top management hierarchy helped to create an effective task force network. By the same token, the task forces provided new "leadership" roles for top management as they reviewed and coached the network leaders. Task force proposals also served as a sponsoring springboard for new hierarchies and businesses.

In this article, we have tried to suggest a way of looking at pluralistic leadership in organizational decision dramas. The ideas are based upon our own research and upon the thoughts and actions of managers involved in this study. The research suggests that executives might consciously consider shoelacing theory as a way to develop multiple and complementary leadership roles. We also suggest that the more typical focus of leadership on the single person leader has not paid off.

Shoelace assumptions of complementarity also have some implications for action. They suggest:

1. We need to stop talking as though executive leadership in decision making is primarily a one-person drama played by CEOs or leaders only. That's an illusion, not an accurate report of how organizational leadership works.
2. We also need to observe and use paradox as a clue for action.[15] For example, it takes a hierarchical leader to take the step toward exaggerated trust. Only such a step can begin the complementary networking process. That means stepping outside of one's hierarchical role to create potentially competitive networks. Hierarchical leadership is needed to create and support useful networking leaderships. Though less obvious, the opposite is also true.
3. Managers need to consider, and work on developing, complementarity skills. They need to create bases of trust across formal boundaries, built more upon what one is willing to give up than upon what one can take away. Managers must also face up to the meaning of networking leadership as complementary to hierarchies, so that people in both roles maintain some autonomy while also looking for ways to shoelace across the gaps. They might begin by looking beyond any critical tension, dichotomy, or opposite.
4. Networking leaderships offer flexibility for exploring uncertainty and ambiguity, as when hierarchical leadership wishes to search out an uncertain environment or explore new areas of opportunity which will eventually need hierarchical leaderships to run them. The two perspectives must be shoelaced actively back and forth so that neither, especially the more dominant hierarchical perspective, prevails when the other would be more useful. The skill is to keep each independent and yet complementary. That is easy to say and very difficult to do.

---

[15]   L.B. Barnes, "Managing the Paradox of Organizational Trust," *Harvard Business Review*, March–April 1981, pp. 107–116.

Managing the Paradox of Organizational Trust

LOUIS B. BARNES

Several years ago, the largest subsidiary in a giant international complex found itself with a new president, a bright young marketing manager named Jones from one of the subsidiary's divisions. Jones soon let it be known that the old days of delegation were over and that he was going to create a strong, centralized head office with himself as its driving force. On more than one occasion, Jones made it clear that he had little respect for either the previous management or some of the managers still in the company. He introduced specific cost, measurement, and reporting procedures; a number of managers and staff members were fired, took early retirement, or resigned. As Jones set his policies in motion, other old-timers were immobilized or bypassed.

Jones spent a good deal of time in the field, and every three months he took a team of headquarters staff with him to area plan-and-review sessions that cynics labeled "jump for Jonesie" shows, "rock 'em, sock 'em" binges, and "point the finger" days. Along with his periodic outbursts about the shortcomings of certain subordinates or reports, Jones's toughspoken demands for tight budgets, detailed action plans, and short-term goals set the tone for management meetings.

As time went on, opposition to Jones appeared within both the company and the parent organization, but it remained underground because his company's measurable benefits seemed to outweigh the obvious costs of his behavior. The performance figures looked good. With increased inflation, cost cutting, and rising demand, the so-called bottom line showed the company to be very successful. Balanced against these positive indicators, high dissatisfaction, high turnover, postponed investments, and little evidence of succession planning all seemed negligible.

After several long, serious strikes in three of the subsidiary's key plants, however, top management finally became concerned with Jones's hard-line approach. Shortly after the last strike, senior managers in the parent company began to review their options—and about a year later replaced Jones with a senior manager from the parent company. No one within the subsidiary appeared capable of taking the job at that time.

This story may sound dramatic, but I suggest that the Manager Joneses of the world are legion. Sometimes the battle lines are more subtly drawn than in this case; sometimes managers are the masters and sometimes the victims, but almost invariably at one time or another managers fall into Jones-like situations.

Like all people, managers behave according to their assumptions of how the world works—whether, for instance, it is a kind or a cruel place. Disastrous behavior such as Jones's follows when a manager's assumptions about the world establish a dangerous and self-defeating pattern.

The pattern develops, I believe, when managers hold three simple assumptions that, in combination, prevent trust from forming. Even though managers like Jones will state that it is trust more than either power or hierarchy that really makes an organization function effectively, these same managers all too often find themselves operating in and sometimes creating an atmosphere of pervasive mistrust in their companies.

Using Manager Jones as representative of all of us at times, I want to explore this mistrust—so subtle, so prevalent, and yet so unproductive—and then to describe how the three assumptions people make daily can create this destructive atmosphere.

I will briefly describe the three "harmless" assumptions, show how they appear in a managerial context, and then explore some alternative approaches and assumptions. In presenting these alternatives, I argue in favor of two fragile but important concepts—namely, tentative trust and paradoxical action.

Too often we fail to go beyond our initial reactions in order to look at an issue's deeper levels and thus avoid the time and the tension that such work entails. Then, as Manager Jones did, later on we pay the price. To see how this happens, let's begin with the assumptions as Manager Jones might have experienced them.

THREE HARMLESS ASSUMPTIONS

The three assumptions are, first, that important issues naturally fall into two opposing camps, exemplified by either/or thinking; second, that hard data and facts are better than what appear to be soft ideas and speculation, exemplified in the "hard drives out soft" rule; and finally, that the world in general is an unsafe place, exemplified by a person's having a pervasive mistrust of the universe around him or her. These assumptions can often be useful and necessary. Separately, they seem so natural that we don't see them as harmful. As a matter of fact, we often see them as healthy; in certain situations, for instance, we think only a fool would not be mistrustful.

Nevertheless, when managers combine all three assumptions at the same time, which we do very naturally as well, the assumptions may benefit us in the short run—but be very destructive in the long. Now let's look at them in turn.

Do or Die

A person holds assumption number one where either/or thinking dominates choices and decision making. Like the rest of us, Manager Jones had to turn complex sets of alternatives into useful prime choices. Under conditions of uncertainty, Jones relied on experience and instinct to help him limit the alternatives, make choices, and then implement them. Using analysis and discussion, managers typically narrow their alternatives into such options as make or buy, act or react, centralize or decentralize, expand or retrench, and reward or punish.

But the problem with this way of thinking is more serious than that it limits options. People often become emotionally attached to a symbol or choice and see it as either good or bad. We set up the alternatives as adversaries and turn them into unions *versus* management, blacks *versus* whites, government *versus* business, theory *versus* practice, and us *versus* them (whoever they are). Despite Lincoln's reminder that a house divided against itself cannot stand, American tradition and history have taught us to separate issues into their two most obvious alternatives—and then to pronounce one of them "good" and the other "bad." It seems that part of what Manager Jones created in those around him was this either/or mentality. By his own definition, his choices were good. Others were to be criticized and attacked.

Even when it occurs, however, either/or thinking by itself is not destined for disaster. The real problem is that the assumption builds certain future expectations. For Manager Jones, these expectations prevented him from stepping outside of each either/or dichotomy to look again at the ingredients—to find an unseen paradoxical alternative or ingenious recombination. In Jones's case, for instance, he never sought to reintegrate the old-timers into his new management scheme. Because he saw them as having caused the problems, that would have seemed absurd at the time. Yet, paradoxically, they might have helped Jones overcome his subsequent turnover, morale, and strike problems.

Other examples of either/or ingredients illustrate the problem as well as a resolution. For example: For several generations now, people have viewed the management versus union dichotomy as a fact of life. One is good while the other is bad, depending on your perspective. If not enemies, the two have been at least antagonistic adversaries bound mainly by a legal contract. In many companies, this view leads to daily frictions between workers and supervisors. These can escalate into formal grievances. Under such conditions, even honest cooperative gestures are seen as dishonest or hostile. In one company, management tried to start some "improvement meetings" with workers. But because of past union-management experiences, the meetings were doomed before they started.

Yet in other companies, workers and managers have bargained hard on some issues and achieved shop floor cooperation on others, beyond the legalities of the contract. They were both bound to but not always limited by the contract.

Are these latter situations an exception to the rule? Probably they are, simply because the rule in most companies seems based on the more prevalent either/or assumption and its traditions. It is easier to take a firm position and act as if us or them, right or wrong, and good or bad were the major real-life options. But again, the villain here is not the either/or assumption itself. It is the distortion that occurs when people assume they need to defend their positions while also adopting the other two assumptions.

A Bird in the Hand . . .

Assumption number two is the principle that *hard is better than soft*, which means that hard drives out soft.* We saw it in Jones; we see it in ourselves. The idea goes as follows. Once Jones began to make either/or choices, he almost "had to" show their superiority and defend them; at least, that's the way he saw it. And to defend his position, he needed hard facts rather than soft feelings, hard numbers rather than soft words, and hard data and concrete steps rather than abstract possibilities. It meant short-term action taking rather than long-term planning, "tell it like it is"

*Author's note: George F.F. Lombard of the Harvard Business School first called my attention to this assumption some years ago as a variant on Gresham's Law that "bad money drives out good money." I have since heard of other similar variations such as one coined by Warren Bennis, recent president of the University of Cincinnati, as Bennis's Principle: "routine work drives out nonroutine work." In the same spirit, I suppose, "hard drives out soft" deserves to be known as Lombard's Law, which is what some of us have affectionately called it in recent years.

statements rather than speculative explorations.

Consequently, Jones became a tough wheeler-dealer manager who needed to win out over the other side. As "they" became the opposition, having the best defense meant having a good offense. In Jones's case, as in many of our own situations, it is easy to see how the dangerous link between the first and second assumptions gets fused.

Holding this second assumption easily leads a person to a hard-nosed, buccaneer management style that turns doubt into action and stirs the hearts of those who idolize such uncompromising figureheads as General George S. Patton, Harold Geneen of ITT, the Ayatollah Khomeini, or the late John Wayne's macho cowboy roles. Such leaders at least *act* as if they know what they're doing. And the shoot-from-the-hip style is not restricted to management; the hard/soft assumption shows up in the hard-nosed skepticism of science and in the lawyer's quest for hard evidence. In the best competitive tradition, people who hold this assumption "get things done," despite later consequences.

Yet both proponents and opponents of hard-is-better-than-soft can make profound mistakes in its name. Both can propel an either/or position a long way toward a disaster of the extremes, as the following example shows: When John F. Kennedy took office in 1961, he was confronted with the CIA's plans for the Bay of Pigs invasion. Although Kennedy semed to have early doubts about the invasion and even though a few advisers like Arthur Schlesinger, Jr. and Chester Bowles expressed reservations, Kennedy went along with the arguments for an attack as presented by Allan Dulles of the CIA, some joint chief of staff members, and other highly qualified advisers.

Schlesinger later wrote about the hard-drives-out-soft mood of those meetings in his book *A Thousand Days*—"Moreover, the advocates of the adventure had a rhetorical advantage. They could strike virile poses and talk of tangible things—fire power, air strikes, landing craft, and so on. To oppose this plan, one had to invoke intangibles—the moral position of the United States, the response of the United Nations, 'world public opinion,' and other such odious concepts.

"But just as the members of the White House Staff who sat in the Cabinet Room failed in their job of protecting the President, so the representatives of the State Department failed in protecting the diplomatic interests of the nation. I could not help feeling that the desire to prove to the CIA and the Joint Chiefs that they were not soft-headed idealists but were really tough guys too influenced State's representatives at the Cabinet table."[1]

The Bay of Pigs example illustrates the power of the hard-is-better-than-soft assumption in combination with its either/or companion. When opposing sides are formed, people feel almost compelled to choose one or the other—and to find tangible ways of defending their choices. The side that usually seems most convincing is the one that is supported by hard evidence and defended by hard tactics, which have both an intellectual and an emotional appeal for the tough-minded and the would-be tough-minded, like Jones.

The danger with people's tendencies to make hard-nosed choices is that, as in the Bay of Pigs discussions, such choices quickly acquire their own momentum. To stop the snowball—to try to reexamine the options—means violating the either/or and hard/soft assumptions, while seeming, as Schlesinger says, to be a "soft-headed idealist." As many

---

[1] Arthur W. Schlesinger, Jr., *A Thousand Days: John F. Kennedy in the White House* (Boston: Houghton Mifflin Co., 1965), p. 255.

managers know, in most tough-guy contexts it can be very hard to appear soft.

Pitting himself and his hard-line approach against both old-line practices and old-time managers, Jones exemplified the tough-guy manager. However, he personified a third assumption as well.

Nice Guys Finish Last

The third harmless assumption forms a basis for and helps contaminate the other two. It holds that the world is a dangerous place requiring that a person adopt a position of *pervasive mistrust* to survive. When held, this assumption dominates the atmosphere and blots out situational factors. Like the other two assumptions, mistrust can be very useful when our safety or well-being is at stake. On other occasions, however, our own mistrust helps set the stage for either/or thinking and hard-drives-out-soft behavior.

According to those who had known him in earlier years, Manager Jones had been taunted in childhood for being weak. To avoid the appearance of weakness, he adopted an aggressive posture and an air of superskepticism, which fit his view of the world. He was bright enough to be a rising star in a company where mutual trust among managers was considered important. Jones, himself, was considered trustworthy by his superiors in the sense of being a predictable producer.

As Jones set one subordinate faction against another, however, and as hard began to drive out soft, the parent company managers saw how destructive Jones's sense of mistrust was and how absent and important the softer, more caring side of trust had become. Not surprisingly, key subordinates reciprocated Jones's lack of caring, which led them to indulge in inconsistent and unpredictable behavior. As a result, any earlier bases for organizational trust disappeared.

Jones's assumption of pervasive mistrust was reinforced by his either/or and hard-drives-out-soft viewpoints. The situation deteriorated even more as Jones's subordinates took sides and added fuel to the fires of mistrust. It took the company more than five years to move out of what was by then commonly acknowledged to be a very difficult situation. This experience suggests how much harder it is to drive out hard with soft than vice versa, even though it can be done over time. It also suggests that we should examine the tenacious roots of trust and mistrust more closely. For this, the work of Erik H. Erikson is instructive (see box on page 337).

Although Erikson's work rests on rich clinical evidence, it seems reasonable to ask, "What do early trust-mistrust patterns have to do with managers like Jones?" In response, researchers would generally agree that we never fully conquer old anxieties or doubts; when we encounter difficult new situations, we often reexperience old tensions. Thus the early major dilemmas of the human life cycle can often return in later years when we meet new tension-filled settings and experiences.

In addition—and most important for managers—even though our earliest and most basic assumptions about trust and mistrust are formed in early infancy, they are affected by new situations and by how a person feels about the immediate situation. Consequently, the trust versus mistrust dilemma constantly confronts us as we face new situations, new people, new adversities, and even new successes.

In this fashion, much of our initial behavior in these new situations is an effort to search for, test out, and initiate a tentative sense of trust or mistrust. When other people see this initial behavior as *both* predictable and caring, they develop an expectation of future hope, which accompanies trust. Such early search behavior also invites similar responses from others.

This exchange creates the giving and

getting-in-return behavior that Erikson pictures and which pervades all cultures in what sociologists call the norm of reciprocity. Its universal pattern gives us (and Jones) a way to check out a test for the presence of trust. When we try to give something, we have a chance to see what we get in return. If the exchange is unsuccessful, for whatever reason, we usually assume it is a situation in which mistrust prevails.

To further show how the trust/mistrust assumption works, though, let me briefly describe three studies by other behavioral scientists.

The first, by James Driscoll, shows how satisfaction in organizations is determined more by the degree of trust present than by either levels of participation or people's inherent trust. In other words, Driscoll suggests that with trust, the immediate environment is more important than either one's background or one's participation in decisions.[2]

The second study of trust and mistrust is Dale Zand's simulation of managerial problem solving, and the third is R. Wayne Boss's replication of Zand's study done some years later.[3] Both studies examine how high-trust and low-trust conditions affect the quality of managerial problem solving involving a company president and three vice presidents. Each study set up teams with sets of instructions; some teams' instructions were filled with high-trust assumptions, others' had low-trust assumptions. The surprising thing in these studies is how easily the simple instructions given to each set created these trust differences. Zand's instructions for the high-trust teams, all of whom were managers attending a course, read as follows (note the words I have italicized):

You have learned *from your experience* during the past two years that *you can trust* the other members of the top management team. You and the other top managers *openly express your differences and your feelings of encouragement or of disappointment.* You and the others *share all relevant information and freely explore ideas and feelings that may be in or out of your defined responsibility.* The result has been a *high level of give and take and mutual confidence in each other's support and ability.*[4]

According to Zand, the instructions given to the low-trust groups were "worded to induce a decrease in trust." This was epitomized by the president perceiving his or her vice presidents as potentially competitive.

The key difference in the two sets may be the specific cues about the give-and-take reciprocity among managers. In the high-trust teams, the norms of reciprocity included expressing differences of opinion, stating feelings of encouragment and disappointment, sharing information, exploring ideas outside of one's own function, providing high give and take, and giving support. For the low-trust teams the opposite was implied.

Both the Zand and the Boss studies indicate that high trust was the key factor in problem-solving effectiveness. Moreover, in his replication study, Boss reports a surprising finding (italics mine):

The fact that trust was the overriding variable was not initially apparent to the subjects. When participants were asked to explain the reasons for the obvious differences in team effectiveness, they offered a number of plausible explanations. . . . When told

[2] James W. Driscoll, "Trust and Participation in Organizational Decision Making as Predictors of Satisfaction," *Academy of Management Journal*, 1973, vol. 21, no. 1, p. 44.
[3] Dale Zand, "Trust and Managerial Problem Solving," *Administrative Science Quarterly*, June 1972, p. 229; and R. Wayne Boss, "Trust and Managerial Problem Solving Revisited," *Group and Organizational Studies*, September 1978, p. 331.
[4] Zand, "Trust and Managerial Problem Solving," p. 234.

of the different instructions, the group members reacted with amazement and relief. *They were amazed that they had not perceived what seemed to them after the fact to be obvious.*[5]

What does all this tell us about the soft assumption of trust?

1. Our concerns about trust apparently begin very early and recur throughout our lives.
2. Trust seems important for both effective performance and high satisfaction.
3. Trust may be easier both to create and to destroy, under some conditions, than we have assumed (it depends on how norms of reciprocity develop and take hold).
4. Managers may gloss over the crucial role of trust and mistrust assumptions and fall back on more convenient explanations for behavior in their companies, such as personality differences and the boss's actions.
5. Perhaps most important, our assumptions of trust and mistrust come at us from both past and present situations.

[5] Boss, "Trust and Managerial Problem Solving Revisited," p. 338.

TRUST VS. MISTRUST

Since 1950 and the publication of Erik Erikson's *Childhood and Society*, many developmental psychologists have viewed trust and mistrust as the cornerstones of human development. Erikson divides the human life cycle into eight stages and suggests that each period is a time for a major developmental dilemma or crisis. The first of these crises is the trust versus mistrust crisis, which faces the human infant on entering a world of confusion and complexity. The determining relationship is, of course, with the infant's mother.

The other seven crises are autonomy versus shame and doubt (during the first year or two), initiative versus guilt (during the remaining preschool years), industry versus inferiority (during the early school years), identity versus identity confusion (during adolescence), intimacy versus isolation (during young adulthood), generativity versus stagnation (during adult hood), and integrity versus despair (during old age).

Working through and tentatively resolving each crisis brings an accompanying strength and a basis for future behavior. Thus viewed very roughly, for example, the young child who works through the autonomy crisis achieves an expected virtue of self-control, which provides a behavioral base for holding on and letting go.

Although Erikson sets up the trust/mistrust dilemma in an either/or form, he is careful to add that variations of the same problem continue on through life despite a tentative and precarious balancing of trust and mistrust during the crucial infancy period. If that tentative balance tilts in the direction of trust, Erikson suggests that the infant gains a basis for expecting the virtue of hope in the future, which in turn lays the groundwork for giving-and-receiving behavior.

Source: Erik H. Erikson, *Childhood and Society* (New York; W.W. Norton & Co., 1950).

We may not be able to do much about the past, but we do have some control over present and future actions. In new situations, once we question the inevitability of pervasive mistrust, then the either/or and hard/soft assumptions also stand on shakier ground. Indeed, if we question all three assumptions enough, it becomes apparent that they no longer need to combine to our detriment. But what can we use to replace them?

ALTERNATIVE APPROACHES

So far I've discussed how—even though separately each may be very useful—long-term problems arise when managers combine the three harmless assumptions. The same is true when we combine their most obvious alternatives, which, in good either/or fashion, happen to come from their exact opposites. Manager Jones would most likely reject the idea that pervasive trust (the obvious alternative to pervasive mistrust) could possibly replace his assumption. His experience has taught him otherwise. And he would surely (and with reason) reject the idea that a prolonged-tolerance-for-ambiguity or a soft-is-better-than-hard viewpoint is a suitable replacement for any more rigorous stance.

Even though Jones might reject these obvious alternatives, others do not. For some people, the concepts of pervasive trust, prolonged ambiguity, and soft-overwhelming-hard fit together and have great appeal. With almost religious fervor, like flower children or sensitivity training converts, they promote their causes to proclaim the new utopias. Typically, that fervor is all it takes for their more mistrustful adversaries to draw new lines and define new battlegrounds.

Ultimately, holders of opposing viewpoints emerge and throw loaded overstatements at the other side, as both parties get drawn into defending fixed positions.

Over the years the management pendulum swings back and forth from liberal to conservative, from centralization to decentralization, from harsh layoff periods to ex-pensive benefit programs, and from severe survival controls to expanded product development and cries for creativity. A major problem is that early dialogue between the opposing viewpoints often triggers defensive thinking within each position, as happened in Jonestown, Watergate, and Iran. In each case, typically—and tragically—either/or, mistrust, and hard-drives-out-soft prevail in the short term.

At the same time, people in organizations can and do learn. What appears to be pendulum behavior isn't merely that. Opposites sometimes converge or change as they develop. Sometimes new managers and new situations phase new assumptions into old issues. Sometimes a wise, experienced manager can rise above a repeated false dichotomy and furnish the impetus for finding new approaches. Such approaches, however, require people adept at a third path, not just a middle way, as well as specific steps toward organizational trust and constructive reciprocities. To do this, managers need to abandon the three assumptions and their opposites in favor of less rigid, more creative combinations.

Things Aren't Always as They Seem

Another example, as follows, might help to illustrate how this third way can work: The faculty and administration of a small college were torn by argument and dissension. The veteran president had recently resigned, and a search committee had chosen a woman with a distinguished academic record as the new president. Not long after the new president arrived, the dean of faculty also resigned.

After conferring with the executive committee of the faculty, the new president appointed a young, recently tenured faculty member as the acting dean of faculty. She also announced three short-term goals: improving the enrollment picture, improving the financial situation, and building new trust. She resisted strong pressures to produce a specific "mission" statement, saying that as soon as she did, it would polarize the college community into those who agreed with the statement and those who didn't. She also chose to keep the new dean of faculty as an acting dean so that he could be tested in his new role while she and the faculty learned to work with him and with each other.

During their first year of working together, the new president and the acting dean took supportive but active roles in faculty discussions, helped to pass legislation that greatly simplified the cumbersome committee structure, improved the enrollment and financial pictures, and tried to strengthen faculty work relationships.

Specifically, the new dean worked hard to reinvolve a number of senior faculty members who were described by others as "burned out" and "losers" of earlier faculty battles. He did this by going to them for advice on important matters, frequently seeking them out in their offices, refusing to let them withdraw, helping them to get money for such mundane tasks as manuscript typing and library research, sending them to conferences on innovative practices in their own fields, asking them to chair short-term task forces, and seeking and finding financial help for them to start new research.

At the start of the second year of the acting dean's appointment, the president still refused to appoint him as the permanent dean until the official search committee was set up and made its own report and recommendation. The acting dean agreed: "I have everything to gain by not having the official title and authority. This way I can still get help from everyone and don't have to act like an official dean." Nevertheless, within a few months a search committee did recommend that his title be made official.

A number of knowledgeable sources have since reported that the college is progressing excellently.

As managers, the new president and her acting dean posed a puzzle to most of their constituents. She was new, an outsider, and wouldn't take a firm position on educational policy; he was young and had little administrative experience. In an institution where protocol, tradition, and gestures of strong leadership had been important, neither administrator leaned on them. Where mistrust had been rampant, she set out to assume and to build trust. In an effort to demonstrate that there was still leadership in the faculty ranks as well, he set out to revitalize burned-out faculty members.

In effect, the president and the dean refused to adopt either set of simple hard or soft assumptions. Instead they assumed a condition of tentative trust and worked toward a set of *and/also* rather than either/or expectations. They did this by behaving in ways that explored, listened, and confronted while exemplifying care for the school and its people. In effect they began reciprocities that could lead to organizational trust.

In doing so, the president and dean created a sense of shared hope for the future. Both gave ample evidence of caring for the school and its individual members. After identifying a set of crucial problems—enrollment, finances, trust, a demoralized faculty, little support for faculty projects, and low student and faculty initiative—both confronted them. As new leaders, they worked on old issues in new ways and surprised some people. They did not initially set forth a master plan or mission. She chose a relatively inexperienced person as dean. They both tried to build and rebuild faculty leadership instead of drawing attention to their own. And even after the acting dean had convinced the faculty of his competence, the president refused to push for his permanent appointment until the faculty also took responsibility for it.

As a result, the either/or power struggles that had existed between the previous administration and the faculty moved toward a set of and/also expectations. The new administration, the senior faculty, the junior faculty, the students, and the subfactions built a new leadership network where the quality of students rose, student turnover and attrition declined, programs expanded, and finances improved. Paradoxically, the president and dean accomplished the expected, or hoped-for, results by creatively pursuing the unexpected—at least in the eyes of many constituents.

These seemingly inappropriate about-faces are what I call paradoxical actions. In using the word *paradox* in this way, I'm borrowing from philosopher W.V. Quine's notion that paradox is "any conclusion that at first sounds absurd but that has an argument to sustain it," although these arguments are often buried, ignored, or brushed over quickly.[6] Paradoxical actions are the "absurd" steps, such as listening hard to the other person when one is trying to win an argument, that break up and bridge false dichotomies. They create working links toward trust where there were few or none before.

Paradoxical Actions . . .

The mysteriousness of paradox has fascinated poets, scientists, philosophers, and laymen for thousands of years. Paradoxical puzzles can both pose unanswerable questions and lead to insightful creative answers; Kierkegaard called paradox the "source of the thinker's passion." The reconciliation of apparent contradictions underlies some of the most truly creative discoveries of science, not to mention most religions, while the suggested unity of opposites permeates the works of great writers, like O'Neill and Conrad. Most important, partly because it is based on an unfamiliar logic or rationale, a paradox's true workings always seem to be just beyond our understanding.

Once we see these same paradoxical situations as and/also propositions rather than either/or contradictions, the reconciliations seem relatively obvious. That awareness, though, doesn't always help us find the underlying unities the next time we face a set of apparent opposites. Manager Jones is not the only one who finds it difficult to break old reciprocities or the patterns that reinforce them. Sometimes, however, change requires the very opposite of what appears to be logically appropriate behavior.

At the same time, paradoxical actions are not foreign to many a modern manager. To buy when others are selling, to ask questions when others expect answers, or to give new autonomy when subordinates expect tighter controls are all actions that make sense under certain conditions. And, without highlighting it, some of the most popular management concepts of recent years have relied on paradox. The work of McGregor, Blake and Mouton, and Lawrence and Lorsch all entail paradoxes (see box).

In a sense, these real and theoretical

---

6   W.V. Quine, *The Ways of Paradox* (Cambridge: Harvard University Press, 1976), p. 1.

examples highlight the almost unnoticed role of paradox in organizational behavior. In similar fashion, I suspect, most readers overlook the crucial role that paradox plays in their own more creative actions. And yet, acting paradoxically constitutes one way to get beyond tentative trust rather than adopting the extremes of pervasive trust or pervasive mistrust.

Likewise, a manager who avoids either/or thinking or its mushy opposite, prolonged ambiguity, must consciously adopt an and/also viewpoint whereby ingredients are kept separate but are not assumed to be in conflict. Finally, and most difficult, managers need to replace the hard versus soft behavior with paradoxical actions that *cope* with new information, *confront* important discrepancies, and *care* for individual people and issues. The goal is not to do one or the other; it is to weave them into a pattern of separate behaviors that sets the basis for new reciprocal patterns.

... and Norms of Reciprocity

Earlier, I suggested that the fragile toughness of trust is a crucial factor in blending extremist hard- and soft-line assumptions into an organizational bonding that holds a company's disparate parts together. Trust that is too tentative, emotional, and fragile will fall back into pervasive mistrust. Trust that is too tenacious, impervious, and tough becomes inflexibly shaped into a pattern of pervasive trust. Organizations with too much mistrust become overly differentiated, with people succumbing to either/or expectations and hard-drives-out-soft behavior. Organizations with too much trust become overly integrated, with people lapsing into prolonged ambiguity and soft-is-better-than-hard behavior. Both extremist patterns depend on emotions more than on data and self-awareness. Both also build up ineffective reciprocity patterns.

The three-path diagram in *Exhibit 1* displays the points I've made so far plus another path that is based on the more modest assumption of tentative trust. The diagram also suggests that the patterns persist because people reinforce them: i.e., attack/defend/withdraw behavior follows from an assumption of pervasive mistrust and win/lose expectations. Such behavior begins a cycle that repeats itself until it becomes a norm of reciprocity and degenerates into a continuing self-oriented need pattern. Obey-

---

PARADOX IN MANAGEMENT THEORIES

More than 20 years ago, Douglas McGregor wrote about two sets of assumptions that he called Theory X and Theory Y. Theory X corresponded with our first three assumptions, the hard ones. But Theory Y was not just Theory X's opposite, although that is what many observers concluded. McGregor did not intend the two sets of assumptions to be forced into the hard versus soft mold. He meant Theory Y to be an integrative set of assumptions, not Theory X's polar opposite. As McGregor notes in describing the paradoxical qualities of Theory Y:

"The central principle of Theory Y is that of integration; the creation of conditions such that the members of the organization can achieve their own goals best by directing their goals toward the success of the enterprise. . . . The concept of integration and self-control [also] carries the implication that the organization will be more effective in achieving its economic objectives if adjustments are made in significant ways to the needs and goals of its members."*

In other words, McGregor is suggesting that each party could meet its own goals best by paradoxically directing them largely toward the goals of the other party. Much to McGregor's disappointment, this was not the way many people came to see Theory Y.

Likewise, five years later, Robert R. Blake and Jane S. Mouton developed the managerial grid. Building on others' thinking, including McGregor's, they originated the concept of organization development and built it around five styles of management. By using the concern for production and the concern for people as two polar extremes, they identified two of the styles (9,1 and 1,9) with these extremes, another style (1,1) as low on both concerns, and two other styles (5,5 and 9,9) as trying to take both production and people concerns into account. Blake and Mouton's major contribution, I believe, was to distinguish the middle path compromise position of 5,5 from the paradoxical fusion style of 9,9. As they wrote about the 9,9 style:

"Unlike the other basic approaches, it is assumed in the 9,9 managerial style that there is no necessary and inherent conflict between the organization purpose of production requirements and the needs of people. Under 9,9, effective integration of people with production is possible by involving them and their ideas in determining the conditions and strategies of work."†

In their writings on differentiation and integration, Paul R. Lawrence and Jay W. Lorsch described another paradox dealing with organizational structure. Lawrence and Lorsch found that active and uncertain organizational environments require specialized and differentiated functions within the organization. However, high differentiation also requires stronger, more elaborate integration efforts to help coordinate the parts of the organization. The paradox lies in the idea that the most effective companies in turbulent environments had both high differentiation and high integration. As Lawrence and Lorsch observe:

"The finding still leaves us with a curious contradiction. If, as we have found, differentiation and integration work at cross purposes within each organization, how can two (of the studied) organizations achieve high degrees of both? The best approach to explaining this apparent paradox beomes evident. . . . If organizations have groups of highly differentiated managers who are able to work together effectively, these managers must have strong capacities to deal with interdepartmental conflicts. . . . Effective integration . . . means that these conflicts must be resolved to the approximate satisfaction of all parties and to the general good of the enterprise."††

*   Douglas McGregor, *The Human Side of Enterprise* (New York: McGraw-Hill, 1960), p. 49.

†   Robert R. Blake and Jane S. Mouton, *The Managerial Grid* (Houston, Tex.: Gulf Publishing, 1964), p. 142; and Robert R. Blake, Jane S. Mouton, Louis B. Barnes, and Larry E. Greiner, "Breakthrough in Organization Development," HBR November-December 1964, p. 133.

††   Paul R. Lawrence and Jay W. Lorsch, *Organization and Environment* (Boston: Harvard Business School Division of Research, 1967), p. 53.

ing a distorted golden rule, people do to others what they perceive is being done to them. Beginning with a pervasive sense of mistrust, they shift eventually into a set of destructive reciprocities and finally to even more divisive and self-oriented needs. As emotions run high, the cycle continues, engendering even more mistrust.

The three-path diagram also suggests that norms of reciprocity need not result in rigid patterns and structures. One way to break those norms, which are perceived as natural by the time they are frozen, is to seek for and initiate paradoxical actions. New norms cannot be set into motion unless the old ones are broken. And the old ones cannot be broken unless paradoxical insights and actions help break old patterns. Some of this paradoxical behavior is subtle and difficult to capture. It hinges on words, gestures, and maybe most of all on careful listening for new clues and knowledge.

But even more, paradoxical actions begin to set up new relationships and in that sense lead to the unexpected. Such actions suggest that, in Lewis Carroll's words, "things aren't always as they seem." Consider one final example where a major company president, reflecting on a turbulent year of employee relations, notes:

"Some of our problems are our own fault. We lost contact with our own employees. Managements in large companies say that they get too big to stay in personal contact with their employees. We swallowed that. Now, however, I think that the opposite is true. The larger we get, the *more* important it is for us to emphasize personal contact by top management down through all levels. We've been doing it all wrong. We stumbled over our own assumptions."

In essence, to prevent mistrust beliefs or their extreme opposites from becoming frozen, we sometimes need, unlike our friend Manager Jones, to live and to create paradoxical actions. We need to know and act as though some things are both certain and uncertain. We need to polarize and synthesize, to see questions in answers, to be both inside and outside of situations, to learn while teaching, and to find unity in opposites as well as opposites in unity. Interestingly enough, excellent managers, though they are not used to talking these ways, *are* used to thinking paradoxically. Our hope for dealing with an increasingly complex organizational future lies in understanding—and making more explicit—the implicit truth in this way of thinking.

EXHIBIT 1 The Assumptions and the Patterns They Create.

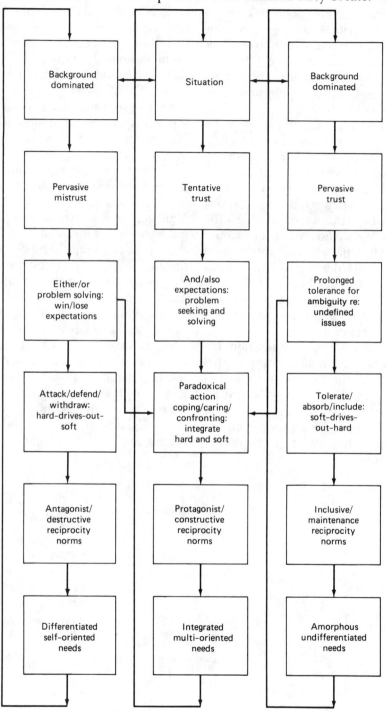

Evolution and Revolution as Organizations Grow

LARRY E. GREINER

A small research company chooses too complicated and formalized an organization structure for its young age and limited size. It flounders in rigidity and bureaucracy for several years and is finally acquired by a larger company.

Key executives of a retail store chain hold on to an organization structure long after it has served its purpose, because their power is derived from this structure. The company eventually goes into bankruptcy.

A large bank disciplines a "rebellious" manager who is blamed for current control problems, when the underlying cause is centralized procedures that are holding back expansion into new markets. Many younger managers subsequently leave the bank, competition moves in, and profits are still declining.

The problems of these companies, like those of many others, are rooted more in past decisions than in present events or outside market dynamics. Historical forces do indeed shape the future growth of organizations. Yet management, in its haste to grow, often overlooks such critical developmental questions as: Where has our organization been? Where is it now? And what do the answers to these questions mean for where we are going? Instead, its gaze is fixed outward toward the environment and the future—as if more precise market projections will provide a new organizational identity.

Companies fail to see that many clues to their future success lie within their own organizations and their evolving states of development. Moreover, the inability of management to understand its organization development problems can result in a company becoming "frozen" in its present stage of evolution or, ultimately, in failure, regardless of market opportunities.

My position in this article is that the future of an organization may be less determined by outside forces than it is by the organization's history. In stressing the force of history on an organization, I have drawn from the legacies of European psychologists (their thesis being that individual behavior is determined primarily by previous events and experiences, not by what lies ahead). Extending this analogy of individual development to the problems of organization development, I shall discuss a series of developmental phases

Author's note: This article is part of a continuing project on organization development with my colleague, Professor Louis B. Barnes, and sponsored by the Division of Research, Harvard Business School.

through which growing companies tend to pass. But, first, let me provide two definitions:

1. The term *evolution* is used to describe prolonged periods of growth where no major upheaval occurs in organization practices.
2. The term *revolution* is used to describe those periods of substantial turmoil in organization life.

As a company progresses through developmental phases, each evolutionary period creates its own revolution. For instance, centralized practices eventually lead to demands for decentralization. Moreover, the nature of management's solution to each revolutionary period determines whether a company will move forward into its next stage of evolutionary growth. As I shall show later, there are at least five phases of organization development, each characterized by both an evolution and a revolution.

KEY FORCES IN DEVELOPMENT

During the past few years a small amount of research knowledge about the phases of organization development has been building. Some of this research is very quantitative, such as time-series analyses that reveal patterns of economic performance over time.[1] The majority of studies, however, are case-oriented and use company records and interviews to reconstruct a rich picture of corporate development.[2] Yet both types of research tend to be heavily empirical without attempting more generalized statements about the overall process of development.

A notable exception is the historical work of Alfred D. Chandler, Jr., in his book *Strategy and Structure*.[3] This study depicts four very broad and general phases in the lives of four large U.S. companies. It proposes that outside market opportunities determine a company's strategy, which in turn determines the company's organization structure. This thesis has a valid ring for the four companies examined by Chandler, largely because they developed in a time of explosive markets and technological advances. But more recent evidence suggests that organization structure may be less malleable than Chandler assumed; in fact, structure can play a critical role in influencing corporate strategy. It is this reverse emphasis on how organization structure affects future growth which is highlighted in the model presented in this article.

From an analysis of recent studies,[4] five key dimensions emerge as essential for building a model of organization development:

[1] See, for example, William H. Starbuck, "Organizational Metamorphosis," in *Promising Research Directions*, edited by R.W. Millman and M.P. Hottenstein (Tempe, Arizona, Academy of Management, 1968), p. 113.

[2] See, for example, the *Grangesberg* case series, prepared by C. Roland Christensen and Bruce R. Scott, Case Clearing House, Harvard Business School.

[3] *Strategy and Structure: Chapters in the History of the American Industrial Enterprise* (Cambridge, Massachusetts, The M.I.T. Press, 1962).

[4] I have drawn on many sources for evidence: (a) numerous cases collected at the Harvard Business School; (b) *Organization Growth and Development*, edited by William H. Starbuck (Middlesex, England, Penguin Books, Ltd., 1971), where several studies are cited; and (c) articles published in journals, such as Lawrence E. Fouraker and John M. Stopford, "Organization Structure and the Multinational Strategy," *Administrative Science Quarterly*, Vol. 13, No. 1, 1968, p. 47; and Malcolm S. Salter, "Management Appraisal and Reward Systems," *Journal of Business Policy*, Vol. 1, No. 4, 1971.

1. Age of the organization.
2. Size of the organization.
3. Stages of evolution.
4. Stages of revolution.
5. Growth rate of the industry.

I shall describe each of these elements separately, but first note their combined effect as illustrated in *Exhibit 1*. Note especially how each dimension influences the other over time; when all five elements begin to interact, a more complete and dynamic picture of organizational growth emerges.

After describing these dimensions and their interconnections, I shall discuss each evolutionary/revolutionary phase of development and show (a) how each stage of evolution breeds its own revolution, and (b) how management solutions to each revolution determine the next stage of evolution.

Age of the Organization

The most obvious and essential dimension for any model of development is the life span of an organization (represented as the horizontal axis in *Exhibit 1*). All historical studies gather data from various points in time and then make comparisons. From these observations, it is evident that the same organization practices are not maintained throughout a long time span. This makes a most basic point: management problems and principles are rooted in time. The concept of decentralization, for example, can have meaning for describing corporate practices at one time period but loses its descriptive power at another.

The passage of time also contributes to the institutionalization of managerial attitudes. As a result, employee behavior becomes not only more predictable but also more difficult to change when attitudes are outdated.

Size of the Organization

This dimension is depicted as the vertical axis in *Exhibit 1*. A company's problems and solutions tend to change markedly as the number of employees and sales volume increase. Thus, time is not the only determinant of structure, in fact, organizations that do not grow in size can retain many of the same management issues and practices over lengthy periods. In addition to increased size, however, problems of coordination and communication magnify, new functions emerge, levels in the management hierarchy multiply, and jobs become more interrelated.

Stages of Evolution

As both age and size increase, another phenomenon becomes evident: the prolonged growth that I have termed the evolutionary period. Most growing organizations do not expand for two years and then retreat for one year; rather, those that survive a crisis usually enjoy four to eight years of continuous growth without a major economic setback or severe internal disruption. The term evolution seems appropriate for describing these quieter periods because only modest adjustments appear necessary for maintaining growth under the same overall pattern of management.

Stages of Revolution

Smooth evolution is not inevitable; it cannot be assumed that organization growth is linear. *Fortune's* "500" list, for example, has had significant turnover during the last 50 years. Thus we find evidence from numerous case histories which reveals periods of substantial turbulence spaced between smoother periods of evolution.

I have termed these turbulent times the periods of revolution because they typically exhibit a serious upheaval of management practices. Traditional management practices, which were appropriate for a smaller size and earlier time, are brought under scrutiny by frustrated top managers and disillusioned lower-level managers. During such periods of crisis, a number of companies fail—those unable to abandon past practices and effect major organization changes are likely either to fold or to level off in their growth rates.

The critical task for management in each revolutionary period is to find a new set of organization practices that will become the basis for managing the next period of evolutionary growth. Interestingly enough, these new practices eventually sow their own seeds of decay and lead to another period of revolution. Companies therefore experience the irony of seeing a major solution in one time period become a major problem at a latter date.

Growth Rate of the Industry

The speed at which an organization experiences phases of evolution and revolution is closely related to the market environment of its industry. For example, a company in a rapidly expanding market will have to add employees rapidly; hence, the need for new organization structures to accommodate large staff increases is accelerated. While evolutionary periods tend to be relatively short in fast-growing industries, much longer evolutionary periods occur in mature or slowly growing industries.

Evolution can also be prolonged, and revolutions delayed, when profits come easily. For instance, companies that make grievous errors in a rewarding industry can still look good on their profit and loss statements; thus they can avoid a change in management practices for a longer period. The aerospace industry in its infancy is an example. Yet revolutionary periods still occur, as one did in aerospace when profit opportunities began to dry up. Revolutions seem to be much more severe and difficult to resolve when the market environment is poor.

PHASES OF GROWTH

With the foregoing framework in mind, let us now examine in depth the five specific phases of evolution and revolution. As shown in *Exhibit 2*, each evolutionary period is characterized by the dominant *management style* used to achieve growth, while each revolutionary period is characterized by the dominant *management problem* that must be solved before growth can continue. The patterns presented in *Exhibit 2* seem to be typical for companies in industries with moderate growth over a long time period; companies in faster growing industries tend to experience all five phases more rapidly, while those in slower growing industries encounter only two or three phases over many years.

It is important to note that *each phase is both an effect of the previous phase and a cause for the next phase*. For example, the evolutionary management style in Phase 3 of the exhibit is "delegation," which grows out of, and becomes the solution to, demands for greater "autonomy" in the preceding Phase 2 revolution. The style of delegation used in Phase 3, however, eventually provokes a major revolutionary crisis that is characterized by attempts to regain control over the diversity created through increased delegation.

The principal implication of each phase is that management actions are narrowly prescribed if growth is to occur. For example, a company experiencing an autonomy crisis in Phase 2 cannot return to directive management for a solution—it must adopt a new style of delegation in order to move ahead.

Phase 1: Creativity . . .

In the birth stage of an organization, the emphasis is on creating both a product and a market. Here are the characteristics of the period of creative evolution:

- The company's founders are usually technically or entrepreneurially oriented, and they disdain management activities; their physical and mental energies are absorbed entirely in making and selling a new product.
- Communication among employees is frequent and informal.
- Long hours of work are rewarded by modest salaries and the promise of ownership benefits.
- Control of activities comes from immediate marketplace feedback; the management acts as the customers react.

. . . and the leadership crisis All of the foregoing individualistic and creative activities are essential for the company to get off the ground. But therein lies the problem. As the company grows, larger production runs require knowledge about the efficiencies of manufacturing. Increased numbers of employees cannot be managed exclusively through informal communication; new employees are not motivated by an intense dedication to the product or organization. Additional capital must be secured, and new accounting procedures are needed for financial control.

Thus the founders find themselves burdened with unwanted management responsibilities. So they long for the "good old days," still trying to act as they did in the past. And conflicts between the harried leaders grow more intense.

At this point a crisis of leadership occurs, which is the onset of the first revolution. Who is to lead the company out of confusion and solve the managerial problems confronting it? Quite obviously, a strong manager is needed who has the necessary knowledge and skill to introduce new business techniques. But this is easier said than done. The founders often hate to step aside even though they are probably temperamentally unsuited to be managers. So here is the first critical developmental choice—to locate and install a strong business manager who is acceptable to the founders and who can pull the organization together.

Phase 2: Direction . . .

Those companies that survive the first phase by installing a capable business manager usually embark on a period of sustained growth under able and directive leadership. Here are the characteristics of this evolutionary period:

- A functional organization structure is introduced to separate manufacturing from marketing activities, and job assignments become more specialized.
- Accounting systems for inventory and purchasing are introduced.
- Incentives, budgets, and work standards are adopted.
- Communication becomes more formal and impersonal as a hierarchy of titles and positions builds.
- The new manager and his key supervisors take most of the responsibility for instituting direction, while lower-level supervisors are treated more as functional specialists

than as autonomous decision-making managers.

. . . and the autonomy crisis Although the new directive techniques channel employee energy more efficiently into growth, they eventually become inappropriate for controlling a larger, more diverse and complex organization. Lower-level employees find themselves restricted by a cumbersome and centralized hierarchy. They have come to possess more direct knowledge about markets and machinery than do the leaders at the top; consequently, they feel torn between following procedures and taking initiative on their own.

Thus the second revolution is imminent as a crisis develops from demands for greater autonomy on the part of lower-level managers. The solution adopted by most companies is to move toward greater delegation. Yet it is difficult for top managers who were previously successful at being directive to give up responsibility. Moreover, lower-level managers are not accustomed to making decisions for themselves. As a result, numerous companies flounder during this revolutionary period, adhering to centralized methods while lower-level employees grow more disenchanted and leave the organization.

Phase 3: Delegation . . .

The next era of growth evolves from the successful application of a decentralized organization structure. It exhibits these characteristics:

- Much greater responsibility is given to the managers of plants and market territories.
- Profit centers and bonuses are used to stimulate motivation.
- The top executives at headquarters restrain themselves to managing by exception, based on periodic reports from the field.

- Management often concentrates on making new acquisitions which can be lined up beside other decentralized units.
- Communication from the top is infrequent, usually by correspondence, telephone, or brief visits to field locations.

The delegation stage proves useful for gaining expansion through heightened motivation at lower levels. Decentralized managers with greater authority and incentive are able to penetrate larger markets, respond faster to customers, and develop new products.

. . . and the control crisis A serious problem eventually evolves, however, as top executives sense that they are losing control over a highly diversified field operation. Autonomous field managers prefer to run their own shows without coordinating plans, money, technology, and manpower with the rest of the organization. Freedom breeds a parochial attitude.

Hence, the Phase 3 revolution is under way when top management seeks to regain control over the total company. Some top managements attempt a return to centralized management, which usually fails because of the vast scope of operations. Those companies that move ahead find a new solution in the use of special coordination techniques.

Phase 4: Coordination . . .

During this phase, the evolutionary period is characterized by the use of formal systems for achieving greater coordination and by top executives taking responsibility for the initiation and administration of these new systems. For example:

- Decentralized units are merged into product groups.
- Formal planning procedures are established and intensively reviewed.

- Numerous staff personnel are hired and located at headquarters to initiate company-wide programs of control and review for line managers.
- Capital expenditures are carefully weighed and parceled out across the organization.
- Each product group is treated as an investment center where return on invested capital is an important criterion used in allocating funds.
- Certain technical functions, such as data processing, are centralized at headquarters, while daily operating decisions remain decentralized.
- Stock options and companywide profit sharing are used to encourage identity with the firm as a whole.

All of these new coordination systems prove useful for achieving growth through more efficient allocation of a company's limited resources. They prompt field managers to look beyond the needs of their local units. While these managers still have much decision-making responsibility, they learn to justify their actions more carefully to a "watchdog" audience at headquarters.

... and the red-tape crisis But a lack of confidence gradually builds between line and staff, and between headquarters and the field. The proliferation of systems and programs begins to exceed its utility; a red-tape crisis is created. Line managers, for example, increasingly resent heavy staff direction from those who are not familiar with local conditions. Staff people, on the other hand, complain about uncooperative and uninformed line managers. Together both groups criticize the bureaucratic paper system that has evolved. Procedures take precedence over problem solving, and innovation is dampened. In short, the organization has become too large and complex to be managed through formal programs and rigid systems. The Phase 4 revolution is under way.

Phase 5: Collaboration . . .

The last observable phase in previous studies emphasizes strong interpersonal collaboration in an attempt to overcome the red-tape crisis. Where Phase 4 was managed more through formal systems and procedures, Phase 5 emphasizes greater spontaneity in management action through teams and the skillful confrontation of interpersonal differences. Social control and self-discipline take over from formal control. This transition is especially difficult for those experts who created the old systems as well as for those line managers who relied on formal methods for answers.

The Phase 5 evolution, then, builds around a more flexible and behavioral approach to management. Here are its characteristics:

- The focus is on solving problems quickly through team action.
- Teams are combined across functions for task-group activity.
- Headquarters staff experts are reduced in number, reassigned, and combined in interdisciplinary teams to consult with, not to direct, field units.
- A matrix-type structure is frequently used to assemble the right teams for the appropriate problems.
- Previous formal systems are simplified and combined into single multipurpose systems.
- Conferences of key managers are held frequently to focus on major problem issues.
- Educational programs are utilized to train managers in behavioral skills for achieving better teamwork and conflict resolution.
- Real-time information systems are integrated into daily decision making.
- Economic rewards are geared more to team performance than to individual achievement.
- Experiments in new practices are encouraged throughout the organization.

... and the ? crisis What will be the revolution in response to this stage of evolution? Many large U.S. companies are now in the Phase 5 evolutionary stage, so the answers are critical. While there is little clear evidence, I imagine the revolution will center around the "psychological saturation" of employees who grow emotionally and physically exhausted by the intensity of teamwork and the heavy pressure for innovative solutions.

My hunch is that the Phase 5 revolution will be solved through new structures and programs that allow employees to periodically rest, reflect, and revitalize themselves. We may even see companies with dual organization structures: a "habit" structure for getting the daily work done, and a "reflective" structure for stimulating perspective and personal enrichment. Employees could then move back and forth between the two structures as their energies are dissipated and refueled.

One European organization has implemented just such a structure. Five reflective groups have been established outside the regular structure for the purpose of continuously evaluating five task activities basic to the organization. They report directly to the managing director, although their reports are made public throughout the organization. Membership in each group includes all levels and functions, and employees are rotated through these groups on a six-month basis.

Other concrete examples now in practice include providing sabbaticals for employees, moving managers in and out of "hot spot" jobs, establishing a four-day workweek, assuring job security, building physical facilities for relaxation *during* the working day, making jobs more interchangeable, creating an extra team on the assembly line so that one team is always off for reeducation, and switching to longer vacations and more flexible working hours.

The Chinese practice of requiring executives to spend time periodically on lower-level jobs may also be worth a nonideological evaluation. For too long U.S. management has assumed that career progress should be equated with an upward path toward title, salary, and power. Could it be that some vice presidents of marketing might just long for, and even benefit from, temporary duty in the field sales organization?

IMPLICATIONS OF HISTORY

Let me now summarize some important implications for practicing managers. First, the main features of this discussion are depicted in *Exhibit 3*, which shows the specific management actions that characterize each growth phase. These actions are also the solutions which ended each preceding revolutionary period.

In one sense, I hope that many readers will react to my model by calling it obvious and natural for depicting the growth of an organization. To me this type of reaction is a useful test of the model's validity.

But at a more reflective level I imagine some of these reactions are more hindsight than foresight. Those experienced managers who have been through a developmental sequence can empathize with it now, but how did they react when in the middle of a stage of evolution or revolution? They can probably recall the limits of their own developmental understanding at that time. Perhaps they resisted desirable changes or were even swept emotionally into a revolution without being able to propose constructive solutions. So let me offer some explicit guidelines for managers of growing organizations to keep in mind.

Know Where You Are in the Developmental Sequence

Every organization and its component parts are at different stages of development. The task of top management is to be aware of these stages; otherwise, it may not recognize when the time for change has come, or it may act to impose the wrong solution.

Top leaders should be ready to work with the flow of the tide rather than against it; yet they should be cautious, since it is tempting to skip phases out of impatience. Each phase results in certain strengths and learning experiences in the organization that will be essential for success in subsequent phases. A child prodigy, for example, may be able to read like a teenager, but he cannot behave like one until he ages through a sequence of experiences.

I also doubt that managers can or should act to avoid revolutions. Rather, these periods of tension provide the pressure, ideas, and awareness that afford a platform for change and the introduction of new practices.

Recognize the Limited Range of Solutions

In each revolutionary stage it becomes evident that this stage can be ended only by certain specific solutions; moreover, these solutions are different from those which were applied to the problems of the preceding revolution. Too often it is tempting to choose solutions that were tried before, which makes it impossible for a new phase of growth to evolve.

Management must be prepared to dismantle current structures before the revolutionary stage becomes too turbulent. Top managers, realizing that their own managerial styles are no longer appropriate, may even have to take themselves out of leadership positions. A good Phase 2 manager facing Phase 3 might be wise to find another Phase 2 organization that better fits his talents, either outside the company or with one of its newer subsidiaries.

Finally, evolution is not an automatic affair; it is a contest for survival. To move ahead, companies must consciously introduce planned structures that not only are solutions to a current crisis but also are fitted to the *next* phase of growth. This requires considerable self-awareness on the part of top management, as well as great interpersonal skill in persuading other managers that change is needed.

Realize That Solutions Breed New Problems

Managers often fail to realize that organizational solutions create problems for the future (i.e., a decision to delegate eventually causes a problem of control). Historical actions are very much determinants of what happens to the company at a much later date.

An awareness of this effect should help managers to evaluate company problems with greater historical understanding instead of "pinning the blame" on a current development. Better yet, managers should be in a position to *predict* future problems, and thereby to prepare solutions and coping strategies before a revolution gets out of hand.

A management that is aware of the problems ahead could well decide *not* to grow. Top managers may, for instance, prefer to retain the informal practices of a small company, knowing that this way of life is inherent in the organization's limited size, not in their congenial personalities. If they choose to grow, they may do themselves out of a job and a way of life they enjoy.

And what about the managements of very large organizations? Can they find new solutions for continued phases of evolution? Or are they reaching a stage where the government will act to break them up because they are too large.

CONCLUDING NOTE

Clearly, there is still much to learn about processes of development in organizations. The phases outlined here are only five in number and are still only approximations. Researchers are just beginning to study the specific developmental problems of structure, control, rewards, and management style in different industries and in a variety of cultures.

One should not, however, wait for conclusive evidence before educating managers to think and act from a developmental perspective. The critical dimension of time has been missing for too long from our management theories and practices. The intriguing paradox is that by learning more about history we may do a better job in the future.

EXHIBIT 1 Model of Organization Development.

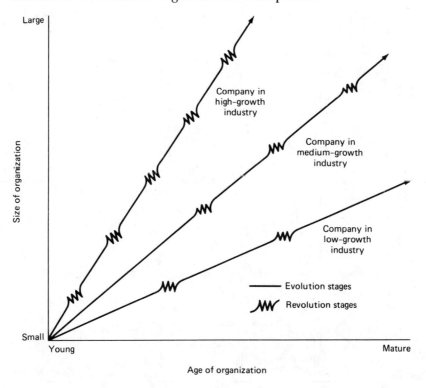

EXHIBIT 2 The Five Phases of Growth.

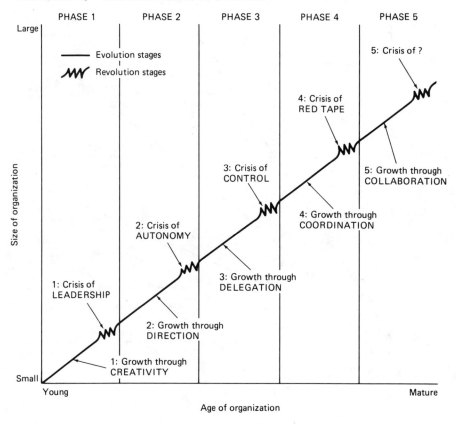

Organizational Transitions

EXHIBIT 3 Organization Practices during Evolution in the Five Phases of Growth.

Category	PHASE 1	PHASE 2	PHASE 3	PHASE 4	PHASE 5
MANAGEMENT FOCUS	Make & sell	Efficiency of operations	Expansion of market	Consolidation of organization	Problem solving & innovation
ORGANIZATION STRUCTURE	Informal	Centralized & functional	Decentralized & geographical	Line-staff & product groups	Matrix of teams
TOP MANAGEMENT STYLE	Individualistic & entrepreneurial	Directive	Delegative	Watchdog	Participative
CONTROL SYSTEM	Market results	Standards & cost centers	Reports & profit centers	Plans & investment centers	Mutual goal setting
MANAGEMENT REWARD EMPHASIS	Ownership	Salary & merit increases	Individual bonus	Profit sharing & stock options	Team bonus